Lynne McKay

FORM
IN
MUSIC

Order gave each thing view.
Shakespeare

The poet's eye, in a fine frenzy rolling,
Doth glance from heaven to earth, from earth to heaven;
And as imagination bodies forth
The forms of things unknown, the poet's pen
Turns them to shapes, and gives to airy nothing
A local habitation and a name.
Shakespeare

I am seeking always . . . the coherent and living
expression of my musical ideas.
Roger Sessions

FORM
IN
MUSIC

Second Edition

An examination of traditional techniques
of musical form and their applications
in historical and contemporary styles

Wallace Berry
PROFESSOR OF MUSIC
UNIVERSITY OF BRITISH COLUMBIA

Prentice-Hall, Inc., Englewood Cliffs, New Jersey 07632

Berry, Wallace.
  Form in music.

  Includes index.
    1. Musical form.   I. Title.
  MT58.B34 1986   781'.5   85-3374
  ISBN 0-13-329285-1

Editorial/production supervision: Mark Stevens
Cover design: Ben Santora
Manufacturing buyer: Ray Keating

Printed in the United States of America
10 9 8 7 6 5 4 3 2

ISBN   0-13-329285-1   01

Prentice-Hall International (UK) Limited, *London*
Prentice-Hall of Australia Pty. Limited, *Sydney*
Editora Prentice-Hall do Brasil, Ltda., *Rio de Janeiro*
Prentice-Hall Canada Inc., *Toronto*
Prentice-Hall Hispanoamericana, S.A., *Mexico*
Prentice-Hall of India Private Limited, *New Delhi*
Prentice-Hall of Japan, Inc., *Toyko*
Prentice-Hall of Southeast Asia Pte. Ltd., *Singapore*
Whitehall Books Limited, *Wellington, New Zealand*

To the memory of

my mother and father

CONTENTS

FOREWORD
to the First Edition

Since music is an art that exists in time, the intelligent listener must face the problem of relating the successive manifestations of the musical discourse to those already heard, and ultimately, through familiarity, to those yet to be heard. Music acquires its meaning through the interaction of all its parts. The unprepared listener is seldom aware of these interactions and may even be unable to identify the protagonists of the musical drama. He listens to music as a succession of individual moments, of greater or lesser beauty, never discovering the larger structures that give these moments meaning.

The study of musical form has been all too often an establishing of textbook patterns, averages of common practice to which few actual compositions conform. In a sense, every piece of music creates its own form out of its individual materials. Comparison of two sonatas by the same composer is likely to reveal more significant differences than similarities; only in the most general sense do the works of different composers agree. It is essential to consider the larger dimensions, which make it possible to categorize; but it is equally important that the individual differences, the unique solutions, be specially considered in the analysis of many works.

In the pages that follow, Wallace Berry has systematically examined the structure of music, mainly instrumental, in the light of historical orientation and aesthetic necessity. He turns the beam of his inquiry upon every facet of the form, illuminating as he penetrates to the essentials. From the smallest elements of music—figure, motive, phrase—he proceeds in an orderly fashion to the most complex musical organizations—sonata, variations, fugue. He ranges widely through the literature of all periods. His terminology is unequivocal; though not always traditional, it may well become standard.

A careful and thorough study of this book will abundantly reward the reader, especially if he brings himself to acquaintance with the vast treasury of music unlocked here, by reading, playing, and listening. I can imagine no more congenial guide through the storehouse than Dr. Berry.

Halsey Stevens

From the PREFACE
to the First Edition

What is form in music? It is the sum of those qualities in a piece of music that bind together its parts and animate the whole. It is the product of intellectual control over the musical ideas which bring a composition into existence. It is a discipline through which the inherent power of the musical materials is realized and directed to an end that is convincing and seemingly inevitable. It is all of these; yet, the complexity of any comprehensive answer is indicated by the fact that books like this are written.

The primary purpose of these studies is the exposition of the fundamental principles of musical form, illuminated by illustration of the techniques by which they are applied. While one cannot, alas, describe music with recourse to its own inexhaustibly rich language of notes, the theorist must conduct his study of musical form with constant, probing reference to musical works of clear but challenging form. That is the reason for the number of musical quotations and citations in these chapters and for my pausing at frequent intervals to take a careful look at the makings of form in complete examples. Observations are shown, I hope with the consistency I have desired, to be based on significant musical practice.

When music theory speaks of *traditional forms,* its reference is to established models which were brought to consummate realization in the eighteenth and nineteenth centuries, and which show remarkable viability today. Most studies in musical form have as their basis of subject matter the literatures which reflect the broad principles of these forms.

As is apparent from the table of contents, this book approaches the question of musical coherence through a systematic investigation of such traditional forms, and is thus adaptable to the usual advanced music theory course commonly designated "Form and Analysis," or "Analytical Techniques." Overemphasis on surface at the expense of more critical and decisive elements of form in much recent music education has produced a reaction against the study of traditional forms in many places, but there survives a just appreciation of their importance as flexible and proven frameworks for the solution of structural problems, and as monuments to human invention and artistic evolution.

I believe that the study of traditional forms is useful and valid so long as it proceeds beyond mere identification and classification into the penetrating analysis of *all* aspects of form in significant works—unorthodox as well as conventional. Such analysis must pursue every detail of form, recognizing that overall schematic design is only a basis, and that the application of a traditional formal plan is no assurance of logic, coherence, and animate substance in music. Therefore, it is crucial that analysis be directed into the investigation and understanding of all relevant principles.

The present study is not conceived as an end. A part of the reason for singling out those forms which are the bases for these essays is their adaptability through changes of musical style and idiom. I choose to deal extensively with fugue, for example, rather than ricercar, which is important for more specialized study. Also excluded are vocal types like the mass, which have no standard musical structure. Thus, I have rejected the inclination to try to discuss all musical genres—with a hasty aperçu of the motet, a page and a half on the oratorio, and so on—in favor of exhaustive treatment of common forms that afford vivid illustration of principles of musical logic and unity, and which, in their immediacy, are the most useful foundation for later, more particularized research. Virtually all Western music derives unity and vitality from one phase or another of a common set of principles, whether or not a conventional total design is employed. Hence, I have been able to draw many illustrations from such genres as the oratorio, the mass, the opera, and the art song, and from a wide historical span which extends well into the twentieth century.

The studies in this book are made with a constant awareness of the dangers of categorization which is too rigid and generalization which is too broad and insistent. At the same time, I believe that any observation of traditional practice leads to the delineation of important parallels among forms and styles, and that classification is therefore possible and reasonable—providing a background of common practice against which to regard the anomalies that are so valuable a source of instruction. Of course, the discussion of classification with respect to any given work must often be content merely to point the way to a rationale, while leaving particular questions unanswered. Such, I think, is one of the arts of pedagogy.

This volume is addressed to the musician—amateur or professional—who has studied basic music theory. In seeking to demonstrate techniques of form and analysis through careful and searching examination of the most tenacious forms and literatures, it does not try to be a history of those forms, nor of their rarer antecedents. And, in analysis, I have tried to restrict myself to objective discussion of musical anatomy in preference to subjective description.

The musical examples are intended to encompass a wide variety of styles and media. The music suggested for supplementary analysis, when not listed for its high intrinsic value, either has some special usefulness or illustrates some particular device or problem. I have not provided a workbook for what is to me a very important reason: the risk of stagnation in the classroom practice of dealing with the same limited frame of reference in course after course, year after year. It seems altogether feasible as well as profitable to refer to a varied selection of moderately priced editions of such indispensable items as Bach fugues and Beethoven sonatas in addition to less familiar works, some of them recent, offering stimulation and broad stylistic variety and often meeting the special needs of a specific situation. Materials for such use are listed throughout this book, and published collections and workbooks will be found to be readily available for conditions in which they are deemed essential, and for individual study. My examples from the early eighteenth century and earlier are, in many instances, drawn from the *Historical Anthology of Music,* whose two volumes are convenient and accessible as well as abundant in range of content.[1]

The exercises are specimens of projects for valuable study beyond the material of the text itself. Rare will be that situation in which the reader can turn his or her attention to more than a few of them, but the listing of many makes possible the choice of an area of investigation of special relevance or special interest. Where group study is involved, several projects might be undertaken, the results of each to be shared with the group. In this as in all respects, specific application of the material is left to be governed by the limitations and demands of particular circumstances.

The value of penetrating musical analysis, having more as its end than the classification of works according to particular terms, is generally accepted wherever music is a serious field of study. I for one would make no apology in pointing to the sheer delight in discovery of all the working parts of a musical organism. But, beyond that, analysis is a vital experience for all musicians, and it is axiomatic that music has only the palest reality apart from the transmissions of its past.

Analysis is, of course, indispensable to the theorist and musicologist who must use its techniques in the evaluation of style and significance. Young composers, for whom analysis is one of the paths to skill in their craft, too often forget, in an impatient search for self-expression, that they must fulfill themselves as musicians (if they are to write music), imbibing deeply the instructions of great musical achievements, learning intimately the principles and techniques that make a musical work a vital unit, remembering that the art they practice is never totally new, and is false if it pretends to be anything but, in the words of Ernest Bloch, a "balance between tradition and evolution."

Performers must, like all musicians, acquire a comprehension and ultimately an intuition of the functions and requirements of form. They must have the means to consider, when necessary, the particular functions of any problematic passage. They have to understand how tension is heightened and released in music; other-

---

[1]Archibald T. Davison and Willi Apel, *Historical Anthology of Music* (Cambridge, Mass.: Harvard University Press, 1949, 1950).

wise, how can they be effective participants in the realization of musical content, and on what basis are their decisions on dynamics, tempo, phrasing, and all elements of "interpretation" to be formed?

The critic is incapable of wisdom respecting musical effectiveness and ineffectiveness without a thorough understanding of the *reasons* behind fundamental failings that inhibit so much musical expression. And how incredible it is that the scholar whose primary concern is the aesthetics and psychology of musical communication is so often ignorant of the technical factors that make for motion, dynamic intensity and recession, dramatic effect, stability and instability, and unity and variety, some of the attributes that enter into the form of music.

Finally, we must recognize the deeper enjoyment that accrues to the listener who makes an effort to understand the anatomy of music. His or her response to emotional stimuli, at a primitive and innocent level, is by no means unimportant; but how much the experience deepens when the listener can participate intellectually as well. Music has a logical, rational organization, and all the vital details brought out in analysis are meant to be heard and felt.

Correlatively, all scholars need to be reminded of the value of listening. It is in the act of listening that analysis is finally understood and confirmed, and listening as a prelude to analysis not infrequently suggests the most fruitful avenue of approach in the study of the music's form.

Many of the musical excerpts and textual quotations reprinted in this book are drawn from works or editions which are restricted by copyright, and I am indebted to the publishers and other copyright owners who have consented to my use of them.

For stimulating and challenging discussion with many colleagues—exchanges that have led me to reexamination and better formulation of not a few ideas—and to that occasional student of searching mind and relentlessly critical inquiry, I would express most earnest thanks.

The staff of the Music Library of the University of Michigan and those of the Libraries of the American Academy and the Accademia Nazionale di Santa Cecilia in Rome have been very helpful, and I am grateful both for their assistance and for the facilities placed at my disposal.

Professors Louise Cuyler and Halsey Stevens read the complete manuscript and made many helpful and important suggestions. My indebtedness to them is inestimable.

It is customary in the final words of his preface for an author to acknowledge the support of his wife. This is a gesture in which I, having so much greater reason than most, can scarcely fail. Her incisiveness of mind, wisdom of critical perception, and inspiriting warmth have been resources upon which I have drawn constantly through the long months in which these studies have taken form.

Wallace Berry
Ann Arbor, Michigan
1965

PREFACE
to the Second Edition

Form in Music has been accorded a very large volume of use since its publication in 1966, and the present, revised edition represents an opportunity to acknowledge the interest and responsive observations of many students, colleagues, and other readers over that time. I hope that the somewhat unsettling experience of probing a work of twenty years past has eventuated in significant improvements in scope and detail, in clarifications of essential formulations, and in the introduction, however tentative, of a number of concepts of musical structure which underlie analytical approaches explored in my publications of the intervening years. It is especially in the final chapter that these concepts are treated in initiatory discussion pointing to their fuller consideration in my *Structural Functions in Music* of 1975.[1] That discussion indicates, in its substance and implication, the vital importance of looking beyond form (as the thematic scenario-narrative of exposition and development) to specific processes by which form unfolds, and thus into *all* elements of content by which structure is articulated.

The second edition of *Form in Music,* while not a new book, is a very serious effort. Work on it has been marked by, and has had to surmount, an inevitable ambivalence between the tendency to reconceive and rewrite and the inclination to leave well enough alone. Often, to be sure, my decisions have been governed by practical considerations, in particular the circumscribing requirements of publication, respecting the physical limits of the original book.

---

[1]This study, first published by Prentice-Hall, has been reprinted as a Dover paperback (New York, in press). It is one of a number of studies of recent years inquiring into the nature and structural implications of rhythm, texture, timbre, motive, and the expressive significances of shaped compositional dispositions of all of music's elements.

The revised edition includes a new chapter on the concerto, a presentation whose chief intent is to expose some particular approaches to form in the special terms of duologue by which the genre is characterized, and to look into some of the unique circumstances of formal articulation in the conditions of timbral-sonorous opposition and complementation especially striking in the concerto but in some respects applicable to other genres, such as the duo sonata.

Partly to compensate for added material but also in the interest of sharper focus and for other reasons, I have made many deletions from the original text. These include the greater part of the original concluding chapter and large segments of the chapters on suite and sonata-rondo, in addition to a large number of less drastic excisions throughout. And while certain definitions of basic concepts have been extended for improved clarity, others—including explanations of elementary theoretical terms (largely in the original footnotes), redundancies, and items of marginal or questionable utility—have been dispensed with altogether. In a few instances I have had to make changes in terminology, as in my effort in the revised text to distinguish consistently between *form* and *structure,* the latter a comprehensive specification of which the former is one aspect, as indicated in the new concluding chapter.

Still, while I have again given much thought and study to the basic terms and concepts explored in *Form in Music,* I have in the end left these substantially intact, while striving for less insistent distinctions than those of certain relatively labored formulations which at times burden the first edition. In rethinking, I have concluded that many troublesome difficulties of classification are indeed inescapable, and that no set of simplistic definitions unequivocally stated, however these might wishfully be sought and glibly pronounced, can be true to the challenging intricacies and purposeful ambiguities of authentic works of art. And fine distinctions of classification are imperative when they suggest functional and substantive disparities in compositional practices and results, however such practices may require *particular* modes of scrutiny as to *particular* elements of form and structure in individual works. For example, differentiation between the concepts of *coda* and *codetta,* however problematic, is unavoidable, deriving from study of the elements of content, scope, and position in the formal narrative. Moreover, forms revealing comparatively incipient conditions of less than full and decisive realization, within stipulated essential attributes, require distinction. Need I argue, as in the original edition, that none of this leads to inflexible and arbitrary categorization, and that gray areas are a necessary and valid aspect of categorization, whether of form, style, or genre? Examples of uncertain identity—for instance, works of the type just mentioned, in which an emergent formal principle or procedure is evident in an incipient state—are indeed often the most provocative, and I have tried here to call attention to many borderline specimens, often without pleading this or that view, placing them within a reasoned—and, I trust, reasonable—perspective according to carefully delineated criteria of classification. Marginal regions of terminology occur at times in the spectrum of continuity from small to large, and at other times (as in the binary-sonata delineation, or that between the simple rondo and sonata-rondo) in a perspective suggestive of evolutionary historical trends.

Some of the musical illustrations quoted in the first edition—references of apparently moot significance or of duplicative content and purpose—have been taken out, and a number of new examples have been introduced in the new segments of the text. In the work of twenty years ago, I included many quotations from works of certain 20th-century composers—Hindemith, Bloch, Schuman, Riegger, Piston, and others—now somehow, and I think unfortunately and unnaturally, shadowed in the arena of serious scholarship and analysis, and to a considerable extent in that of public performance, perhaps in part for reasons of exaggerated attention to a more spectacular (and at times bewildering) creative output of recent years. I have pondered these references, which occur along with many from Schoenberg, Webern, Bartók, Berg, and Stravinsky—the prime, proven figures—and have decided to retain most of them, as specimens of good music illustrative of cited points concerning traditional formal prototypes. Indeed, one senses a notable resurgent interest today in works embodying tonal methods of relatively forthright, quasi-conventional, explicit harmonic and melodic basis, where elements of tonally oriented content are adapted to the requirements of strong individual ideas and idioms such as many of those of the composers mentioned above. My assumption, as before, is that teachers and other readers will introduce supplementary examples for examination as particular forms are considered, as well as supplementary reading—in sources I have cited and in others—by which to enlarge the framework of study.

In the chapters dealing with large forms, extended examples of reference and partial quotation are again at times unavoidable. Some (as in the new section on concerto) are quoted only minimally, others are referred to and discussed briefly, and still others are merely named in particular connections. Often, I have had to assume the reader's access to a complete score, as in my commentary on the finale of Bartók's Piano Concerto No. 3. My own pedagogical practice of placing such items on library reserve during the period of their investigation surely parallels that of many colleagues. In any event, detailed text reference without musical quotation is as exceptional in the revised text as in the original, the Bartók movement being the most extreme case.

Many of the exercises at the ends of chapters have been deleted or modified, and some have been added. As before, the suggested exercises are intended for two purposes. One is that of group study, in an overt sharing of conclusions of analysis and research; the other is that of individual inquiry, possibly culminating in papers or projects. In order to provide a latitude of choice, there are again many more exercises—some general, some specific in focus of reference—than can be accommodated in any given situation. (An editorial note, not explicit in the first edition, is that I state the given names and dates of a composer at the first citation only.)

It is my premise, again, that student readers of this book have been through basic studies in music theory and history, and will thereby have been exposed at least moderately to some of the terms and concepts pertaining to tonal forms. No sequence of presentation can be suitable to the requirements of readers having variously broad and deep preliminary experience, and users of this book will undoubtedly often follow an ordering of chapters and sections other than that of its printing. For the reader who needs to look back or ahead for a particular reason, the index should provide ready access to definitions and other elements sought out of the established sequence. In the revision, the subject index has been thoroughly reconsidered, and there is now a complete index to citations of composers and works.

My hope in an overdue re-edition of this sober and comprehensive study, whose origins seem so distant in (my) time, is to have achieved its significant revitalization: by the infusion of elements of subsequent thinking, where that has been feasible; by reformulations of originally problematic, inconclusive, or otherwise deficient items; and by a vast amount of editing, in evidence on every page. In making this exacting effort, I am, again, keenly aware of indebtedness to many readers of *Form in Music* who have by their faithful regard and encouragement sustained its undiminished circulation over these two decades, and certainly to those who have made suggestions for improvements, many of which have been taken into account in the new edition. Finally, I wish to acknowledge, with warm appreciation, a very large number of helpful and insightful suggestions provided by Mr. Mark Stevens, my production editor for this book.

Wallace Berry
Vancouver, British Columbia

1

MOTIVE, PHRASE, PERIOD

Just as a novel, a play, or a ballet is divided into chapters or acts, scenes, episodes, and such smaller elements as paragraphs, lines, and gestures, so the progress of music in time achieves form and intelligibility through small groupings, each making its particular contribution to the development of the whole. The small units which are the building stones of music are, ideally, bound together into a logical succession by (1) the common rhythmic, harmonic, and melodic features which they share; (2) the techniques by which they are joined; and (3) their use in the development of accumulative points of climax (and repose) in the musical work.

Words, the smallest meaningful structural units in language, convey distinct and intelligible impressions when purposefully combined into phrases and clauses. The larger units (phrases, clauses, sentences, stanzas, paragraphs) usually relate to one another and to the whole of which they are portions by virtue of the central, larger *meaning* to which they contribute, even though other unifying factors may be involved—as, for instance, meter and rhyme.

Music, however, lacks discursive and concise meaning. This is not to say that music has no meaning: it may impart a sense, a mood, an impression of states or qualities. But it is essentially abstract, and its structural components achieve integration chiefly by their corroboration through *repetition,* often in varied form and new combinations, as well as by lending appropriately to the general direction and expressive character of the work or passage of which they are a part.

Some guides to identifying and characterizing the smaller, integral units of form in music are discussed in this chapter. It is from these units—especially motives and phrases—that large forms evolve. Although this book will present descriptions of a number of conventional designs, the features of which are shared by

1

multitudes of musical works, it must be recognized that these surface forms find unique application in nearly every specific example. For the form is not predetermined and then filled with musical ideas. The opposite is true: the ideas of the composer, coming out of the richness of the imagination and through a mastery of the musical language, become the material from which the specific directions of the form emerge. A vital musical motive, like a living cell, has a pregnancy and energy of its own and often stimulates its own immediate continuation; the rest is up to the composer's craft. Combining small units into a convincing and persuasive whole, with a balance between forces of tension and release and a sense of logical and inexorable course, requires the highest degree of technical command.

Part of the coherence of almost any piece of music lies in the fact that it rests upon a succession of regularly spaced impulses, or beats, against which the rhythmic patterns play, and in relation to which, as to one another, they enter into coherent form. The frequency of the fundamental pulsations and the amount of activity superimposed on them determine the tempo of the music, one of the most basic factors governing its character. Beats fall into groups, or measures, often of the same length throughout a given piece or movement. In some music the length of the measure changes frequently during the course of a work, and such metric change lends a quality of its own.

Similarly, phrases and periods made up of odd numbers of measures can constitute an effective element of asymmetry in music. Still, many composers have almost consistently written in units of 2, 4, 8, and 16 measures. While a predictable regularity of this kind can easily dispel the listener's interest, there are, of course, many ways of achieving contrast and asymmetry in music within a regular rhythmic structure. The fact that thematic phrases are entirely of 4-measure lengths may be offset by asymmetry in "free" developmental passages, and by devices such as overlapping, or *elision,* in the joining of adjacent units.

Musical form invariably involves division into interrelated segments. The lines of distinction, especially between motive and phrase, are often a question of subjective impression; precise, absolute definitions that will apply for all listeners in all cases are not possible. Yet there is no question of the existence of these units in music, and it is important to consider their qualities and the manner of their delineation even if we cannot always fit examples into invariable nominal categories.

THE MOTIVE   *punctuation, significance—thematic —developmental*

A *motive,* as is suggested by its etymological source, is a motivating idea in music—the small cell out of which the music evolves. The French composer Vincent d'Indy (1851–1931) labeled the essential motives in his scores as *cellules* (cells), a term suggestive of small, organic units of building material. Also worth noting is the definition of motive given by André Coeuroy: "It is an element, ordinarily short—shorter than the theme—from which the composer draws a musical development.''[1] (For ''theme'' in Coeuroy's statement, we should substitute ''phrase''; the phrase, discussed later in this chapter, incorporates motives or employs a single motive with its repetitions and variants.)

Ernst Toch, in *The Shaping Forces in Music,* describes with rare insight and sensitivity the functions of the motive: the ''motive power'' of a composition—reviving, animating, bridging, splicing, feeding movement. ''It lives on repetition and yet on constant metamorphosis. . . .''[2] Toch cites as an example of such a propelling force the opening motive of the first movement of Brahms's Second Symphony; this motive sounds unassuming indeed when it is first heard below the theme melody, but becomes a prime motivating force as the movement develops.

Ex. 1.1   Brahms, Symphony No. 2 in D, Op. 73, first movement.

Thus, the potential and significance of a thematic fragment may be unapparent until it is subjected to manipulation in the course of a work. In other words, the significance of a motive in a given example usually depends on the extent of its development by the composer. Example 1.2 shows a motive which is announced

Ex. 1.2   Beethoven, Sonata in B-flat, Op. 22, first movement. [3]

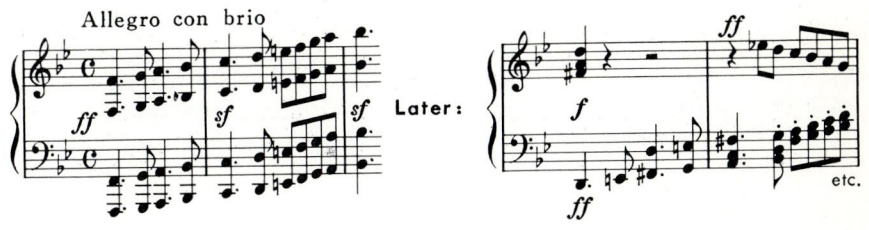

inconspicuously in the final measures of the exposition; it would hardly be predicted that this motive would later form the basis for nearly all of the development section.

[1]André Coeuroy, *La Musique et ses formes* (Paris: Les Editions Denoël, 1951), p. 19. Passage translated by the author.
[2]From *The Shaping Forces in Music* by Ernst Toch, copyrighted 1958 by Criterion Music Corp.
[3]''Sonata'' is throughout understood to mean ''sonata for piano.''

The motive might be defined, then, as the smallest characteristic unit, *distinctive* in melodic and rhythmic content, whose significance is established in development. The motive is a stimulus to its own development and continuation.

Motives are not necessarily delineated by explicit cadential formulae. Often, they are punctuated by means of metric division, by rests, by articulation, or by a momentary cessation of movement on a longer note. Or, as suggested above, a motive's identity may become apparent only in its later appearances and development, or by its immediate repetition. Some of these principles are apparent in Exx. 1.3-1.6.

Ex. 1.3 Brahms, Sonata in A, Op. 100, for violin and piano, second movement.

Ex. 1.4 Aaron Copland, Symphony No. 1, Prelude.

Copyright 1931 by Cos Cob Press Inc., renewed 1958 by Aaron Copland. Reprinted by permission of Aaron Copland, copyright owner, and Boosey & Hawkes Inc., sole licensees.

Ex. 1.5 Mozart, Sonata in D , K. 284, third movement.

Ex. 1.6 Beethoven, Trio No. 4 in B-flat, Op. 11, for clarinet, cello, and piano, first movement.

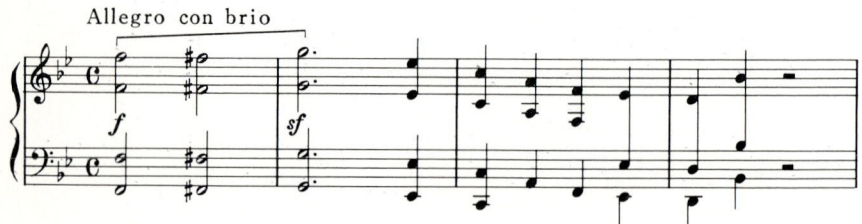

The rhythmic anacrusis, or upbeat, is an element commonly found in the motive; it acts as a preliminary "inhalation" which sets the motive in motion.

Ex. 1.7 Paul Hindemith, Pittsburgh Symphony, first movement.

The length of a motive depends on a number of factors, especially the tempo of the music. Obviously, in a slow succession, fewer notes will combine into a single total impression, while if the notes are faster a greater number can be perceived as a single unit. The motive in Ex. 1.8 contains 12 notes in its first appearance; in subsequent extensions it incorporates as many as 21 notes, appreciable as a totality by virtue of tempo, articulation, and derivation from a simpler source.

Ex. 1.8 Stravinsky, Le Sacre du Printemps, Part I (Danse de la Terre).

If they are of distinctive quality, and if they have importance in later development, as few as 2 notes may constitute a motive (Ex. 1.9).

Ex. 1.9 Debussy, Nocturnes, No. 1 (Nuages).

Permission for reprint granted by Editions Jean Jobert, Paris, France, copyright owners, and Elkan-Vogel Co., Inc., Philadelphia, Pa., agents.

Of course, any musical segment is arbitrarily divisible into small fragments. But, having recognized the factors of punctuation and significance in our definition of the motive, we can see at once that a musical segment does not necessarily fall into motivic units. In Ex. 1.10, phrase 7 is a repetition of the final motive of phrase

Ex. 1.10 Chorale, Ich ruf' zu Dir, Herr Jesu Christ.

6; and the motive of m. 2 occurs in various forms. But, for the most part, the phrase is the smallest unit of structural significance. Unity is produced by similarities among the phrases (between phrases 1 and 5, 2 and 6, in rhythm only; between phrases 1 and 3, 2 and 4, in every respect), and by motion toward D, the final of the modal scale.

Motives enter into the larger musical structure by their literal restatement, by their sequential repetition (repetition at other pitch levels), by modification of rhythm or some other feature, by imitation[4] in other voices, by combination with other motives, and by many other devices. A few of these are shown in Exx. 1.11–1.14.

---

[4]Imitation is treated at length in Chapter 12.

Ex. 1.11   Brahms, Quartet in A, Op. 26, for piano and strings, first movement.

Ex. 1.12   Mozart, Sonata in E-flat, K. 282, third movement.

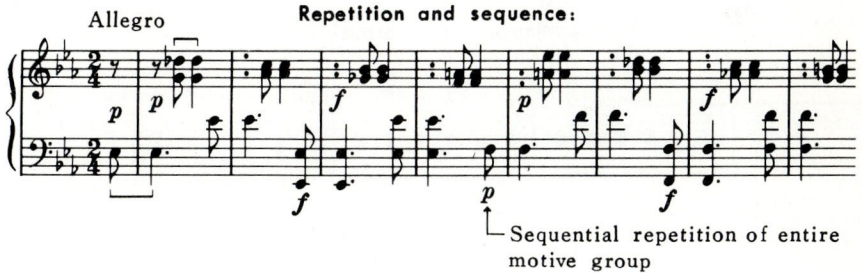

Ex. 1.13   Bartók, String Quartet No. 1, Op. 7, second movement.

Ex. 1.14   Schubert, Der Einsame, Op. 41.

THE FIGURE

It will be useful to make a distinction between that kind of fragment which is of thematic and developmental significance in a work and that which is used accompanimentally or episodically. The latter is a *figure*. The episodic figure is sometimes found in the connective passages, or *transitions*, although these passages are often based upon motives from the thematic groups which they bridge. The figure is generally of secondary importance, hardly comparable to the motive, from which an entire form can arise. Examples 1.15 and 1.16 illustrate accompanimental and episodic figuration.

Ex. 1.15   Mozart, String Quartet in C, K. 465, third movement.

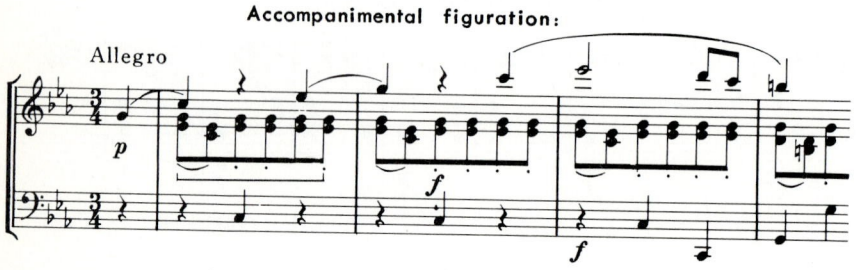

Ex. 1.16   Beethoven, Trio in G, Op. 1, No. 2, for piano, violin, and cello, fourth movement.

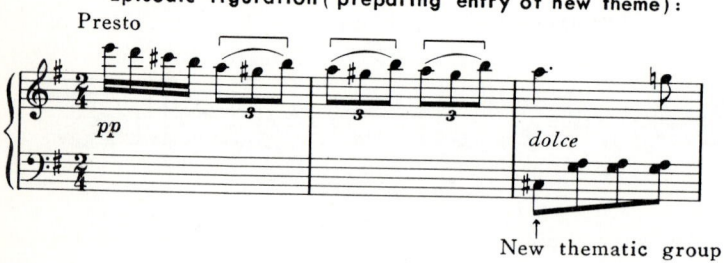

THE CADENCE

Units larger than the motive commonly end with a formula called a *cadence:* a kind of musical punctuation, usually both melodic and harmonic, conveying a sense of close or of interruption in the rhythmic motion of the musical line.

The harmonic composition of a cadence, in addition to other factors, has much to do with the impression of finality which it imparts. Thus, some types are relatively conclusive in effect (especially the authentic cadences) while others are tentative and incomplete (especially the half-cadence).

It is important to consider each cadence not only in its broad technical classification, but also as to its relative strength or weakness in context, and on its own particular terms. The same basic cadential formula can be affected in its degree of finality by a number of subtle factors, such as the metric positions of the harmonies, the use of nonharmonic dissonances, the directions of individual lines, and other circumstances including dynamics, texture, register, and orchestration.

The standard types of cadence in tonal music (authentic, half-, plagal, deceptive, and variants among these) are treated in many basic sources in music theory, and will not be defined here. But the reader will find in the following pages a multitude of examples in which to study the general criteria by which cadential formulae are classified and in which to evaluate the highly variable properties of individual cases. The consideration of cadential qualities and relations is a vital aspect of the analysis of form in music, and thus a matter of recurrent concern throughout this book.

A cadence is said to be *elided* when it marks the end of one unit and the simultaneous beginning of another. The continuity of the music is thereby maintained and the feeling of punctuation obscured; the impression is that something (often a measure of pause) has been left out. Example 1.17 illustrates this.

Ex. 1.17   Mozart, Sonata in F, K. 280, first movement.

One of the common devices for extending a phrase or other unit is to substitute abruptly an unexpected harmony at the moment the ear expects the prepared cadence. An *avoided cadence* is illustrated in Ex. 1.18.

Ex. 1.18   Mozart, Sonata in F, K. 280, first movement.

In the absence of functional harmonic relationships (harmony supporting the impression of a key center), a cadence may—as is often the case in twentieth-century music—be achieved by a pause on a longer note, by an actual rest, or by a descent in the melodic line. Or there may be a sense of harmonic resolution in the arrival upon a relatively consonant harmony. The harmony may be functional, of course, without being of traditional triadic construction. In turn-of-the-century French and other impressionist music, as well as in more recent works, the basic harmonic scheme is often traditional, especially at cadence points, despite ostensible "freedom" of harmonic movement around the basic scheme (see Exx. 13.3, and 13.4). Examples 1.19–1.21, cadential passages from Bartók's First String Quartet, illustrate some of the above points.

Ex. 1.19 Bartók, String Quartet No. 1, Op. 7, first movement.

Example 1.19 quotes the final measures of the Quartet's first movement. The longer note-values, the falling motive (see superimposed stems), the diminishing dynamic level, the thinning of the texture, and the consonance of the final intervals are some of the factors establishing the movement's final cadence.

Example 1.20, a quotation from the second movement of the Quartet, shows a cadence achieved by an abrupt stop, rest, and change of material. The music is made to stop suddenly in the midst of the heightening tension created by rising pitch, more severe dissonance, quicker rhythmic activity, and *forte* articulations.

Ex. 1.20 Bartók, String Quartet No. 1, Op. 7, second movement.

Many cadences of a conventional order are found in the work as well, despite the generally unsettled and ambiguous tonal context of the whole. An example may be seen in the measure before rehearsal no. 9, a cadence on the dominant of A.

Finally, Ex. 1.21, from the third movement, is a cadence in which tonic feeling is strongly conveyed by the insistence upon the note E (preceding bars have dwelt upon its leading-tone, D♯). There is no rest here, but an abrupt abandonment of the syncopated motive after a high degree of momentum has been developed. The fact that the motive is not triadic does not weaken the sense of E as a tonic note. Tempo change heightens the sense of formal articulation between the two quoted measures.

Ex. 1.21 Bartók, String Quartet No. 1, Op. 7, third movement.
    © 1949 by Rozsavoelgyi & Co., Budapest. Copyright 1954 by Edizioni Suvini Zerboni. Used by permission.

THE PHRASE

If the motive is comparable to a syntactical unit of 2 or 3 words, such as a prepositional phrase, the musical *phrase* may be compared to the clause, which, whether or not it is complete enough to warrant a period at its close, contains at least a subject and a predicate. The phrase typically includes motives of potential significance, or a single such motive repeated, usually in varied form. R. O. Morris describes the phrase in this way, and states that it "comes to a stop (and is to that extent self-subsistent) yet cannot stand by itself."[5]

A phrase is marked by a distinct beginning, a clear course of continuation, and an ending (cadence), however tentative. It thus manifests, melodically and harmonically, integral unity in a controlled course of action, followed by an arrival, normally conveying some sense of completeness without finality. A phrase, while an identifiably self-contained unit, requires the corroborating and complementary interactions of other phrases with which it is interdependent. Indeed, the phrase is ultimately comprehensible only in association with other phrases, and in relation to the larger formal units which motives and phrases combine to produce. The concept

[5]R. O. Morris, *The Structure of Music* (London: Oxford University Press, 1956), p. 10.

of phrase, including that of the cadential punctuation by which phrases are marked, is sometimes regarded as related to the natural intervals of breathing in singing or in playing wind instruments.

The *underlying* harmonic content of a typical phrase of tonal music can usually be described very simply. Often it consists of a basic succession (I–V or V–I, for example) modestly elaborated, or even a "single" basic harmony prolonged by surface elaboration. The melodic-rhythmic features of the upper voice are usually of primary effect and immediacy, to both ear and eye; here the phrase's beginning, progress, and end, as well as the motives into which it is divisible, are usually most readily apparent.

The length of the phrase cannot be specified since it varies widely, depending on such disparate factors as tempo, the possible extension through deliberate avoidance of cadence, and the perceptual capacities of the listener. In traditional music, especially that of the late eighteenth and nineteenth centuries, the phrase often consists of even-numbered multiples of 2 measures, and is very commonly 4 measures long (or 2 measures in slow tempo, 8 in quick tempo). But by no means is this to be taken as a rule for even the classical period. In considering phrase length, meter is also a factor: a 2-measure unit in 12/8 has the same "length" as a 4-measure unit in 6/8, if the 8th-note is of the same value.

The phrase is often composed of a 2-measure motive in sequence (Ex. 1.22).

Ex. 1.22   Beethoven, Sonata in B-flat, Op. 22, fourth movement.

Like the motive, the phrase often begins with an anacrusis. Here again, the approach from weak to strong, or "inhalation" to "exhalation," is a generative one; the upbeat affords a "push" that sets the phrase in motion (Ex. 1.23).

Ex. 1.23   Beethoven, Sonata in D, Op. 10, No. 3, first movement.

Occasionally, the upbeat may be considerably prolonged, constituting an elaborate preparation for the first strong downbeat in the phrase.

Ex. 1.24 Beethoven, Sonata in B-flat, Op. 22, first movement.

Many phrases are of irregular length—3, 5, or 7 measures, for example (see Ex. 1.25). This disruption of perfect symmetry has been discussed earlier as more than a rare exception even in the works of composers of the classical period.

Ex. 1.25 Mozart, String Quartet in F, K. 590, third movement.

The irregular phrase may be a basically symmetrical one which has been extended in some manner. There may be internal extension by repetition of a pattern within the phrase (Ex. 1.26), by repetition of the final pattern (Ex. 1.27), by avoidance of cadence (Ex. 1.18), or by repetition of the opening motive (Ex. 1.28). In the

Ex. 1.26 Haydn, Symphony in B-flat, No. 102, first movement.

Ex. 1.27 Brahms, Trio in C minor, Op. 101, for piano, violin, and cello, first movement.

Ex. 1.28 Mozart, Sonata in E-flat, K. 282, second movement.

last instance the feeling may be that the phrase actually begins with the second statement of the motive and is in that sense regular in length.

Note the clear relationship between the asymmetric phrase and the asymmetric measure. Just as beats are grouped into measures to form a primary level of meter, measures group into larger units to form *intermensural meter,* or *hypermeter.*
Thus, a 5/4 measure is, on another scale, comparable in effect to a 5-measure
phrase.

REPETITION OF THE PHRASE

Phrases normally combine into periods or phrase groups, both to be discussed presently. Occasionally, however, the phrase is simply repeated, possibly with variation
in timbre, dynamics, or texture, or with minor changes in the notes themselves, but
with the essential melodic and harmonic outlines left unchanged (Ex. 1.29).

Ex. 1.29 Beethoven, Sonata in D, Op. 10, No. 3, first movement.

The repeated phrase may be in sequence (Ex. 1.30).

Ex. 1.30 Beethoven, Trio No. 9 in E-flat, for piano, violin, and cello, WoO 38, second movement.

THE PERIOD

The single period (as distinct from enlarged forms to be discussed presently) is a pair of consecutive phrases, the second ending with a cadence which is more final and positive in effect than that of the first. Often the phrases are in parallel construction—i.e., of the same motivic material, although this is not always the case. The first phrase (*antecedent*) has an interrogative, tentative character as compared to the second (*consequent*), which is more affirmative in effect. This relationship is achieved, for the most part, by the contrast of cadences: by far the commonest cadential relationship is that of dominant (the most common half-cadence) ending the first phrase to tonic (authentic cadence) ending the second.

Parallel construction within an 8-measure period usually implies a correspondence in motivic material between mm. 1 and 5, 2 and 6, and 3 and 7, as in Ex. 1.31. In the following examples, cadences are marked as half- (H.C.), perfect authentic (P.A.C.), and imperfect authentic (I.A.C.).

Ex. 1.31 Beethoven, String Quartet in B-flat, Op. 130, second movement.

Ex. 1.31 (continued)

P.A.C.

But the phrases of a period are not necessarily in parallel construction. The well-known theme which opens the second movement of Beethoven's Sonata in C minor, Op. 13, is an example of a period whose phrases lack such explicit motivic correspondence. Unity is achieved in the Beethoven theme by the cadential antecedent-consequent relationship, as well as by such factors as the complementary melodic curves (first an underlying prolongation of the essential eb^1, then a descent from this pitch to ab), common accompanimental patterns and rhythmic consistency, and integral unity of basic harmonic content (I-V-I), in addition to equality of phrase lengths. Example 1.32 is another specimen of period form without parallel motivic construction, but also without the symmetry of equal phrase lengths.[6]

Ex. 1.32   Robert Jones, What if I Seek for Love (Book of Ayres, 1601).

Coeuroy speaks of the middle cadence as "a transient point of repose on the dominant"[7] but such a prescription excludes examples such as the following, in which an imperfect authentic cadence occurs at the end of the first phrase.

Any tonal fluctuation in the period is likely to be transitory, and certain to be

---

[6]While Ex. 1.32 clearly does not embody the explicit formula of motivic parallelism seen in Ex. 1.31, it does employ less obvious motivic relations. Thus, the ascending-3rd motive of the first part of the consequent phrase is an inversion of the descending-3rd pattern seen twice in the antecedent phrase.

[7]*La Musique et ses formes*, p. 26. Passage translated by the author.

Ex. 1.33 Mozart, Sonata in F, K. 332, first movement.

so in expository and concluding (as opposed to developmental) sections of forms. Such fluctuation usually may be conceived as referring, by tonicization, to secondary tonal regions extending the primary tonality, as by the introduction of F♯ in Ex. 1.34. In Ex. 1.35, the consequent phrase fluctuates toward a secondary tonic cadence on A, a 3rd removed from the primary tonic.

Ex. 1.34 Beethoven, Sonata in C, Op. 2, No. 3, fourth movement.

Ex. 1.35 Brahms, String Quintet in F, Op. 88, first movement.

Ex. 1.35 *(continued)*

The period relationship can also be observed at lower structural levels, as suggested by Ex. 1.22. The following example does not constitute a period (since its parts are not phrases); however, the antecedent-consequent principle is clearly implied in the relationship of the motives.

Ex. 1.36 Mozart, Sonata in E-flat, K. 282, second movement.

ENLARGEMENT OF THE SINGLE PERIOD

Just as phrases are frequently 4 measures long, periods are often twice that length. The majority of the examples quoted above have been 8 measures long, containing two phrases of equal length.

Example 1.37 is a 16-measure period made up of two 8-measure phrases, in quick tempo.

Ex. 1.37 Beethoven, Sonata in C, Op. 2, No. 3, third movement.

Example 1.37 is only apparently longer than the norm, by virtue of its tempo and meter; it is not an enlarged period. Moreover, a period of 5-, 6-, or 7-measure phrases can only be said to be "enlarged" where some explicit principle of extension is discernible. In Ex. 1.38, the 6-measure phrases would properly be thought of as extended only if conceived in relation to some simpler, normative model—for example, a basic 4-measure phrase, with two measures of "upbeat."

Ex. 1.38   Bartók, Mikrokosmos, Book II, No. 62.
Copyright 1940 by Hawkes & Son (London) Ltd. Reprinted by permission.

There are various ways in which the period may be distinctly enlarged. (1) Either phrase may be repeated. An example, too long for quotation, is the opening theme of the third movement of Beethoven's Sonata, Op. 13. Here, the consequent phrase is not only repeated but extended to more than twice its original length. (2) Either phrase may be extended. An example is the opening theme of Mozart's Sonata in G, K. 283, whose consequent phrase is extended 2 measures beyond the "normal" terminal point, m. 8. Example 1.39 illustrates a period in its symmetrical

Ex. 1.39   Schubert, Frühlingsglaube, Op. 20, No. 2.

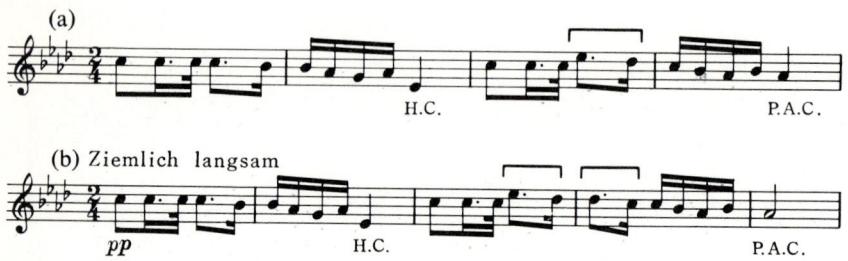

form, and in its extended form (b) as Schubert actually wrote it. (3) There may be a number of antecedent phrases (Ex. 1.40), or more rarely, consequent phrases. Ex-

Ex. 1.40   Thomas Ford, Come, Phyllis (Musicke of Sundrie Kindes, 1607).

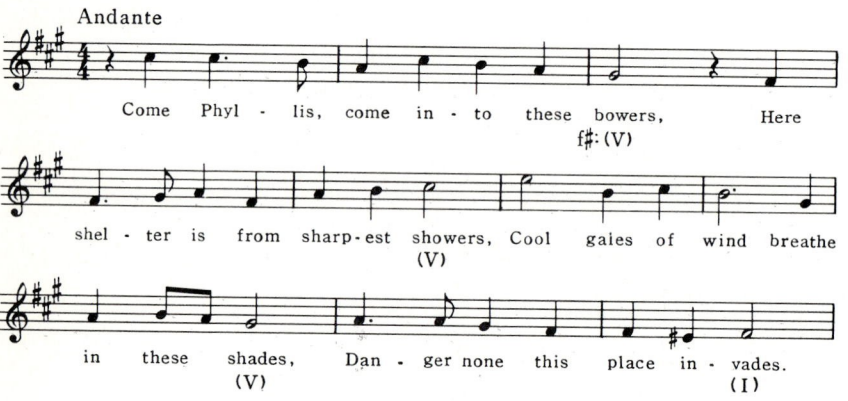

ample 1.41 illustrates enlarged antecedent and consequent segments. As harmonized by Bach[8] for the conclusion of his Cantata No. 130, the chorale is a period with two antecedent phrases (imperfect authentic cadence, half-cadence) and two consequent phrases (perfect authentic cadences). The four voice parts and continuo bass are quoted, with trumpets and timpani omitted. A pair of antecedent phrases, as in the chorale, no doubt implies the necessity for a comparably enlarged, balancing consequent.

---

[8]When the family name is used without given names or qualifying initials, it refers to Johann Sebastian (1685–1750).

Ex. 1.41 Bach, chorale, Herr Gott dich loben alle wir (from Cantata No. 130)

Example 1.42, whose first antecedent phrase is not quoted, includes two consequent phrases, both ending in strong cadences on the tonic.

Ex. 1.42 Irish Folk Song, Bendemeer's Stream.

THE DOUBLE PERIOD

In a double period the bipartite structure is expanded so that the antecedent element is of two phrases, as is the consequent part, with a perfect authentic cadence delayed until the end of the final phrase. Frequently all four phrases share the same, or very similar, motivic material; especially the first and third phrases are likely to have motives in common.

Since the two halves of the double period exist in the same relationship as the two phrases of a single period, an incomplete cadence ends the first two-phrase element, as well as the first and third phrases. A typical double period is shown as Ex. 1.43.

Ex. 1.43 Mozart, String Quartet in B-flat, K. 458, fourth movement.

Percy Goetschius makes the analogy between a double period and a four-line stanza of poetry.[9] In the stanza quoted below, the final line ends in a period—the period marking a point analogous to the perfect authentic cadence, the most emphatic punctuation in traditional music. Each line of the stanza consists of four met-

[9]Percy Goetschius, *Lessons in Music Form* (Bryn Mawr, Pa.: Theodore Presser, 1904), p. 80.

rical feet, a parallel to the common 4-measure phrase and 16-measure double period. The rhyme scheme parallels the frequent correspondence between the first and third, and second and fourth, phrases of the double period. Obviously, further analogy could be drawn between the couplet and the period. The example is from "The Definition of Love" by Andrew Marvell (1621–1678).

> And yet I quickly might arrive
> Where my extended soul is fixt,
> But Fate does iron wedges drive,
> And always crowds itself betwixt.

Example 1.44 shows a double period whose final phrase is substantially extended by sequential development of its initiating motive.

Ex. 1.44   Tchaikovsky, Symphony No. 4 in F minor, Op. 36, second movement.

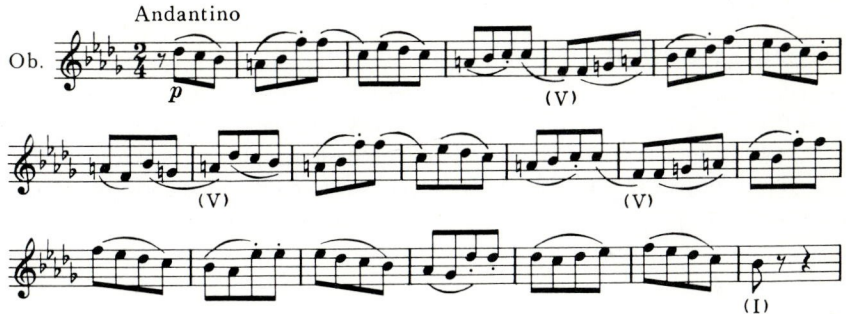

REPETITION OF THE PERIOD

Sometimes a period is repeated immediately, in which case there may be changes of orchestration or other elements without alteration of the basic structure and material. The two consequent cadences are thus harmonically equivalent. In Ex. 1.45,

Ex. 1.45   Haydn, Symphony No. 102 in B-flat, first movement.

Ex. 1.45 (continued)

the two periods are in strict correspondence except for changes in dynamics and orchestration, and omission of the nonharmonic c^2 in the final cadence. The repeated period should not be confused with the double period, in which the final cadence is *harmonically* superior to all of the preceding cadences.

THE PHRASE GROUP

Two disparate phrases, both of which end on the dominant, obviously constitute neither a period nor a repeated phrase. Such a succession of phrases is described as a *phrase group*, or part of a phrase group. A phrase group lacks the correspondence and antecedent-consequent cadential pattern of period form. Example 1.46 is from

Ex. 1.46 Beethoven, String Quartet in B-flat, Op. 130, fifth movement.

mm. 10–26 of the Cavatina movement of Beethoven's Quartet, Op. 130. The movement begins with a period whose consequent phrase is considerably elongated. The phrase group which begins at m. 10 is representative of a kind of musical syntax perhaps analogous to prose rather than verse.

A succession of phrases ending in perfect authentic cadences also forms a phrase group, as in Bach's harmonization of the chorale "Auf dass wir also allzugleich" (from Cantata No. 176, *Es ist ein trotzig und verzagt Ding*). When a series of phrases ending in incomplete cadences is directly followed by a corresponding phrase with tonic cadence (as in the aria "Mein Verlangen," mm. 31ff., from Bach's Cantata No. 161), the analyst will likely conclude that the final tonic is a complement to and affirmation of the preceding incomplete cadences, and completes a period having several antecedents.

Phrase groups are relatively common in pre-classical and recent music, and in developmental sections in music of all periods.

IRREGULAR EXAMPLES

Needless to say, interesting musical situations often lack clear conformance with the norms upon which definitions, classifications, and generalizations are based. Many passages employ motivic fragments interspersed among larger units, or repeated developmentally. The concentration upon short motives and figures, as in Ex. 1.47,

Ex. 1.47 Beethoven, Sonata in F minor, Op. 2, No. 1, first movement.

contributes to the relatively unstable character of typical developmental passages.

In a polyphonic texture, phrase and motive divisions usually overlap among the several voices. This is illustrated in Ex. 1.48, a transitional section in which

Ex. 1.48 Mozart, String Quartet in D minor, K. 421, first movement.

motives of varying sizes overlap, sometimes in imitative fashion, obscuring "seams" and imparting a feeling of forward movement without definite punctuation, a quality basic to imitative textures.

The type of rhetoric in which regular phrase divisions are suppressed in favor of a more proselike structure, as in Ex. 1.48, affords valuable contrast to such regularity. Examples of this kind are, however, best regarded in comparison with the distinct phraseology characteristic of original expository statements of themes in tonal forms.

THE JOINING OF CONTIGUOUS UNITS

A unit of form may come to a complete stop, followed after a break by continuation into the following section. However, maintenance of motion over the cadences is always significant and of interest. Without skillful bridging, especially between small units, a form can become disjointed and fragmentary. The methods by which a composer achieves an effect of cadential punctuation without a full stop in the surface flow are numerous, and the careful analysis of these is always instructive.

Consecutive units may be joined simply by drawing them into the closest proximity, causing the new unit to begin concurrently with the end of the one preceding; the so-called *elided* cadence has already been introduced (see Ex. 1.17).

At the point of cadence, a motive of the succeeding phrase may be introduced as a means of establishing a palpable connection between the two units (Ex. 1.49).

Ex. 1.49 Bach, Christmas Oratorio, Part III, No. 31 (Alto aria: Schliesse, mein Herze).

Rarely, a new section enters before the preceding part has ended; the entry of the new material may even be concealed within the framework of the cadence ending the preceding section. A justly celebrated example, representing a highly ingenious if rather uncommon procedure, is the "hidden entry" of the reprise of the theme in the first movement of Mozart's G minor Symphony (Ex. 1.50).

The most common method of joining contiguous units is that of filling in the measure of the cadence with a figuration or line of some kind. This affords a contin-

Ex. 1.50 Mozart, Symphony No. 40 in G minor, K. 550, first movement.

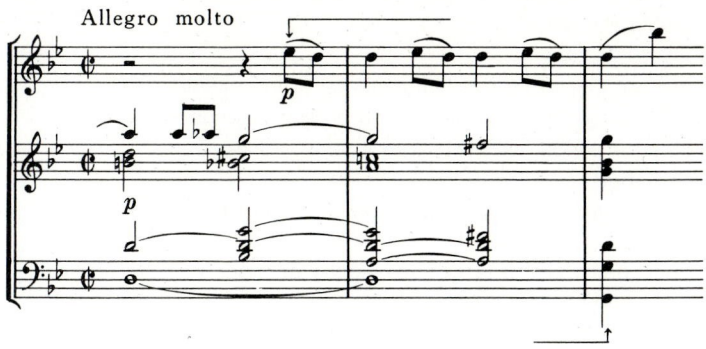

uation of rhythmic activity, often in a single voice, but does not impair the sense of cadence (Ex. 1.51).

Ex. 1.51 Bartók, Mikrokosmos, Book II, No. 66.
    © Copyright 1940 by Hawkes & Son (London) Ltd. Reprinted by permission.

New phrase

    For further examples, and for a full and perceptive discussion of this problem, the student is again referred to Toch's *The Shaping Forces in Music,* Chapter 11.

EXERCISES

The activities suggested at the end of each chapter, most of them in the nature of research, will consolidate and illustrate the principles learned by reference to the literature itself, and will prove of inestimable value. It is not assumed that all of the exercises will be undertaken; benefit will derive from the completion of any number. Various exercises can, at times, be divided among the members of a group with a common sharing of the results, or the exercises may be taken as specimens upon which further projects are to be developed.

1.   Look for examples of units of form discussed in Chapter 1. Do not limit yourself to the literature of any single period. Include examples of irregular proportions.

2. Try writing each of the following—at least the melody, indicating the appropriate cadential harmonies below the melodic line.
   a) a 4-measure phrase
   b) a 5-measure phrase
   c) an 8-measure period, with a half-cadence at the middle
   d) a 10-measure period, with the second phrase extended
   e) a 12-measure period, with two antecedent phrases
   f) a double period
3. Prepare an examination covering the material in Chapter 1. Include examples for analysis.
4. Find (or invent) passages in language—poetry or prose—which compare, in structure, meter, and punctuation, to specific types of phrase and period.
5. Find examples of consecutive phrases and other adjacent units. Consider how the cadential points are bridged. Try to imagine another way of accomplishing the same purpose.
6. Analyze the first 24 measures of Beethoven's Sonata in E minor, Op. 90. Classify the cadences and identify the key levels. Do you feel that the half-cadence at m. 16 is a period division? What elements of symmetry do you observe? Would you describe the passage as a phrase group or an enlarged period?
7. Analyze phrase and period form in the folksongs "Arkansas Traveler" and "Blue Bells of Scotland."

2

BINARY

An almost invariable principle in the forms of traditional music has been division, by one or more strong cadences, into two or more contrasting but related sections. As suggested in Chapter 1, such segmentation is an aid to coherent organization.

The binary is a two-part form. It is a magnification of the period and thus a larger manifestation of the antecedent-consequent idea, and it may constitute an entire movement. Its two parts (sections, divisions) are in themselves periods or phrase groups, and the half-cadence of the antecedent element is a relatively pronounced reference to the dominant or another closely related key. By extension, the period, and its characteristic, definitive principle of antecedence-consequence, may be regarded as the embryonic basis for single-movement sonata form, the ultimate evolution of binary form (see Chapter 6).

THE INCIPIENT TYPE; STANDARDS
OF CLASSIFICATION

When considering the relations of smaller to larger forms, one sometimes comes upon ambiguous examples in which more extended types can be seen in incipience in forms of relatively small dimension and limited developmental amplitude. It is often difficult, for instance, to distinguish clearly between period and binary form, and terminology must therefore be flexible.

In a sense, the *incipient binary* is a period of inflated implications within either of two dimensions by which scope in tonal forms is measured. One is the obvious criterion of length. The other is the "depth" of modulatory import, the extent of tonicization of the secondary key at the point of bisection.

As to the first of these, the distinction must be somewhat arbitrary. Since it does seem reasonable to make such a distinction recognizing an interim condition between period and binary, we may assert that in full binary form each of the two parts contains more than two phrases. The second criterion is problematic in that the evaluation of tonal fluctuation is considerably subjective: the significance of occurrences of the secondary leading-tone must depend upon rhythm, tempo, and other factors. The theoretical "meaning" of chromatic deviance in any particular tonal structure is also problematic. Gradations of effect range from the totally diatonic through surface chromaticism to relatively emphatic cadences on the tonicized dominant or other degree. This last condition, of pronounced reference through the secondary dominant to the secondary tonic as an explicit focus of cadential direction, *is germane to the binary principle*.

An incipient binary is, then, a two-part form in which one of these two standards is applicable, but not the other. Some examples show relatively strong reference to a secondary key (tonal amplification, depth of tonal import[1]), while their length suggests period form. In other examples, despite the absence of even superficial tonal deviance, the number of phrases exceeds the period norm. Of course, an imperative criterion for binary of any kind is bisection by distinct cadential punctuation.

Example 2.1 is an extreme case in which each of the two sections is but a

Ex. 2.1   Beethoven, Sonata in F minor, Op. 57, third movement.

single phrase, repeated, the second extended to 10 measures. The cadential reference to the dominant minor (c) is substantial, and is achieved partly by the occur-

---

[1]The idea of "depth" of implication inherent in a particular tonal occurrence can be thought of in one sense as to the temporal span over which it applies, as a measure, with that of exposure at cadences, of significance *under*lying the elaborative surface. The applicable temporal span associated with the occurrence includes its harmonic preparation as well as its literal duration and repetition.

rence of e♭¹ in m. 7 (from which the melodic line descends by step to c), representing momentary cancellation of the tonic leading-tone, in addition to emphatic harmonic preparation at least from m. 6. In this restricted sense, the example reflects a tonal amplitude beyond that of the simple period. A further aspect of this is, incidentally, the modest inflation of the second part, which leads ephemerally toward the relative major, showing an incipient developmental tendency which will presently be seen as characteristic of full binary form.

A further example of this type of incipient binary is quoted as Ex. 2.2. Here,

Ex. 2.2 Beethoven, Sonata in G, Op. 79, second movement.

each of the two parts is 4 measures long, divided into *two 2-measure phrases*. Each 4-measure group is a period. The designation ''incipient binary'' is again based on the brevity of the passage (here, individual sections of two phrases each) combined with a pronounced reference to a secondary tonic (here, the relative major) at the middle point.

An example of incipient binary of the second type is the ''Air'' from Bach's Partita No. 6 in E minor, in which larger proportions are in evidence (a total of seven phrases, excluding the codetta, comprising a first part of 12 measures and a second part of 16) but without modulation at the conclusion of the antecedent part. The half-cadence ending the first part is shown as Ex. 2.3.

Ex. 2.3 Bach, Air from Partita No. 6 in E minor.

An example like the Bach Air is obviously closely allied to the typical enlarged period, but more extensive and digressive.

Occasionally, the analyst may come upon a specimen which, while definitely in two parts, defies classification on any of the bases outlined above. Such an example is the variation theme from the second movement of Beethoven's Sonata in F minor, Op. 57. It conforms to neither condition of binary as we have defined it. It is neither a double period nor a repeated period, it is entirely homogeneous tonally, and the two principal cadences are of the perfect authentic type. It is best described either as two periods, each repeated, or as a period followed by an extended phrase in which a 2-measure motive undergoes variation.

BINARY: THE FIRST PART

The first part of a binary form, often ending with a repeat sign, may be a double period, an enlarged period, or a group of phrases.

The tonal motion which we have established as a characteristic of binary form normally occurs early enough to allow emphatic tonicization of the secondary tonic before the bisecting cadence, its implication often extending into the second part of the form. There may be a series of brief, superficial modulations leading to the cadence. The key in which the first part ends is very often the dominant when the example is in the major mode, and the relative major if the primary key is minor. Exceptions to the rule for major mode are rare (see Ex. 2.4); in minor, the goal of

Ex. 2.4   Schubert, Sonata in A minor, Op. 42, third movement.

the first part is occasionally the dominant rather than the relative major (Exs. 2.1 and 2.7).

Goetschius speaks of the occasional use of an "introductory phrase."[2] In Ex. 2.4 the opening segment is introductory, with the binary form proper beginning at m. 5. Only portions of the first part, which modulates to the mediant key of A minor, are quoted here.

Another example of the introductory phrase in binary form is seen in No. 9 of the Schumann *Papillons*, Op. 2 (see mm. 1–8).

Often the material centers on the treatment of a particular motive, developed in various ways throughout the form (Ex. 2.5).

Ex. 2.5   Handel, Allemande from Suite IX in G minor.

Sometimes the texture is fugal, as often in the gigues of Bach suites and partitas.

Ex. 2.6   Bach, Gigue from French Suite No. 1 in D minor.

The cadence ending the first part commonly forms a decisive punctuation, most often a perfect authentic cadence on the secondary tonic. It constitutes a pronounced interruption and is followed by a clear sense of resumption.

[2]*Lessons in Music Form*, p. 85.

Ex. 2.7 Froberger, Plainte from Suite in A minor.

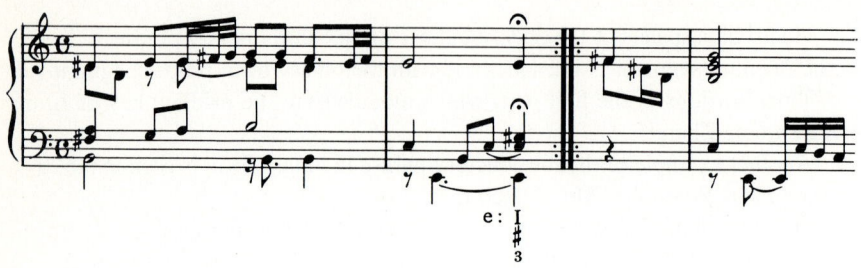

THE SECOND PART

The form of the binary's second part is likely to be comparable, and may even be identical, to that of the first. Often it is a phrase group in which there is somewhat free development of a basic motive. The second part is thus frequently longer than the first (resulting in an asymmetrical binary), and more modulatory within the range of closely related keys. The diagram in Ex. 2.8 illustrates some of these fac-

Ex. 2.8 Geminiani, Concerto in C minor, Op. 2, No. 2, for strings, fourth movement.

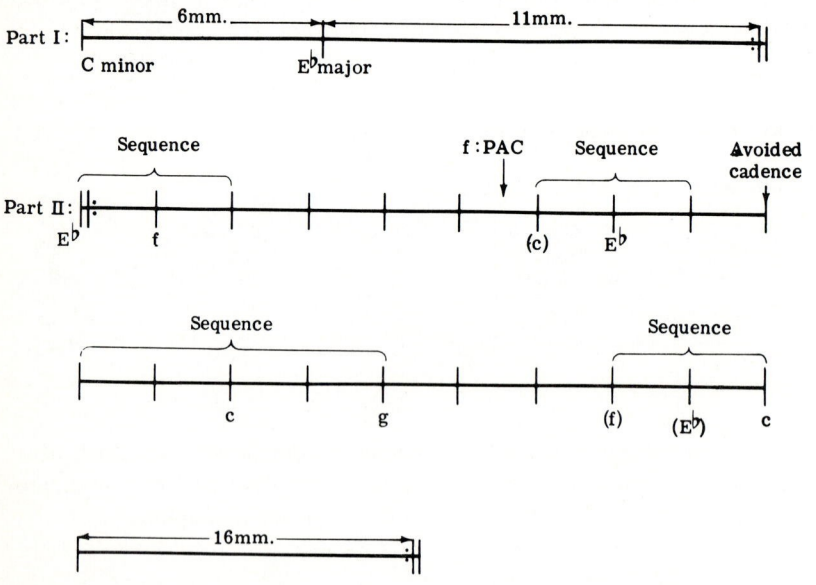

tors. The main tonal areas are the tonic, relative major, subdominant, and dominant minor; tonal levels indicated in parentheses are touched on only fleetingly.

There may be considerable difference in the relative lengths of the two parts (see Ex. 2.8), although the symmetrical binary is not uncommon. Greater length in the first part is, however, extremely rare. Perfectly symmetrical examples of binary form are the Corrente from Bach's Partita No. 5, with 32 measures in each section, and the theme of Bach's *Goldberg Variations,* in which each half is made up of two periods totalling 16 measures.

Bach's fourth Partita contains interesting examples of asymmetrical binary—for example, the Allemande, which has 24 measures in Part I and 32 in Part II. In the same Partita, the Sarabande is extremely asymmetrical: its proportions are 12–26. One can see in this movement some of the emerging principles of later single-movement sonata form. Not only is there a developmental quality in the opening measures of the second part, but in m. 17 in Part II there is an allusion to the original material.

During Part II of binary form, the tonic key returns early enough so that it is strongly established and reaffirmed before the final cadence. Example 2.9 is from another Bach suite movement—a relatively short, very asymmetrical example. There are 24 measures in all; the second part is exactly twice the length of the first, but lacks the ternary feature of thematic restatement. The quoted excerpt shows the point of modulation back to the tonic; this is preceded by passing references to E, B minor, and E minor, in addition to a strong reference to the key of D.

The aspect of the form discussed above—that of modulation from the original key and its reaffirmation in the final bars—is exceedingly significant and characteristic. Binary form has in this sense a ternary attribute: the opening and closing tonic sections create a kind of three-part structure tonally, even if this is not confirmed by actual segmentation and thematic design.

Ex. 2.9 Bach, Courante II from English Suite No. 1 in A.

There is nearly always a strong motivic correspondence between the two divisions, lending a pervasive unity to the form. Often, the second part begins quite like the first (as in Ex. 2.5), except for the difference of key, and the cadences ending the two sections are likewise frequently identical in every respect except key (see Ex. 2.10).

Ex. 2.10 Hindemith, Ludus Tonalis, Interludium between second and third fugues.

Pastorale, moderate

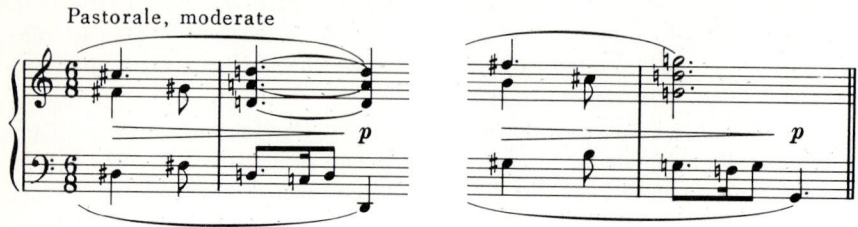

Occasionally, especially in eighteenth-century examples, the parallel construction described above is realized by the use of an inverted form of the common motive at the beginning of the second part. Example 2.11 shows such a motive and its inversion; the second quotation (inversion) is the beginning of Part II.

Ex. 2.11 Bach, Gigue from French Suite No. 2 in C minor.

The diagrammatic designation often given for binary form is *AB*. It can now be seen that this representation is not altogether proper. The use of the letter *B* usually denotes a substantial change of character, of materials, or of texture; none of these is likely in binary form. The rule is a second part which is simply a new arrangement of the motives of the first, with the same rhythmic pace and content, even though more fluctuant tonally.

THE CODETTA

Frequently the form ends with a short closing section or *codetta* (from the Italian *coda*, meaning ''tail'') commonly only a few measures in length.

A codetta may close the first as well as the second part. It is typically set off by a cadence—in some sense inconclusive—in the key in which the section is to end; the ensuing material adds a stamp of finality. Example 2.12 shows a deceptive cadence setting off a codetta of 2½ measures. The example closely parallels the corresponding point in the first part of the form.

Ex. 2.12   Bach, Allemande from French Suite No. 3 in B minor.

In the movement shown in Ex. 2.13, from Carl Philipp Emanuel Bach (1714–88), the 8-measure codetta recurs in the second part in a precise transposition. The mild, surface chromaticism reveals in a germinal manifestation a common device of elaboration, around I, which is idiomatic in large codas, at times in expansive prolongations: the developmental tonicization of IV and V.

Ex. 2.13   C. P. E. Bach, Prussian Sonata No. 1 in F, third movement.

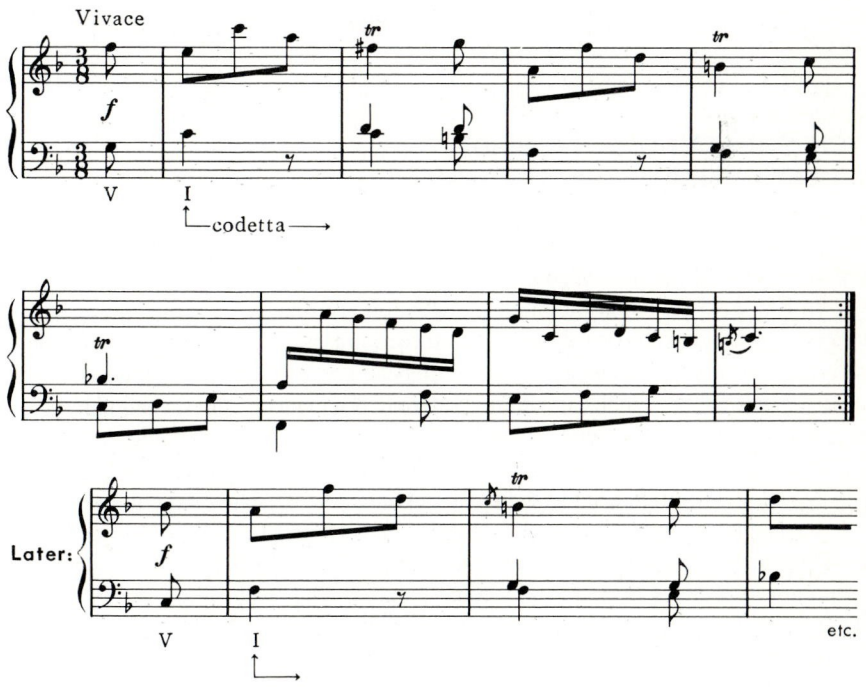

Rarely, a codetta may be in two distinct parts. It is clear in Ex. 2.14 that the final section (set off by the perfect authentic cadence at m. 72) is matched by the preceding material. The two segments are obviously divisions of a larger unit, and parallel in construction; this is thus a two-part codetta.

Ex. 2.14   D. Scarlatti, Sonata in E minor, K. 263 (Longo 321).

BACH, SONATA NO. 2 IN A MINOR
FOR VIOLIN ALONE, THIRD MOVEMENT

The outline of one complete example will serve to summarize the features of binary form as discussed in this chapter.

In Ex. 2.15 principal points of punctuation are marked as authentic or half-cadences. Each large binary division has three phrases, whose periodic relations, appreciable at more than one level, are of unusual interest. The first phrase of each part is distinctly antecedent, concluding with a half-cadence.[3] The second phrase of each part is pivotal, its cadence in some sense imperfect although tonic, so that it functions at once as consequent to the preceding and further antecedent to the third. In each part, the third phrase has the most emphatic arrival. The final phrase of Part I is at the same time transitional, effecting the expected progression to the dominant key. The cadence of Part II is much extended, appropriately, and the most emphatic in duration as well as in its primary tonal content. The final phrase starts, at the upbeat to m. 20, with development of a motive varied in melodic content while of a

---

[3]Classification of the cadences is with respect to the *immediate* tonal context.

Ex. 2.15   Bach, Sonata No. 2 in A minor for solo violin, third movement.[4]

fixed, 1-measure length, this development being a means of extension. Seen in the context of the entire form, the final phrase is a consequent to all the preceding phrases. This is a way of seeing the binary as an inflation of period form; another similarity with the period can be seen in the fundamental content of the two major divisions: I–V; V–I.

The first measures of Part II are, as so often, the most modulatory area in the form.[5] Its tonal regions are indicated in the quotation by identification of the first *dominant* of each: the passage touches the relative minor, and its dominant and sub-dominant levels.

The reader will observe the manner in which Bach maintains surface continuity, arresting rhythmic motion only at the two primary cadences. The strongest of the subordinate cadences (m. 8) is attenuated by reiteration of the tonic root; another authentic cadence (m. 19) is weakened by dissonance (the $f\sharp^2$). Further factors contributing to forward momentum are a general prevalence of melodic and harmonic dissonance, the infrequency of root-position tonic harmony, and chromatic harmony (for example, in m. 24).

Additional study of this movement might take up the recurrence and variation of characteristic motives which lend unity to the form. Further analysis would note, too, the rise and fall to and through secondary and primary high points of pitch; for example, in Part I, the upper-voice melody ascends through e^1, g^1, c^2, e^2, and g^2 (to its neighbor, a^2)—an underlying linear expression of the tonic triad, followed by phased descent to the g^1 of the cadence. A comparable view of framing harmonic content, following the basic I–V motion of Part I, would regard the tonicized elements of Part II as comprising an orthodox 5th-succession toward the final tonic: VI–(III)–II–V–I.

SIGNIFICANCE OF THE REPEATS

The two parts which make up binary form are generally repeated. The question may properly be raised as to the effect upon the form, which we have described as being in *two* parts, when such repeats are practiced.

The essential content and nature of the form are not really affected by the repeats; in general form and substance, though not in length, *AA′* is the equivalent of *AA,A′A′* (as *AB* is the equivalent of *AA, BB*). It is clear that the significant division is still at the "middle" point. The result is thus a two-part form in which each part is repeated, usually literally; the total length is affected but not the "scenario" of form-defining content, particularly where the form lacks significant motivic digression.

But the problem is more complex when one considers tonal outlines, which might be represented by the symbols TD, DT. Here, despite the literality of repeti-

---

[5]This passage is further illustration of a pregnant binary feature mentioned before, in which one sees a foreshadowing of the development section of single-movement sonata form (Chapter 6).

tion, the frequency of *tonal digression and return* has been multiplied in a way that does have an impact upon the formal scenario, conditioned by tonal as distinct from thematic events.

In practice, both of performance and of composition, the repeats are not always used. Even when indicated, they are often ignored in performance; sometimes, illogically, one is ignored and the other observed. When repeats are practiced, binary form is magnified, and its tonal outlines altered. Binary repeats normally employ *retransitions*,[6] with the result that continuity is uninterrupted.

THE ROUNDED BINARY

A two-part form in which material of the opening section is formally and substantially recalled, in its original key, in the final bars of the second part is sometimes termed *rounded binary*. Preference is given here, however, to the synonym *incipient ternary*, which is discussed in the following chapter.

EXERCISES

1. Compose a small binary form that includes at least a melody line and an indication of cadential formula.
2. Look for examples of the following:
   a) incipient binary form
   b) full binary form
   c) codetta in a binary example
   d) binary in which the first part modulates to a key other than the dominant
   e) binary illustrating parallel construction, including parallel cadential patterns in the two parts
   f) asymmetrical binary form
3. Take one example of binary and discuss its form according to the procedure followed in this chapter with relation to the Bach Solo Violin Sonata movement.
4. Diagram a hypothetical example of binary form to show basic features and tonal levels.
5. Answer the following questions concerning either a binary example of your selection or one of the examples mentioned in the text.
   a) What is the basic key?
   b) Where is the modulation to the key in which the first part ends?
   c) Characterize each cadence as to its type and relative strength.
   d) Write out the principal motive or motives on which the music is based.
   e) Describe the form of each of the two main parts.
   f) Is there a codetta? What is its length? What is its content?

---

[6]*Retransition*, discussed in Chapter 6, denotes a bridge passage (transition) preparing the return of previously stated material—a connective link leading back to material already featured.

g) What are some of the techniques for joining individual units within each part—for keeping up a constancy of motion and obscuring "seams"?

h) Is the form symmetrical?

i) Locate the modulation in which the basic key is reaffirmed in the second part.

j) Are there other tonal references than those involving the principal keys?

k) What deeper lines of melodic and harmonic continuity do you observe?

6. What opportunities for variety are implicit in binary form?

7. Look for examples of binary form in one or more of the following sources:

a) suites and partitas of Bach

b) suites of George Frideric Handel (1685–1759)[7]

c) eighteenth-century sonata and concerto movements

d) keyboard pieces of Henry Purcell (1659–95) and his English contemporaries

8. What unusual element of asymmetry is often found in binary sonatas of Domenico Scarlatti (1685–1757)?

9. Examine the slow movement of the Piano Sonata in D (Hob. XVI:37) of Franz Joseph Haydn (1732–1809). Why does it end on the dominant of the tonic key?

10. In each of the examples of Béla Bartók (1881–1945) cited below, carefully compare details of harmonic, motivic, and other elements of content in Parts I and II.

11. The text of Chapter 2 refers for illustration to many examples of binary form—examples that may be used for further analysis. Additional works are listed below, and the reader is urged to study binary form in a number of them.

Bach, Prelude No. 22 in B-flat minor from the *Well-Tempered Clavier,* Book I
Sinfonia (Three-Voice Invention) No. 6 in E

Bartók, *Mikrokosmos,* Book II, Nos. 42 and 51; Book III, No. 69

Ludwig van Beethoven (1770–1827), String Quartet in C minor, Op. 18, No. 4, trio of third movement
Variations on a Theme of Diabelli, Op. 120, theme
String Quartet in G, Op. 18, No. 2, second movement, mm. 29–52
Sonata in D, Op. 28, trio of third movement
Sonata in G, Op. 79, last movement, mm. 1–16

Johannes Brahms (1833–97), Waltz in G-sharp minor, Op. 39, No. 3

François Couperin (1668–1733), harpsichord pieces *L'Aimable Thérèse,* *L'Anguille* (an incipient binary), and *Les Tricoteuses*

Haydn, Sonata in E-flat (Hob. XVI: 28), trio of second movement and theme of last movement
Symphony No. 73 in D (*La Chasse*), trio of third movement

Paul Hindemith (1895–1964), *Ludus Tonalis,* Interludes preceding Fugues 3, 6, and 12

Wolfgang Amadeus Mozart (1756–91), *Variations on a Theme of Salieri,* K. 180, theme
Eight Variations on a March from Mariages Samnites by Grétry, K. 352, theme
String Quartet in E-flat, K. 428, trio of third movement (unusual tonal plan)

---

[7]A composer citation is given with full name and dates at only the first listing in text or exercises.

Jean-Philippe Rameau (1683–1764), harpsichord piece *L'Entretien des Muses*

D. Scarlatti, Sonata in E minor, K. 263 (Longo 321)
    Sonata in E, K. 46 (Longo 25)

Franz Schubert (1797–1828), Sonata in A minor, Op. 42, second movement, mm. 1–32

3

SIMPLE TERNARY

Since music unfolds in time, consisting of contiguous events, the faculty of memory is necessarily engaged in its perception. As an aid to tying together the successive components, it has been customary to use the device of recalling a particular, significant idea after its initial appearance. Thus, a theme or motive, A, may be repeated immediately—creating a relationship of perfect identity between two contiguous segments—or it may be repeated after a contrasting idea has been introduced (*ABA*).

Repetition of some kind—of rhythmic pattern, of cadence, of tonal reference—has been pertinent to each of the forms and small units discussed so far, with the exception of the motive, which is so small that the mere temporal proximity of its parts relates them, assuming as well a compact, gestural integrity of idea by which motive is defined. Motivic repetition in period forms is explicit in parallel construction between phrases. In binary form, the use of a characteristic motive throughout has been seen to be usual. Of course, repetition is often not literal; the recurrence of an idea commonly involves modifications of the original pattern while its essential identity is preserved.

The concept of *ternary* form is that of repetition (return) after digression, represented by *ABA*, or *ABA'* when the restatement is a modification of the original. This principle was discussed briefly in connection with tonal levels of the binary (Chapter 2); its further implication in the period is evident, although analogous contrasting areas are of course harmonic (with reference to a single tonic) rather than tonal in the smallest forms.

The idea of *repetition after digression*, the basis for ternary form, is very old. It can be seen, for example, in such early musico-poetic forms as the medieval *vire-*

lai. A famous example of early sixteenth-century ternary form is the chanson "Faulte d'argent," by Josquin des Prez (c. 1440–1521). This piece falls into three nearly equal sections with a codetta at the end (m. 64). The third part is recapitulative.

Ex. 3.1   Josquin des Prez, Faulte d'argent.

> Reprinted by permission of the publishers from Archibald T. Davison and Willi Apel, *Historical Anthology of Music: Oriental, Medieval, and Renaissance Music* (Cambridge, Mass.: Harvard University Press, copyright, 1946, 1949, by the President and Fellows of Harvard College, © renewed 1974 by Alice D. Humez and Willi Apel).

Beginning of Part I, 24 measures:

Beginning of Part II, 21 measures:

Restatement (Part III), 21 measures:

Our basic definition of ternary form will stipulate the following features: (1) three sections; (2) a clear relationship between the first and third parts, so that the third is felt to be a return of the first; and (3) contrast—tonal, thematic, textural, developmental, or any combination of these or other factors—in the second part. The ternary principle thus signifies more than mere tripartition. For example, the third and last part of Brahms's *Alto Rhapsody,* Op. 53, does not represent a return of the first and thus the whole does not constitute ternary form.

SIGNIFICANCE OF TERNARY DIVISION
AS A PRINCIPLE OF FORM

The practice of making a musical statement, following it with a contrasting statement, and then restating the original material can be an extremely satisfactory solution to the problem of producing both unity and variety in musical form. The possible variation of the material in its return in the third part is a further treatment of the same problem—at once a provision for unity and variety. The digressive material of the second part must, of course, be complementary to that of the first (therefore like it in many respects) and, while contrasting, never contradictory.[1]

The recapitulation of original thematic materials in a third section—a conscious relating of events separated in time, for the purpose of binding the whole into a perceptible and logical unity—is often described as a "rounding" of the form. The flanking of a middle section with two similar outer parts circumscribes and contains that material. Ideally, ternary thus conveys the logic and unity of a "circular" form. It is a fundamental principle in the history of form in music, and remains as viable now as ever before. *Most highly developed traditional forms are in one way or another a manifestation or extension of the ternary principle.* A twentieth-century illustration of that principle is shown in an example from Anton Webern (1883–1945).

Ex. 3.2   Webern, Variations for Piano, Op. 27, first movement.
Copyright 1937, Universal Edition.   Used by permission.

[1]Implied here is an exceedingly provocative issue in the study of musical form. In works commonly accepted as great, juxtapositions of contrasting materials are assumed to be other than arbitrary.

Ex. 3.2 (continued)

Beginning of Part II (at m. 19):

Modified Restatement (Part III), at m. 37:

PARTITION WITHOUT REPRISE; OTHER TYPES OF MULTIPLE SEGMENTATION

As stated above, tripartition in music does not necessarily mean an ordering of sections in the pattern *ABA,* although that pattern is apparent in the vast majority of tripartite examples. For instance, there may be three sections with no contrasting part—that is, three identical or nearly identical sections (or a larger number), as is the case in many *strophic* songs, in which, with minor variations to fit the changing text, the basic pattern is clearly *AAA* . . . , or *AA'A''* . . . , etc. Folk and art songs of this type are very numerous; examples include Schubert's "An Mignon," "An die Musik," and "Der Fischer," in each of which the music of the strophe is repeated unchanged. Each stanza (strophe) of "Der Fischer" is a double period.[2]

A further example, Schubert's "Der Schiffer," recalls essentially the same music with each stanza, but in variation. The stanza consists of a period, a repeated phrase, and another period.

An example in three sections, with some sharing of motives but no true reprise, is the first part (*Premier acte*) of Couperin's *Les Fastes de la Grande et Ancienne Ménestrandise* for harpsichord. When, as in the Couperin, the form comprises strongly contrasted sections, related by the sparse occurrence of common motives yet lacking systematic sectional returns, it is sometimes described as *additive.* Such a procedure (*ABC* . . .) is rare in musical form.

---

[2]Strophic form is clearly comparable to variation form, treated in Chapters 9 and 10.

Other arrangements of three sections are possible (*AAB, ABB*); where the number of sections is greater, the number of potential permutations increases. But the use of recapitulation in works where there is formal segmentation involving three or more parts is almost universal.

THE INCIPIENT TERNARY

Incipient ternary form (mentioned in the preceding chapter as *rounded binary form*) occurs most commonly as a subsection within a larger form.

The general, definitive characteristics of incipient ternary form are three. (1) The form is in *two* principal parts, of which the second is comparable to the first in length, though often slightly longer. (2) The close of the first part, as in binary form, is often in a closely related key. (3) The second part contains, in its closing measures (before the codetta, if there is one), a formal return of a significant part of the material of the first section, substantially in its original condition. Partial reprise is of the essence, and in many cases only one of two phrases is brought back, sometimes extended.

Thus, incipient ternary form demonstrates its relationship to binary form in its proportions (division into two major sections of comparable length) and often in its tonal structure (where there is modulation at the end of the first part and a return to the tonic in the second part). The second part includes the contrasting elements, of whatever degree, and the gesture of reprise.

It is apparent in Ex. 3.3 that the feeling of thematic return in the final mea-

Ex. 3.3   Brahms, Liebeslieder Walzer, Op. 52, No. 4.

sures is convincing even when there has been no pronounced motivic contrast preceding it. The opening phrase of the second part uses motives of Part I, varied in a context of underlying dominant implication.

There are occasional examples of incipient ternary whose sectional proportions are problematic as to clarity of classification. For example, the first 22 measures of the second movement of Beethoven's Sonata in D, Op. 28, suggest incipient ternary form in a scheme whose overall proportions, in numbers of measures, are 8–8,6. (Note that the second part is lengthened by extension; there is a reprise of only one phrase, but it is 6 measures long as compared to its original 4 measures.)

In Ex. 3.4 incipient ternary form is implicit in the equal proportions of the two main parts and the clear feeling of reprise at the end. But the first part ends in the original key. Examples 3.3 and 3.4, and the excerpt from Beethoven's Op. 28, can all be characterized as incipient ternary forms, even though only Ex. 3.3 conforms to the stereotype in all three respects. Examples 3.3 and 3.4 are symmetrical; the Beethoven example is asymmetrical.

Ex. 3.4   Attrib. to Spilman, Flow Gently, Sweet Afton.

Analysis of any of the following examples will help to illuminate the nature of incipient ternary form: trio of the second movement of Frédéric Chopin's (1810–49) Sonata in C minor, Op. 4 (proportions 16—8,8; keys of E-flat minor and G-flat); Beethoven, Bagatelle, Op. 119, No. 4 (8—4,4; in A and E); first 16 measures of the Mozart Concert Rondo for piano and orchestra, K. 382 (8—4,4; entirely in D; two periods whose consequent phrases are identical); Robert Schumann (1810–56), *Album for the Young,* Op. 68, No. 2 (16—8,8; in G and D); and Mozart, Sonata in A, K. 331, theme of the first-movement variations (8—4,6; entirely in A; the single phrase of the reprise enlarged by 2 measures).

SIMPLE TERNARY FORM FURTHER DEFINED

Simple ternary form has three sections of which at least the first and third are of comparable length. Occasionally the second part is, while large enough to establish its contrasting character, considerably smaller than the flanking sections. (See the trio of the second movement of Mozart's String Quartet in G, K. 387. Its proportions are 25–8–25; there is modulation to the dominant minor at the end of Part I.)

Example 3.5 embodies the standard, normative features of ternary form: the

Ex. 3.5   Beethoven, Sonata in B-flat, Op. 22, third movement.

usual conclusion of Part I in the primary tonic, the modestly digressive content of Part II, and the function of Part III as restatement. Its proportions are symmetrical, 8–8–8.

In some cases (for example, the Mozart excerpt referred to in the first paragraph of this section), Part I ends, like that of binary form, in a related key. An example of simple ternary having three nearly equal parts (20–22–20), with modu-

Ex. 3.6   Bach, Invention No. 6 in E.

Part I, beginning and end:

Part II, beginning and end mm.21–42 **:**

Part III, beginning and end mm.43–62 **:**

lation to the dominant at the end of Part I, is Bach's two-voice Invention No. 6.

Simple ternary form, like incipient ternary, occurs commonly as part of a larger form, although it is not infrequently the organizational principle underlying a complete piece. Very often the first part is repeated, perhaps reflecting binary practice. Often the combined second and third parts are repeated as well, giving the formula A‖: BA‖:, again suggesting binary procedure (Ex. 3.7).

While hoping to avoid any misleading implication with respect to *historical evolution*, one can draw a *conceptual* line linking simple ternary with other forms, in a summary which renders visible the fundamental relations of extent and complexity by which the various small forms are to be compared. Such a line would start with the period and continue through the incipient binary, the binary, the incipient ternary, and the simple ternary form. It will be useful to pause at this juncture to review definitive features of each of these forms, as well as qualities which can be seen in all of them, from the smallest to the largest.

The following chart (Fig. 3.1) will aid such a review. For obvious reasons the

Ex. 3.7   Haydn, String Quartet in B minor, Op. 64, No. 2, third movement.

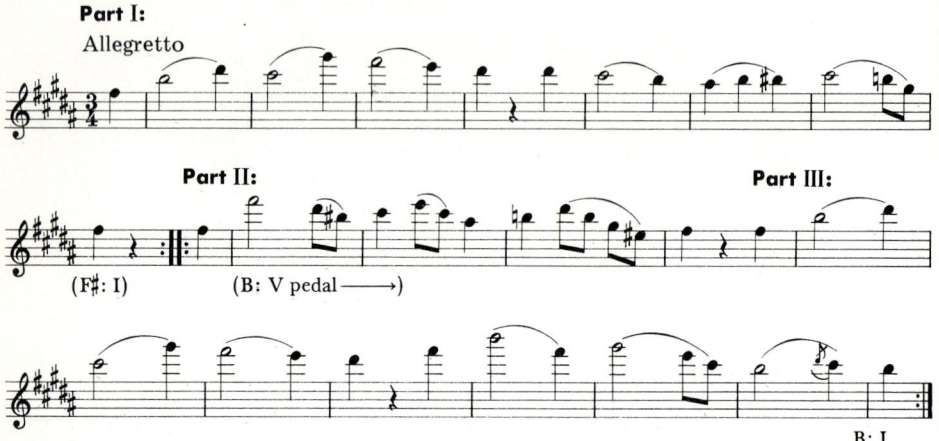

Fig. 3.1

SUMMARY OF
DISTINGUISHING FEATURES
OF SMALL FORMS

PERIOD	A	(Antecedent phrase)		A¹ or B	(Consequent phrase)
		T:V			T:I

INCIPIENT BINARY (1)

More than two phrases

A	B (on A)
T:V	T:I

(2)

One or two phrases

A	B (on A)
R:I	T:I

BINARY

More than two phrases

A	B (on A)
R:I	T:I

INCIPIENT TERNARY

A	B	A
R:I		T:I

TERNARY

A	B	A
T:I R ⟶ T:V		T:I

many variants discussed in the text are omitted and only the prototypes are represented. Neither repeats nor codettas are shown, and the symbols at cadences indicate the most probable arrival harmonies. The symbols *R* and *T* refer to related and
tonic keys, respectively.

THE FIRST PART

Rarely, the first part begins with a short introductory gesture—conceivably as much
as a complete phrase (Ex. 3.8).

Ex. 3.8   Ernst Křenek, Twelve Short Piano Pieces, Op. 83, No. 4.
Copyright, 1939, by G. Schirmer, Inc. Reprinted by permission.

The first part is based throughout on a common motive or set of related
motives, and it is traditionally also homogeneous in tonality. Here, of course, the
basic material of the form is presented; the later reprise of this material in the tonic
key is the form's fundamental basis. Example 3.9 shows the main motivic substance

Ex. 3.9   Brahms, Sonata in F minor, Op. 5, second movement.

of Part I of a simple ternary. The first section actually continues to m. 20, and is
involved throughout with the material shown here. In this work, the entire ternary
form takes up 46 measures of the movement.

The form of Part I may, like that of binary form, consist of a group of phrases,
or some variety of period form—a single period, double period, or enlarged period.
Rarely is it a single phrase. Example 3.10 is a very common type, consisting of a

Ex. 3.10 Mozart, Piano Concerto in B-flat, K. 595, third movement.

symmetrical period of two phrases. The quoted excerpt, together with its immediate tutti repetition, constitutes Part I of a small ternary.

An example of an opening section in which a phrase group occurs is found in the Menuet from *Le Tombeau de Couperin,* a suite by Maurice Ravel (1875–1937). Measures 1 to 8 consist of two phrases which do not form a period.

As already indicated, and as is borne out, for instance, in Exx. 3.5 and 3.10, Part I most often ends with an authentic cadence in the tonic key. (For an example of a first part ending on a secondary tonic, see Ex. 3.6 and its explanatory paragraph.) In many cases, especially in the late eighteenth and early nineteenth centuries, the first part is followed by a repeat sign with two endings. Or, especially in more recent examples, Part II follows immediately without the repeat of Part I. In Ex. 3.11 not only is there no repeat, but Parts I and II are joined by an elided cadence.

In simple ternary form, there is usually no transition between Parts I and II, but perhaps for an adjusted second ending when Part I is repeated. Now and then the

Ex. 3.11 Elgar, Enigma Variations, Op. 36, opening theme.
     Reproduced by permission of Novello & Co., Ltd.

Ex. 3.11 (*continued*)

End of Part I,
beginning of Part II

first part moves unobviously, by dissolution,[3] into Part II. In this regard, the student may examine the Chopin Prelude in G-sharp minor, Op. 28, No. 12. Part I begins with an 8-measure phrase. At the repetition of this phrase (m. 9) the music moves off into a long, digressive, modulatory middle section, with a reprise at m. 41. Thus, the form is ternary despite the absence of clear cadential separation between Parts I and II.

THE SECOND PART

The principal structural function of the second part is to provide contrast—a sense of departure as a basis for the restatement of the original thematic material in the tonic key. In the simple ternary, the second part is frequently based on the same motivic material as Part I. In such cases there will be contrast of melodic contour, of texture, of key, or of some other element. In most cases there is at least contrast of secondary tonal reference. If the original tonic persists, there is likely to be harmonic contrast in the form of dominant prolongation, or by other means.

In Ex. 3.12, the basic motives are carried into Part II, but they are turned to different melodic effect (see the inversion of mm. 2–3), and the tonal level is changed.

An imaginative composer has infinite possibilities for variety in the second section; the problem is to achieve variety without introducing contradictory elements—for example, extreme changes of rhythmic motion and pattern. In other words, in the small dimensions of the form, the middle section ideally offers contrasting attitudes and substance which are at the same time complementary to Part I. Of all the possibilities of variety, surface tonal change is the most common in the traditional ternary.

Again, the most likely keys for the middle section are the dominant, relative

---

[3]The *dissolution* of a unit is its failure to continue on an established course, to an expected conclusion, or in a previously implied direction. Often the material disintegrates into thematically insignificant figuration. Or it may stop at a certain point, a fragment then repeated in variants, reaching a tentative cadence, or avoiding a cadence. Example 4.14 is a particularly clear illustration.

Ex. 3.12   Ravel, Le Tombeau de Couperin, Menuet.

> Permission for reprint granted by Durand et Cie., Paris, France, copyright owners, and Elkan-Vogel Co., Inc., Philadelphia, Pa., agents.

major, and relative minor. Examples of each, including one irregular relationship, are shown in Exx. 3.13, 3.14, and 3.15. In each of these examples, the end of Part I and the beginning of Part II are shown.

Other tonal relationships are, of course, possible (see Ex. 3.18). In Chopin's Prelude No. 15 in D-flat the middle section is in the parallel enharmonic minor.

The form of Part II is occasionally merely a single phrase; more often it is a phrase or motive group. It is most commonly comparable in length to Part I. Because the second part often ends on dominant harmony (T:V),[4] in anticipation of the

Ex. 3.13   Schumann, Album for the Young, Op. 68, No. 3.

[4]*T:V* denotes dominant of the tonic (fundamental, or original) key.

Ex. 3.14 Schumann, Papillons, Op. 2, No. 3.

Ex. 3.15 Schubert, Die Liebe hat gelogen.

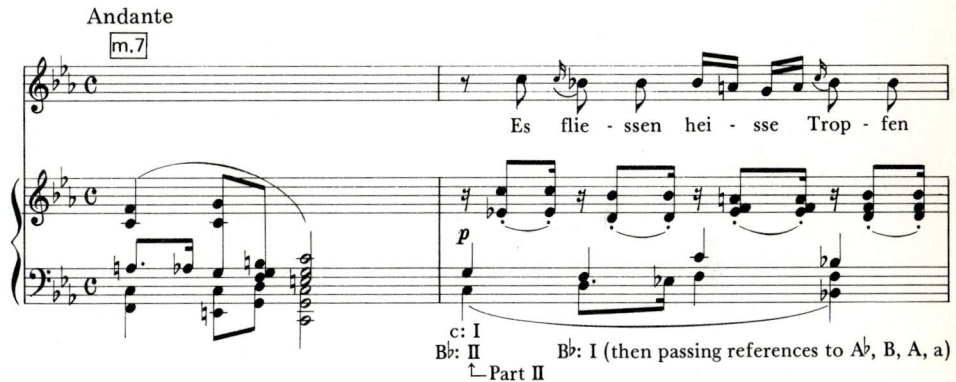

return, period form is uncommon. (A rare example may be seen in the trio of the second movement of Haydn's Sonata in G, Hob. XVI:27, whose middle section is in B-flat.) An example of Part II as a single phrase, in this case of 4 measures, is seen in Ex. 3.7. The Menuet from Ravel's *Le Tombeau de Couperin*, cited above, affords a good example of a second section constructed as a phrase group (mm. 9–24).

Rarely is a new theme introduced in the middle section of a simple ternary. An exception occurs in the scherzo of Beethoven's Sonata in A, Op. 2, No. 2, where a new theme, in G-sharp minor, begins in m. 19.

The character of the second part, even in simple ternary, is often of particular interest, being more tentative, less settled, less likely to be punctuated with firm cadences than either of the flanking sections. This relative mobility often takes the

Ex. 3.16 Chopin, Prelude in D-flat, Op. 28, No. 15.

form of restrained sequential development (Ex. 3.16) of a motive or phrase. (See also the theme of Mozart's *Ten Variations on an Air of Gluck,* K. 455.)

The second part may close with a strong cadence in the contrasting key, followed directly by the third part. This means, of course, that the final harmony of Part II would function as a pivot for the return of the tonic key (Ex. 3.17).

Part II may dissolve into a retransitional passage which prepares the return of the original material and key, or such a retransition may follow a cadential ending of the second part (Ex. 3.18).

It is also possible for the second part to contain within itself, without any disruption of its formal structure, a modulation back to the original key. The specimen

Ex. 3.17 Tchaikovsky, Symphony No. 6 in B minor, Op. 74, second movement.

Ex. 3.18   Beethoven, Bagatelle, Op. 119, No. 1.

Part I beginning:

End of Part II :

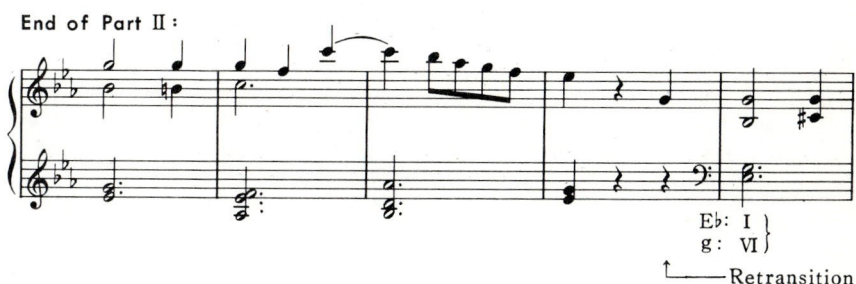

from which Ex. 3.19 is taken is of the proportions 4–7–7, part of a larger form. As is not unusual in freer styles, the music is characterized by tentative cadences.

The question of transition (and retransition) is here a focus of attention for the first time. It is useful to consider three factors of preparation in the function of retransition.

1. Tonal preparation: modulation to the tonic of the forthcoming material.
2. Thematic preparation: anticipation of the motivic material of the next section.
3. Harmonic preparation: often involving an extended passage on a dissonant form of dominant harmony, intensifying the expectation of the approaching section.

As an example of retransition, necessarily brief because of the limits of the form under discussion, Ex. 3.20 illustrates all three principles of preparation. The modulation is indicated; motives appearing in the thematic preparation are brack-

Ex. 3.19 Debussy, Suite Bergamasque for piano, Menuet.

Permission for reprint granted by Editions Jean Jobert, Paris, France, copyright owners, and Elkan-Vogel Co., Inc., Philadelphia, Pa., agents.

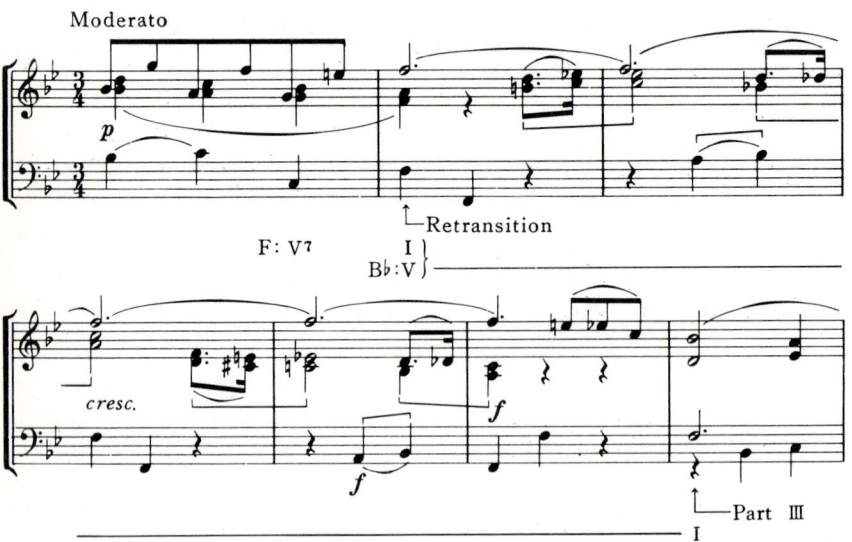

Ex. 3.20 Mozart, String Quartet in B-flat, K. 458, second movement.

eted; the 5 measures of dominant harmony, finally yielding to the tonic B-flat, represent the harmonic preparation. Of course, it should not be assumed that all three factors are present in all cases.

A notable example of harmonic preparation of unusual intensity and effect occurs in the scherzo of Beethoven's Sonata in A-flat, Op. 26. The preparation of the return in Part III of this simple ternary comprises no fewer than 20 measures of dominant harmony (mm. 25-45).

THE THIRD PART

In the restatement in Part III, the almost invariable rule is the return of the tonic key, usually before the beginning of this section. Example 3.21, from Brahms's String Sextet, Op. 18, is highly exceptional in this respect. Only important points are shown here. Part I is 10 measures long and Part II consists of a mere 4 measures. Measure 15 begins a restatement which is at the same time elaborately developmental. This section is 26 measures long, returning to the key of F only 3 measures before the end of the trio (at m. 38).

All possibilities relevant to the form of Part I apply to Part III. The return may be a literal *da capo,* as in the Beethoven Bagatelle, Op. 119, No. 3. However, now and then (more often in larger ternary forms) the material of the first part is varied in

Ex. 3.21   Brahms, String Sextet in B-flat, Op. 18, third movement (trio).

Part I:

some way in its return. Theoretically, any aspect of the material—formal, harmonic, melodic, rhythmic, timbral, textural—is subject to change. In practice, however, the return in simple ternary form is usually quite literal, with variation generally limited to changes in accompanimental motion, slight embellishments of the melody, and small excisions or extensions. A few of these possibilities are illustrated in Exx. 3.22 and 3.23. A further type of treatment is seen in Exx. 3.6 and 3.8, in which the first and third parts are in double counterpoint.

An abbreviated return is found in Beethoven's Bagatelle, Op. 126, No. 5, whose proportions are 16–16–8. Haydn often develops the basic material after the feeling of return is established; an example of this is the second movement of the Sonata in G (Hob. XVI:27) after m. 29. For a final example the reader may look into No. 3 of the Schumann *Papillons*, Op. 2, in which the theme is made into a canon in Part III.

Part III normally ends with a strong authentic cadence, and at times with a codetta. However, when the simple ternary is part of a larger form, there may be a dissolution or transition leading into the following section.

Ex. 3.22   Beethoven, Allegretto für F. Piringer (WoO 61).

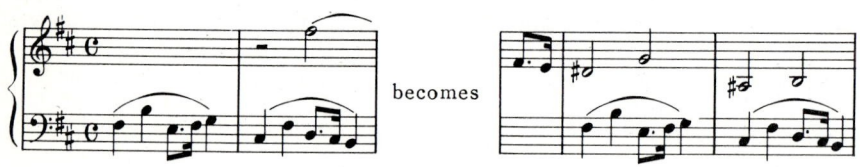

Ex. 3.23   Bartók, Mikrokosmos, Book V, No. 128.
Copyright 1940 by Hawkes & Son (London) Ltd. Reprinted by permission.

THE CODETTA

A codetta may or may not occur at the end of Part III (or of Part I, since it, too, usually ends with an authentic cadence). The codetta has been described (see Chapter 2) as the final section of a part or small form, set off by the last cadence in the key in which the part or form closes. This cadence is clearly punctuative, yet tentative by comparison with the more positively conclusive cadence which ends the codetta. A codetta in simple ternary form is brief and only rarely sectional, in view of the limited scope of the total form. (See pp. 38 and 84-85 for discussion of the sectional codetta.)

Example 3.24 quotes a codetta ending Part I of a simple ternary; Ex. 3.25 shows a codetta at the close of Part III of a further example. The codetta material of the Beethoven example, extended to 9 bars, is later used as a codetta to the complete ternary, whose proportions are 16–20–34 (codettas included). (The final section is a good basis for study of variation and extension in the return.) The second movement

Ex. 3.24 Beethoven, Trio in G, Op. 1, No. 2, for piano, violin, and cello, third movement.

Codetta

Ex. 3.25 Mussorgsky, Pictures at an Exhibition (The Ox-Cart).

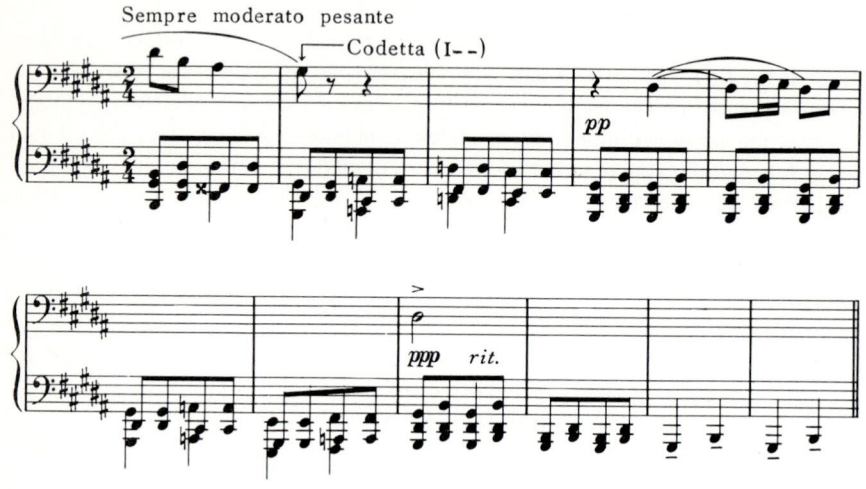

of Haydn's Sonata in G (Hob. XVI:40), mm. 8–10, affords another example of a codetta to Part I.

BRAHMS, BALLADE IN G MINOR, OP. 118, NO. 3, MEASURES 1–40

The reduced representation included as Ex. 3.26 summarizes graphically the features of simple ternary form. This example of ternary is typical in that it is an excerpt from a larger form. Indications of the main divisions and materials, as well as of phrases and motives, are given. Cadences and key levels are shown, together with other important features. The conclusion, as noted, is superseded by transitional movement into the next part of the piece. Here, the melodic G becomes the root of a dominant 7th-chord, treated enharmonically as an augmented-6th to lead into the key of B, an unusually remote tonality for the next section in the larger form.

Individual features of the work should be studied with the complete score in hand. Brahms uses the opening motive as the thematic basis for Part II, varying it tonally and in dynamics and articulation. A striking feature is the compelling thrust which propels the music over the joint linking Parts II and III: crescendo, chromatic harmony (augmented-6th on E♭, again as a device of modulation), syncopation, articulative accents, extension of the anacrusis and upward drive in pitch, and the cadential elision itself. The irregularity of the 5-measure phrases in the opening period and the asymmetry of the total form are elements of interest. The reader is urged to continue the analysis of the factors making for unity, contrast, and vitality in these 40 measures.

INCIPIENCE OF THE RONDO PRINCIPLE

We have reached a convenient point for anticipation of the rondo principle in musical form. The rondo is characterized by a pattern of several recurrences of the opening thematic material, as will be discussed fully in Chapter 5. While a rondo

Ex. 3.26 Brahms, Ballade in G minor, Op. 118, No. 3.

design involves at least three statements (two restatements) of the principal theme or group, the simplest rondo form (*ABABA* or *ABACA*) is clearly conceivable as an extension of the ternary principle of return after digression. Or, put another way, the rondo idea is implicit in the ternary. Moreover, when a small three-part form is practiced with the most usual pattern of repeats (*AABABA*) its effect comes close indeed to embodying the rondo principle.

EXERCISES

1. Try to think of as many ways as possible in which the restatement of material can be varied, without confusing its original identity. How is this problem significant in ternary form?
2. Write a paragraph explaining the significance of the ternary principle.
3. Find an example among the string quartets of Mozart illustrating simple ternary form. Analyze it thoroughly according to the procedures developed in this chapter.
4. Find an example of small ternary form in which Part III is not a strict duplicate of Part I. Compare the two sections minutely, and discuss the relationships and differences between them.
5. Compose at least the melody line and sketched harmonic basis of a small ternary according to the following plan.

    Part I: A period of irregular length in the key of D.

    Part II: A passage employing a motive derived from Part I which is treated sequentially, followed by a single phrase with a cadence on the dominant of D. Begin this section in B minor and arrange it to lead back to D.

    Part III: An abbreviated version of Part I. Be sure that it is adequate to balance the form. Follow it with a short codetta, possibly modeled after an example you have studied.

6. Study some of the musical examples in Chapter 3. Consider precisely what each of them is intended to illustrate.

    Try to find additional examples in the music of the eighteenth, nineteenth, and twentieth centuries to illustrate some of the same features. Do this with as many of the examples as possible.

7. Examine the simple ternary form of Schubert's song "Schäfers Klagelied." Why might this be described as a musical *arch form?*
8. Study the methods by which simple ternary form is linked to the subsequent section of the tonal form in some of the slow movements of sonatas of C. P. E. Bach. An example is the second movement of his *Württemberg Sonata* No. 6.
9. A few supplementary references to simple ternary form will point the way to further study. In addition to the following, the examples cited in this chapter can form the basis for independent analysis. A vast source can be found in the movements with trios (scherzos, minuets) of symphonies, sonatas, and chamber works of the eighteenth and nineteenth centuries; individual sections of such movements are very often in simple ternary form. After observing the outlines of the total form, examine the means by which the composer unifies its parts, introduces contrast, maintains interest and vitality, joins sections, and

prepares tonal and other changes. List individual, striking features in at least one or two specimens.

Bach, *English Suite* No. 6 in D minor, both gavottes
Beethoven, *Bagatelles*
    Variations in F, Op. 34, theme
Brahms, Symphony No. 2 in D, Op. 73, third movement, mm. 1–32
    Waltz in E, Op. 39, No. 2
    Waltz in E minor, Op. 39, No. 4
F. Couperin, *Les Baccanales* for harpsichord, No. 1, "Enjouements Bachiques"
Zoltán Kodály (1882–1967), Piano Pieces, Op. 3, Nos. 2, 4, and 7
Ernst Křenek (b. 1900), Piano Pieces, Op. 83 (Which are ternary in form?)
Mozart, *Twelve Variations on a Minuet by Fischer,* K. 179, theme
Schubert, "Am Strom" (song)
    Sonata in E-flat, Op. 122, second movement, mm. 1–20
Schumann, *Album for the Young,* Op. 68 (Which are ternary in form?)
Igor Stravinsky (1882–1971), Concerto for violin and orchestra, arias–second and third movements
Peter Ilyich Tchaikovsky (1840–92), Symphony No. 5 in E minor, introduction to first movement, mm. 1–37

4

COMPOUND TERNARY

The significance and wide application of the principle of recapitulative tripartition in music, emphasized in the preceding chapter in connection with the simple ternary, is further attested by the common occurrence of a ternary of broader and more intricate design—*compound ternary form*.

The important features of contrast and unity, and of the distribution and equilibrium of unifying and contrasting features, are evident here in an expanded pattern; the possibilities of variety and diversity in compound ternary form are greater than in any of the forms discussed so far, and with this wider framework a new flexibility emerges.

Ernst Toch discusses the importance of ternary form persuasively and succinctly:

> To it [the principle of tripartition] most of the forms can be traced, regardless of their substructures, proportions, standards, terms. . . . whence we came, thither we return, after all the blooming and climaxing, after all the turbulence and trepidation. The principle of tripartition is rooted in nature . . . , in our very existence.[1]

Ternary forms are sometimes reasonably described as *arch forms* because of the archlike image suggested in the concept of progression and return. The same analogy is applicable to any form embodying sections whose ordering is duplicated in reverse (for example, *ABABA*). (The analogy of "circularity," also understandable, is less apt in that no tonal-thematic return, after digression, quite reproduces the

---

[1] *The Shaping Forces in Music*, pp. 163–64. (Copyright 1958 by Criterion Music Corp.)

effect of the original; even when the repetition is literal, the reprise reexposes the early material in a new contextual light.)

The importance of the ternary principle through several periods of music history was pointed out in Chapter 3. *Da capo* arias of the baroque period are sometimes in compound ternary form (examples are cited in the following pages). Examples of early *da capo* arias will be seen to embody the ternary principle clearly, and in many cases to approach compound structure. The reader may investigate examples in the Davison-Apel *Historical Anthology of Music*,[2] Volume II; examples 203, 244, and 258—by Luigi Rossi (1598–1653), Agostino Steffani (1653–1728), and Alessandro Scarlatti (1659–1725), respectively—are *da capo* arias. Even the earliest of these has a first part which may be described as an incipient binary; other examples from this period bring back the opening phrase at the end of the first part, yielding a suggested simple ternary in the first section of the larger ternary whole.

Eighteenth-century *da capo* vocal and choral forms in full-fledged compound ternary form are readily found. An example is the alto aria "He was despised" from Handel's *Messiah*. Part I of this aria is a binary form in the keys of E-flat and B-flat, with a return to E-flat in its second section. Part III is a literal *da capo* repeat. Another example is the chorus "Ruht wohl, ihr heiligen Gebeine" from Bach's *St. John Passion*.

Occasionally composers of the eighteenth-century suite included contrasting dance pairs, with instructions for the performer to repeat the first dance after playing the second. The indication *alternativo* (It.) or *alternativement* (Fr.) was understood to mean that the first dance of the pair was to be played again after the second, resulting in a compound ternary form, each component of which would usually be a binary. An example is the pair of bourrées in Bach's *English Suite* No. 2 in A minor. The third and sixth of the *English Suites* have gavotte pairs played in *alternativo* form, and the minuet and passepied pairs of the *English Suites* Nos. 4 and 5 are further examples.

Compound ternary form, because it is an expanded, more diverse pattern, makes possible relatively strongly contrasting moods and thematic ideas. With this potential for more pronounced change in Part II, compound ternary form was a popular vehicle in the nineteenth century for character pieces written for the piano by Beethoven, Schubert, Schumann, Felix Mendelssohn (1809–47), Chopin, Brahms, and many other composers, under such labels as *bagatelle, nocturne, prelude, fantasy,* and *intermezzo.* Also included among the many piano pieces of this genre are dances and dance-derived compositions of a great variety of types—waltzes, mazurkas, polonaises, and others. Nineteenth-century salon pieces for the piano are almost invariably in simple or compound ternary form, often the latter.

Finally, the slow movements of symphonies, sonatas, and chamber works are sometimes in compound ternary form, and the minuet and scherzo movements of

---

[2]In subsequent references, the title is given in abbreviation (*HAM*).

the classical and romantic multimovement works of these types are more often than not in compound ternary form.

The above notes underscore the universality and importance of ternary form, especially since the early eighteenth century.

COMPOUND TERNARY FORM

Compound ternary form can best be defined as a recapitulative tripartite form in which each of the three parts, or any one of them, is itself a complete or incipient type of binary or ternary design. The following is an outline of the normative compound ternary. The symbols *T* and *R* denote tonic and related keys, respectively; possible introductory phrase, transitions, and codetta or coda are not represented.

aba (or ab)	*cdc (or cd, or c)*	*aba (or ab)*
A	B	A
T	R	T

Part II is sometimes centered in the parallel major or minor. A further observation concerning the tonal plan is that each of the three parts is often ''closed'' tonally—that is, each frequently begins and ends in the same key. (The second part may end in the tonic in preparation for the return; more often its final harmony is a direct pivot or is followed by a retransition.)

Example 4.1 illustrates three common features: the second part's initial reference to a closely related secondary tonic (here V), its incorporation of developmental sequence, and a concluding brief codetta (here casually retrospective of the motive of Part II evident in Ex. 4.1a).

Ex. 4.1a Chopin, Prelude in F-sharp (portion of Part II).

Ex. 4.1b Chopin, Prelude in F-sharp (final codetta).

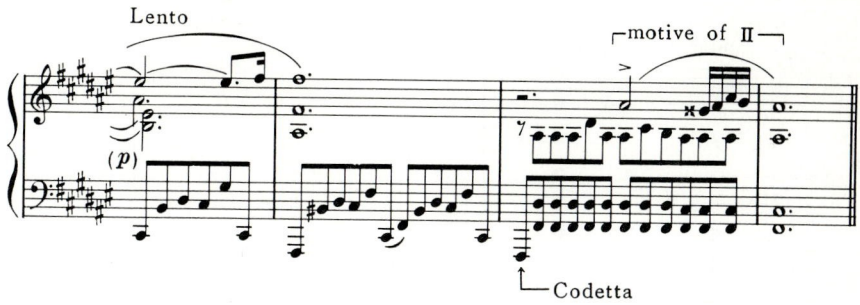

While the simple ternary is in general smaller than the compound type the essential distinction is in the degree of complexity, not of size. And in twentieth-century music, in which ternary form is important indeed, strict tonal organization into smaller binary and ternary substructures is less usual than in the tonal periods, and relatively large simple ternaries are to be found. An example is Charles Griffes's (1884–1920) *The White Peacock,* which must be described as a simple ternary because of the simple organization of its separate parts, which do not form two- or three-part designs. Yet, its proportions are quite large. Part I rests mostly on the dominant of the key of E; Part II (m. 19), extensive and fluctuant, is somewhat developmental of material of Part I; Part III (the last 20 measures), recapitulates the opening material.

THE INTRODUCTION

Although it is more likely in a larger form that some sort of introductory material will precede the form proper, the introduction is still relatively uncommon in the compound ternary.

The concept and function of the introduction, already presented briefly, will be discussed fully in Chapter 6 with regard to single-movement sonata form, where the introduction is sometimes very significant and highly developed. It will suffice here to point out a few examples of introductions to compound ternary forms and to discuss some possibilities of structure and content.

There may be a device of no more than a chord or two, or a single brief motive, pointing to the thematic entry to follow (Ex. 4.2).

Examples 4.3 and 4.4 are slightly more extensive. The first, which is very familiar, is a series of harmonies amounting to a single phrase. The imperfect plagal cadence into m. 4 is extended for 2 measures of tonic harmony. The same phrase is used in the closing section at the end of the movement.

Ex. 4.2 Chopin, Nocturne in B, Op. 62, No. 1.

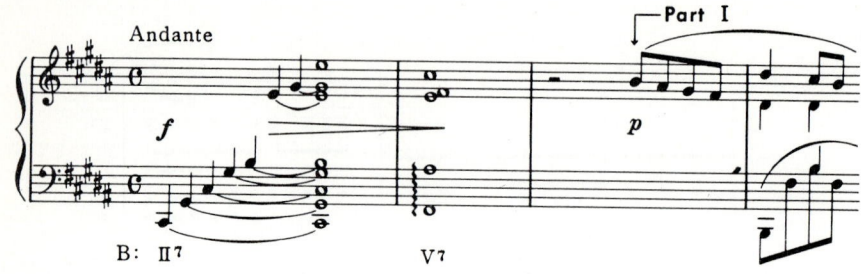

Ex. 4.3 Dvořák, Symphony in E minor, Op. 95, second movement.

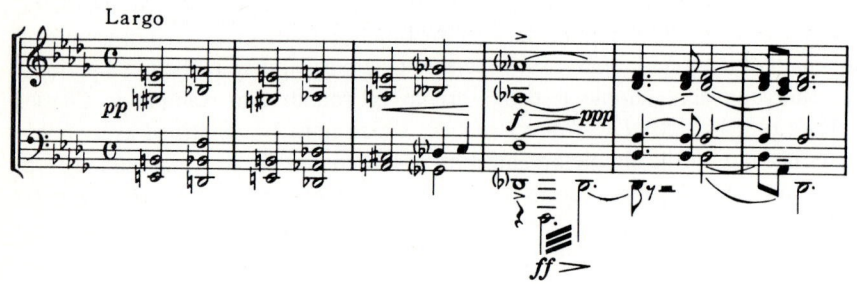

Ex. 4.4 Chopin, Etude in A minor, Op. 25, No. 11.

Example 4.4 is an introduction consisting of two short phrases, the second a harmonized repetition of the first leading to a half-cadence in A minor. Only very rarely does an introduction to compound ternary form exceed 8 measures in length. However, an unusually large example of the form may have a correspondingly long introduction: the second movement of the *Symphonie Fantastique* by Hector Berlioz (1803–69) has an introduction of 38 measures.

Because an introductory passage is a preparation for the main body of the form, it normally ends in an unresolved fashion, establishing at its close an air of expectancy, often by means of a half-cadence, as in Ex. 4.4. Further, the introduction may anticipate the thematic material of the form proper. Example 4.5, a brief introduction to Part II of a compound ternary, illustrates both points.

Ex. 4.5   Brahms, Sonata in E minor, Op. 38, for cello and piano, second movement (trio).

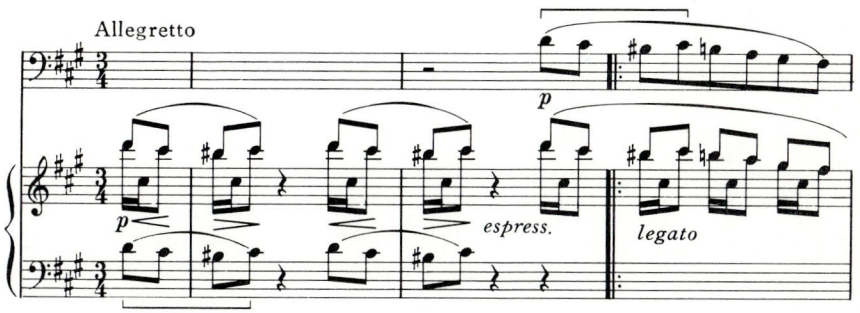

THE FIRST PART

The principal thematic content is stated in Part I. Since thematic contrast is likely in Part II, the first section is most often of similar motivic material throughout, even when it is itself a simple ternary.

Again, several possibilities of form exist. In most cases, the first part is binary, incipient ternary, or simple ternary. An example of the last type is quoted in melodic outline as Ex. 4.6; the beginning of Part II, in the subdominant, is included. A good example of incipient ternary as Part I of the compound form is the trio of the third movement of Beethoven's String Quartet in B-flat, Op. 18, No. 6. Its proportions are 8—4,4; to this is added a 4-measure codetta in the parallel minor. Both of these examples include the conventional binary-like repeats.

Measures 9–12 of the following Schubert example (Ex. 4.6) are of interest. In one sense, mm. 9–10 fortify the cadence of the opening period; in another, they prepare the contrasting section starting in m. 13, by means of motivic anticipation. Measures 11–12 further foreshadow the next section by beginning the process of tonal change. Measures 9–10 thus look both ways, in cadential function and motive, while mm. 11–12 act transitionally in modulation to C minor.

It is possible, but not usual, for the first part to be a period or a phrase group. According to the foregoing definition of compound ternary form, this would mean that Part II is a binary or ternary design, as illustrated in Ex. 4.31.

Obviously, there is often some modulation—of at least an ephemeral sort—in the course of Part I, although in incipient forms this may be lacking. An example marked by consistent tonal stability is the first part of the second movement of

Ex. 4.6   Schubert, Sonata in E-flat, Op. 122, third movement.

Beethoven's Sonata in C-sharp minor, Op. 27, No. 2, where Part I of a larger compound form consists of an 8-measure period repeated in variation, a V-oriented contrasting segment of 8 measures, and a return of the initial period not repeated but extended, all in D-flat. Where there is tonal fluctuation, the traditional relationships, tonic to dominant or relative, usually pertain. Part I usually ends in the tonic, with an authentic cadence.

At the end of the first section, there may be a transition of one or more measures (see pp. 90–96). When there is no transitional passage, the final harmony of Part I functions as a pivot into the following section. This is seen in the Schubert (Ex. 4.6), in which the final harmony (E♭:I) becomes a dominant in A-flat, leading directly into Part II.

Occasionally Part I of a compound ternary is even larger in scope than any of the examples cited; for example, the complete movement may exhibit the form *ababa—cdc—ababa*. This type of compound ternary is discussed on pp. 96–97 under the heading *extended compound ternary*. In some instances, Part I appears with its various component sections written out in repeats with variations, so that it takes on an unusual size. Part I of the Chopin Nocturne in B, Op. 9, No. 3, is 87 measures long, but it boils down to an incipient ternary in which individual sections are repeated in variation.

THE SECOND PART

Part II, as in the simple ternary, has a primary function of contrast. In most cases different motivic material is introduced; however, if the motives themselves are not unlike those of Part I, there is contrast of other kinds. In Ex. 4.7, which shows the beginnings of Parts I and II of a compound ternary, the thematic substance changes while the imitative technique is retained.

Ex. 4.7   Chopin, Sonata No. 1 in C minor, Op. 4, second movement.

Example 4.8 shows an unusual change of meter in Part II, with increased dynamic emphasis and urgency.

In most cases, however, Part II does not depart radically in basic features (tempo, meter) from Part I. A change of key is usual, or there may be an emphasis *on* the dominant harmony rather than *in* the dominant key. An instance of changed mode over the retained tonic is shown as Ex. 4.9. When this happens, the second part is sometimes labeled *maggiore* or *minore* as the case may be.

Ex. 4.8   Beethoven, Symphony No. 6 in F, Op. 68, third movement.

Part I

Allegro

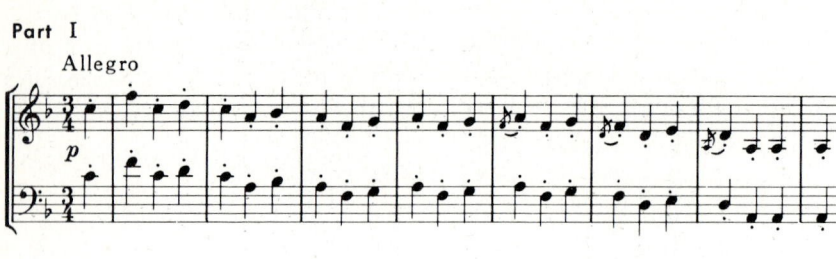

Part II

In tempo d' allegro

Ex. 4.9   Haydn, Sonata in E-flat (Hob. XVI: 49), second movement.

Part I

Adagio cantabile

Part II

When Part II is in a different key, the original tonic tends to be avoided until the point of preparation for Part III. Again, the traditional key relationships apply. An exceptional case is shown as Ex. 4.10, where Part II is in the dominant of the relative major.

Ex. 4.10 Bach, St. John Passion, chorus, Ruht wohl (upper part and figured bass).

All the possibilities of form discussed with respect to Part I are applicable here: Part II may be either a two- or three-part design or free in form. An example of a second part in simple ternary form is seen in Brahms's *Capriccio* in G minor, Op. 116, No. 3 (proportions of 12–14–7). A symmetrical simple ternary can be seen in Part II of the Chopin Nocturne in G minor, Op. 37, No. 1. A portion of the vocal part of a lied is quoted below with indications of cadential harmonies; this is a middle part of freer structure, a phrase group. The overall form is unusual in that the ternary implications of Part I (not shown) are not actually realized until its recurrence as Part III. Thus, Part I may be represented by the symbol *ab* — (in G and D); Part II as a phrase group; Part III as *aba* (in G, D, and G). A relatively large coda is included, incorporating all of the basic material.

Part II is usually comparable in length to Part I. Overall symmetry is rarer in compound ternary form than in smaller forms, as one might expect. Some proportional relationships between Parts I and II are listed below.

Beethoven, Sonata in C minor for piano and violin, Op. 30, No. 2, third movement.

       Part I —48 measures
       Part II—36 measures

Beethoven, Trio in E-flat for piano, violin, and cello, Op. 70, No. 2, third movement.

       Part I —56 measures
       Part II—52 measures (including transition starting at m. 43 of Part II)

Ex. 4.11 Wolf, Epiphanias (No. 19 of the Goethe-Lieder).

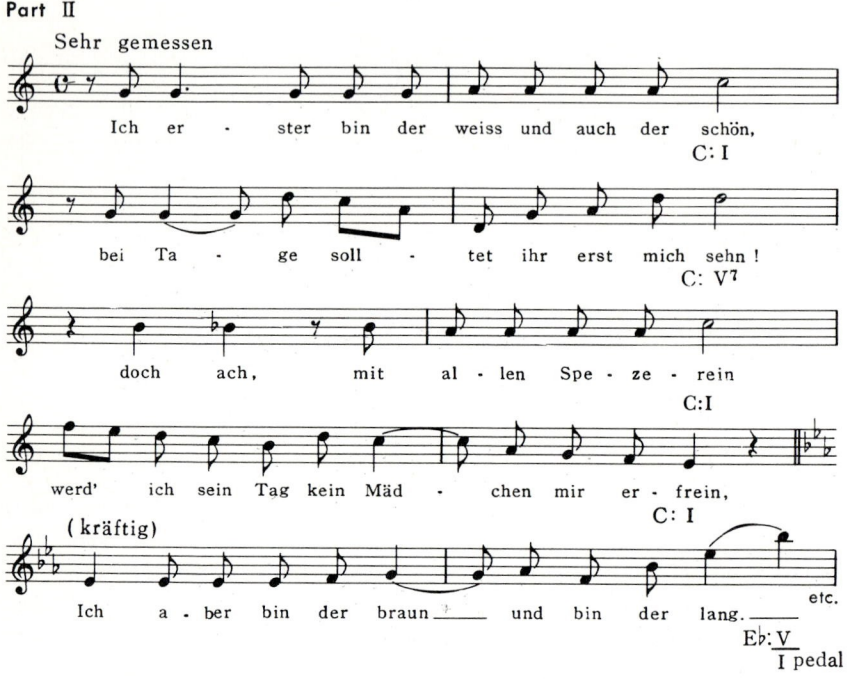

Haydn, Sonata in B minor (Hob. XVI:32), second movement.

Part I —22 measures
Part II—18 measures

The second part may be taken up with the development of motives of the first part. In such a case, sequential fluctuation is likely. Example 4.12 shows a group of motives as they originally appear in Part I, then their development in a sequential passage in Part II. Part I in this movement is in binary form, its first part moving to the dominant key and its second part (using the same theme in mirror inversion) returning to the tonic. The second part of the binary in Part III, the recapitulation, starts in the unexpected key of F and works its way back to B minor. The student will observe that the motive labeled *a* is developed in its mirror inversion in Part II.

Again, the final cadence may lead directly into the next section (Ex. 4.13) or there may be a passage of retransition to reintroduce the tonic key and otherwise lay the basis for the return of the original material. Retransitional functions are discussed more extensively later in this chapter (p.96). In the case of a second part in the parallel major or minor, there is, of course, no issue of tonal preparation.

Ex. 4.12 Walter Piston, Sonata for violin and piano, second movement.
© 1940 by Associated Music Publishers, Inc., New York. Used by permission.

Ex. 4.13 Brahms, Capriccio in G minor, Op. 116, No. 3.

THE THIRD PART

Part III, as a restatement of the first part, is normally of the same form, thematic material, and tonality.

Frequently, especially in late eighteenth- and early nineteenth-century works, the middle section is followed by the indication *da capo* (from the beginning), denoting a precise repeat of Part I.[3]

When written out, the third part is subject to variation, as in simple ternary form. Embellishment of the upper-voice melody is especially common. Variation possibilities were treated briefly in Chapter 3 and will be discussed in subsequent chapters in connection with other forms. It will suffice here to quote from examples of compound ternary form to show a few such possibilities.

The return may be abbreviated. This is what happens in the Chopin Prelude No. 13 (Ex. 4.1). A further example is quoted as Ex. 4.14. In this Prelude the return of Part I, originally 27 measures long, is limited to 6 measures, at which point there is a dissolution into the final cadence. This point is marked in the example.

Ex. 4.14 Chopin, Prelude No. 15 in D-flat, Op. 28.

Point of
dissolution

---

[3]This instruction to repeat Part I may take any of the following forms: *da capo e poi la coda* (repeat the first part and then play the coda); *da capo al fine* (repeat the first part "to the end"—to the point marked *fine*); *dal segno* (repeat from the sign 𝄋, used when the repeat of Part I does not begin with the first note); *da capo senza repetizione* (repeat the first part but do not observe the repeats of its separate sections; this is often practiced in performance even when not stated).

Ex. 4.14 (*continued*)

Example 4.15 illustrates the return of a theme with a new contrapuntal associate in Part III, the original theme taken into a different register with the harmony essentially unchanged.

Sometimes an element of Part II continues into Part III, merging with the ma-

Ex. 4.15   William Schuman, Anticipation, No. 1 from piano cycle Voyage.
Copyright 1954 by Howard Music Company. Reprinted by permission.

terials of the first part. This seems inevitable in Ex. 4.16, a quotation from the Mendelssohn Violin Concerto, Op.64. Here, the rhythmic motion in 32nd-notes, established in the second part, is maintained well into Part III. An excerpt from each of the three parts is shown.

Ex. 4.16 Mendelssohn, Concerto in E minor for violin and orchestra, Op. 64, second movement.

THE CODETTA; THE CODA

A distinction should be made between the terms *codetta* and *coda*, the former a diminutive of the latter. The coda is defined as the final section of an entire piece or movement—a section in which something more than mere cadential iteration, extension, or elaboration occurs. We shall not attempt to specify that a coda must be of a certain minimum length, but obviously length is a factor in the distinction be-tween a real coda and a codetta.

A coda must be judged as having *significant* substance—thematic statement or development. A codetta, on the other hand, is defined as: (1) the closing section to a major *part* of a movement; (2) the closing section to the entire piece or movement when the material of which it is composed is of minor significance, serving chiefly to intensify the decisiveness of the final cadence, and of inferior dimensions as well; or (3) the simple repetition of an earlier closing section (codetta) which had occurred within the body of the overall form.

The codetta is often defined simply as the closing section for a part of a move-ment and the coda as the final closing section, regardless of other factors. But this simple distinction breaks down when one considers that often (as will be remem-bered from preceding chapters) the two are in fact identical. It is therefore unreason-able to describe one by one term, the other by another term.

The experience of studying the content of a closing section, and the conclu-sions drawn from such study, are more important than the specific label assigned to the example under consideration. But on the basis of the distinction established here, the use of the term *codetta* bears definite and important implications as to character, scope, and content. Therefore, there is a point in the use of the two terms and the distinction drawn between them.

In tripartite forms, closing sections occur more commonly in Parts I and III than in Part II, as was observed in the simple ternary. An important point should be repeated here: If a closing section is attached to Part III it is often an enlarged ver-sion of the codetta to Part I. In Ex. 4.17 the ''final'' tonic of the original codetta is followed, at the end of the movement, by several additional measures of chromatic

Ex. 4.17 Brahms, Trio in C, Op. 87, for piano, violin, and cello, third movement.

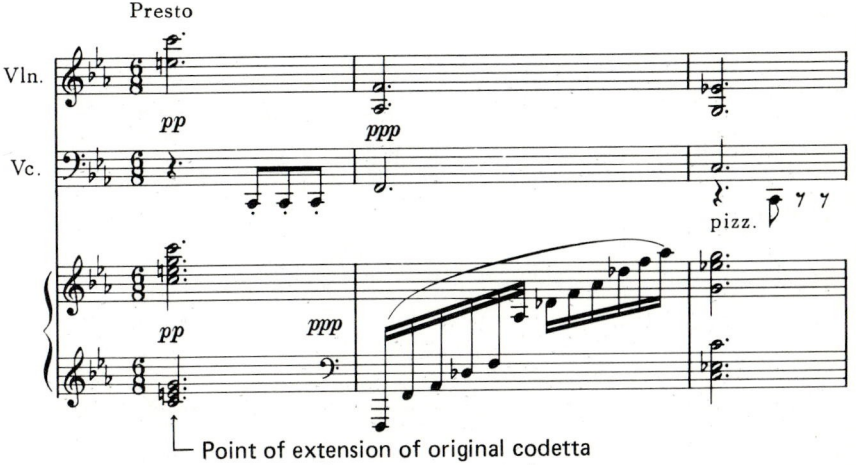

└─ Point of extension of original codetta

Ex. 4.17 (continued)

cadential harmonies, within an elaborated tonic. The beginnings of the two codettas are identical, as the reader will see in comparing mm. 52 and 161.

Example 4.18 illustrates a sectional codetta.[4] The various sections of the codetta are parts of a single division in the form *in view of obvious identity of content and function*. This material is appended to Part I, a simple ternary form. It is set off by an elided imperfect authentic cadence, weakened by use of the first inversion of the tonic. A similar cadence occurs 4 measures later. At the next cadence point, indicated in the quotation, the tonic is avoided by the use of VI, followed by a strong cadence (IV-V-I) in the final 2 measures. Example 5.23 (p. 132) is a comparable instance, also from Mozart.

Ex. 4.18   Mozart, String Quartet in B-flat, K. 589, third movement.

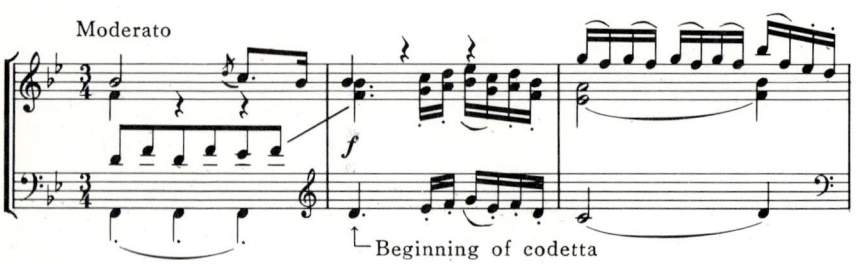

---

[4]See page 38 for additional discussion of this concept. The fact that codettas may be sectional must be understood in view of the definition of the codetta as set off by the latest cadence of the form to which it is appended.

Ex. 4.18 (continued)

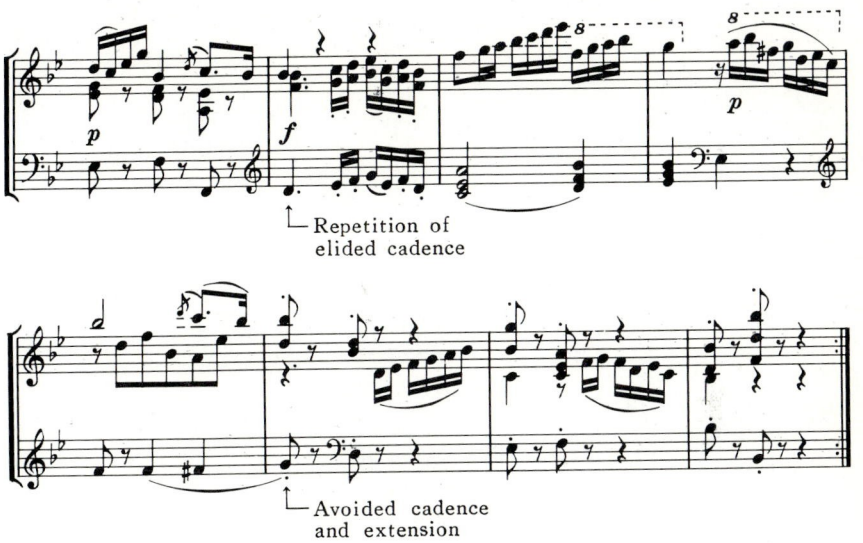

└─ Repetition of
    elided cadence

└─ Avoided cadence
    and extension

In the first movement of Mozart's Violin Concerto in D, K. 218, mm. 34–41, segmentation of the codetta is again marked by a series of authentic cadences. Unequivocal cadential harmony prevails among the sections, which lack significant motivic content and development, concentrating rather on typical cadential gestures of tonic elaboration and emphasis.

The larger the form, the more likely it is to have a coda at its close rather than a codetta. Compound ternary form is the first in our discussion which occasionally has a real coda. Excerpts from such a coda are shown as Ex. 4.19d-g. Part I of this example ends with a perfect authentic cadence in A minor (4.19a). At the end of the reprise (Part III) this becomes a half-cadence (b) which is repeated three times, sustaining the dominant. At this point, the second part of the cadential formula is repeated twice (c), after which the dominant is continued through 3 measures of figuration (d) in piano and violin (only the piano part is shown). The basic theme of the movement returns briefly, developed in a short sequence (e). A perfect authentic cadence 3 measures later sets off a new section of free imitation between the two instruments (f). This leads to the final cadence, in which the tonic is repeated twice (g). Obviously this example, because of size and the significance of its material, is a coda.

Another example is found in the second movement of the Berlioz *Symphonie Fantastique*. Its large sectional coda begins at m. 256, with ''seams'' at mm. 272, 288, 302, 320, 338, and 353, from which point there is rapid *stringendo* movement to the end. A further example is the third movement of Beethoven's Piano Trio in E-flat, Op. 70, No. 2; in this movement the coda, consisting of the final 24 measures, is formed of materials from Parts I and II.

Ex. 4.19 Beethoven, Sonata in A, Op. 12, No. 2, for piano and violin, second movement.

Ex. 4.19 *(continued)*

COMPOUND TERNARY FORM WITH DA CAPO

Further mention should be made of that species of compound ternary form, common in the eighteenth and nineteenth centuries, known as *minuet* or *scherzo*, whose middle section is often called a *trio* and whose last section is a literal *da capo* restatement of the opening section.

The term *trio* as applied here is in most cases inapplicable in any strict sense, but it is so firmly established that it can be accepted and understood to have this as well as its more literal meaning. Its use stems from a type of baroque dance pair (performed *ABA*) in which the second dance has a texture of three voices, and thus is literally a trio. The final movement of Bach's *Brandenburg Concerto* No. 1 in F is a case in point, actually containing two such trios, which provide digressions for the rondolike repetition of the minuet.

Ex. 4.20   Bach, Brandenburg Concerto No. 1 in F, final movement.

Trio No. 1

Trio No. 2

In sonatas, symphonies, and chamber works of the eighteenth and nineteenth centuries, the compound ternary form with *da capo* occurs principally as either the second or (more commonly) the third movement in a four-movement scheme. In the late eighteenth century the minuet with trio is more common; in the nineteenth century, the scherzo with trio.

An important structural feature of the compound ternary with *da capo* is that it is most often characterized by decisive cadential separations, rather than transitional sections, between the three major divisions. An example is shown as Ex. 4.21; only

Ex. 4.21 Handel, Why do the nations so furiously rage?, bass aria from Messiah.

the ends of Parts I and II are quoted. This is not, of course, to say that such separations are peculiar to the form with *da capo,* nor that transitions never occur in this type of ternary form (see Ex. 4.25).

Another type of procedure is shown as Ex. 4.22. Here, the decisive close of Part II is followed by a segment which may be termed a *transitional codetta:* it is at the same time an emphatic cadential appendage to Part II and, in its modulatory function, a preparation for restatement of Part I. Often, in examples with repeats, the simple expedient of first and second endings is used to effect adjustment from one section to another.

Ex. 4.22   Pergolesi, La Serva Padrona, bass aria "Sempre incontrasti" from Act 1.

d: I }
F: VI }

(*Dal segno al fine*)

└─Transitional codetta

An extension is brought about by the insertion, after the reprise of the first part, of a second trio, which is followed by a further restatement of Part I. Thus, a five-part rondo form emerges. The second trio may be identical to the first, as in the Beethoven Fourth Symphony. In the third movement of this work, the pattern of repetition is: scherzo, trio, scherzo, trio (identical to the first), scherzo, and coda. The scherzo and trio are initially of almost equivalent lengths; in its final appearance, the scherzo is less than half its original length.

An example of a movement with two *different* trios is the D minor scherzo of Schumann's Symphony No. 1. Its first trio, in duple meter, is in the parallel major key of D; the second, in triple meter, is in B-flat. Both restatements of the original scherzo are shortened—especially the final one, which is followed by a coda.

Bach's *Brandenburg Concerto* No. 1 (Ex. 4.20) carries the principle even further. Its final movement, a compound form, is in seven major parts (though the minuet is notated only once): minuet, trio I, minuet, polacca,[5] minuet, trio II, minuet.

REPEATS IN THE TERNARY WITH DA CAPO

The component binary and ternary forms of the compound ternary often occur with their usual repeats, especially in the sonata movement with trio and *da capo*. While the pattern of sectional form and tonal change is elaborated by the repeats, the fundamental large ternary, with its compound internal features and overall recapitulative design, remains the essential point. Yet the number of surface tonal and thematic "turns" is at times greatly increased, and the form complicated by a resultant enhanced frequency of redirection.

[5]The *polacca* (It.) is usually understood to be a *polonaise,* although the term may refer also to other Polish dances.

The use of repeats in movements of more than one trio varies considerably. For example, in the third movement of Beethoven's Fourth Symphony, the initial statement of the scherzo is in simple ternary form with the usual repeats, but no further repeats are used. In the scherzo of the First Symphony of Schumann, only the first part and the *second* trio (both simple ternaries) have repeats.

Even in the more common ternary with one trio, the use of repeats varies a great deal. Thus, in the Schubert Impromptu in A-flat, Op. 90, No. 4, no repeats are used in Part I, while the second part employs the standard repeats of the simple ternary form. Sometimes, especially in examples lacking the literal *da capo*, repeats may be omitted altogether, or they may be written out, frequently with variation. In Chopin's Nocturne in A-flat, Part I is an incipient ternary (*a–ba*, of which the *ba* is written out a second time without variation); when this material returns as Part III, the same portions are repeated, this time with variations (Ex. 4.23).

Ex. 4.23   Chopin, Nocturne in A-flat, Op. 32, No. 2.

TECHNIQUES OF INTEGRATION IN THE COMPOUND TERNARY; TRANSITION AND RETRANSITION

In a well-integrated compound ternary, literal repeats are less likely, and instead of pronounced cadential interruption at the ends of Parts I and II, the parts are usually bridged by transitional material. The adjective "integrated" thus applies *as a matter of degree* where major cadential seams are qualified or obscured by elision or transition. A written-out recapitulation, commonly involving variation, is often associated with transitional integration.

A case in point, the third movement of Brahms's Symphony No. 3 in F, is outlined as Ex. 4.24, which should be read with score in hand.

Ex. 4.24

Part I (Simple ternary)

a—Measures 1–24. Double period, with half-cadences at mm. 8, 12, 20, and a perfect authentic cadence at m. 24; there are motive punctuations within each phrase, as in mm. 2 and 4 in the first phrase.

b—Measures 24–36. Brief development of motive

in C major and A minor, ending on half-cadence in A minor.

Transition—Measures 36–41. Anticipates motive of *Ia* and modulates back to C minor.

a—Measures 41–52. A single period, only half of the original statement.

Transition—Measures 52–53. Very brief link between Parts I and II, yet clearly transitional, entering abruptly on the second beat of m. 52, anticipating the harmony with which Part II begins.

Part II (Incipient ternary)

a—Measures 54–61. Phrase or 2-phrase unit, introduces key of A-flat, ends with half-cadence.

a—Measures 62–69. Same material in variation.

b—Measures 70–78. Contrast touching G-sharp minor and B major, by enharmonic change, before returning to A-flat; ends on half-cadence.

a—Measures 79–86.

Transition—Measures 87–98. On material of *II-b,* dissolving and modulating to C minor; ends on German 6th-chord in C minor, having anticipated the motive of Part I.

Part III

Measures 99–150. Same form as Part I, but with changes of accompanimental pattern and orchestration.

Coda

Measures 150–163. Leans toward A-flat at outset but quickly reaffirms C minor; material is reminiscent of both Parts I and II.

An example of a *da capo* ternary with transitions is cited as Ex. 4.25. Here,

Ex. 4.25   Brahms, Trio in E-flat, Op. 40, for piano, violin, and horn, second movement.

Ex. 4.25 (*continued*)

the transition into Part II is distinct from the strong cadential ending of Part I, rather than emerging out of it. This type of transition thus does not effect as high a degree of integration as, for example, those cited in Ex. 4.24.

It will be instructive at this point to illustrate important features of some transitional passages. In a form of this scope, transitions are normally not more than a few measures in length, and they may even be as short as a single measure or two. Example 4.24 illustrates a transition consisting of a single measure, a single chord. Example 4.26 shows a transitional measure from a twentieth-century aria. In this

Ex. 4.26   Stravinsky, *Persephone*, aria of Eumolpe (Rehearsal No. 140).

aria, Part I is a simple ternary; at the end of Part I an expected cadence in C is altered by the sudden tonicization of D. This is an aspect of transition in which chromatic succession leads into the key of F, for Part II.

Often a transition, instead of following the cadential close of the preceding section, occurs in lieu of such a cadence—that is, out of the dissolution of the form of the preceding section and the avoidance of the expected cadence. In Ex. 4.27,

Ex. 4.27   Berlioz, Symphonie Fantastique, Op. 14, second movement.

Ex. 4.27 *(continued)*

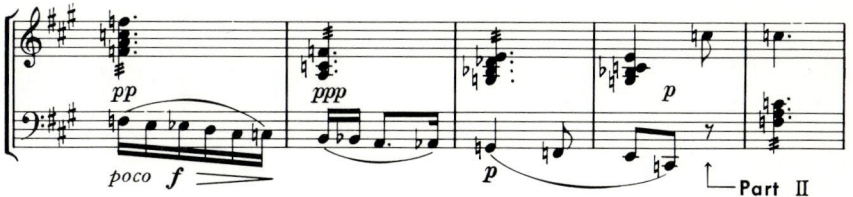

dissolution begins at the end of m. 6 of the quotation, where the motive last heard is taken up in development leading eventually into F, the key of the following section.

The material of the transition may be any of a number of types, as will be discussed more thoroughly in Chapter 6. It may consist of figuration having no thematic importance. It may be related motivically to either of the adjacent sections and not to the other. Or it may be motivically related to both of the two sections between which it forms a bridge. The logic of this last type of transition is apparent. Example 4.28 is a transition joining Parts I and II; motive *a* is from Part I, motive *b* from Part II.

In the Chopin Nocturne from which Ex. 4.29 is taken, Parts I and II are in parallel keys. Not only is there no transition but the cadence ending Part I is actually

Ex. 4.28 Brahms, Ballade in G minor, Op. 118, No. 3.

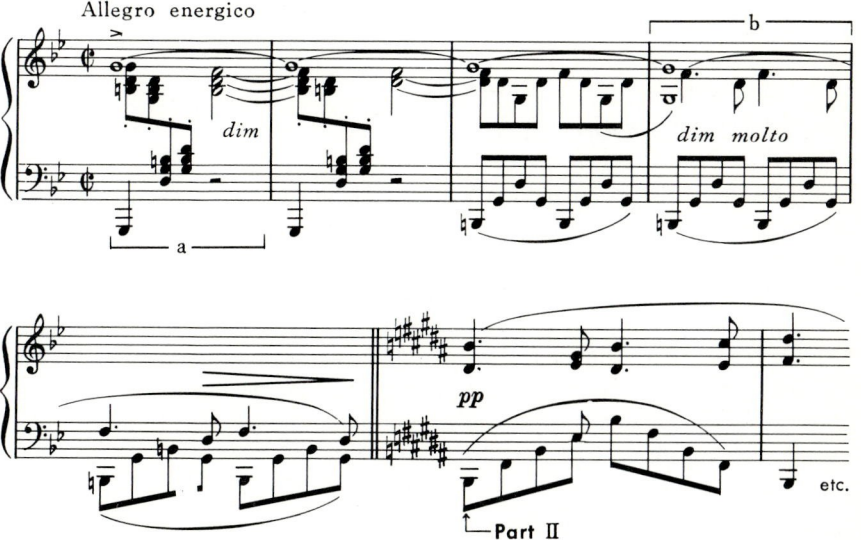

Ex. 4.29 Chopin, Nocturne in B, Op. 9, No. 3.

elided to the beginning of Part II. This must be considered another kind of integration in ternary form, an avoidance of cadential break.

The transition into Part III was explained briefly in Chapter 3 as a *retransition* involving preparation of the original key and the original material, and often characterized, especially in larger forms, by the prolongation of a point of tonal instability (V, usually) as a tension-building device. Example 4.30 illustrates these retransitional procedures: tonal preparation (modulation to E-flat minor by enharmonic-chromatic progression), preparation of an element of content (the steady triplet motion of Part III), and sustained dominant harmony, longer than it appears in view of the *ritardando*. The tonal relationship between Parts II and III is astounding on the surface (B minor to E-flat), until one realizes that the E-flat minor tonic is, enharmonically interpreted, the mediant harmony in the key of B. A further illustration of this type of transition is to be seen in the Schubert Impromptu No. 4 in A-flat, also of Op. 90.

Integrated compound ternary forms are common among nineteenth-century piano pieces and slow movements of multimovement sonata forms.

EXTENDED COMPOUND TERNARY FORM

There is a species of compound ternary in which one of the three parts is more extensive than either binary or simple ternary. The total effect is comparable to that of the standard type with individual sections repeated, but the extensions are generally of greater diversity and significance than direct, literal repeats.

An example is the adagio movement from Haydn's Sonata in E-flat (Hob. XVI:49). Its first part is in the pattern *ababa*, the digression, *b*, occurring on dominant harmony (see m. 17). Part II is in the parallel minor and its relative major; the reprise, Part III, is a simple ternary, *aba*, followed by a sectional, 16-measure coda set off by a deceptive cadence.

The second movement of Brahms's Trio in E-flat, Op. 40, is another example. Its first part, the scherzo, may be represented as *abacab(a);* it is followed by a

Ex. 4.30 Schubert, Impromptu in E-flat, Op. 90, No. 2.

transition into the trio (Ex. 4.25). A final example is the "Queen Mab Scherzo" from Berlioz's *Romeo and Juliet*.

In each of these examples, Part II is larger and substantively more contrasting than the digressions within Part I, so that Part II gives a feeling of proportional balance in relation to Part I. Thus the overall form is ternary.[6]

---

[6]A useful supplementary reference for compound ternary is to be found in Chapter 8, where the slow movement from Brahms's Double Concerto is treated in detail with respect to concerto applications.

DEBUSSY, STRING QUARTET IN G MINOR, OP. 10, THIRD MOVEMENT

The third movement from the String Quartet by Claude Debussy (1862–1918) is a beautiful specimen of compound ternary form, and may serve as a summary example for this discussion. Its essential outline is given as Ex. 4.31.

Ex. 4.31   Debussy, String Quartet in G minor, Op. 10, third movement.

Permission for reprint granted by Durand et Cie., Paris, France, copyright owners, and Elkan-Vogel Co., Inc., Philadelphia, Pa., agents.

Ex. 4.31 (continued)

Ex. 4.31 (*continued*)

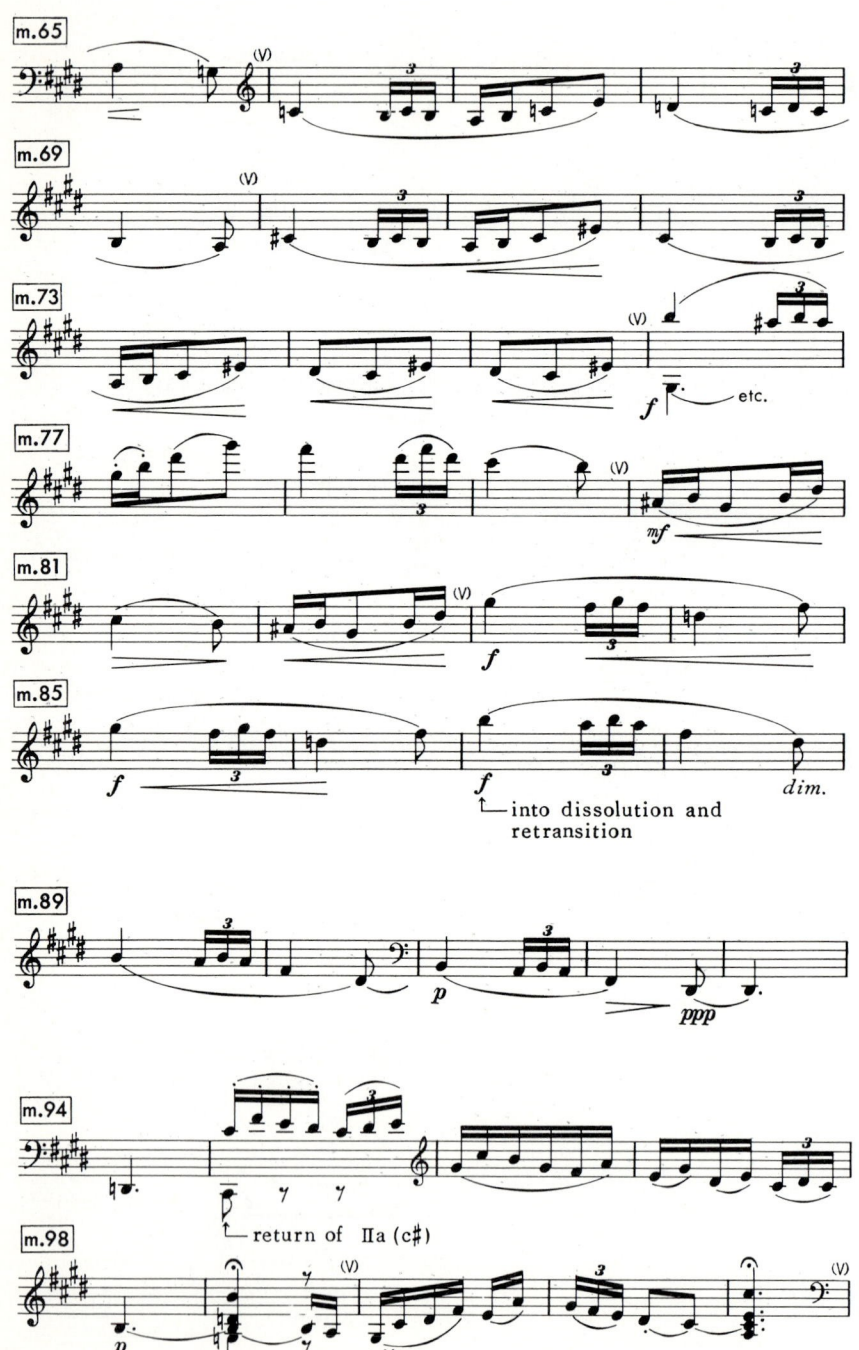

Ex. 4.31 (*continued*)

Part I, following a brief introduction, consists of a phrase group centered in D-flat; Part II begins with a modal theme, also a phrase group, in C-sharp, the enharmonic parallel. At m. 21 of Part II (m. 41 of the whole) a characteristic and mildly contrasting idea enters and undergoes modulatory development, some of it sequential, finally dissolving into a transition which leads chromatically back to C-sharp for the return, its content reduced to two phrases. The reprise of Part I in the overall form is also abbreviated. The movement is extremely asymmetrical, with proportions of 23–75–17; however, since the middle part is slightly faster, and in

3/8 rather than 6/8 meter, the three parts are of similar lengths in actual performance time.

The Debussy movement is a rewarding basis for the study of subtle variations from phrase to phrase. The variations in phrase length in Part II are striking. The long extension of the final phrase of Part I is effectively climactic just preceding the pronounced cadential settling before the middle section.

The means by which units are joined—by elision, by maintenance of internal movement—should be studied in the complete score. A point should be made of listening for the unusual harmonic and instrumental colors within a framework of traditional form and tonal function.

While there is no codetta, the final cadence is broadened into a perfectly conclusive gesture. The phrase in which the theme returns in octaves is dissolved (*un peu retenu*) by continued ascent in unsettled, syncopated rhythms. At the restoration of tempo, on the steadier rhythm of the principal motive, cadential feeling is initiated: 2 measures of "dominant," 3 measures of "tonic" (see all four parts), and the final plagal motion to I from an altered II_7.

RELATIONSHIPS TO THE RONDO

The rondo principle (Chapter 5), as has been suggested, may be said to be incipient in the compound ternary, more decidedly than in the simple ternary form. And when the first part of a compound ternary form is a simple ternary, a design results which is, on the surface, quite like that of the sonata-rondo form, treated in Chapter 7.

But the extended rondo form is more often and more thoroughly integrated; the scope of each minor segment in the ternary (*a, b,* etc.) is normally smaller than corresponding sections in the rondo; the final *b* digression in the sonata-rondo is most often in the primary tonic; in rondo the first digression, *b,* is more digressive both in tonality and in material than in the typical ternary; and the middle section in the large rondo form is frequently developmental, a tendency not characteristic of the ternary form.

Still, despite the most careful attempt at clarity of definition, problems of classification will persist. As an example, we may cite the final movement of Haydn's String Quartet in D, Op. 64, No. 5. This movement is normally described as a rondo (sonata-rondo, extended rondo) and it clearly is of a design which we may represent by the symbol *aba c aba*. The *b* section is digressive in tonality more than in material, and when it returns in the final division it is in its original key, unlike the usual practice in sonata-rondo form. The movement is modest in length. The opening theme, *a,* is only an 8-measure period. But the middle section, *c,* which is in the parallel minor, is fairly extensive; while it maintains a thematic relationship to the opening materials, it sets out on a vigorous, fugal development before a retransition prepares the return of *a.* While there is a pronounced cadence at, for example, the end of the initial ternary, there is compelling integration throughout the movement, one aspect of which is the incessant 16th-note motion up to the final measures. The best description of this movement, as in many other cases, is that which points out those of its features which relate it to the rondo, and those which relate it to compound ternary form. Nothing is gained by insistence upon a particular classification, although much is gained in consideration of the problem of classification, even when it results in the finding that no major category satisfactorily suits the example at hand. Analysis of the question of classification will eventuate, if conducted with perception and in depth, in an understanding of many aspects of the form of the music.

EXERCISES

1. Find an example of compound ternary form in which no codettas are present. Try writing some codettas, limiting yourself to a few measures of cadential elaboration.

2. Try inserting brief transitional passages into an example in which the main divisions are not bridged.

3. Find a Part III which is a literal reprise. Write out the first two measures three or four times, showing possible variations on the material.

4. Write the melody line of a compound ternary of your own, showing key levels and harmony at principal cadence points.

5. Find examples of an integrated compound ternary form to demonstrate various procedures of transition.

6. Analyze the second movement of Mozart's Sonata in C, K. 330, according to the following points:
   a) Mark the three major parts.
   b) Are there codettas?
   c) Is there a coda?
   d) Outline the tonal structure by listing the key levels and telling where each is evident.
   e) Identify the basic motivic materials of each section.
   f) Classify the cadence forms according to terminology you have learned.
   g) Consider symmetry versus asymmetry in the overall design and within each of the sections.
   h) What motivic relationships, if any, are there between Parts I and II?

7. Explain, in a paragraph of your own, the differences between simple and compound ternary forms.

8. Try writing a 2- or 3-measure introduction (ending on the dominant) to a specific compound ternary which has none. Consider carefully what the effect of the introductory passage should be, and try to make it "set the stage" for the beginning of the form proper.

9. Find an example of compound ternary form from one of the following genres. Be prepared to discuss its important features, considering all points discussed in the chapter to the extent that they are relevant to the example you select.

a) Dances in *alternativo* form from eighteenth-century suites.

b) *Da capo* arias from seventeenth- and eighteenth-century operas and oratorios.

c) Piano pieces of the nineteenth century.

10. Consider whether either or both of the following are compound ternary forms. Assemble the best possible arguments to support your view. If you feel that firm classification is not possible, explain why.

a) Debussy, *Prélude à l'après-midi d'un faune.*

b) Ravel, "Menuet" from the *Sonatine* for piano.

11. The following are suggestions for further study and are intended to supplement the many works cited in Chapter 4.

Bach, *French Suite* No. 3 in B minor, minuet
Bartók, Concerto No. 3 for piano and orchestra, second movement
Brahms, Concerto in D, Op. 77, for violin and orchestra, slow movement
Beethoven, Sonata in E-flat, Op. 7, slow movement
   Symphony No. 3 in E-flat, Op. 55, slow movement
Debussy, "Feuilles Mortes," from *Préludes,* Book II
Mozart, String Quartet in B-flat, K. 589, final movement
Arnold Schoenberg (1874–1951), Suite for piano, Op. 25, minuet
Giuseppe Verdi (1813–1901), *Falstaff,* dance from Act III, Scene II
Hugo Wolf (1860–1903), "Nimmersatte Liebe," from *Mörike-Lieder*

5

RONDO

The rondo can be conceived as an expansion of ternary form in which there is a further contrasting section and a second reprise. Rondo form thus comprises a recurring theme alternating with contrasting material. It occurs commonly as the final movement of a multimovement work—symphony, sonata, chamber piece, concerto. Examples cited in this chapter will show that it also appears in other positions in the multimovement scheme, and as an individual piece.

The application of principles of unity and contrast remains fundamental, and the larger the form the more complex the issues of balance and integration. Occasionally a composer deliberately places side by side materials of exceedingly different, seemingly contradictory character, for dramatic effect. Such extreme contrast is evident in Ex. 5.1. Not only are the two strongly dissimilar themes abruptly contiguous, but Beethoven has also avoided any suggestion of transition or preparation of the contrasting material. A crescendo precedes the new section, emphasizing and

Ex. 5.1 Beethoven, Sonata in E, Op. 109, first movement.

intensifying the change, which includes a severe slowing of tempo. Chromatic successions have an important function in the dramatic effect, and also in linking the opposed materials through such inner-voice lines as E-D♯-C♯-B♯, and B-A♯-A♮. The movement as a whole is a rondo form (*ABA'B'A''*) in which the opening material is, at its returns, transposed and elaborately developed.

In the following pages, particular examples of individual parts of the rondo will be cited and quoted, with attention to the content and significance of each in the form from which it is extracted.

HISTORICAL BACKGROUNDS
OF THE RONDO PRINCIPLE

Any speculation as to the early origins of the rondo would be out of place in this book, but it may be of value to point out some sources for study of its history and of antecedent examples and genres.

There is a clear analogy between the rondo, with its series of statements alternating with digressive materials, and that type of song which alternates between stanza and refrain. This is a familiar scheme in many songs from popular sources, some of them very ancient. And the medieval *rondeau,* a poetic form found in many of the monophonic songs of the French *trouvères,* is an embodiment of the principle of repetition after digression, although its relation to later developments of the rondo is uncertain. Examples can be found in the first volume of *HAM* (see Nos. 19d and 19e). No. 14 of this volume contains Gregorian *responsoria* in which alternation between solo verses and choral responses embodies an analogous principle, as pointed out by the editors.

A further example in this same volume is the three-voiced *Deix soit* (No. 36c) by Adam de la Halle (c. 1230–1287). This piece follows the scheme *ABABA* and is thus, in the editors' words, "interesting as an early instance of the modern rondo, ababa, a form which did not come into general use until after 1650."[1]

THE SEVENTEENTH-CENTURY RONDEAU
AND OTHER ANTECEDENTS

An important precursor of the eighteenth-century rondo is the seventeenth-century instrumental *rondeau.*[2] Like the rondo, it consists of a recurrent refrain (*A*) separated by *couplets* (*B, C* . . .) of changing substance contrasting also with the mate-

---

[1]*HAM*, Vol. I. p. 219.

[2]This use of the term *rondeau* is not to be confused with that pertaining to the unrelated medieval poetic-musical form mentioned above. See Willi Apel, *Harvard Dictionary of Music,* 2nd ed. rev. (Cambridge, Mass.: The Belknap Press of Harvard University Press, 1969), p. 739.

rial of the refrain; thus: *ABACAD . . . . A*. The term *rondeau* (like *ritornello,* discussed in the following section) is applicable both to the formal procedure and to the recurring theme itself.

The seventeenth-century rondeau appears in orchestral and dramatic works, as well as, most importantly, in French keyboard pieces of the period. A convenient specimen from opera can be cited first, again from *HAM* (Vol. II, No. 277). Entitled "Sommeil" (subtitled "Rondeau tendre"), it is from the opera *Dardanus* by Rameau. It divides into five segments: the rondeau theme (G minor, mm. 1–14); a contrasting *première "reprise"* of 8 measures in B-flat (imitative, like the opening rondeau, and motivically related to it); a literal repetition of the rondeau; a second reprise of 14 measures in D minor (whose motivic content and imitative texture are shared with the other sections); and a final literal recurrence of the rondeau.

"Soeur Monique," for harpsichord, is one of the many *pièces de clavecin* by the organist-harpsichordist François Couperin; it appears as No. 265b of the second volume of *HAM*. Its main subject is an 8-measure period in F. The first digression, or *couplet,* is a 6-measure period in C (its surface rhythms resemble those of the rondeau theme, while its period form consists of a 2-measure antecedent and a 4-measure consequent). The return of the rondeau theme is literal. The second couplet, initially in D minor, is an 8-measure period followed by another of 6 measures, proportions in the latter again of 2 and 4 measures, its tonics F and C; this couplet is explicitly derived from motivic material of the rondeau. A further rondeau statement is again literal; it yields to a third couplet in F, this time a 12-measure period (divided 4-8, each segment repeated) with sharply contrasting surface rhythms but clear motivic relation to the rondeau. A final rondeau appearance is, again, literal. Notable here is palpable motivic interrelation of rondeau and couplets throughout.

A harpsichord Chaconne (No. 212 in *HAM,* Vol. II) by Jacques Champion de Chambonnières (c. 1597–1672) has theme recurrences separated by couplets to form a total of eleven parts. In the same volume (No. 240), a set of organ variations by Georg Muffat (c. 1645–1704) has the original theme returning after variations 5, 11, 17, and 23, thus suggestive of the rondo principle.

Finally, a directly preclassical antecedent of the rondo may be cited, the familiar gavotte from the Bach Partita No. 3 in E for solo violin. This movement contains five statements (four returns) of an 8-measure, symmetrical rondo theme. The form may be represented by the diagram *A:‖ BACADAEA*. The first digression is in C-sharp minor, the second in B, the third in F-sharp minor, and the fourth in G-sharp minor. The final statement of the theme is a *da capo* repetition.

RITORNELLO

An important historical procedure which bears upon the rondo principle is that of the *ritornello,* commonly evident in allegro movements of the baroque concerto (see pp. 228-30).[3] The word is a derivative of the Italian *ritornare* (to return, to reappear).

In this rondo-related procedure, the orchestral tutti is commonly pitted against solo passages, the two in alternation; the term "ritornello" is applicable to the recurrent orchestral material as well as to the principle of alternation itself. The ritornello usually appears three or four times, often in variants, and in various keys, with at least the first and final occurrences in the tonic.

A vivid example may be seen in the last movement of the Violin Concerto, Op. 8, No. 8, by Giuseppe Torelli (1658–1708) (*HAM,* Vol. II, No. 246). A distinct pattern of ritornello alternation can be observed here: tutti (C minor to G minor); solo (m. 17, elided with the G minor cadence); tutti (E-flat to F minor, mm. 27–34); solo (F minor, G minor, C minor); tutti (mm. 47–66, essentially in C minor but referring also to G minor). The orchestral ritornello thus appears at the outset, at m. 27, and at m. 47, and in the tonic, dominant, relative major, and subdominant.

The ritornello concept is evident also in specimens of the later baroque, often in intriguing individual and sophisticated patterns where the lines of distinction between tutti and solo (in contrast to those of the Torelli) are subtly obscured by rapid alternation between the two, by the overlapping of entries and exits, and by the phased emergence of the tutti at its recurrences—for example, by the anticipation of its leading motive(s) in preparatory interjections, as in the Handel movement traced below. (During the ritornello sections, the solo parts often double the upper orchestral voices; in the solo sections, members of the tutti typically accompany the soloists.)

For further illustration, the following course of events can be traced in the first movement of Handel's Concerto Grosso in G, Op. 3, No. 3 (these comments require reference to the score).[4] Following a slow 5-measure introduction ending on V, the fugal tutti, *allegro,* leads to a largely figural[5] solo (flute or oboe) entry at m. 12, accompanied by a texturally sparse, slower-moving orchestral violin component. Tutti recurrences on the original subject are at the upbeat to m. 21 (consisting of a single subject entry anticipated motivically in the preceding 2 bars), at m. 35 (also a single subject entry, which overlaps the solo's return less than 3 bars later), at m. 44 (here anticipated by three fragmentary motivic interjections, and yielding quickly to the solo), at m. 48 (a substantial episode, beginning with material from m. 5, then gradually introducing the fugal subject), and finally at the end of m. 65 (a

[3]See Donald Jay Grout, *A History of Western Music,* 3rd ed. (New York: W. W. Norton and Co., Inc., 1980), p. 129, concerning a "ritornello" principle applicable to certain fourteenth-century Italian genres fundamentally different from that under consideration here. Neither is the present discussion concerned with the term as applied to certain seventeenth-century operatic, vocal, and choral idioms.

[4]See Chapter 8, pp. 228-30, concerning the concerto grosso. All of Handel's concerti grossi are available in full score in a single-volume reprinting from the Deutsche Händelgesellschaft Edition, ed. Friedrich Chrysander (New York: Dover, 1981).

[5]One essentially of figuration rather than motivic content.

5-measure tonic conclusion featuring the subject and a brief, partially imitative development in a strongly cadential context).

In one sense, the Handel movement is relatively limited in interest in that the solo, when it is not doubling the material of the ripieno, consists largely of episodic passagework rather than significant thematic content, often in brief interludes which interrupt the tutti's substantive statements. On the other hand, provocative features, at times of notable subtlety, can be discerned in vital continuities of form. Among these are the variation and development of ritornello material, sometimes in passing recollection (e.g., m. 44) during the course of an episodic solo; discreet motivic preparation of the ritornello, the tutti arising gradually (see its first return); and the pervasive continuity effected in part by overlapping tutti and solo entries and cadences as opposed to deliberate segmentation (as at mm. 19–20, and in the solo entrance at m. 37, just prior to the tutti cadence). The tutti returns employ closely related keys: tonic, dominant, relative minor.

Chapter 8, which is concerned with applications of various formal procedures in the concerto, includes further discussion of the ritornello principle in Handel, Bach, and other composers of the baroque and later periods.

RONDO FORM FURTHER DEFINED

The type of rondo form with which this chapter is chiefly concerned has five essential parts and might be labelled a "five-part rondo" to distinguish it from rondos of similar principle but of seven or more parts.

In this form, there are three appearances of the basic thematic material separated by two similar or dissimilar contrasting sections, or *digressions* (also called *episodes*). The form proper may be preceded by introductory material and may be followed by a codetta or coda. It may include bridging passages between sections.

The usual diagrammatic symbol for this form is *ABABA,* when the second digression is built of the same theme or themes as the first, and *ABACA* when the two digressions are of different materials.

Example 5.2 illustrates part of a rondo of small dimensions. It is of the type *ABABA,* and its initiating theme is related to the digression. At the same time, there is strong tonal contrast: the digression occurs both times in the mediant major, by direct chromatic modulation. The divisions between parts are clearly marked by double bars and changes of key signature. Only the first two parts are shown; the repetitions proceed with perfect regularity.

Another Schubert song in rondo form is the first of the lieder on Scott's *Lady of the Lake:* "Raste Krieger, Krieg ist aus." In this song, Schubert uses enharmonic change to shift from five flats to three sharps. The reader will find it helpful to examine this clear specimen of rondo form.

Ex. 5.2 Schubert, Der Musensohn.

ELEMENTS OF RONDO FORM

The introduction

The introduction, if present at all, may consist of anything from a single chord or other brief gesture to several phrases, and may be of simple, figural content or important motivic material.

In Ex. 5.3, the introduction is a mere attention-calling sounding of the dominant root, of indefinite length.

Ex. 5.3   Schubert, Impromptu in C minor, Op. 90.

The final movement of Mendelssohn's Piano Concerto in G minor begins with a 39-measure introduction before the rondo theme appears. (This introductory passage also serves to link the second and third movements, leading from A minor to G major in preparation for the rondo.) Nineteen measures of the introduction are on and immediately around the tonic six-four harmony and the dominant in G. Except for its beginning, the introduction consists mainly of figuration. In Ex. 5.4, the

Ex. 5.4   Mendelssohn, Concerto in G minor, Op. 25, for piano and orchestra, third movement. Reduction by Adolf Ruthardt.

Ex. 5.4 (continued)

chief passage of tonal and thematic change is quoted, including the strong approach to the G: I_4^6, which is introduced by a chromatically derived augmented-6th chord. The omitted 16 measures steadfastly maintain a pedal on the dominant of G, established at the entrance of the solo part.

The introduction may have broad significance in the form proper. In Ex. 5.5, the introductory material extends to 18 measures, leading ultimately to D-flat for preparation of the rondo theme. In the course of the movement, the same material forms the basis for transitional passages from digression to theme and theme to digression.

The rondo theme

The rondo theme may be a period, an enlarged or double period, a phrase group, or a small binary or ternary. When it is a binary or ternary form, the overall design is a *compound rondo*.

In a compound rondo in which the theme is a small ternary form, any digression *within* the rondo theme is likely to be brief and of limited divergence, having a close relationship to the flanking parts. The effect is that the whole of the small

Ex. 5.5 Berry, Four Movements for Chamber Orchestra, fourth movement.

Ex. 5.5 (*continued*)

Rondo
proper

ternary is bound, in length and likeness of material and tonality, into a single unit in the overall form.

In the final movement of Haydn's String Quartet in E-flat, Op. 33, No. 2, the first 36 measures constitute the rondo theme—a small ternary form. The theme returns in its complete form after the first digression, but is abbreviated in its final statement. The above observations concerning the strong consistency of the ternary theme—a unity to be viewed against the background of the two digressions and the total form—are borne out in this movement.

In Ex. 5.6, the rondo theme is a period followed by two variations preceding the entry of the first digression, which appears without transition at m. 27. The two complementary phrases of the theme are quoted here; the first ends with a half-cadence, the second with a perfect authentic cadence. Two measures of the first variation are shown. Also shown is the beginning of the consequent phrase of the second variation, which should be compared with mm. 5 and 6 of the original period. A rondo theme of this type is unusual.

In the continuation of the Prokofiev movement, the rondo theme is reduced in

Ex. 5.6   Prokofiev, Piano Sonata No. 9 in C, third movement.

size with each appearance. Thus, the second statement consists of only two periods, and the final statement is a single period.

The rondo theme may end with a brief codetta. An example can be seen in the final movement of Schumann's Piano Sonata in G minor, Op. 22 (Ex. 5.17).

Transition

A rondo transition, like transitions in other forms, may have any of a variety of shapes, lengths, and materials. (See Chapter 4.)

Whether the transition is modulatory depends primarily on the key of the first digression. If that approaching section represents, for example, merely a change of mode, tonal adjustment is obviously unnecessary. But the digression may also enter in a diatonically related key without modulatory preparation, proceeding from a diatonically related final harmony of the theme. Examples of this have already been seen. The finale of the Schumann Sonata in G minor, Op. 22, has no transition of any kind between rondo theme and digression: there is an authentic cadence, a fermata, and an immediate entry of the contrasting section.

The transition may begin out of a dissolution of the rondo theme, as in the final movement of the Beethoven Sonata in C, Op. 2, No. 3. A comparison of m. 4 with m. 22 will indicate how the dissolution takes place: at the latter point an abrupt substitution of a chromatic harmony leads sequentially into G, the key of the first digression.

In Ex. 5.7, the first digression enters directly following the rondo theme, taking the original tonic as dominant. In effect, there is no transition. The cello and second violin parts, both *forte,* preclude any sense of relaxation, pointing directly into the digression.

Ex. 5.7   Haydn, String Quartet in E-flat, Op. 33, No. 2, final movement.

In Ex. 5.8, the composer arrests the rondo theme on a strong tonic cadence, after which the music proceeds sequentially through B minor to A. The material used in the transition is based on the opening of the theme:

Ex. 5.8   Clementi, Sonata in D, Op. 26, No. 3, final movement.

The A:V to which the transition leads is sustained, elaborated by *its* dominant, and enhanced finally by a *ritardando* and fermata. The digression begins with, but is not limited to, material of the rondo theme in the dominant key.

The transition may, as we have seen, have the character of a codetta. In the final movement of Schubert's Sonata in A minor, Op. 143, the transition begins with a phrase repeated with variation, confirming the initial key and strengthening the cadence of the rondo theme. Then, in its final 5 measures, there is a modulation to F (see mm. 45–50). The transition, at m. 31, introduces a distinctive 2-measure motive of its own. There is a good deal of emphasis on F as the submediant of A minor in anticipation of the modulation to the key of F.

The first digression

The first digression usually presents a substantial contrast in motivic material, character, mode, tonality, rhythmic quality, texture, or any combination of these factors, with the extent of contrast generally more pronounced in romantic than in classical style. The digression is normally comparable to the rondo theme in length.

Occasionally the digression, for dramatic effect, contrasts sharply in all its basic attributes, as in Ex. 5.1. More commonly, there is thematic and tonal contrast while the tempo and meter of the rondo theme are maintained.

If the motivic content of the digression is derived from the rondo theme, the factor of tonal contrast has special significance (as in Ex. 5.8). Often, as in many Haydn movements, analysis tends to center on tonal rather than thematic outlines as definitive for the form. In Ex. 5.9, there is tonal contrast while the thematic material carries over from rondo theme to digression.

Ex. 5.9   Haydn, Sonata in C (Hob. XVI: 48), final movement.

Ex. 5.9 (*continued*)

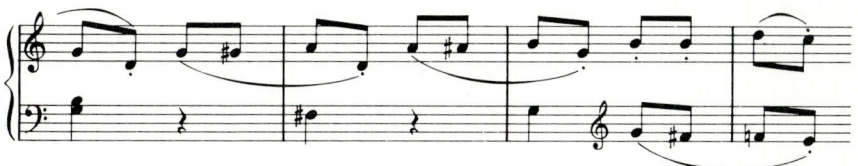

While, as noted above, the digression may be expected to be comparable to the rondo theme in length, differences in form are usual. The tonality of the first digression is, conventionally, closely related to that of the rondo theme, often entering in the dominant (Ex. 5.9) or relative major or minor. The digression may, on the other hand, assert its function of contrast by change of theme while adhering to the tonality of the opening, venturing only later into other tonal regions. (See the closing movement of the Mendelssohn Piano Concerto in G minor, whose first digression enters at m. 32 in the tonic key of G, but modulates subsequently.)

The digression in Ex. 5.10 begins without transitional preparation, and consists of one long phrase—7 measures in slow tempo. It leads from F minor to E-flat, after which a retransition brings in at the last instant the note D♭ over the E♭:I to effect a reaffirmation of the primary tonic.

Ex. 5.10   Beethoven, Sonata in C minor, Op. 13, second movement.

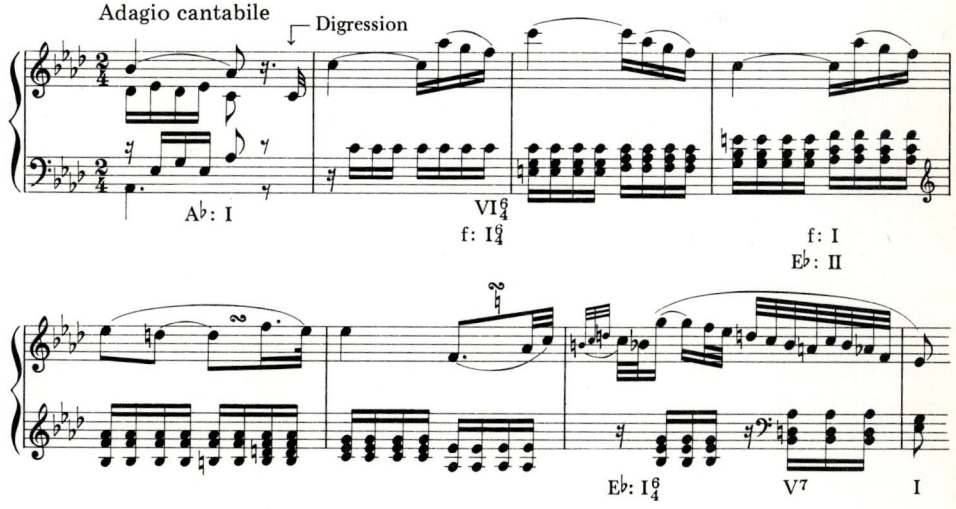

Example 5.11 illustrates a first digression in simple ternary form whose motivic material is clearly derived from the rondo theme, as is that of the second

Ex. 5.11   Haydn, Sonata in E minor (Hob. XVI: 34), final movement.

digression. The principal contrasting elements are of melodic direction and mode, with secondary tonicizations in the digression's ternary form. Indeed, the entire movement is on an E tonic, with changes to the parallel major at points of digression. There are no transitions. Simple ternary form in the digression renders the whole a compound form.

Retransition; the restatement of the rondo theme

Like transitions, retransitions vary greatly in length, and may be dispensed with altogether. Again, the retransition may have real thematic substance, or may be a mere continuation of motion through the cadential seam. The retransition in Ex.

5.12 carries on the accompanimental figuration of the first digression, effecting a rapid modulation to the tonic for return of the rondo theme.

Ex. 5.12 Schubert, Sonata in A minor, Op. 143, final movement.

The retransition shown in Ex. 5.13 clings to the note G, which appears first as the E-flat mediant, thence becoming the dominant in C minor. The motive of the rondo theme is anticipated, with rests intensifying the feeling of expectation; there

Ex. 5.13 Beethoven, Sonata in C minor, Op. 30, No. 2, for violin and piano, final movement.

Ex. 5.13 (continued)

└ Restatement

is a brief dialogue between the instruments, after which the rondo theme enters almost imperceptibly. The rondo statement which follows is developmental in character, and considerably extended, but it remains in the tonic key of C minor.

Example 5.14 includes fragments of the rondo theme and the first digression

Ex. 5.14   Ravel, String Quartet in F, final movement.

> Permission for reprint granted by Durand et Cie., Paris, France, copyright owners, and Elkan-Vogel Co., Inc., Philadelphia, Pa., agents.

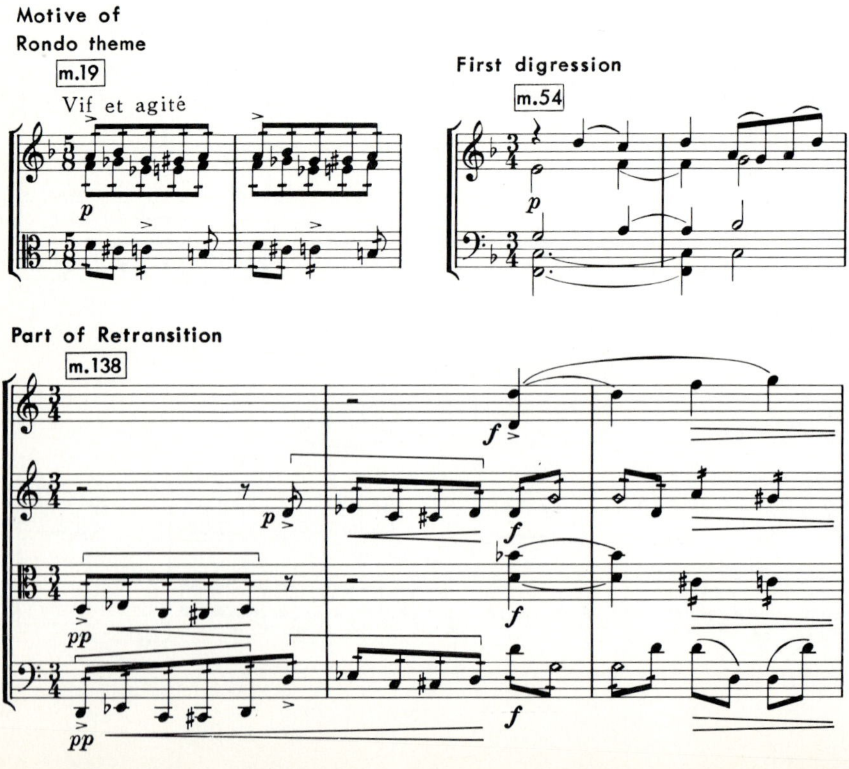

Motive of
Rondo theme
m.19

Vif et agité

First digression
m.54

Part of Retransition
m.138

Ex. 5.14 (continued)

(derived from the first movement), thus relating to both of the sections which it links. The retransition (not shown in its entirety) is entered by dissolution of material of the first digression (see m. 135) with a gradual emergence of the motive of the original thematic complex.

Another example of this type, incorporating materials of both the *A* and *B* sections, is the final retransition in the fourth movement of Beethoven's Octet for winds, Op. 103. In m. 142, following the fermata, there occur materials of the section just past as well as of that which is approaching.

With rare exceptions, the return of the rondo theme is in the tonic key, and usually varied in some way. Example 5.15 shows a small fragment of a rondo theme, and the corresponding point in its first return, to illustrate the variation technique used.

Ex. 5.15 Schubert, Sonata in D, Op. 53, final movement.

The expansion of the theme by developmental procedures is illustrated in the final movement of Beethoven's Sonata in C minor for violin and piano (Ex. 5.13), an excellent example for study. In the development, Beethoven concentrates on a seemingly unimportant phrase of the rondo theme, taking it into far tonal regions with extraordinary control. The particular portion of the rondo theme thus developed is omitted altogether in the final return.

An example of restatement in a key other than the tonic is seen in the Schubert Sonata in A minor, Op. 164, second movement. The opening rondo is in E major, its first return in F.

The second transition

As with the first transition, the content of the second depends on the character and key of the digression which follows it. As before, the transition may be omitted.

Example 5.16 is a quotation from the first and second transitions—one a vari-

Ex. 5.16 Brahms, String Quartet in G, Op. 111, fourth movement.

Ex. 5.16 (continued)

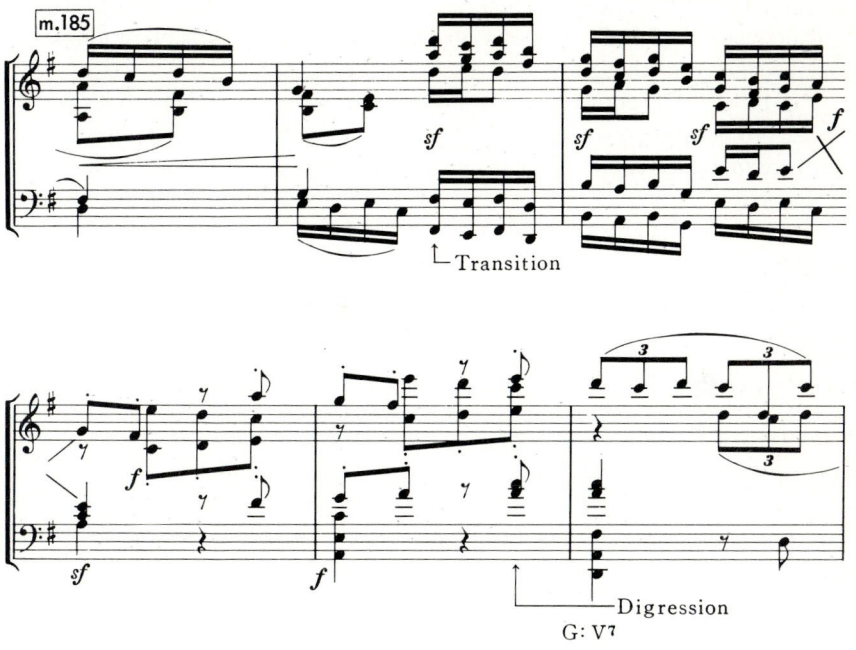

Ex. 5.17 Schumann, Sonata in G minor, Op. 22, final movement.

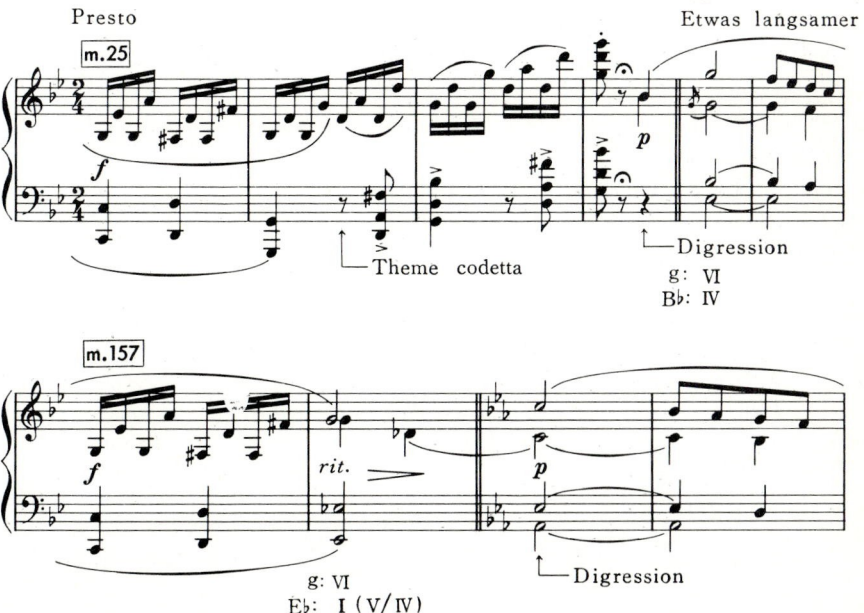

ant of the other—in a rondo of Brahms; both lead to the same digressive material
(*B*), and both use motives of the rondo theme. Characteristic of both is a rhythmic
and harmonic-rhythmic deceleration, an aspect of the preparation for approaching
thematic material. But the first leads to the dominant and is somewhat longer; the
second requires no change of key.

In Ex. 5.17, there are no transitions, in the true sense of the word, but the
approach to the *B* digression differs because the material of the first digression returns here in a different key. The codetta to the rondo theme appears as part of the
first quotation.

In a rondo with dissimilar digressions (*ABACA*), the passages by which they
are approached are likely to differ in important respects. In such a case, the manner
in which transition is entered may be the principal basis of comparison.

The second digression as a repetition of the first

When the material of the first digression is brought back in the second, some variation is probable, although this is perhaps less common than in the case of the rondo
theme, presumably because the digressive material has fewer appearances. There is
often contrast of tonality, although we have seen that the contrast is sometimes
merely of mode. Some nineteenth-century examples of key relations appear below.

Work	Tonic of movement	Key of first digression	Key of second digression
Beethoven, String Quartet, Op. 18, No. 1, second movement	D minor	F	D
Schubert, Impromptu, Op. 90, No. 1	C minor	A-flat	G minor
Schubert, Sonata, Op. 143, final movement	A minor	F	C
Schumann, Sonata, Op. 22, final movement	G minor	B-flat	E-flat

Ex. 5.18 Schubert, Impromptu in C minor, Op. 90, No. 1.

Ex. 5.18 (*continued*)

In the Schubert Impromptu (Ex. 5.18), the second digression, while restating the theme of the first, introduces a modification in rhythmic motion, as well as the change of key, as a source of variation.

The second digression as a contrast to the first

The rondo in which the second digression is thematically unlike the first (*ABACA*) is somewhat less common. Below are listed some key relationships between unlike first and second digressions.

Work	Tonic of movement	Key of first digression	Key of second digression
Mozart, Horn Quintet, K. 407, final movement	E-flat	B-flat	C minor, E-flat
Beethoven, Piano Trio, Op. 1, No. 1, second movement	A-flat	E-flat	A-flat minor, F minor
Beethoven, Sonata for violin and piano, Op. 30, No. 1, second movement	D	B minor	B-flat
Beethoven, Rondino for wind octet, WoO 25	E-flat	C minor	E-flat minor
Schubert, Sonata, Op. 53, final movement	D	A	G

The two digressions in the Beethoven Violin Sonata movement present extreme contrasts. (The first begins at m. 17, the second at m. 44.) In the Trio movement, *C* is more extensive and more digressive than *B*. In the Mozart, the second digression is a simple ternary form—again a strong contrast to the first, which had been based on motives of the rondo theme. In the Mozart, as well as in the Beethoven Rondino and Piano Trio, transition is omitted at the point where the second digression enters; in all three examples, however, retransition is used following this section. The Mozart retransition, following the second digression, is a good one for study, having as its motivic basis the final fragment of the second digression. The coda to this movement might also be mentioned as especially worthy of investigation; it begins at m. 143, and includes a modest canon on the rondo theme.

Example 5.19 gives a fragment of the first digression and the entire second digression from a Haydn sonata movement. This example is in simple ternary form

Ex. 5.19 Haydn, Sonata in D (Hob. XVI: 37), final movement.

Ex. 5.19 *(continued)*

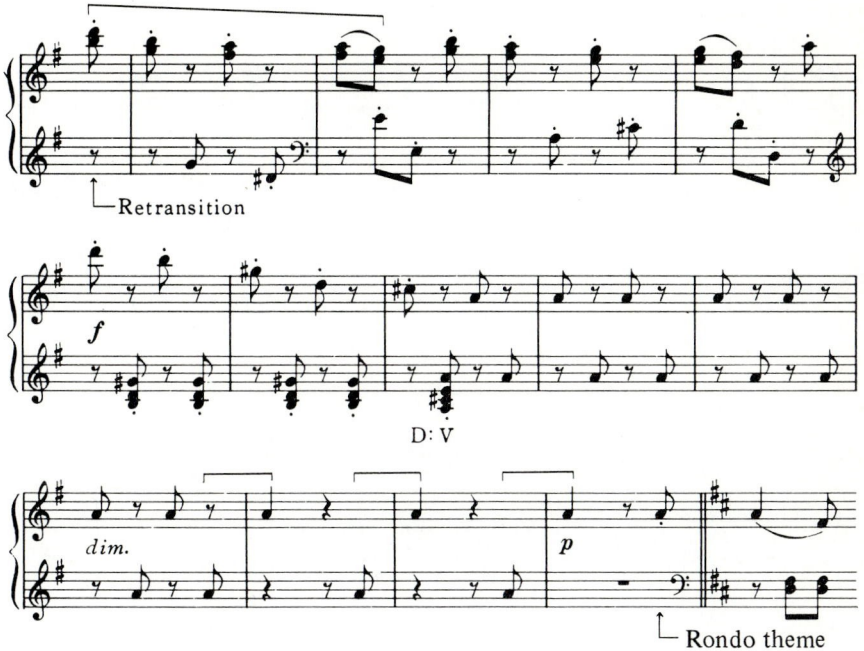

—Retransition

D: V

— Rondo theme

(period–phrase–period) and in the major subdominant key, and is followed by a simple but excellent example of retransition, employing dominant prolongation and anticipation of the opening motive of the rondo theme.

An example of highly unusual and very segmented form in a second digression is that of the Mozart Serenade for winds in B-flat, K. 361, final movement (in *ABACA* form, with coda). This digression, mm. 57-88, contains *four* contrasting sections, each repeated, in the keys of E-flat, C minor, G minor, and D minor. The tonic key of the movement is B-flat.

Final statement of the rondo theme

Differences in the two retransitions, if any, are usually attributable to the nature of the preceding material. For example, the adagio movement (in D) from Beethoven's Sonata in A, Op. 30, No. 1, for violin and piano, has scarcely any retransition after the first digression, which is in the relative minor. Following the second digression, which is in B-flat, there is a lengthy retransition in which the music leads first from B-flat to D minor, wavering around the dominant of that key for the last 8 measures. The hesitations in rhythmic motion and the fermata (mm. 60-63) add to the heightened effect of reappearance of the rondo theme. The motive of m. 52 is from the opening theme of the movement.

Ex. 5.20 Beethoven, Sonata in A, Op. 30, No. 1, for violin and piano, second movement.

An example which has *no* retransition after the second digression is the final movement of Beethoven's Sonata in G minor, Op. 49, No. 1. The retransition following the first digression (see m. 65) leads from B-flat, the key of the first digression, through G minor, to G major for the return of the rondo theme. The second digression, however, is in G major and thus requires no modulation into the final appearance of the rondo theme (see mm. 135-136).

The final statement of the rondo theme is in the tonic and is often a variation on earlier statements. Not uncommon is the abbreviation of the final return, as seen in Ex. 5.21, which dissolves at the point indicated into the coda.

Ex. 5.21   Beethoven, Sonata in G minor, Op. 49, No. 1, final movement.

The codetta; the coda

The codetta or coda begins after the final statement of the rondo theme has reached its cadence, or at the point of its dissolution. Example 5.22 shows the beginning of a coda set off by the theme's cadence; there is an immediate resumption of the dotted rhythms with which the movement began, along with an essentially new theme of quiescent character.

Ex. 5.22   Beethoven, Sonata in A, Op. 30, No. 1, for violin and piano, second movement.

Example 5.23 shows the 12-measure codetta of a rondo movement. The theme's cadential tonic appears in first inversion. It is followed by the codetta's II_5^6-I_4^6-V_7-I_6; this succession is repeated, arriving finally on the tonic in root position, initiating a tonic pedal which expresses decisive finality. The harmonic content of the codetta is thus entirely cadential.

Ex. 5.23 Mozart, Sonata in D, K. 576, final movement.

A short (9-measure) coda to a rondo form is illustrated as Ex. 5.24; this concluding section relates to much of the movement's major content. In the overall form, the first digression (m. 20) features an inversion of the rondo theme in a contrasting key, while the second digression brings in an independent theme. The coda's beginning, from m. 77, is articulated in an unorthodox manner by a sudden rest (Ex. 5.24a), followed by precipitate, rapid movement. The fourth bar of the coda (see 5.24b) finds the horn recalling the second digression theme (see m. 37). Immediately following this, there is reference to the rondo theme (cello, m. 81), a motive of which also occurs in flute and bassoon at the final cadence (5.24c).

Ex. 5.24a   Toch, Concerto, Op. 35, for cello and chamber orchestra, second movement.
© 1925 B. Schott's Soehne/Mainz, Germany. Renewed 1952. Used by permission.

Ex. 5.24b

Ex. 5.24c

A rondo movement built on the design *ABABA,* in which the coda uses materials of both *A* and *B,* is the final movement of Schubert's Sonata in A minor, Op. 143. A highly unusual coda concludes the Prokofiev movement cited in Ex. 5.6. In this coda, the theme of the subsequent movement appears prominently just before the end.

REPEATS IN PARTICULAR EXAMPLES

While many examples of rondo form have no repeated sections, it is not difficult to find examples which do contain such repetitions. Any part of a rondo movement may be repeated.

For example, in the final movement of the Haydn Sonata in C (Hob. XVI:48) both parts of the incipient ternary theme are repeated at the beginning, after which there is a lengthy transition. No other repeats occur in the movement. A similar case is the finale of the Schubert Sonata in D, Op. 53, whose ternary theme is repeated at the outset. Again, no further repeats are used.

In the second movement of Schubert's Sonata in A minor, Op. 164, only the second part of the theme is repeated at each appearance; in addition, both digressions are followed by repeat signs.

In each of these cases, the repeat is immediately applied to a particular component in the form and does not have significant effect on the formal design except to extend it. (Where tonal fluctuation occurs within a repeated segment the sequence of tonal events is complicated, as we observed in connection with smaller forms.) As has been pointed out, notated repeats are not invariably observed in performance; thus, the issue of their implications is confused by the uncertainties of actual realization.

THE RONDO PRINCIPLE IN DA CAPO FORMS

In the chapter on compound ternary form, the point was made that the traditional minuet or scherzo with "trio" and *da capo* is sometimes extended to include two trios and a second *da capo*. We observed that this kind of enlargement of the compound ternary results in a rondo form. (See Chapter 4, pp. 87-89.) Such a rondo is invariably of the compound type, often with distinct separations between parts.

A further example is the Mozart Serenade in B-flat for winds, K. 361, which includes two movements (the second and fourth) in which the addition of second trios results in rondo forms. In the second movement, each of the five major parts —Menuetto, Trio I, Menuetto, Trio II, Menuetto—is a simple ternary. The movement is basically in B-flat, while the trios are in E-flat and G minor, respectively.

TECHNIQUES OF INTEGRATION IN RONDO FORM

Integration is often achieved in the rondo, as in other forms, by the use of bridging passages—transitions and retransitions—and by interrelations among materials of the various sections. We have already seen illustrations of both features. A third technique is that of concealment, by rhythmic means or elision, of points separating sections.

Example 5.25 shows the juncture of the first return of the rondo theme and the second digression. Although there is no transition, continuity is enforced by the use of a common motive (bracketed) and by elision at the cadence, where the tonic suddenly appears as a minor triad, introducing a new phrase. The *sforzato* attack is a further factor in forward impulse. The effect of the elision seems especially significant in view of the pronounced cadence and rest which had separated the opening rondo statement from the first digression (m.22).

Ex. 5.25 Haydn, String Quartet in C, Op. 33, No. 3, fourth movement.

Just as there can be a high degree of integration without a transitional passage, there can be transition in conjunction with marked cadential breaks. Thus, in the second movement of the Schubert Sonata in A minor, Op. 164, the theme and both digressions are clearly "closed" units, with transitions *following* their strongly articulated cadences.

The movement from the Cello Concerto of Ernst Toch (1887–1964), referred to in Ex. 5.24, is a good example of a rondo form with tight integration of its various parts. Another is the finale of the Haydn Symphony in E-flat, No. 103. This movement should be studied with care. Note that (1) the entire movement is based on , the digressions' contrast deriving only from motivic development and tonal change; and (2) the motion is continued vigorously at every cadence, except for two fermatas preceding the returns of the rondo theme and another near the end of the movement.

Silences can, somewhat paradoxically, be persuasive factors of continuity, where cessations in rhythmic motion occur in conditions of harmonic instability. When the interruption is of indefinite length, the feeling of intensity is particularly strong.

Ex. 5.26 Haydn, String Quartet in C, Op. 33, No. 3, fourth movement.

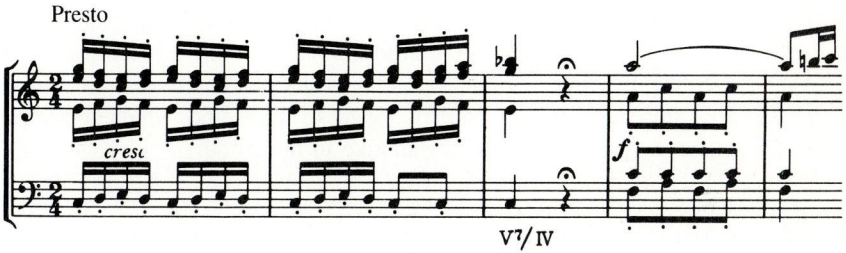

In many instances it is clearly a compositional choice that contrasting sections should be sharply delineated. And in a lengthy movement, points of clear punctuation—of "breathing"—may seem necessary. In the Haydn movement cited in Exx. 5.25 and 5.26, the few pronounced interruptions are significant; in relation to them the general continuity and vitality of the music are all the more compelling. And in the Haydn as in most tonal music, interruptions are relatively rarely on perfect tonal consonances.

EXTENSIONS OF RONDO FORM

Taking the five-part rondo scheme as a standard of the type discussed in this chapter, extension is possible by the addition of theoretically any number of further digressions and rondo returns. The Bach Gavotte discussed on p. 107 illustrates this.

Another example of this type of rondo extension is from Schumann's piano work *Faschingsschwank aus Wien,* Op. 26; its allegro first movement has five statements of the rondo theme. The fourth movement of the Ravel String Quartet is a rondo design consisting of four statements of the rondo material (not a "theme" in the usual sense): its basic form may be represented as *ABABABA*. A further example is the final movement of Bach's *Brandenburg Concerto* No. 1, to which reference is made in Chapter 4, p. 89.

A traditional seven-part rondo form much used by composers of the eighteenth and nineteenth centuries, the *sonata-rondo,* is discussed in Chapter 7, following the chapter on single-movement sonata form, to which it bears certain important resemblances.

BEETHOVEN, TRIO IN E-FLAT, FOR PIANO, VIOLIN, AND CELLO, OP. 70, NO. 2, SECOND MOVEMENT

For summary study of a complete movement, we may examine the second movement of the Beethoven Piano Trio in E-flat. Certain key points in the movement will be illustrated by quotation; the reader should, however, make reference to the complete score.

The movement begins with the rondo theme, stated without introduction. The theme is a 16-measure enlarged period—enlarged by the repetition and variation of each of the two basic phrases; the variation technique is simply a redistribution of voices and instrumental parts, with the essential outlines and harmonic structure of the two phrases preserved. A characteristic aspect of the theme, which appears in Ex. 5.27a, is the rhythm of the opening motive in the piano.

Ex. 5.27a Beethoven, Trio in E-flat, Op. 70, No. 2, for piano, violin, and cello, second movement.

Ex. 5.27a *(continued)*

The first digression, in the parallel minor, follows without transition. It consists of three phrases; the first two (mm. 17–24) are similar except for their cadences, the second phrase being an ornamental variation of the first (5.27 b,c). The keys of C minor, A-flat, and F minor are touched at the three cadences. The motive

takes on a special significance here; it is later to become

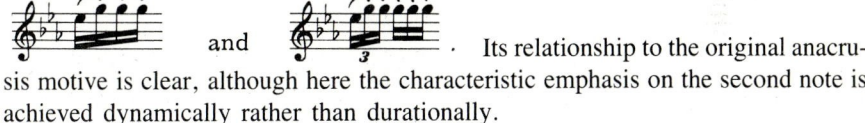

and . Its relationship to the original anacrusis motive is clear, although here the characteristic emphasis on the second note is achieved dynamically rather than durationally.

Ex. 5.27b (piano only).

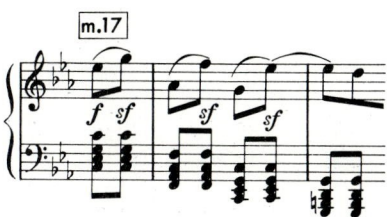

Ex. 5.27c

In the second half of m. 28 the opening motive returns for retransition to the rondo theme. Throughout the retransition (6 measures) the harmony vacillates between tonic and dominant of F minor. In the last measure, an implied f:I becomes C:IV by the chromatic change of A♭ to A♮ (5.27d).

Ex. 5.27d

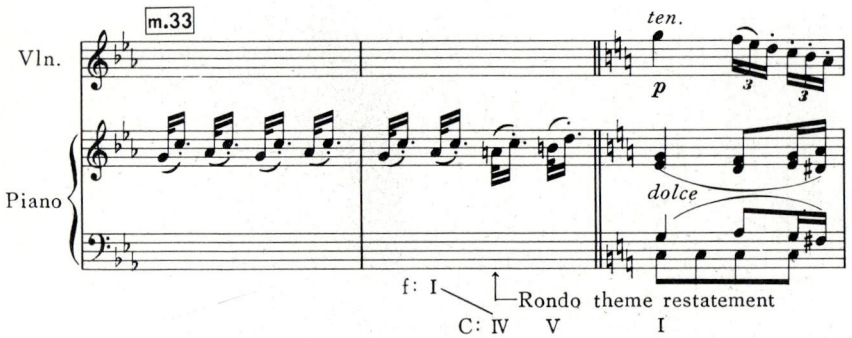

In its first return, the rondo theme is repeated, thereby extended to 32 measures. Several variations are developed, as may be seen by comparing the fragments given in Ex. 5.27e with the first measure of the original theme (see also m. 35, Ex. 5.27d).

Ex. 5.27e

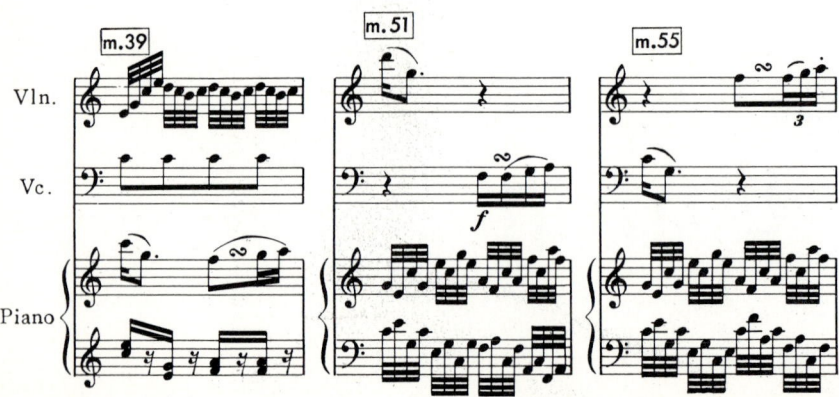

The second digression, a variation on the first, is similarly introduced without transition. In form, tonality, and harmonic structure, it is precisely parallel to the first digression, but the characteristic motive (see Ex. 5.27b, c) now takes on more rapid rhythmic motion, as in the preceding variation of the rondo theme. The technique of ornamental variation applied here can be seen by comparison of fragments (5.27f) with the first measure of the first digression (5.27b,c).

Ex. 5.27f

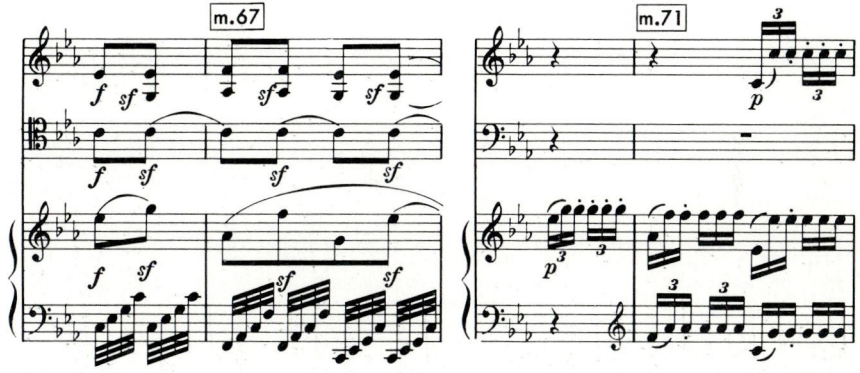

The retransition is now cut from 6 to 4 measures. Again, it anticipates the anacrusis motive of the theme, although in steady 32nd-note motion which echoes rhythms developed in the second digression. Just before the theme appears, the cello enters with a descending anacrusis figure of three 8th-notes, helping to prepare the slower motion of the theme (5.27g).

Ex. 5.27g

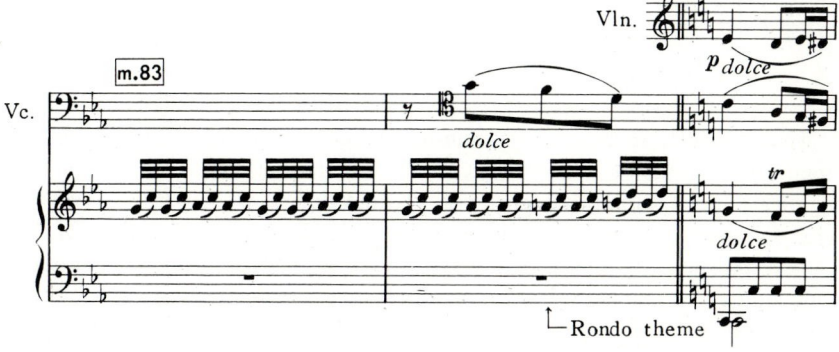

In its final statement, the theme is reduced to two phrases—the basic antecedent and consequent of the original period—and it appears as at the beginning of the
movement, without variation (5.27g). It is followed by a transition of 4 measures,
based on the original anacrusis motive, introducing a change of mode and leading to
the coda in C minor. The transition might be conceived as an inflated upbeat to the
assertive beginning of the coda proper at m. 98 (Ex. 5.27h).

Ex. 5.27h

The coda is 42 measures long, unusual in view of the 138-measure length of
the total movement. In key and mode, it is reminiscent of the digressions; in thematic material, it is varied. It begins with a repeated phrase which has a somewhat
tenuous relationship to the rondo theme (5.27i); its anacrusis is the familiar first
measure of the theme. Following the first 8 measures, there is a development of the
opening motive of the first digression, a portion of which (the development) is
quoted as Ex. 5.27j.

Ex. 5.27i

Ex. 5.27j

The coda continues in 4-measure phrases, with a perfect authentic cadence in C minor concluding each. The last of these reaches its cadence at m. 120 and is extended by repetition of the tonic and dominant cadential harmonies, stopping on the dominant at m. 123, and prolonging that harmony with a gradual reduction in dynamic intensity, in texture, and in rhythmic motion over the next 4 measures, at which point the characteristic anacrusis motive of the theme returns again (5.27k).

There is a brief, renewed development of this motive, with a sudden, dramatic *forte* at m. 129, followed by a pause of half a measure. Now the first 2 measures of the theme, first in major, then in minor, make a final appearance (5.27l), with hesitations in tempo.

With a few further, capricious appearances of the motive in brief dialogue between piano and strings, the coda reaches a final cadence in C minor. A particularly striking aspect of the movement is its realization of form combining the rondo principle with pervasive variation technique.

Ex. 5.27k

Ex. 5.27l

Ex. 5.27m

EXERCISES

1. Find examples of the following:
   a) A historical antecedent of the classical rondo.
   b) A rondo theme of period form.
   c) A transition linking the rondo theme to the first digression.
   d) A retransition preparing the return of the rondo theme.
   e) A highly integrated rondo. (Describe its particular properties of connection and interrelation.)
   f) A piece, possibly a song, illustrating the rondo principle in an extended form.
   g) A rondo using variation techniques in the restatements of the theme.

2. Select an example cited in connection with the first question, or choose an example from the text of this chapter. Write, in outline form or in an expository paragraph, an analytical discussion of its form, referring to some of the points discussed in this chapter.

3. Compose a theme which might form the basis for a traditional rondo. Show two or three ways in which the theme might be varied in its reappearances.

4. Analyze the second movement (Adagio) of Beethoven's Sonata in C minor, Op. 10, No. 1. Give special attention to the following points.
   a) Study the retransition preparing the first return of the theme.
   b) To what extent does the music fall obviously into sections, and to what extent are demarcations bridged? (For example, the first transition is an integrating factor, but it follows a well-marked cadential division.)
   c) Would you describe the last 11 bars as a codetta? Why, or why not?

5. Find an example of coda in a rondo movement.
   a) What is its length?
   b) What is its proportion in relation to the entire movement? To the rondo theme?
   c) Can it be said to be in any degree developmental? Explain.
   d) From what sources is its thematic material drawn?
   e) Is there any departure from, or modulatory expansion of, the basic tonality?
   f) Is it sectional? Explain.
   g) Is a considerable portion taken up with repetitions of cadential harmonies in elaboration and extension of the final cadence?
   h) Is there any use of sequence in the coda? Of contrapuntal imitation?

6. Prepare a list of questions that might be used in an examination on rondo form.

7. How would you characterize the form of the Mozart Rondo in D, K. 485?

8. Prepare an analysis of the Concerto in C minor for clarinet and orchestra, Op. 26, by Louis Spohr (1784–1859). Why is this a compound form? Give special attention to transitions and to the coda (m. 295) produced by the dissolution of the rondo theme.

9. Study techniques of variation in the restatements of digression and rondo theme (ABA'B'A'') in Haydn's Sonata in D (Hob. XVI: 33).

10. Many specimens of the five-part rondo have been used for illustration or mentioned in the text of this chapter. A few supplementary works are listed below for further study.

Johann Christian Bach (1735–82), Sonata in E-flat, Op. 5, No. 4, second movement

Beethoven, Polonaise, Op. 89 (introduction and two contrasting digressions)
Sonata in G, Op. 49, No. 2, final movement

Gabriel Fauré (1845–1924), Prelude No. 3 in G minor for piano

Haydn, Sonata in E-flat, Hob.XVI:49, third movement
Sonata in D, Hob.XVI:19, final movement
Sonata in D , Hob.XVI:51, final movement
Sonata in E, Hob.XVI:22, final movement

Johann Nepomuk Hummel (1778–1837), Rondo, Op. 11, for piano (interesting transitional passages)

Mozart, Serenade in B-flat for winds, K. 361, second, fourth, and seventh movements
Quartet in F for oboe, 2 violins, and cello, K. 370, final movement
Sonata in C, K. 545, third movement
Rondeau in F, K. 15hh, for piano (Is the Rondeau in D, K. 15d, in rondo form?)
Rondo in A minor for piano, K. 511

Rameau, "Air en rondeau" from *Hippolyte et Aricie*
"Musette en rondeau" from *Les Indes Galantes*

Schubert, Sonata in C minor (D. 958), final movement (note extensive and highly contrasting digressions)

Stravinsky, Concerto in D for strings, third movement

Tchaikovsky, Concerto in D for violin and orchestra, Op. 35, final movement (rondo theme developed in later appearances)

11. Find examples of extended rondo in piano works of C. P. E. Bach—for example, the Rondos in C and D (Wq 56/1,3; Helm 260–61).

12. Consider the ritornello principle as evident in the final movement of Bach's *Brandenburg Concerto* No. 4.

   a) Sections of the movement featuring the ripieno (orchestra) on the one hand and the concertino (solo group of violin and two flutes) on the other are sharply distinguished in texture, timbre, and sonority. Are they also contrasted in thematic content?

   b) Show that ritornello occurrences articulate a tonal scheme of tonic, dominant, subdominant, relative minor; identify the principal ritornello cadences.

   c) At the concertino's first appearance as a solo group (m. 41) flutes have the subject. How would you characterize the solo violin part?

   d) The full orchestra emerges gradually at mm. 63–67. In what sense do the violins prepare the tutti of m. 67? Is this technique of preparation evident elsewhere?

   e) In mm. 87–127, the principal violin is very active. How would you describe its content here, and what is the role of the concertino flutes during their brief appearance in this section?

   f) Do the flutes ever double orchestral voices, as does the principal (solo) violin? What is notable in the flute parts following m. 159?

   g) In what area(s) of the movement does the frequency of concertino-tutti alternation accelerate, and what might this "mean" in the structure?

6

SONATA

The term *sonata* has its origin in the Latin verb *sonare,* to sound, and initially referred to a work to be played (''sounded'') on an instrument or group of instruments, as opposed to a vocal work, or *cantata* (from the Latin *cantare,* to sing). In its evolution from this obvious connotation, the word has at various times assumed various meanings. Thus, in addition to medium of performance, it has to do with particular types of multimovement composition as well as with the specific formal design of certain single movements and single-movement pieces.

In the latter sense, denoting a specific single-movement form, the term applies to many movements of symphonies, quartets, concertos, piano sonatas, and other multimovement orchestral, chamber, and solo types. Single-movement sonata form occurs often in the overture as well. In the sense of multimovement composition, the use of the word *sonata* is usually limited to works for solo instrument, or for piano and another instrument.

This chapter is concerned chiefly with single-movement sonata form as it is commonly represented in at least one of the movements of a multimovement sonata, whether for orchestra (symphony), chamber ensemble (quintet, quartet, trio, etc.), or solo instrument. There are several terms which relate, with various confusing implications, to this particular form. The simple designation *sonata form,* as already stated, refers both to single-movement and multimovement designs. The term *sonata-allegro form,* also in common usage, bears a misleading inference of tempo. Finally, the term *first-movement form* wrongly implies that the form is restricted to opening movements. A solution to the problem of terminology lies in the designation *single-movement sonata form.*

A detailed tracing of the historical development of the sonata does not lie within the scope of the present study, which is concerned with the description and analysis of single-movement sonata form as it ultimately evolved late in the eighteenth century. Moreover, despite its independent history, the symphony is regarded as an orchestral manifestation of sonata form.

While single-movement sonata form is associated in part with the keyboard sonatas of such composers as C.P.E. Bach and J. C. Bach, in whose works it is at least incipient, it was not until the time of Haydn and Mozart that the classical conventions of single-movement sonata form became firmly established. Those conventions are: (1) *contrasting thematic complexes in two tonal regions* (commonly tonic and dominant), followed by (2) *increasingly fluctuant thematic development* of scope and significance as a major division in the form, and, following such development, (3) *the restatement of themes in the tonic,* a procedure signifying resolution of the original condition of tonal opposition.

THE MULTIMOVEMENT SONATA

Certain general observations can be made as to the usual movement types in the multimovement sonata. The first movement, for example, is usually in single-movement sonata form. Works such as the Mozart Sonata in A, K. 331, and the Beethoven Sonata in A-flat, Op. 26, are exceptions; in each of these works the opening movement is a theme with variations. Another exception is the first movement of the Beethoven Sonata in C-sharp minor, Op. 27, No. 2, labelled *quasi una Fantasia.*

The second movement of the four-movement scheme is frequently in a slow tempo. The slow second movement may have any of several forms: theme with variations, ternary form, rondo, binary, single-movement sonata form, or some combination or modification of one or more of these. The Sonata, Op. 26, of Beethoven here again departs from the norm: its second movement is a scherzo. The slow movement of his String Quartet in E minor, Op. 59, No. 2, is in single-movement sonata form. That of the Haydn Sonata in D (Hob. XVI:37) is in binary form. Slow variations as the second of three movements may be seen in the Beethoven Sonata, Op. 57, while the slow second movement of the same composer's Sonata, Op. 13, is in rondo form. An example of large ternary form in a slow movement occurs in the Brahms Piano Quintet in F minor, Op. 34.

The third movement of the four-movement scheme is very often a minuet or scherzo with contrasting trio (see Chapter 4). This type of movement is very common in classical symphonies. Beethoven's Symphonies Nos. 1, 2, 3, 4, 5, and 8 are examples; in Nos. 4 and 5 the restatement of the first part is written out with some variation. The Beethoven Sonata, Op. 26, is again exceptional: its third movement is a slow funeral march. Haydn and Mozart piano sonatas are not usually in four movements, although the minuet with trio can sometimes be found as the second of three movements in these works. Other instances of scherzo or minuet with trio as the third of four movements are found in the Beethoven Sonatas, Op. 7; Op. 10,

No. 3; Op. 22; and Op. 28. Further examples may be seen in the piano sonatas of Schubert: Op. 42, Op. 53, and Op. 122, to name a few.

The final movement is commonly fast, often in rondo form or single-movement sonata form, although other forms are to be found. The last movement frequently embodies strong rhythmic momentum, often with simpler textures than the first (although it may contain passages of fugal imitation in rapid tempo, a favored finale device), and typically with vigorous dynamic qualities appropriate to its position as the concluding movement. The finale to the Haydn Symphony No. 102 in B-flat is in single-movement sonata form with a characteristic fugal passage at m. 188. The final movement of the Beethoven Quartet, Op. 59, No. 2, is a rondo. An example of a fourth movement which is neither is that of Beethoven's Third Symphony, in variation form; another is that of Brahms's Fourth Symphony, a set of variations on an 8-measure harmonic theme.

Many sonatas contain only three movements, as noted above, or even fewer than three. Generalizations as to the nature of the movements are difficult because of wide variance. Still, the first movement is in most cases in single-movement sonata form, and the second contrastingly slow in tempo when it is part of a three-movement work. Three-movement sonatas are so numerous, especially in the solo literature of the classical period, that specific examples hardly need mention. The Mozart Sonata in F, K. 547a, and Haydn's Sonata in G (Hob. XVI:40) are examples of two-movement sonatas, as are the Beethoven Sonatas of Op. 49, Op. 53 (whose Adagio is an introduction to the second movement), Op. 90, and Op. 111.

RELATIONSHIPS AMONG THE MOVEMENTS

The question of relationships among the various movements of the multimovement sonata is a difficult one. Of course, there are cases in which the movements are bound together by transitional passages, and there are numerous examples whose movements are related by the employment of common thematic materials. In the former category are such works as the Mendelssohn Piano Concerto in G minor and the Beethoven Violin Concerto, whose second and third movements are bridged by the passage quoted as Ex. 6.1.

The sharing of common thematic materials among all the movements reaches its most extensive application among French composers of the middle and late nineteenth century, notably in the music of Berlioz and César Franck (1822–90). The Debussy and Ravel string quartets are *cyclical* in this sense, and the technique is to be observed as well in such earlier works as the Schubert *Wanderer Fantasy,* Op. 15, Beethoven's Fifth Symphony, and the Schumann Piano Quintet. Example 6.2 shows the reappearance in the fourth movement of the principal motive of the first movement of the Schumann Quintet.

Another means of relating the several movements is the insertion, without deep integration, of momentary reminders of materials of early movements late in a multimovement work. Thus, the final movement of Beethoven's Ninth Symphony

Ex. 6.1 Beethoven, Concerto in D, Op. 61, for violin and orchestra.

Ex. 6.2 Schumann, Quintet in E-flat, Op. 44, for piano and strings.

First movement excerpt:

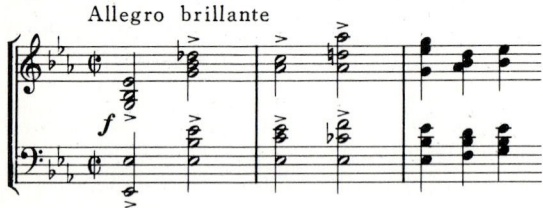

Fourth movement excerpt:

is preceded by brief reappearances of materials of the first three movements and an anticipation of the theme of the fourth movement.

But in the absence of such palpable relationships of common motives and themes, or the binding of one movement to another through bridging material, how does one explain the coincidence of two apparently independent movements in the same work? Given the important conditions of surface unities, especially of tonality and style, balanced conditions of contrast (especially of tempo), and the obvious requirement that two movements of the same work not be so contradictory in character as to be mutually negating (e.g., whimsical and funereal), there are perhaps many instances in which two movements of similar nature from two multimovement works of the same style (hence, probably of the same composer) might be convincingly interchanged—for example, the third movements of the Haydn Symphonies Nos. 101 and 104, both in D. The relationship that we sense between or among movements of a large work may often be one of conditioned association.

SMALLER AND LARGER EXCEPTIONS TO THE MULTIMOVEMENT NORM

A few examples of two-movement sonatas are given on p. 149. One-movement sonatas, representing regular or modified single-movement sonata form, or some kind of condensation of multimovement form, occur in the present century as a symptom of the tendency toward greater compactness in musical form. Yet, if we exclude symphonic poems and overtures, one-movement sonatas are relatively uncommon, even in the twentieth century. Examples of twentieth-century symphonies in one movement are the Seventh of Jean Sibelius (1865–1957), the Third of Roy Harris (1898–1979), and the Sixth of William Schuman (b. 1915). An example of a one-movement piano sonata is the Op. 1 of Alban Berg (1885–1935).

Sonatas comprising a greater number of movements than the normal three or four are also to be found, although relatively rarely. Examples of these are the Beethoven Quartet in B-flat, Op. 130 (six movements), the Schumann Symphony No. 3 in E-flat (five movements), the Piano Trio in E minor, Op. 90, of Antonín Dvořák (1841–1904) (five movements), and the Brahms Sonata in F minor, Op. 5 (five movements).

SINGLE-MOVEMENT SONATA FORM

The introduction

Our attention now turns to the principal subject of this chapter—the important design which we have termed *single-movement sonata form*. Basic features of the form are, as noted on p. 148, the statement of themes or thematic complexes at contrasting tonal levels (exposition), development of some or all of the exposition material, and restatement (recapitulation) of that material in the tonic.

An introductory section, preceding but not necessarily distinctly separated from the main body of the movement, is not unusual, although it is by no means a standard feature. Moreover, its content, size, structure, and other characteristics are largely unpredictable. Each introductory section has to be studied in terms of its own content, which is determined by its function as prefatory material as well as by the nature of what is to follow.

Lengthy slow introductions are not hard to find. The First, Second, and Fourth Symphonies of Beethoven have formal introductions, and the Seventh has an especially extensive and elaborate introduction with a well-delineated form of its own. Many symphonies of Mozart have introductions—for example, the Symphonies in C, K. 425 (*Linz*); in D, K. 504 (*Prague*); and in E-flat, K. 543. Haydn's symphonic introductions are so common that specific examples need not be cited. Other examples of introductions to first movements of symphonies are the "Great" C major Symphony of Schubert, Brahms's First Symphony, and, in the twentieth century, the First Symphony of Sibelius. In the literature of chamber music the following examples may be mentioned: Mozart's Sonata in G, K. 379, for violin and piano, and Quartet in C, K. 465, with its extraordinary chromatic introduction; Beethoven Quartets, Op. 59, No. 3, and Op. 74; Haydn's Quartet in D, Op. 71, No. 2; Schubert's Octet, Op. 166 (whose final movement also has an introduction); Franck's Piano Quartet in F minor, whose slow introduction is worked subtly into the following Allegro and returns in its original tempo late in the first movement; and, in the twentieth century, the Second Quartet of Walter Piston (1894–1976). Another twentieth-century example of an introduction to the first movement of a large work is found in the Piano Concerto No.3 by Serge Prokofiev (1891-1953).

Apart from introductory sections of such scope, many movements have brief opening figures which arrest the listener's attention prior to the statement of the principal thematic material. Such a work is Beethoven's Third Symphony, with its two full tonic chords introducing the opening theme, or Haydn's Quartet in G, Op. 76, No. 1, with its simple but commanding I-V-I progression at the beginning of the first movement. A further example is quoted as Ex. 6.3, from the opening of Chopin's Sonata in B-flat minor.

Ex. 6.3   Chopin, Sonata in B-flat minor, Op. 35.

The function of the introduction is to set the stage for what follows, to prepare the ear for the principal materials of the movement. The reason for an introduction may be found in the nature of the opening theme of the exposition: its decided importance in the movement's future course and content, its unpretentious or very active beginning, its tonal ambiguity, or simply the swiftness of its general impression. It is sometimes revealing to omit the introduction from an example (the first movements of the Beethoven Sonata, Op. 13, and the Schubert Octet are good illustrations); the beginning of the form proper often appears awkwardly abrupt without it.

Although the opening movement of a work is the movement most likely to be preceded by an introductory section, such sections sometimes introduce last movements as well. Introductions to final movements are found in the Beethoven First Symphony (a slow passage of 6 measures), the Brahms Piano Quintet, the Brahms First Symphony, and the Tchaikovsky Fifth Symphony.

Very often, the materials used in the introduction are not explicitly recalled in the movement proper. This is the case with most introductions of Haydn, Mozart, and Beethoven.

It may be argued, however, that a greater degree of integration is achieved when materials of the introduction are developed or restated later in the movement. An example of this procedure is Beethoven's Sonata, Op. 13. Here, the theme of the slow introduction not only returns in rhapsodic fashion in its original form and tempo during the movement proper, but the principal motive of the introduction actually merges with the opening theme of the exposition during the development. The introduction motive is indicated in Ex. 6.4.

Other works in which introductory materials are used subsequently are the Beethoven Quartets, Op. 130 in B-flat and 132 in A minor, the Haydn Symphony No. 103 in E-flat, the Schubert C major Symphony, the Tchaikovsky Fourth and Fifth Symphonies, and the Brahms First Symphony, whose introduction supplies the chief subject matter of the first movement. Related passages from the introduction and exposition are quoted in Ex. 6.5. Many other examples could be cited.

Because it usually introduces comparatively fast material, the tempo of the

Ex. 6.4 Beethoven, Sonata in C minor, Op. 13, first movement.

Ex. 6.5 Brahms, Symphony No. 1 in C minor, Op. 68, first movement.

introduction is in most cases slow. The effect of its length, relative to the balance of the movement, is thus often greater than the number of its measures would suggest.

The exposition

In the exposition, the themes and motives are normally set forth in their most direct form. The terms "principal theme" (or "principal subject") and "subordinate theme" (or "subordinate subject") have been applied to these materials, which often consist of two major thematic ideas; however, a group of motives or themes may be presented in either section of the exposition, or in both. There may, indeed, be distinct contrasts within each exposition area. These materials are best referred to as *theme groups* or *theme complexes,* unified in tonality but not necessarily by explicit motivic means.

For example, the first movement of Mozart's Sonata in F, K. 332, begins with a 12-measure period, followed by a very different thematic element in mm. 13–22. This second theme is to be considered a part of the first section in that it shares the tonic key with the opening theme. The second group (in C) is even more diverse, with individual thematic entities entering at mm. 41, 56, and 71, all in the dominant key.

The more universally applicable point to be made concerning the traditional exposition is that its content is centered first in one tonality, the principal key of the movement, and then in a second. In each of these tonal regions—that of the primary tonic and that of the close secondary tonic—significant expository activity takes place. There are thus two centers of considerable tonal stability; the first *tonal group* is usually followed by a modulatory transition, after which there is a provisional settling at the second tonal level for statement of (again, usually) contrasting materials. To be sure, exceptions can be found; either complex may be tonally unsettled as part of its essential character (Beethoven, *Waldstein Sonata*, Op. 53, first movement, first tonal group).

In traditional eighteenth- and nineteenth-century sonatas, the two keys of the exposition are normally very closely related. The most usual relationship is that of tonic and dominant. In instances in which the tonic is minor, it is likely to be paired with its relative major. The Beethoven *Waldstein Sonata* offers an exception: the first tonal group is in C (despite its tonal fluctuation, mentioned above), while the second is in the mediant key, E.

Ex. 6.6   Beethoven, Sonata in C, Op. 53, first movement.

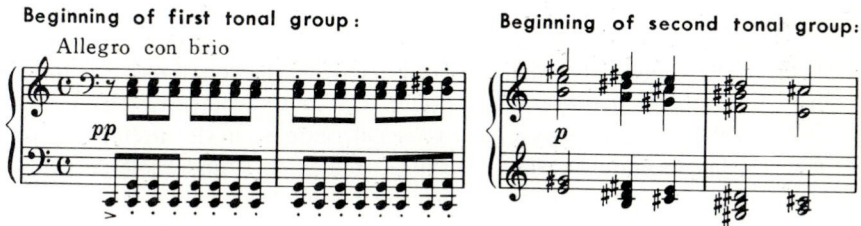

The thematic materials of the first tonal group in the exposition are usually substantially different from those in the second group, but occasionally the same ideas will be the basis for both. Example 6.7 illustrates this point, where pronounced change of articulation is nevertheless evident.

Ex. 6.7   Haydn, Sonata in C-sharp minor (Hob. XVI: 36), first movement.

In classical style, periodic forms are exceedingly common as the basis for either tonal group; other possibilities are numerous, however, and include relatively free orderings of ideas in no particular formal scheme, especially in later examples. Binary and ternary forms are infrequent here, in view of their aspect of tonal change, and the usual uniformity of tonality within each of the two expository complexes.

However, simple ternary form may be seen within the first tonal group of the first movement of Schubert's Sonata in A, Op. 120 (mm. 1–20). The first movement of the Ravel String Quartet begins its first tonal group with a simple ternary followed by a phrase based on a rhythmic permutation of the original motive. This phrase, entering at m. 24, is immediately repeated in sequence. The Mozart Sonata in C, K. 296, for violin and piano, begins with a repeated phrase (mm. 1–8), followed by three statements of a 2-measure motive (mm. 9–14) and an 8-measure period (15-22), ending the first tonal group. The opening of the Piano Quintet, Op. 34, of Brahms is a good example of a phrase group in the first tonal complex: mm. 1-11 are introductory gestures, followed in mm. 12-26 by a group of phrases, with cadences at mm. 17, 22, and 26. Measure 27 begins a new phrase which dissolves into a transition establishing the new tonal area.

A characteristic of many early works in single-movement sonata form is the absence of fully confirmed modulation prior to the introduction of the second tonal group. This can be seen in Mozart quite often (first movements of K. 280, K. 283, K. 284, and K. 311, to list only a few cases) and, at times, in Haydn (for example, the first movements of the Sonatas in D and G, Hob. XVI: 19 and 27, respectively). In such cases the transition out of the first tonal group leads only to the dominant harmony of the original tonic. The second group, which follows directly, simply takes up this harmony as its tonic, as in Ex. 6.8.

Ex. 6.8   Mozart, Sonata in F, K. 376, for violin and piano, first movement.

The technique of tonicizing the 5th beyond the projected tonal destination is often seen in Haydn and Beethoven, among others. An instance is shown in Ex. 6.9, where the modulation from G to D reaches slightly beyond by the subsidiary reference to A. This use of a passing G♯ enhances the effect of the final yielding to the secondary tonic, D.

Ex. 6.9   Beethoven, Sonata in G, Op. 14, No. 2, first movement.

The transition linking the two tonal groups thus has the important function of modulation. Even though, as we have just observed, the modulation is not always clearly manifest, the second group will have some degree of tonal preparation, and other kinds of preparation as well, as in transitions studied in connection with other forms. The transitional passage is approached in various ways: the first group may be concluded on a strong cadence, followed by the transitional material, as in Ex. 6.10; the transition may begin simultaneously with the cadence ending the first

Ex. 6.10   Beethoven, Sonata in C minor, Op. 10, No. 1, first movement.

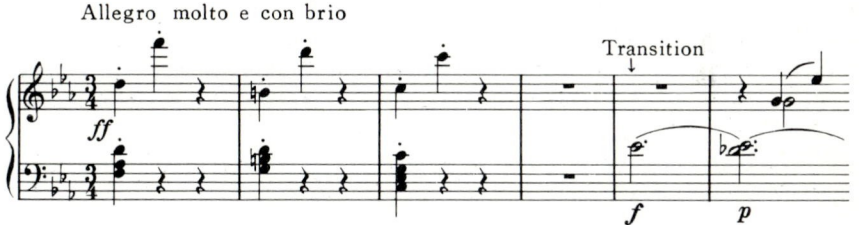

group (Ex. 6.11); or the final element of the first group may dissolve into figuration which leads without even a tentative cadence into the transition. An example of this may be observed in the first movement of Beethoven's Second Symphony (see mm. 16–22). This situation, a small part of which is quoted as Ex. 6.12, develops the primary motive of the first group.

    The transition may contain ideas of the first tonal group, from which it departs, as well as of the second, which it approaches. Thus, in the Beethoven Quartet

---

[1]The symbol in which two harmonic elements are separated by a horizontal line denotes that the upper (here, V/V) occurs *over* and in conjunction with the lower (here, V, represented by its root).

Ex. 6.11   Schubert, Sonata in E-flat, Op. 122, first movement.

Ex. 6.12   Beethoven, Symphony No. 2 in D, Op. 36, first movement.

in C, Op. 59, No. 3, the transition linking the two groups employs, in mm. 71–75, a motive of the first, and in mm. 65–66, a motive of the second.

Occasionally the transition appears to be freely composed, bearing no explicit thematic relationship to the elements surrounding it; see, for instance, Mozart's Sonata in C, K. 309, first movement (mm. 21–32), and the final movement of his Sonata in F, K. 332 (mm. 36–49).

The transition is frequently built fully or in part on a pattern of harmonic sequence. This technique is apparent in the first movement of Haydn's Symphony No. 102, to be discussed at length later in this chapter. The transition is in this case based on two motives of the opening theme. The technique of sequence is used again later in the same transition (mm. 53–54; see Ex. 6.37c). The first movement of the Beethoven Sonata in C minor, Op. 10, No. 1, uses sequence through almost the entire transition between the two tonal groups (mm. 32ff.)

Beyond the possibilities mentioned above, it is difficult to generalize regarding the transitional material. It should be remembered that this segment often has the function of effecting a convincing change of character (which may involve texture, rhythmic activity, and even tempo) in addition to that of modulation. Since the art of joining two disparate formal sections is one of the most challenging aspects of composition, the reader should if possible examine carefully transitional passages of a number of periods and composers.

Following the statement of thematic materials in the second tonal region, there is usually a brief concluding section. This codetta has the appearance of an appendage to the main body of the exposition, and is normally set off by an authentic (or deceptive) cadence, at times elided. The codetta often includes some motivic material of the first group, in casual, perfunctory references, or it may derive from other parts of the exposition. An example of a codetta taking its motives from the first group is that of the first movement of Mozart's *Prague Symphony,* K. 504, after m. 136.

But the codetta is often a mere flourish of cadential chords, as in Ex. 6.13, where its 2 measures consist of nothing more than repetitions of the secondary tonic. The codetta to the exposition of the first movement of the Haydn Quartet in G, Op. 76, No. 1, is a similar summary flourish of cadential harmonies, here tonic and dominant at the secondary tonal level.

Ex. 6.13   J. C. Bach, Sonata in E-flat, Op. 17, No. 3.

In some examples the second tonal group leads into a distinctive new theme of relatively resigned character and restricted content, or into a codetta containing such a theme. A thematic entity of this kind, set apart from the main body of the second group by a transitional passage (Mozart Sonata in F, K. 332, m. 71), by decisive cadential punctuation, possibly including rests, or appearing as part of the codetta, is called a *closing theme.* The closing theme in Ex. 6.14 arises in the codetta (m. 82). The codetta, not quoted in full, leads into a retransition preparing the repeat of the exposition.

Ex. 6.14   Beethoven, Sonata in E-flat, Op. 31, No. 3, first movement.

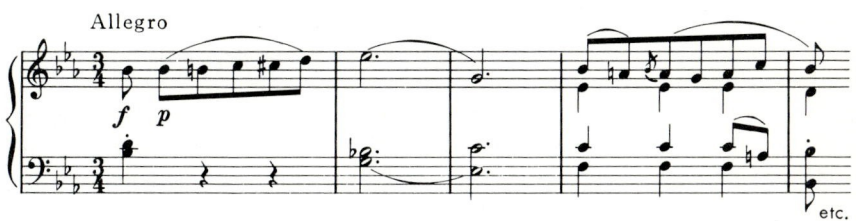

In the first movement of the last Haydn Symphony a closing theme affords the only material contrast to the theme of the first group, which is also used as the basis for the second group. The theme which is shared by the two tonal groups is quoted in Ex. 6.15, together with the closing theme, which occurs as part of the codetta (m. 84).

Ex. 6.15 Haydn, Symphony No. 104 in D, first movement.

The exposition of Beethoven's Sonata, Op. 7, first movement, may be mentioned as a further example of a work containing a distinctive closing theme, in this case as part of the codetta, the final 10 measures of the exposition.

Distinguishing between late elements of the second tonal group and an actual closing theme is at times difficult, and by no means necessarily crucial. If the theme in question actually closes the section (i.e., is part of the codetta), there is no question of the appropriateness of the term *closing theme*. But any thematic element occurring earlier than the codetta itself is, as a closing theme, set off substantially from the second group, even by transition, as a distinct, temporally separate element. The closing theme is, too, comparatively resigned in character, as suggested above, and confined to essentially cadential harmonic content, as is apparent in Exx. 6.14 and 6.15.

The exposition codetta closes in the secondary key and there is traditionally a repeat of the entire exposition, especially in eighteenth- and earlier nineteenth-century examples. The codetta is thus sometimes followed by a retransition to the repeated first group. Such retransition is often unnecessary because of the ease with which the usual secondary key is reinterpreted as the dominant of the opening. The beginning and conclusion of the exposition of a J. C. Bach sonata are shown as Ex. 6.16 to illustrate this point.

When the exposition opens in a minor key and ends in the relative major, the situation may in fact be much the same, even though the tonic of the relative major is not as functional a pivot as is the tonic of the dominant major. Thus, retransition is not particularly common following the exposition, even in movements beginning in the minor mode. Examples in which retransition *are* found in such contexts are

Ex. 6.16   J.C. Bach, Sonata in D, Op. 5, No. 2.

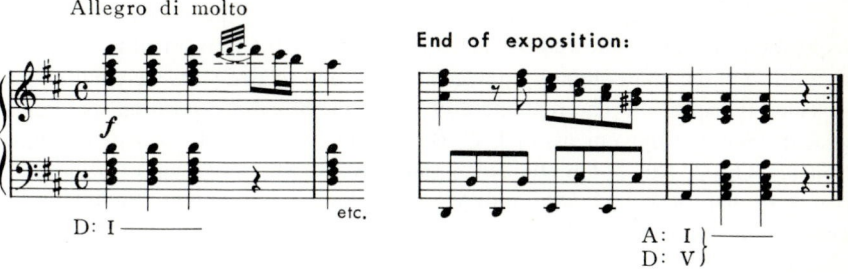

the Haydn G minor Sonata (Hob. XVI: 44), first movement, and the Mozart Sonata, K. 457, first movement. The first movement of Mozart's G minor Symphony, K. 550, uses the principal theme of the first group as codetta material at the end of the exposition, followed by a "retransition" consisting of a single chord to prepare the repeat (Ex.6.17).

An elaborate retransition is found in the Beethoven Sonata, Op. 13; another can be seen in his Sonata, Op. 31, No. 2. In the first movement of Beethoven's Fifth Symphony, there occur two extremely effective measures of silence just preceding the repeat.

Retransitions are found in all of the A minor Sonatas of Schubert; see the first movements of Op. 42, Op. 143, and Op. 164. In Op. 143, the second tonal group is in the dominant rather than the more usual relative major.

Ex. 6.17   Mozart, Symphony in G minor, K. 550, first movement.

Retransitional passages are also found in movements in the major mode. An example is the Mozart *Dissonance Quartet*, K. 465, first movement; this retransition contains a motivic preparation for the repeat of the first group. Many excellent transitional passages can be seen in the chamber music of Brahms; the rule in many of these works is motivic as well as tonal preparation of the repeat. A model example of complete retransitional preparation of the first tonal group can be seen in the String Sextet in G, Op. 36, first movement (m. 213).

A word should be said regarding the usual repeat (repeat sign and double-bar) at the end of the exposition. The composer's use of the repeat sign following the exposition, at times followed by repeat of the rest of the movement as well, is an outgrowth of the earlier binary, in which the first and second parts were individually repeated (Chapter 2). The remainder of the form, like the exposition, is often repeated. (See first movements of J. C. Bach and C. P. E. Bach sonatas; Beethoven Sonatas, Op. 2, No. 2, Op. 10, No. 2, and Op. 79; Mozart Sonatas for violin and piano, K. 301, 302, 304, etc.; most Mozart piano sonatas; and the Haydn *Emperor Quartet* in C, Op. 76, No. 3, to name only a few examples from works of the classical period.)

When the repeats are regarded as a survival of an earlier practice relating to a different formal concept, their relevance to mature single-movement sonata form becomes questionable. They are, in fact, often omitted in actual performance and are not even indicated in many later examples of the form: Beethoven's Ninth Symphony; his Sonatas, Op. 54, Op. 57, Op. 90, Op. 101, Op. 109, and Op. 110; and most works of the later nineteenth century. The repeat principle does persist through many works of Schumann, Schubert, Chopin, and Brahms. (In the Brahms symphonies such repeat signs persist until the fourth movement of the Third Symphony.)

The often-repeated explanation of this practice—that it insures that the themes of the exposition are firmly impressed upon the listener's mind—is of uncertain validity and fails to take into account the evolution of single-movement sonata form from binary antecedents. Perhaps the sense in which such repetition is most significantly useful is in demonstration of the interrelationship of the two tonal levels; yet even this has been amply demonstrated in the course of the exposition.

One may well ask what effect such repetition, when practiced, has on the form of the music. The relative dimensions of the form are of course substantially affected. Moreover, the repeat of the exposition follows contrast; there has been a change of tonal direction and considerable activity in the related tonality. In that sense, the design is altered when the repeat is practiced. The essentials of single-movement sonata form—the statement of thematic materials at contrasting tonal levels, followed by their development and recapitulation—are not compromised. But the relative proportions and the ordering of tonal-thematic events in the scenario are modified.

The development

The section following the exposition usually comprises a free manipulation of the ideas presented earlier. Occasionally, however, this section may introduce materials which are not derived from or motivically related to those of the exposition. In the Beethoven Sonata in C minor, Op. 10, No. 1, first movement, the theme occurring and developing sequentially at mm. 188ff. is essentially new, even though some relationships to the exposition can be traced—for example, the appoggiatura figure with which the theme phrases end. In extreme cases, the entire middle section may be devoted to the statement of new material. An example of this is seen in the final movement of the Beethoven Sonata, Op. 2, No. 1, where the materials of the exposition are avoided completely until the preparation for the recapitulation. The analyst must thus be prepared for the possible appearance of materials which are not directly related to those of the exposition.

What is usually found here, however, is a working out (in German, *Durchführung*, ''leading through'') of the themes and motives of the exposition—not necessarily all of them—in a section which is in most cases tonally unstable to a much higher degree than anything which has occurred before. Many tonal regions may be traversed in the development, and the range of relations among them is often wide. The single tonality which is often avoided, except occasionally at the beginning, is the primary tonic, reserved for the subsequent formal recapitulation.

The retransitional preparation for the recapitulation is often a climactic point of the development and of the movement, commonly featuring arrival on and prolongation of the dominant harmony of the tonic key. The frequent sustained dominant at the end of the development creates an impression of suspended dissonance, often quite lengthy, relieved only by the return of the first tonal group in the original key at the point of recapitulation. A portion of such a passage is reproduced as Ex. 6.18. Dominant harmony has actually been established several measures earlier, and is continued in figuration, as shown, even beyond the point quoted. A further excellent example of this technique is to be seen in the Schubert Piano Trio in E-flat, Op. 100, first movement. In the preparation for the recapitulation, dominant harmony begins at m. 329 and continues, with only superficial interruption, to the beginning of the recapitulation at m. 385. After m. 337 the 7th and minor 9th are added to the dominant, rendering it increasingly dissonant as the tension of its protraction mounts.

Development is of primary importance in the sonata, for in no other traditional form is the free manipulation of musical ideas so emphasized, nor is there in any other conventional form a major division for treatment of this kind. The development may be fantasylike with frequent and abrupt changes of key, of material, even of tempo. That of the first movement of Beethoven's Sonata in E-flat, Op. 81a,

Ex. 6.18 Mozart, Sonata in F, K. 332, final movement.

is short (40 measures) but intense, almost entirely involved with two motives of sharply opposed character, alternating at an agitated pace in an atmosphere of severe dissonance and chromatic-enharmonic ambiguity and mobility.

The development often contains the movement's most exciting events; it is the scene of conflicting moods, of restlessness, of drama, of the unexpected. It affords important contrast to the more direct and stable presentation of themes which occur earlier and later. This contrast is afforded by relative freedom of form and texture, by the mixture of opposing elements (often merged in fascinating ways, as in Ex. 6.4), and by tonal fluctuation. The middle section has assumed increasing importance during the evolution of the form; witness the comparative insignificance of the developmental principle as applied in very early examples, indistinguishable from simple binary except for possibly greater diversity of ideas (see the discussion of *sonatina* later in this chapter). In many recent examples, by contrast, the techniques of development are operative through the greater part of the movement. Thus, in the Sextet for strings, clarinet, and piano (1937) by Aaron Copland (b. 1900), the opening materials of the first movement are set forth and then developed continuously with very little restatement.

The techniques of development are not, of course, restricted to the development section. It has already been observed that transitional passages in the exposition may involve development of earlier motives, and developmental techniques are often applied in other sections of the sonata movement as well, notably in the coda.

Often, the development begins with a forthright statement, generally abbreviated, of the opening material of the exposition, as a reminder of what is to be treated. This is especially likely when no repeat of the exposition is indicated. When this is done, especially in the tonic key, the form becomes more closely allied to the so-called *sonata-rondo* (Chapter 7), but for the likely partial statement of the theme here, and absence of formal final restatement, as in rondo, before the coda. An example of this is the first movement of Brahms's Fourth Symphony, in which the main theme of the first tonal group returns in the development section in its original key (m. 145). Examples in which an abbreviated version of the theme appears at the corresponding point are the movements of the Beethoven Quartets, Op. 59, No. 2, and Op. 74, and the Haydn Quartets, Op. 64, No. 5, and Op. 76, No. 1. In the first of these Haydn examples, the theme of the first group is stated in the subdominant key (G); in the second, a good share of the opening theme is recalled, with a contrapuntal voice added. In the Beethoven examples are more fragmentary reminders of the original materials.

It is difficult to generalize as to the key of the development's beginning, except that it may be expected to relate closely to that of the end of the exposition. Sometimes the development begins by taking up a motive with which the exposition has ended. This is shown in Ex. 6.19.

At some point near the end, the development is directed toward the primary tonic, usually its dominant harmony. Example 6.20, by Haydn, shows the end of the development and beginning of recapitulation.

Ex. 6.19   Brahms, Sextet in B-flat, Op. 18, for strings, first movement.

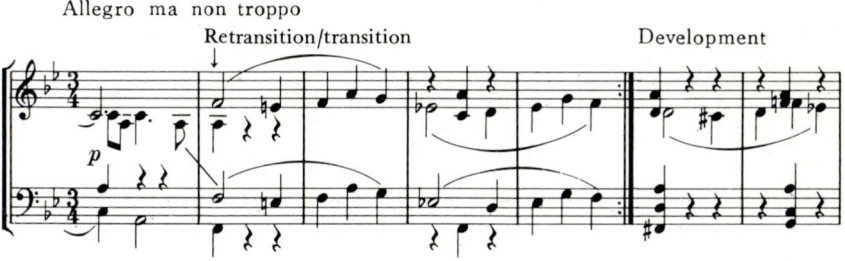

Ex. 6.20   Haydn, String Quartet in E-flat, Op. 9, No. 2, first movement.

The durational extension of dominant harmony, usually in dissonant form, is perhaps the most basic tension-producing harmonic device in tonal music. In the retransition toward the recapitulation, it sets up an air of expectancy to be fulfilled by the forthcoming tonic entry. Other devices for evoking tense expectancy are common at this point: extreme diminuendo or crescendo, rise in pitch, and motivic preparation in the form of tentative, anticipatory repetitions of motives with which the recapitulation is to begin. In the first movement of Beethoven's *Waldstein Sonata,* Op. 53, the development gives way to the recapitulation at m. 156. As early as m. 136 the dominant of the original tonic (C) enters, and an intense preparation

for recapitulation gets underway, involving crescendo, rise in pitch over an insistent, unmoving bass, and steady recurrence of one of the basic motives of the first
group in various forms.

The preparation for recapitulation is thus always of particular interest. In this
process, the character of the opening theme as well as its specific motivic content
are anticipated by often resourceful means.

Occasional examples show the interpolation of the opening theme (even in the
tonic key) in the midst of the development, as a sort of ''false reprise'' which is then
abandoned in favor of further development. Haydn is associated with this procedure, which is seen, for instance, in the D major Quartet, Op. 64, No. 5. In the first
movement of this work the principal theme of the first group appears, complete and
in the tonic form, in the middle of the development at m. 105. The actual recapitulation does not occur until 37 measures later. Even when such a false reprise is made
in a key other than the tonic, the effect may be analogous. In the Haydn Symphony
No. 102, in B-flat, an entry of the complete first theme in the key of C (Ex. 6.37h)
interrupts the development at m. 185; the recapitulation arrives 42 measures after
this point.

Listed below, in summary, are some techniques of thematic and motivic development often encountered in development sections.

1. The literal statement of material from the exposition, even entire phrases and larger
    units, is not uncommon.
2. Segmentation and repetition of thematic fragments, often at changing pitch levels (se-
    quence), seen in Ex. 6.21, must be seen as fundamental. Such disjunction and repeti-
    tion, especially when extended in an environment of dynamic change, can have inten-
    sifying effect.

Ex. 6.21 Haydn, Sonata in E-flat (Hob. XVI: 49), first movement.

Source of motive (exposition, first tonal group):

Development of motive in sequential repetition:

3. The ideas may be employed in imitation. The fugato (Chapter 12) is a frequent device in development and the whole range of contrapuntal-variational techniques—augmentation, inversion, stretto, and others—is available to the composer in this connection. Example 6.22 is a quotation of the opening theme of the Quartet No. 2 of Walter Piston, and a later developmental passage on the theme. In the development, the theme is treated in augmentation and in canon between the outer parts.

Ex. 6.22 Piston, String Quartet No. 2, first movement.
      Copyright, 1946, by G. Schirmer, Inc. Reprinted by permission.

Example 6.23 illustrates the diminution of an exposition theme in the development section of Prokofiev's Quartet in B minor. Only a portion of the original theme is quoted, followed by its diminution as it appears at m. 127.

Ex. 6.23 Prokofiev, String Quartet in B minor, Op. 50, first movement.
      Reprinted by permission of the copyright owners, Boosey & Hawkes Music Publishers Limited.

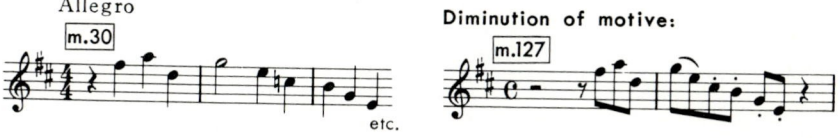

4. The thematic material may be subjected to such techniques of variation as change of mode, change of rhythm with melodic outline preserved, change of melodic outline with rhythm preserved, change of dynamics, of register, of instrumental color, of meter, or of any other theme element. The first theme of the Brahms Piano Quintet is recalled (Ex. 6.24) in the development with striking alteration of mode (A♮, A♭).

Ex. 6.24   Brahms, Quintet in F minor, Op. 34, for piano and strings, first movement.

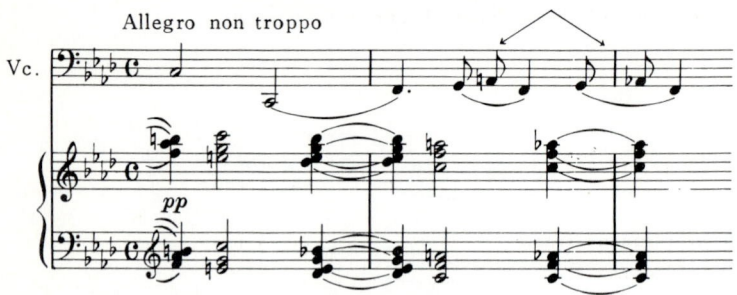

Beethoven's Symphony No. 8 affords another illustration of modal change in the appearance of the primary motive at m. 161 of the first movement.

Both rhythm and melodic contour may be altered, with some distinctive feature retained. Thus, in the first movement of the Schubert Sonata in A minor, Op. 42, the use in the opening of the development section of a characteristic ornament from the original theme is enough to recall the first tonal group (Ex. 6.25).

5. Various motives may be combined contrapuntally or even merged into the same melodic entity (Ex. 6.4); or they may alternate so that one motive is abruptly abandoned for another.

Example 6.26 shows a rapid alternation between the two motives, widely sepa-

Ex. 6.25   Schubert, Sonata in A minor, Op. 42, first movement.

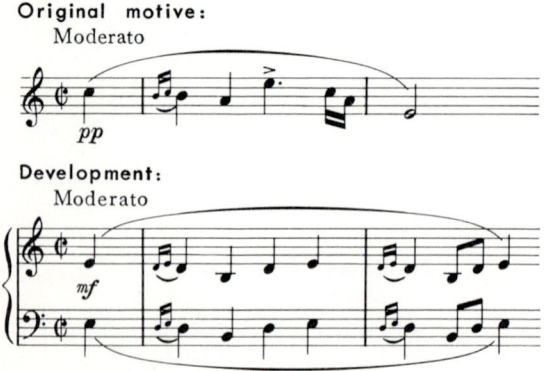

Ex. 6.26   Beethoven, Sonata in C, Op. 53, first movement.

rated in register, from the opening measures of Beethoven's *Waldstein Sonata*, Op. 53; the second excerpt shows a related passage from the development.

6.   An idea, or a pair of ideas, may be used in a manner of rapid "dialogue"—a kind of imitation—between opposing voices or bodies of sound. This is seen in Ex. 6.27, a passage from the Debussy String Quartet.

Ex. 6.27   Debussy, Quartet in G minor, Op. 10, first movement.
       Permission for reprint granted by Durand et Cie., Paris, France, copyright owners, and Elkan-Vogel Co., Inc., Philadelphia, Pa., agents.

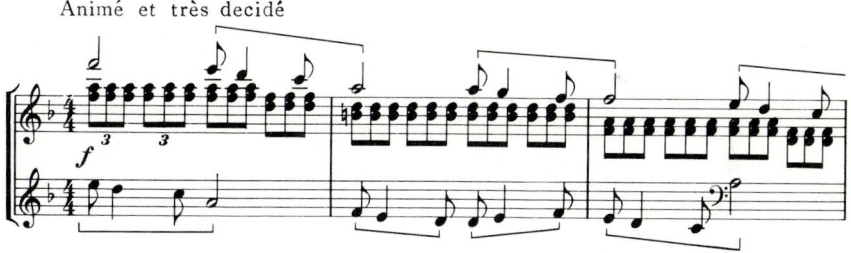

7.   A thematic element may be stated in part and then dissolved into its individual motives or mere figuration, its continuation thus altered in negation of an apparent, direct statement. This is seen in Ex. 6.28.

8.   The use of a rapid pace of modulation, often in sequential patterns, is itself a basic resource of development. Tonal contrast continues in importance in much current tonal and quasi-tonal music, in which traditional key relationships are, of course, often inapplicable.

It is impossible to list all the techniques used in the development of themes and motives, since the only limit to possibilities is the creative imagination. One cannot overemphasize the importance of subjecting a wide selection of development sections to the most careful scrutiny. Such analysis should include the following questions: Is the material under consideration new or does it derive from the exposition? Precisely what is being done with it? The answer to the second question should

Ex. 6.28   Haydn, Symphony No. 101 in D, first movement.

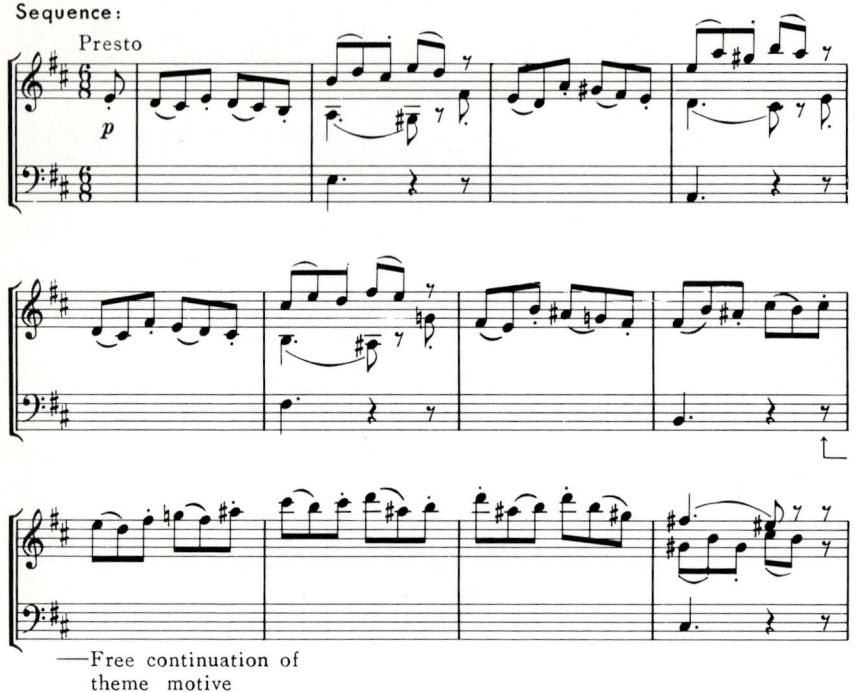

—Free continuation of
theme motive

address many aspects, including tonality, harmony, dynamics, texture, and potentially all elements of structure.

The recapitulation

The recapitulation is the formal return, or restatement, of the materials of the exposition. The presence of a fluctuating and complex development—commonly a wide departure from the character of the expositon—makes such a return fitting and important. The idea of rounding a structure has been discussed in an earlier chapter as a fundamental device of artistic coherence. It is questionable whether convincing form is possible in a work which proceeds tonally, motivically, dynamically, and dramatically from a certain point and is then simply left in flux, without some reference to the original conditions. The sense of return, of restoration, may of course be achieved in other ways than by the complete and literal restatement of the original themes. The technique of brief, summary recapitulation is one occasional solution to the need for stability at the end; it is a device which, obviously, circumvents the risk of redundancy in full reprise, although the issue of necessary balance arises at the same time.

The entry of recapitulation is sometimes an element of surprise, although the usual procedure is clear tonal, harmonic, and motivic preparation already described. Two examples of recapitulation lacking conventional preparation may be mentioned: the first movement of the Beethoven Second Symphony, and the first movement of the Haydn Quartet illustrated in Ex. 6.29. In the Beethoven example, the development is in F-sharp minor until the very last moment; the tonic key (D) is suggested only one measure before the recapitulation. In the Haydn work the tonic key of C is not corroborated until the recapitulation of the first exposition theme is underway; the usual preparation is altogether lacking. A further example is the first movement of Brahms's Sonata in A, Op. 100, for violin and piano, whose recapitulation (m. 158) is entered abruptly through a chromatic succession without the usual tonal preparation.

The arrival of the recapitulation may thus be disguised by elision (Ex. 6.29), by change of harmonization, or by change in some other theme characteristic, as variation, in addition to the factor of avoidance of the usual retransition. The beginning of the recapitulation in the first movement of Mozart's G minor Symphony, K. 550, emerges only melodically over an apparently cadential harmonic progression which in some degree draws attention away from the thematic entry; the effect is one of elision.

The themes of the exposition are often abbreviated somewhat in the recapitulation. Repetitions, for example, which had occurred initially, are likely to be eliminated. In the first movement of Haydn's Symphony No. 102 the first theme of the exposition is repeated, but stated only once when it appears in recapitulation. (See pp. 187-88.)

Movements in which the two groups of materials are motivically related especially require a changed recapitulation, usually shortened or turned here and there into flights of development. The reason is obvious: the movement has already, in exposition and development, seen much of the content shared by the two tonal groups. In this connection, the reader may review the Haydn example cited in Ex. 6.7, or any comparable movement.

It is probable too that materials used in the development will be stated only partially in the recapitulation. An extreme case of this is the first movement of the Beethoven Sonata, Op. 31, No. 2, in D minor, in which the principal thematic sub-

Ex. 6.29   Haydn, String Quartet in C, Op. 33, No. 3, first movement.

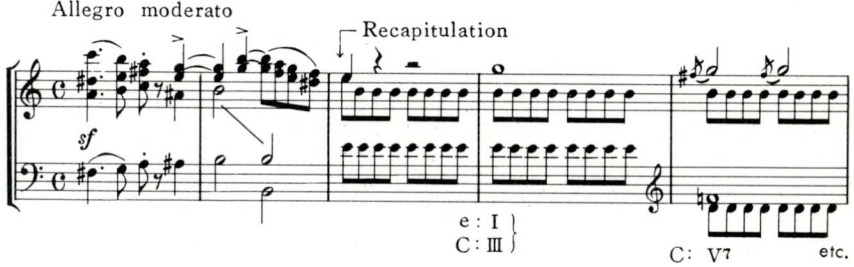

stance of the first tonal group is thoroughly avoided in the recapitulation because of its extensive use in the development.

Occasionally the first theme of the exposition is stated in a more grandiose manner in the recapitulation, becoming a climactic point toward which the developmental processes have led. Typical of such cases is a crescendo just before the recapitulation begins, followed by the first theme in a delivery which is bigger, dynamically and texturally, than at its original appearance. The Beethoven symphonies are interesting to study in this regard, especially the first movements of the Third, Fourth, Fifth and Sixth. In the first movement of the Third, the recapitulation is preceded by a preparation of scope and intensity; however, the most potent delivery of the theme is delayed until later during the recapitulation, which is interrupted several times for passages of prolonged dominant harmony followed by repeated theme statements. In the Sixth Symphony's first movement, the formal reprise begins regularly with changed accompaniment patterns and counterpoints and continued developmental attitudes leading toward a *forte,* fully orchestrated appearance of the first theme in m. 34 of the recapitulation.

A unique and interesting specimen is the first movement of the Mozart Sonata in D, K. 311, in which the materials of the two complexes are reversed in the recapitulation, that of the second tonal group occurring first. Thus, the recapitulation begins in m. 79, but the theme of the first group is withheld until m. 99.

Variation techniques of all kinds can be applied to the recapitulation, to avoid any possible tedium of literal and full restatement. Such variation does not, ordinarily, reach the level of development, except possibly in the coda and, to a limited degree, in transitional passages. In the main body of the recapitulation, there is normally a steadiness of tonality and an integrity of formal units characteristic of the exposition and unlike the typical development.

As implied above, the recapitulation is in a very important sense even compact and unified than the exposition, for the function of the restatement in bringing secure balance to the overall form is underscored by the traditional practice of *stating the second thematic complex in the tonic key,* a factor in the functional implication of resolution.

The relative constancy of tonality in the recapitulation often necessitates a change in the transition connecting the two tonal groups, since its function in the exposition was partially one of modulation. The bridge passage is here likely to be redirected to end in the tonic key. Comparison between this section as it appears in the exposition and as it appears in the recapitulation is instructive. The general character and substance of its motives are not normally altered, since the function of bridging elements of opposing character is applicable here as before. Reproduced as Ex. 6.30 is the complete transition in the first movement exposition of the Haydn Sonata in E (Hob. XVI: 31). The first group reaches its cadence in E; the transition begins in C–sharp minor, modulating to the dominant key (B) in preparation for the second tonal group. Following the example appears its counterpart (beginning only) in the recapitulation. Here, at the point where the first group ends, again in E, the music is directed toward F-sharp minor, which is to E as C-sharp was to B. Again,

Ex. 6.30 Haydn, Sonata in E (Hob. XVI: 31), first movement.

the tonal adjustment is made quickly; the two transitions thus closely resemble each other.

The only cases in which the transition can be expected to be exactly the same in both parts of the movement are those, already referred to, in which the transition in the exposition does not actually tonicize the dominant, but simply ends on the primary dominant harmony. The second group may then enter, more or less convincingly, either in the dominant key, as in the exposition, or in the tonic, as in the recapitulation. (See Ex. 6.8 for such a transition.)

Another way in which the transition materials might theoretically remain intact is for the first group in the recapitulation to be stated in the subdominant key, with the transposed transition then leading back to the tonic. In the Mozart Sonata in C, K. 545, first movement, the first theme appears in the recapitulation in F rather than in C. However, in this movement the transitions are dissimilar in structure, rather than following the obvious procedure of strict transposition up a 4th in the recapitulation. The transition in the recapitulation is 4 measures longer, in fact, than that of the exposition, and contains a much stronger reference to the key of the second tonal group. It is an interesting specimen for study.

Often the transition is much abbreviated in the recapitulation—especially when the motives which it contains have been used a great deal in development. In the first movement of Schubert's Sonata in E-flat, Op. 122, the transition is eliminated entirely in the recapitulation. (Compare mm. 28–40 with the approach to m. 186.)

In contrast to the above, the transition may in the recapitulation be expanded into a sort of subsidiary development, traversing new tonal regions before ultimately returning to the tonic. This is the case with the final movement of the Beethoven Sonata, Op. 31, No. 2. In the recapitulation, the reprise of the first group is dissolved in a context of tonal digression at m. 233. The transitional passage following, which leads into the second tonal group, is more than twice as long as the corresponding passage in the exposition, broadened by the application of renewed developmental procedures.

In summary, the recapitulation may be an exact copy of the exposition, apart from change of key, or it may in any of a number of ways be a new version of the materials. It may be merely a token restatement of the original themes. It is always important to determine precisely how the two flanking sections of the movement compare in a given case. Some sort of recapitulation will be in evidence, however incomplete. Its structural role as a release from the fluctuation of development and as a binding, unifying formal component—a part of the frame within which the development is cast and with reference to which it has meaning—is a vital one.

The coda

The form's final division centers, of course, in the tonic, yet often with superficial fluctuations involving at times apparently distant tonal references within a binding tonic implication; such fluctuation has the effect of intensifying the sense of release at the ultimate point of conclusion.

In some way the coda adds emphasis to the close of the movement: by summing up its major thematic content, by a final development of its motives, by increasing the pace of movement, or by underscoring the final cadence through broad elaborations of its harmonies. Most often it begins as a restatement of the codetta of the exposition, following the recapitulation of the second tonal group, with the material extended to serve a larger function. In examples in which the original codetta does not return, the coda may be understood to begin after restatement of the original thematic complexes, usually following distinct cadential punctuation of any type, sometimes with rests enhancing the punctuative effect.

In a movement which is not highly developed there may, however, be nothing more than repetition, in the tonic key, of the material of the earlier codetta. This is the case in many Mozart and Haydn sonatas, in the Beethoven Sonatas of Op. 49 and Op. 22, and in numerous other works. When the final section is of such modest proportions and calculated merely to add weight to the final cadence, it is, like the section closing a single division of the form, best termed *codetta* rather than *coda*.

In nineteenth-century examples there is usually more of substance at the form's conclusion than the terse cadential gestures associated with codetta.

The term *coda* denotes an extensive peroration, having the quality of an appendage to the main body of the form, while integral to it. Several examples are given (6.31–6.34) to show cadential punctuation separating recapitulation and coda. Example 6.34 cites a coda which is *not* an extension of the original codetta.

Ex. 6.31   Beethoven, Sonata in E, Op. 14, No. 1, first movement.

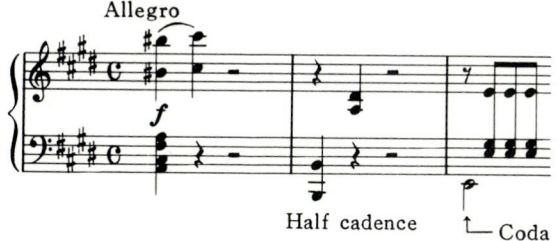

Ex. 6.32   Schubert, Symphony No. 9 (Great) in C, D. 944, first movement.

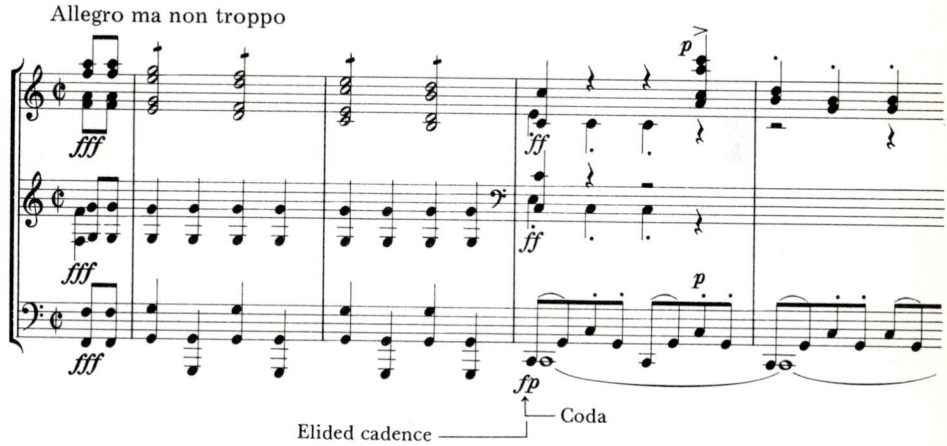

Beethoven is the first composer especially associated with the large developmental coda, sometimes so substantial as to be regarded as a terminal development. It can be seen in his works as early as the Sonata, Op. 2, No. 3 (m. 211, corresponding to the closing theme of the exposition at m. 77). Other examples of Beethoven codas of important size and significance are those of the *Waldstein Sonata*, Op. 53 (both movements), and the Third Symphony, whose first movement has an enormous coda of 145 measures.

Ex. 6.33 Mozart, Quartet in A, K. 464, first movement.

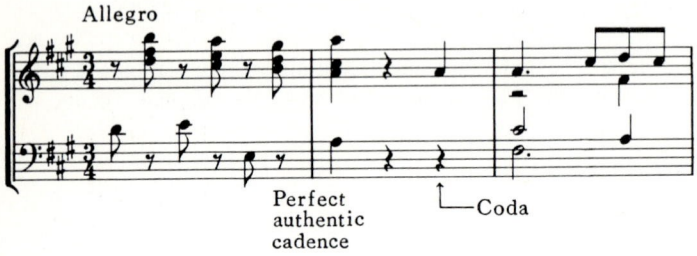

Ex. 6.34 Haydn, Quartet in D minor, Op. 76, No. 2, first movement.

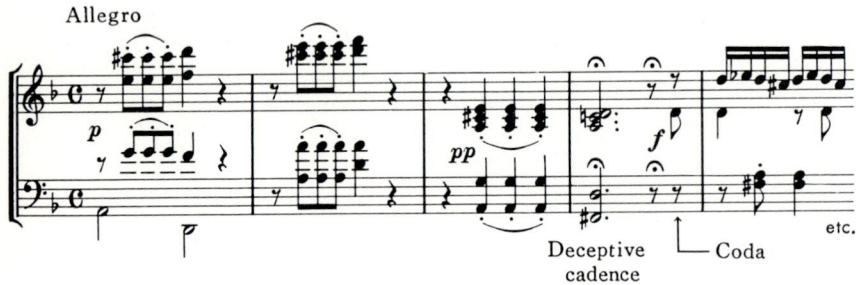

A highly developed coda gives the impression of a fourth major division in the form—a full, new commentary upon what has gone before. The coda is then a final view of the materials, cast in a new frame, conveying a basic sense of epilogue despite any occasional digressiveness at the surface, and developmental within a restricted harmonic amplitude. The expansive developmental coda, while a major dimension in the form, does not seriously contend with the development section itself: were it to constitute another comparable departure, it would imply still further conclusive processes on a major scale. An extensive coda is, indeed, often sectional, with a subordinate concluding division of its own. This is seen in the Schumann Piano Quintet, whose first movement coda begins at m. 314, comes to a very emphatic cadence at m. 332 (Ex. 6.35), and then continues into a final segment which is, in a sense, to the coda as the coda is to the movement.

In their quality of peroration, or summing up, as well as in their inexorable momentum, many of the Brahms codas are without equal. The student should study the Brahms symphonies in this connection. In addition to the codas of the first movements of all four, that of the final movement of the Third Symphony (beginning at m. 217) is a splendid example. Occasionally the coda begins without a pronounced cadential break, contrary to the norm cited earlier, yet commonly, in such cases, with some manner of clear signal: the coda to the first movement of the First

Ex. 6.35 Schumann, Quintet in E-flat, Op. 44, for piano and strings, first movement.

Symphony is marked by sudden rhythmic change (m. 430); that of the first movement of the Second Symphony—a big sectional coda of great power—is merged
with the return of the first theme of the second group (m. 424), yet also unmistakable in its rhythmic implication. The coda to the closing movement of Beethoven's
Waldstein Sonata, Op. 53, is a very ample, complex example entered by dissolution; the form is a rondo, whose final thematic statement merges with, becoming an
element of, the coda. Here, insistent pedal points (I and V, mm. 343–400) mark an
amplified cadence followed by a quickened tempo signalling a headlong final drive.
In the last section, *prestissimo*, Beethoven introduces further allusions to the theme,
as well as such tonal references as A-flat and D-flat, neighbor auxiliaries to the fundamental G and C.

For obvious reasons, the coda rarely introduces new themes or motives of any
distinction; the appearance of such elements, unless perfunctory or quiescent in
character, raises the expectation of further treatment of the new material. Often the
movement's chief motives are stated rather directly in the coda, especially at its
beginning, as an aspect of summation. This too is illustrated by the Schumann coda
cited above.

Each division in a sectional coda tends to add drive to the pace of the preceding, each cadence more emphatic than the one before, with a cumulative effect
which is progressively more resolved and definite. Again the Schumann Quintet is a
case in point. A further example is the coda to the first movement of Mendelssohn's

Ex. 6.36a   Mendelssohn, Trio in D minor, Op. 49, for piano, violin, and cello, first movement.

P.A.C.   └ Succeeding section

Ex. 6.36b

P.A.C.

Ex. 6.36c   FINAL MEASURES OF MENDELSSOHN CODA

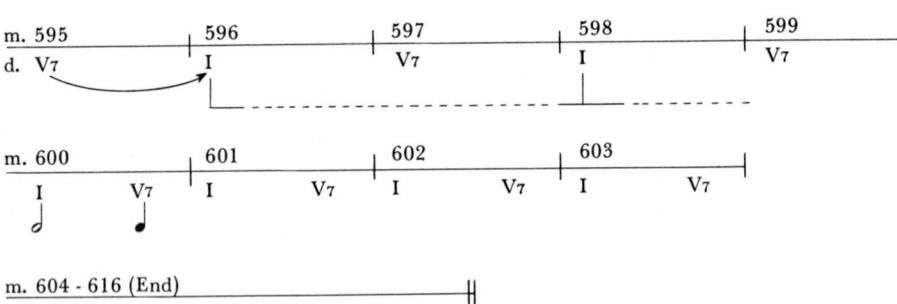

Piano Trio in D minor, Op. 49. At first (mm. 479ff.) it is developmental, treating motives of both groups. At m. 530, it reaches a strong tonic cadence, shown as Ex. 6.36a. There are further cadences, of increasingly affirmative implication, at mm. 580 and 596. The first of these is quoted as Ex. 6.36b. After m. 596 there occurs a series of rapid dominant-tonic cadential progressions according to the pattern shown below. The harmony in this last section changes first from measure to measure, and then within the measure, in conditions of accelerated harmonic rhythm and increasing intensity. The 13 bars remaining after m. 604 are simply an extended animation of unchanging tonic harmony.

Further examples of coda are cited and discussed in connection with large forms traced in Chapters 7 and 8.

HAYDN, SYMPHONY NO. 102 IN B-FLAT, FIRST MOVEMENT

The first movement of Haydn's Symphony No. 102 is a manifestation of single-movement sonata form. It is typical of the form, yet unique in many respects.

Ex. 6.37a   Haydn, Symphony No. 102 in B-flat, first movement.

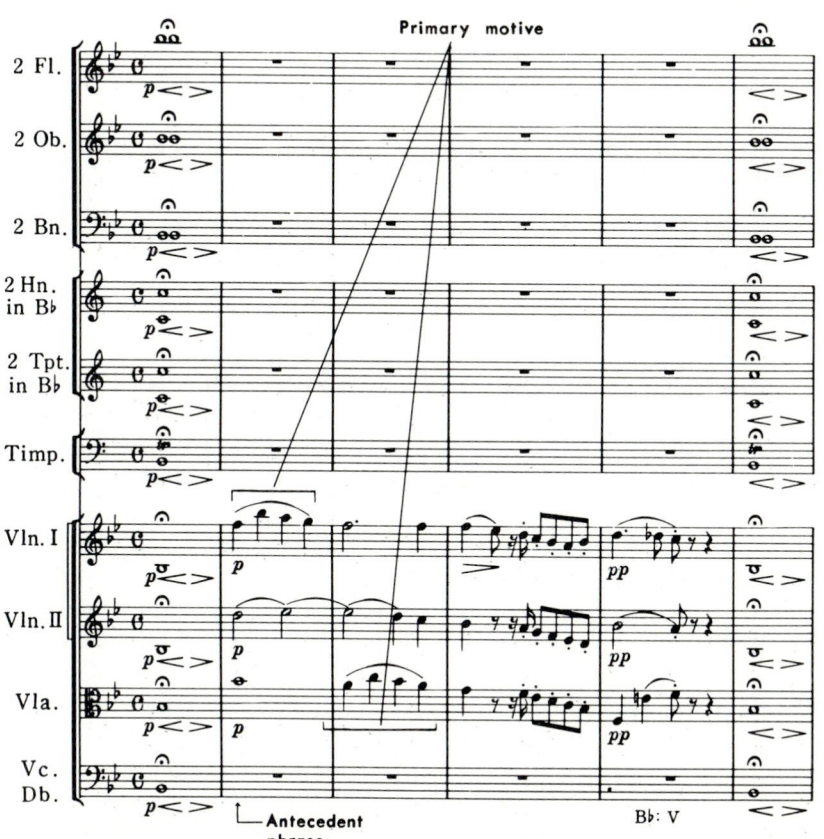

Ex. 6.37 a   *(continued)*

Consequent
phrase

F: I

Haydn's slow introduction, mm. 1–22, is dominated by the motive of m. 2, a part of the opening 8-measure period theme. This motive, marked in the quotation (Ex. 6.37a), appears in nearly every measure once the initiating theme is stated. The doubled B♭, of indefinite duration in its assertions in mm. 1 and 6, emphasizes the tonality, and is an effective element of irregularity against the parallel 4-measure phrases of the theme. It is notable that the period cadence on F (m. 10) is elided with and countered by the entrance of the basic motive in the bass; and the passage which follows (mm. 10–20, not fully quoted) is an excellent illustration of the driving force of motive repetition, here stimulated by syncopations and a rising chromatic pitch line above. The thematic material of the introduction is not explicitly referred to again in the rest of the movement.

The first tonal group of the exposition extends from m. 23 to m. 38, its single theme a symmetrical period repeated with changed orchestration. There are three motives that prove to be of profound significance in later development; these are bracketed in Ex. 6.37b.

Ex. 6.37b

181

Ex. 6.37c

The melodic line of each phrase begins at a high point (toward which the ana-crusis is a motivating thrust), descends to a midpoint level on f^2, and then descends further to the cadence, where it turns up slightly, dropping again. (Compare the first phrase of the allegro theme with that of the period which begins the introduction; although the two melodies are of strongly contrasted character, they are strikingly similiar in line.)

The transition begins with a sudden tutti, and a strong, *forte* impulse (see Ex. 6.37j, the identical passage in recapitulation). It develops all three of the theme motives cited earlier, occurring here in the order of their initial appearance in the theme itself. They are in the prominent upper voice, alternately soaring and plung-ing in a highly turbulent context, at first over a tonic pedal. The use of the typical

Ex. 6.37c *(continued)*

Mirror of primary
motive

Motive of first theme

Fragment of
primary motive

device of sequence should be noted; that of mm. 47–50 is not quoted, but Ex. 6.37c includes mm. 53–54 in which sequence appears.

The excerpt also includes the beginning of the second tonal group, in the dominant. The initial motive of mm. 57–58 dominates most of this section (see vln. 1 and vc., one the mirror of the other). Clearly there is no "theme" here in the conventional sense in which we see it in the first group. A development of the motive, and of two of its fragments, leads to a firm cadence (7 measures of cadential tonic six-four), to be followed by a new theme—part of the present complex.

Example 6.37d shows the arrival point for the extended cadential formula mentioned above. Now, contradicting the deceptive "finality" of the cadence, strings and winds, *fortissimo,* sound A, mediant of the dominant and dominant of the forthcoming D minor. (This bar looks like m. 1 but occurs in a radically different context; yet it plays a comparable role, introducing the antecedent of a period

Ex. 6.37d

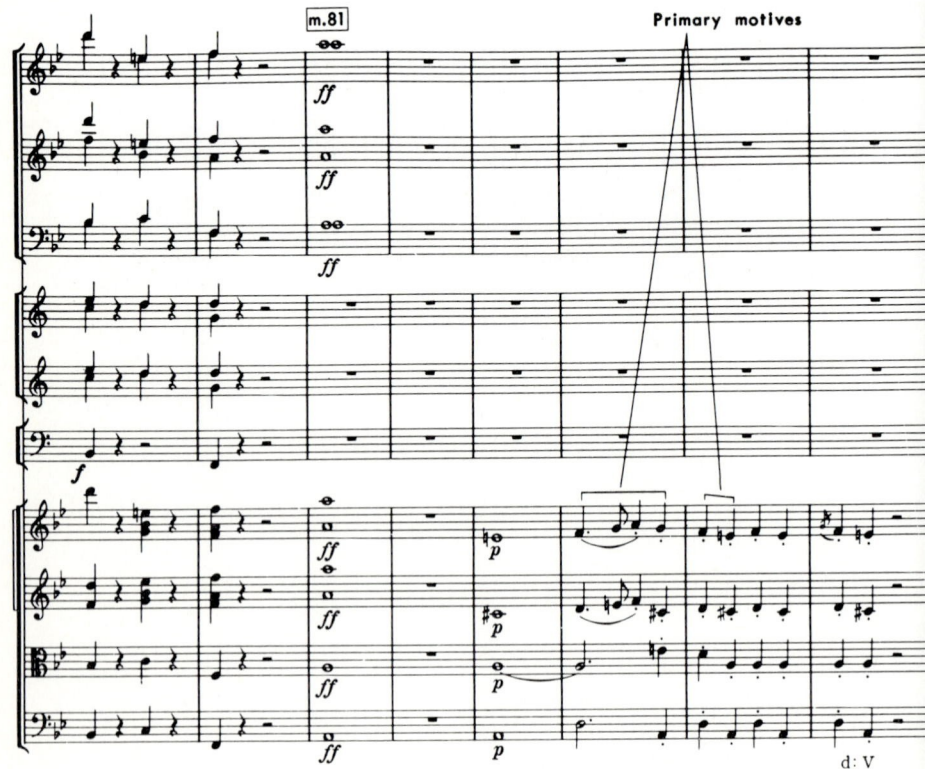

Ex. 6.37d *(continued)*

F: I   Resumption of earlier motives

theme. As in the introduction, the consequent phrase is similarly introduced.) A bar of silence, m. 82, underscores the contrast between the outburst of m. 81, by which the preceding cadence had been unsettled, and the continuation of the antecedent phrase, subdued and in strings alone.

The period theme takes the second group on a momentary excursion toward D minor, its consequent phrase reaffirming F. The perfect authentic cadence which closes the period is subdued, as was that of the initial allegro theme, by the sudden tutti and the rush of 8th-notes, now in the bass. The basic motive of the second group returns, making of the total thematic complex a small ternary form. The quotation shows in the bass a motive of the opening allegro theme—that of m. 24—here used accompanimentally, as at mm. 57ff. (See Ex. 6.37d.)

The exposition codetta, in F, is set off by cadential punctuation at m. 100. Over a tonic pedal (see Ex. 6.37e), it capriciously treats another motive of the first

Ex. 6.37e

m.100

Restricted
imitative
development
of m. 25
motive

Codetta on I pedal

M.24 motive

Cello

F: I
B♭: V

theme (that of m. 25) in rapid dialogue between the violin sections. The motive of m. 24 is also used, as indicated in the quotation, followed by a very strong cadence at m. 110. Repeat of the exposition is specified, without retransition; F:I, as B♭:V, points directly to the return.

Space permits only a brief résumé of the events of the development, one of Haydn's best. All the exposition materials appear, and there is a good deal of tonal fluctuation, touching in rich elaborative mobility the tonal regions of C major and minor, E-flat, F major and minor, A-flat, (B-flat major and minor), D minor, and G minor—except for A-flat and the modal variants, all based on triads diatonic to B-flat.

The period theme at the middle of the second group is developed extensively, especially following m. 132. A 2-note fragment is taken down and up the A-flat diatonic scale (Ex. 6.37f). The continuation of this development, in which a 2-measure motive is manipulated imitatively and sequentially, in vigorous tonal movement, is partly shown above. A bit later, the principal motive of the same

Ex. 6.37f

Development of 2-note fragment
of second group theme

Ex. 6.37f (*continued*)

Development of
m.84 motive

Sequence pattern, repeated
4 measures later

theme undergoes extreme variation of intervallic structure—variation in which its identity is nevertheless clearly preserved:

becomes

The beginning of a canon (see Chapter 12) on the first second-group motive (mm. 57–58) is reproduced as Ex. 6.37g. Canonic development continues from m. 161 to m. 184, all of it on the same material, ending with a fermata. Now Haydn jests with a "false" return of the opening theme—its complete period—in the "wrong" key of C. The end of that statement, presented by the flute, and succeed-

Ex. 6.37g

ing tutti development of a motive of the same theme are shown in Ex. 6.37h. The score should be consulted concerning the use of modulating sequence in this phase of the development.

The end of the development, and the retransition preparing the recapitulation, appear in Ex. 6.37i. The approach to B♭:V is seen. Once achieved, the harmony is prolonged for 10 measures. The upper voice rises, contributing to anticipatory feeling, repeating the opening motive of the approaching theme—now restrained, and in quickly changing timbres—over the sustained dominant harmony. The recapitulation enters assertively, *forte*, releasing the tension of the dominant. The development has been of impressive scope, comprising more than a third of the total form.

Ex. 6.37h

Conclusion of
"false" return

Resumption of development
(m. 24 motive, mirror form)

The restatement of the original allegro theme is without change except for the elimination of the repetition of the period, as may be observed in mm. 227–234. The transition linking the first and second groups, its original modulatory functions no longer valid and its material now exhaustively developed, is considerably reduced in length. It touches the secondary tonic E-flat (through the V₇ of IV) but does not significantly digress from the fundamental tonic. It is seen in full as Ex. 6.37j, which includes the beginning of the second group.

The reprise of the second group, which is not quoted (see mm. 243–288), is abbreviated in some areas, extended in others. It is fundamentally in B-flat, but its middle theme refers momentarily to G minor, paralleling the corresponding refer-ence to D minor in the exposition. The tonic cadence toward which the second com-plex seems to move (see Ex. 6.37k) is upset by deceptive progression to VII$_7$ of V (a diminished-7th chord) in mm. 281–282. This leads to half-cadence, and return of the anacrusis motive which opened the exposition, in mm. 286–288. The coda fol-lows, as marked in Ex. 6.37k.

The coda does not, as is often the case, begin with the material of the former exposition codetta. Example 6.37k shows that it begins with the first group theme. The example does not, however, show the dissolution of the theme, the motive of whose second bar is repeated, haltingly, finally in augmentation (increased note values), coming to a full stop and fermata—a last point of irresolution before the movement rushes to its close:

Ex. 6.37i

Ex. 6.37i (continued)

Thematic preparation
(continued in oboe and flute)—
concurrent with
reduction in texture

Recapitulation

The dissonance on which the music pauses at this point (VII$_7$ of II) contributes to the instability of the moment, mildly deviant in relation to the firmly conclusive B-flat tonic.

Example 6.37l shows the end of the coda. There is further, contained development of theme motives, some of it over a tonic pedal, paralleling the content of the earlier codetta. As before, the imitative toying with the motive of m. 25 and the vacillation of harmony (chiefly I and V) over the insistent pedal, drive the music vigorously to a decisive conclusion.

One could continue in many important analytical directions. In the foregoing account, we have been able to see the main outlines of the movement's form, and to

Ex. 6.37j

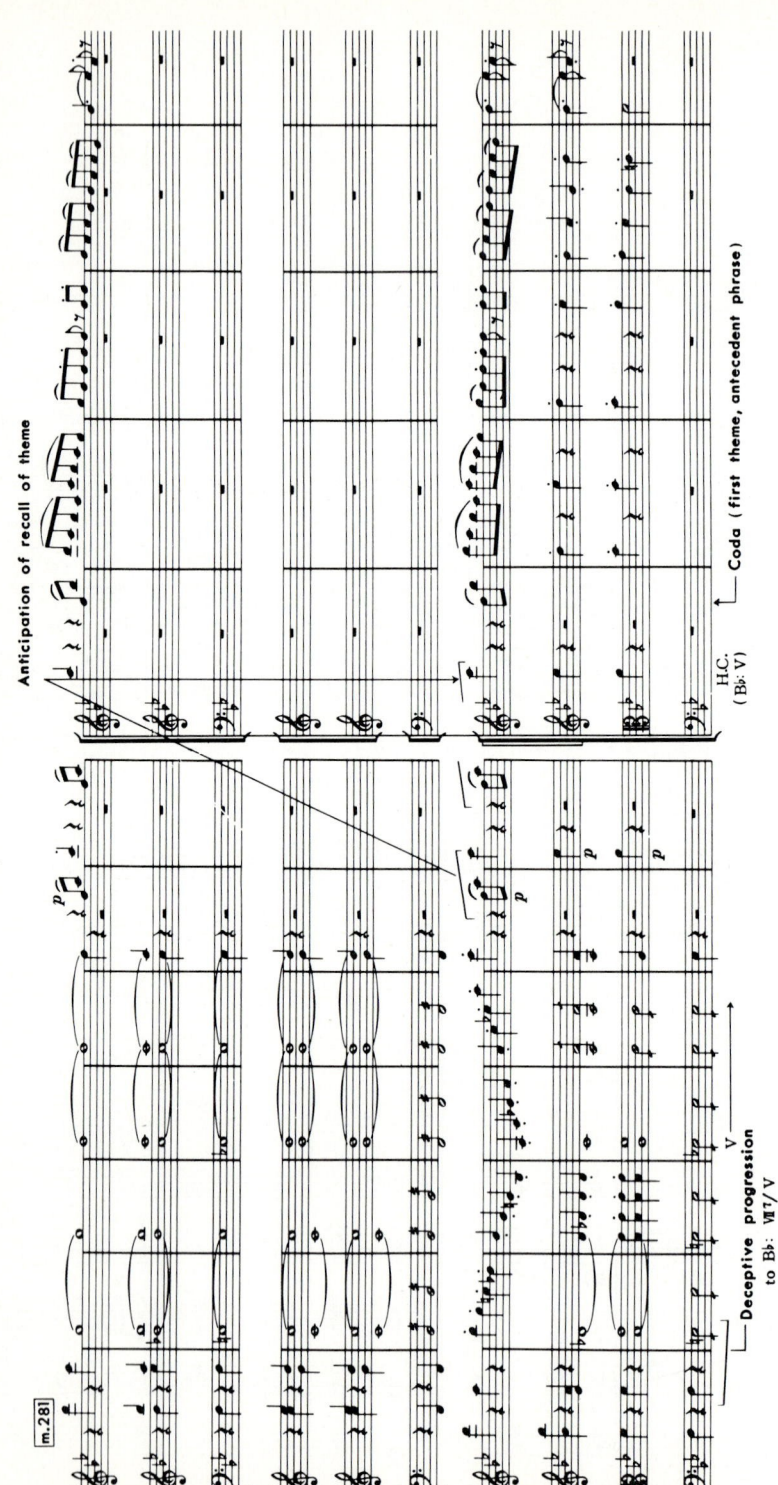

Ex. 6.37k

Ex. 6.37|

point out some of the elements by which form is shaped in one of Haydn's greatest symphonies.

A BINARY OR TERNARY DESIGN?

The question often arises whether single-movement sonata form is basically a two- or three-part form. The fact is that no clear and universal distinction is possible for all cases, and that many examples display properties of both types.

Single-movement sonata form is, as has been suggested, a derivative of binary form; the sonatas of the pre-classical composers often represent an intermediate stage of its evolution. The first part of the binary, ending on a secondary tonic, corresponds to the exposition of single-movement sonata form. The binary's second part corresponds, in its tonal return, to the development and recapitulation in the larger form. It is because of these parallels that single-movement sonata form is often said to be essentially a two-part, or binary, design. Yet it is idle to insist that the later, more expansive structure accordingly and necessarily embodies the vestigial binary principle.

The argument for binary is more persuasive with respect to the *sonatina* type (see pp. 194-98); with its minuscule development, this is rather like a binary form with a slightly inflated second part, but also usually with a greater measure of thematic diversity and at least a token reprise. In fact, many such examples of early classical movements in which the developmental area is restricted, even negligible, in scope and importance, can be cited as relating very distinctly to binary antecedents; see the first movements of Mozart's Sonatas in E-flat, K. 282, and C, K. 545. In the latter, the "development" comprises only 13 measures and is entirely of figuration, not even touching the principal thematic material of the exposition. Moreover, durationally and substantively subsidiary middle sections are, in such examples, an aspect of smaller overall dimensions. In some instances of this kind, the relationship to binary form is significant too in the use of a single thematic resource throughout the exposition.

But when, in its mature stages, the form contains contrasting thematic complexes and a highly resourceful and extensive development, it is meaningless to insist that it bears the same relationship to binary design. The fully expanded development becomes a middle section of considerable scope, and the matter of comparable dimensions of the three principal sections is pertinent. In the characteristic single-movement sonata form, the principle of tripartition is thus expanded considerably: departure and return occur not only tonally, as in the binary, but thematically and in other ways as well. The middle section brings new textures, tonal expansion, a substantially altered character, and often new materials. The development represents an active, mobile phase in the form, as we have seen—a significant contrast to the relatively straightforward statement of materials in the exposition and recapitulation. Thus, the recapitulation is a "return," a third major division, the rounding-out of an essentially tripartite structure.

The preceding example illustrates this well. The middle section of the first movement of Haydn's Symphony No. 102 is 117 measures long, as compared to a total number of 311 measures in the movement (including the introduction, not really integral to the form proper). The development provides a thorough contrast in character and in other respects, and there is a pronounced sense of return at the beginning of the recapitulation. Obviously it is meaningless to insist that this is binary form. Proportionately comparable departure and return constitute the essential basis of the tripartite scheme.

THE SONATINA AND SINGLE-MOVEMENT SONATINA FORM

A piece or movement displaying incipient properties of single-movement sonata form, whose "development" is of modest scope, and whose general dimensions are more nearly bipartite than tripartite, is often characterized as of *sonatina form*. And a work of several movements of minor proportions, relatively incipient forms, and restricted thematic content and development, is described as a *multimovement sonatina*, or simply *sonatina*.

Two extremes from the sonatas of J. C. Bach may be mentioned: the Sonata in E, Op. 5, No. 5, first movement, states the reprise of opening materials immediately at the beginning of the second division; the E-flat Sonata, Op. 5, No. 4, first movement, is on the other hand an example of quite developed single-movement sonata form. Certain sonatas of Beethoven—those, for example, of Op. 49, especially the second, are properly identified as sonatinas. Mozart examples have been cited.

It is thus chiefly the factor of restricted development which is the indicator of single-movement sonatina form. Sonatina types may contain certain areas in restricted development, but there is little of the vigorous wrestling with ideas in fluctuant contexts that one associates with, say, a characteristic Beethoven example. Moreover, slow movements in the classical and early romantic sonata often are in single-movement sonatina form, resembling the sonata type except for the absence or relative insignificance of formal development. Examples are the second movement of the Mozart Sonatas in F, K. 280, and G, K. 283, the Beethoven F minor Sonata, Op. 2, No. 1, and the Haydn Sonatas in E minor and C (Hob XVI: 34 and 35), second movements.

In place of development there may be a brief interlude; more often there is only a retransition leading at once into the recapitulation. Thus, in the Haydn Quartet in F, Op. 3, No. 5, second movement, the "development" of 8 measures merely serves, by statement of the main theme of the first group around the $\substack{G: I \\ C: V}$] harmony, to return to the tonic (C) for the recapitulation in m. 42.

Single-movement sonatina form is distinguishable from binary in that the former manifests a degree of sonatalike diversity between thematic complexes, as well as subsequent formal restatement in a context of tonal unity. Still, it is as impossible to establish an absolute line of distinction between the sonatina and the sonata as it is between either of these and binary form. The analytical consideration of *reasons* for classification, inducing an understanding of distinguishing properties of an example in question, is always of value.

THE VITALITY AND ADAPTABILITY OF SINGLE-MOVEMENT SONATA FORM

Single-movement sonata form is of extraordinary vitality. There has been no period in music history, since the inception of the form, in which it has been neglected. Based as it is on the technique of development through transformation and imaginative manipulation of motivic materials, single-movement sonata form, strictly or freely applied, presents an invigorating challenge to the creative mind.

One can see continuing strong signs of the vitality of the form and its governing principles in later repertoires. Debussy and Ravel, although representing in their aesthetic a considerable denial of the disciplines of traditional procedures, did not altogether neglect sonata forms, as we have seen in their string quartets. Gustav Mahler (1860–1911) and Anton Bruckner (1824–96), in their symphonies, expanded the form into something unprecedentedly large. Certain composers—for example, Max Reger and Alexander Scriabin (1872–1915)—are thought by some to have forced their ideas inappropriately into sonata molds.[2]

We may note in passing some relevant works of twentieth-century composers who have made extensive and effective use of the principles of single-movement sonata form; in some cases interesting variants have appeared. The Sonata, Op. 1, of Berg is a single-movement work applying the principles of the form even to the traditional repeat at the end of the exposition, although there is irregularity in the tonality of the return of the second group. The first movements of Hindemith's Second Trio for strings and Second Piano Sonata are clear examples of the form. Walter Piston's Quintet for flute and string quartet, first movement, employs even the traditional key relationships, E minor and B minor, for the two tonal groups. Further examples can be found in the Quartet in C, Op. 36, of Benjamin Britten (1913–76); the Symphony No. 4 in F minor of Ralph Vaughan Williams (1872–1958), whose first movement presents interesting changes in the materials in the recapitulation; and the Prokofiev Quartet, Op. 50, first movement, whose recapitulation omits a

---

[2]See, for example, Aaron Copland's comments on Scriabin in *What to Listen for in Music* (New York: McGraw-Hill, 1939), pp 189–90.

large portion of the second tonal complex. Many of the symphonic movements of Dmitri Shostakovich (1906–75) might be included here: for example, the first movements of the First and Fifth Symphonies. In the former, the recapitulation states the first theme last, very simply and briefly; in the latter, the recapitulation is a vast development with continued vigorous treatment of the themes, much of it canonic.

Bartók's employment of single-movement sonata form, often provocatively unconventional, may be seen in, for example, the first movements of Quartets No. 1, No. 5, and No. 6; Sonata No. 1 for violin and piano; the Sonata for two pianos and percussion; and Piano Concerto No. 3; and in the exterior movements of the Violin Concerto. The reader is referred to Halsey Stevens's analyses of these and other sonata movements of Bartók.[3]

The Stravinsky Concerto for piano and winds (1924), first movement, brings back in its recapitulation the original thematic complexes in their original keys, and restates its introductory material as a closing section at the end of the movement. The idea of rounding by very summary restatement is illustrated in Stravinsky's *Symphony in Three Movements,* first movement.

Sibelius, in his symphonies, applied sonata form at times very freely and at times conventionally. There is in certain of these contexts a problem of unconvincing succession and grouping of themes (the beginning of the Second Symphony; the first and last movements of the Fourth, the middle section of the former seeming to have little to do with the balance of the form). Single-movement sonata form unfolds in quite regular fashion in, for example, the first movements of the first three symphonies. One can observe resourceful, varied treatment of the principles of the form in, for instance, the first movement of the Fourth Symphony; here the design is archlike, with the original thematic complexes reversed in their restatement at the end. The second movement of the Second Symphony is an example of the form modified in that its modal themes are restated in the development, which thus becomes a combination, so to speak, of development and recapitulation. Sometimes the recapitulation slights or omits altogether certain thematic elements, as in the first movement of the Sixth and final movement of the Fourth. While there is much to question in Sibelius's forms, it cannot be denied that this music is often persuasive and interesting, nor can one fail to recognize the singular power and individuality of many of Sibelius's thematic concepts.

The contemporary application of single-movement sonata form being freer, with the divisions to which tradition accustoms us less clearly marked or not marked at all, one is sometimes at a loss to decide whether a particular work is more akin than alien to the principles of the form. In such cases, it is important to consider the question but often unwise to insist upon a categorical answer; one may assume that some works will be seen to embody one essential feature of the form but not other features, or some characteristics less explicitly than others. It is helpful to keep in

---

[3]Halsey Stevens, *The Life and Music of Béla Bartók* (New York: Oxford University Press, 1953), Part II.

mind that the cardinal principles of single-movement sonata form are: *statement* of thematic materials at contrasting tonal levels, *development* of these materials, and *return* in the original key. The function of recapitulation is not necessarily impaired when the reprise is radically reduced; often a mere gesture of stability, a reminder of the original materials, is adequate to round the form, and to consummate the resolution which is the main point of recapitulation.

EXERCISES

1. Looking among a variety of works of all relevant periods, find examples to illustrate the following items, discussed in this chapter.

   a) An introduction which is motivically related to the balance of the movement.

   b) A tonal group consisting of two or more distinct thematic entities.

   c) Tonal groups conforming to some of the various possibilities of form.

   d) Tonal relationships between the two complexes which are not the usual tonic-dominant or relative major and minor.

   e) Two tonal groups unified by the sharing of common motives.

   f) A transition containing no real modulation, ending on dominant harmony in the tonic key.

   g) A transition modulating beyond the actual tonal destination.

   h) Transitions embodying some of the specific techniques mentioned in the chapter.

   i) An exposition codetta which is a brief cadential elaboration.

   j) A closing theme.

   k) A codetta returning material of the first group.

   l) Examples of single-movement sonata form containing one repeat, two repeats, and no repeat.

   m) An exposition ending in a retransition into the repeat.

   n) The appearance of new themes or distinctive new motives in the development.

   o) Extended dominant preparation of the recapitulation, and exceptions to this practice.

   p) Statement of the first theme at the beginning of the development.

   q) "False recapitulation" of the first theme during the development.

   r) Examples of the various developmental techniques listed.

   s) The "unprepared" recapitulation.

   t) Irregularities in the recapitulation of the original materials (explain possible bases for these alterations).

   u) Use of variation techniques in the recapitulation.

   v) Expansion (or reduction) of the transition in the recapitulation.

   w) Tonal fluctuation in the coda (consider how it is controlled within essentially cadential directions).

   x) Literal repetition of the exposition codetta at the end of the movement.

   y) A coda not growing out of the original codetta.

   z) A developmental coda.

2. Find examples among movements of early sonatas to show (a) binary form, (b) single-movement sonatina form, and (c) well-developed single-movement sonata form.

3. Discuss some of the implications of the term *sonata*.

4. List examples of four-movement sonatas whose arrangement of movements conforms, and does not conform, to the norm discussed.

5. Find works whose movements are linked or otherwise related in one of the ways described in the chapter.

6. Consider examples of introduction with the purpose of evaluating the apparent necessity for, and special importance of, introductory material preceding the main body of the form.

7. Find further examples of slow movements which are in single-movement sonatina form.

8. Outline an example in single-movement sonata form from one or more of the following sources.
   a) C. P. E. Bach or J. C. Bach
   b) Haydn or Mozart
   c) Beethoven
   d) Mendelssohn, Schubert, Schumann, or Chopin
   e) Brahms or Tchaikovsky
   f) Mahler or Bruckner
   g) Debussy, Ravel, Fauré, or Franck
   h) Other composers of the twentieth century

9. Answer the following questions concerning one or two examples of single-movement sonata form of your own selection.
   a) What is the fundamental key?
   b) What is the form of the first tonal group?
   c) How long is the transition? Where is the modulation to the new key? How does the transition begin?
   d) How would you describe the form of the second tonal group?
   e) How are the tonal groups contrasted? How related?
   f) What is the length of the codetta? What is its content?
   g) Is there a retransition preparing the exposition repeat?
   h) What are the tonal levels, motivic materials, and techniques of motivic transformation used in the development section?
   i) How is the recapitulation prepared?
   j) How does the recapitulation compare with the exposition? What is eliminated or shortened? What new versions of the materials do you find?
   k) Is the coda an expansion of the codetta? Is it merely, or essentially, a repetition of the earlier codetta? What kind of cadential separation sets it off? Is the coda developmental?
   l) What irregularities, if any, do you find in the movement as a whole?

10. Try composing original examples of some of the following:
    a) A short, introductory figure, motive, or phrase.
    b) A transition leading from tonic to dominant.
    c) A transition leading from minor to relative major.
    d) Both transitions (b) and (c), as they might appear in recapitulation.

e) A developmental sequence on a given motive.

f) Illustrations of various developmental techniques, using quoted or original motives.

g) A codetta that is a simple extension of the cadence.

h) A typical preparation for the recapitulation of a first theme of vigorous character in the key of E-flat.

11. Prepare an analysis of Schubert's Octet in F, Op. 166, final movement. Consider the form of the Andante and the role its materials play in the movement.

7

SONATA-RONDO

In preceding chapters, we have drawn on large numbers of works to illustrate particular features of each of the forms under consideration. In this chapter, we shall set forth the outlines and characteristics of the sonata-rondo by explanation in the following paragraphs and, on subsequent pages, by analysis of form in two complete examples.

As its name suggests, the sonata-rondo incorporates features of two major traditional forms—rondo and single-movement sonata form. It is in that sense a hybrid. In the practices of composers, the sonata-rondo is confined almost exclusively to final movements in sonatas, chamber works, symphonies, and concertos. This fact is borne out in the examples cited in this chapter, all of which are finales of such works.

In Chapter 4, pp. 102–03, it was pointed out that the compound ternary, represented as *A B A* when its first part is a simple ternary, bears a superficial
(*aba*) (*aba*)
resemblance to the sonata-rondo, represented as *ABACABA*. The principles postulated in that discussion are not repeated here. We may, however, further emphasize one of the primary conditions establishing a line of distinction, albeit not an inflexible one, between simple and compound types: Does the degree of differentiation of materials in such a scheme suggest three or seven parts? Or, are the initial three sections (*aba* or *ABA*) related through compactness, similarity of material, and brevity to the point of constituting a cohesive unity in the overall form?

SONATA-RONDO FORM DEFINED

The concept of an arch is again suggested in sonata-rondo design. The diagrams below demonstrate this, and show further that the scheme is not parallel in the distribution of tonal areas. The symbol R again denotes a related key; D denotes the dominant.

Fig. 7.1   THEMATIC MATERIALS AND TONAL LEVELS IN SONATA-RONDO FORM

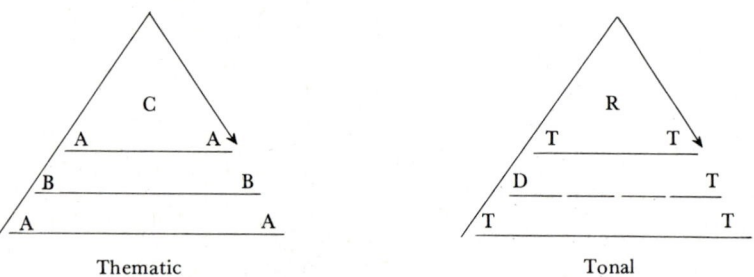

Thematic   Tonal

Of the seven chief parts of the design, four are statements of the rondo theme, A. There are three digressions—two of them of like material (B) and the middle one of contrasting character and/or material (C). The full sequence of parts, excluding transitional elements, is thus: rondo theme—first digression—rondo theme—second digression—rondo theme—repetition of first digression—rondo theme.

As with other forms, the plan may include an introduction. Transitions and retransitions are frequent—especially the latter, and a coda is usual.

The key of the first digression is, predictably, closely related to the basic key of the movement, often the dominant or relative. That of the second digression is a different related key, often the subdominant or parallel; or the tonality of the second digression, especially when it is developmental, may fluctuate, often with sequential movement, from one tonal region to another. The rondo theme, barring rare exceptions, returns in the tonic key for each of its major appearances. The first digression, in its return near the end of the form, appears in the tonic key, as is seen in the diagrams above.

It has by now become clear that recurrences of material may be expected to involve variation, including abbreviation, which may be quite extreme. This is particularly true of the form in which the rondo theme occurs *four* times. In fact, the final statement of the rondo theme in the sonata-rondo is very frequently reduced to a simple (but clear) reminder, or omitted altogether, with the coda recalling its principal motives.

It has been implied that the second digression, C, may be of a developmental character; indeed, this is often true. When the middle section is developmental, it may treat materials of A or B, or both. When it is not developmental, it commonly introduces a new theme or complex and is often longer than the other parts. The rondo theme and first digression, as well as any introductory, transitional, and closing sections, are analogous in content to corresponding sections in forms studied earlier.

RELATIONSHIPS TO SINGLE-MOVEMENT SONATA FORM

Two major factors relate the sonata-rondo to single-movement sonata form: (1) the final appearances of rondo theme and first digression in the tonic key, corresponding to the recapitulation in single-movement sonata form; and (2) the frequent occurrence of a developmental middle section in which the principal thematic material is taken through paces similar to those which are characteristic of development in single-movement sonata form.

One can cite further obvious characteristics which the two forms share. Both may have introductions, and both very often have codas—sometimes extensive, developmental codas. Both involve contrasting themes and thematic complexes which first appear at two related tonal levels and are often developed before formal recapitulation. Often the line of distinction is blurred; again, one errs in approaching the problem of classification with rigid preconceptions.

The finale of Beethoven's Sonata in F minor, Op. 2, No. 1, is a case in point. The opening material does recur following the first digression (see m. 50), but in the ''wrong'' key—the dominant, rather in the manner of an exposition codetta. Further, the middle section is primarily taken up with a new theme in the relative major—not uncommon in rondo form but an anomaly in true single-movement sonata form. The initial theme does *not* occur following the third digression, although there is reference to it in the coda. (See p. 163, where this movement is discussed in connection with single-movement sonata form.)

MOZART, TRIO IN B-FLAT FOR PIANO, VIOLIN, AND CELLO, K.502, FINAL MOVEMENT

The rondo theme of the finale of Mozart's B-flat Piano Trio, K.502 is 18 measures long, consisting of a double period whose consequent, which parallels the antecedent, is extended by 2 measures using the inversion of a motive from m. 5. In Ex. 7.1a, this and other significant motives are bracketed. (Once again, it is important that the student employ the full score while following this analysis.)

The transition to the first digression securely tonicizes F by repeating F:V, I (mm. 19–20, 22, 24). Using rhythms and articulative patterns from the rondo theme (Ex. 7.1b), the transition leads into piano figurations repeating F:V and V of V, thus reaching slightly beyond the actual tonal destination for stronger modulatory effect (c). Near the end of the transition, B♭ is added to the C triad (mm. 30–32), turning the harmony back toward the provisional F tonic before the first digression appears.

Ex. 7.1a   Mozart, Trio in B-flat, K. 502, for piano, violin and cello, final movement.

Ex. 7.1b

Ex. 7.1c

The rests convey a sense of tentativeness, of rhythmic (but not harmonic) relaxation in preparation for the new thematic material (d).

Ex. 7.1d

The first digression is, of course, in the dominant, F. It consists of two phrases of irregular lengths (7 and 10 measures) forming a group rather than a period; the second phrase—see m. 45—is extended by varied repetition. There are two half-cadences, one on V, the other on IV. The example shows, in outline, the first phrase in its entirety; the corresponding point is shown to illustrate how the second phrase is extended. Again, characteristic and important motives are bracketed (Ex. 7.1e).

The retransition (mm. 50–79), which suddenly reintroduces the motive of the rondo theme (7.1f), adheres at first to the key of F; although the example shows some tonal digression, it is all transitory, and there is a strong cadence in F at 56–57 (7.1g). Measures 57–58 are reminiscent of the conclusion of the first digression; at m. 59, the rondo motive returns in a variation of the opening phrase of the retransition (compare 7.1f and h). There is some anticipatory development of two motives of the rondo theme, ending on F:I, to which E♭ is added (m. 74) to point toward the primary tonic and the formal return of the rondo theme.

The second statement of the rondo theme (the first return), mm. 80–93, recalls the first three phrases in their original form, the fourth phrase undergoing dissolution by motive repetition in sequence (7.1j).

The middle section (the second digression) is developmental. The sequence which dissolved the preceding rondo statement (7.1j) has led to G minor. From this point, the primary motive,

Ex. 7.1e

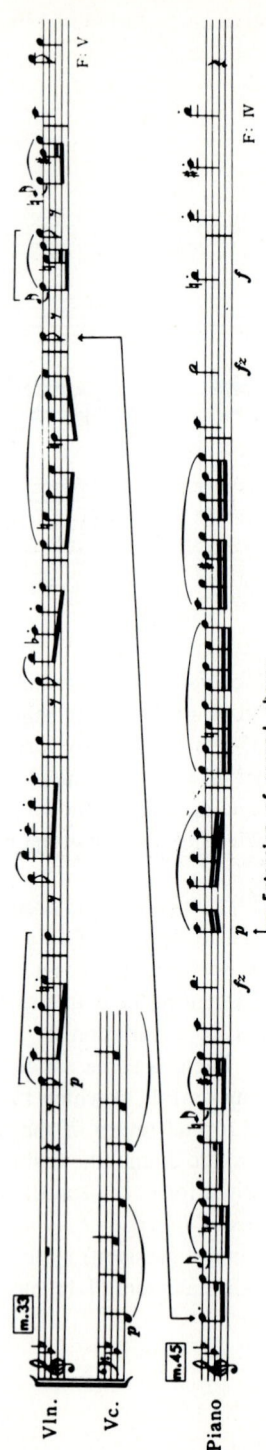

Vln.

Vc.

Piano

Extension of second phrase

Ex. 7.1f

Ex. 7.1g

Ex. 7.1h

Ex. 7.1i

Ex. 7.1j

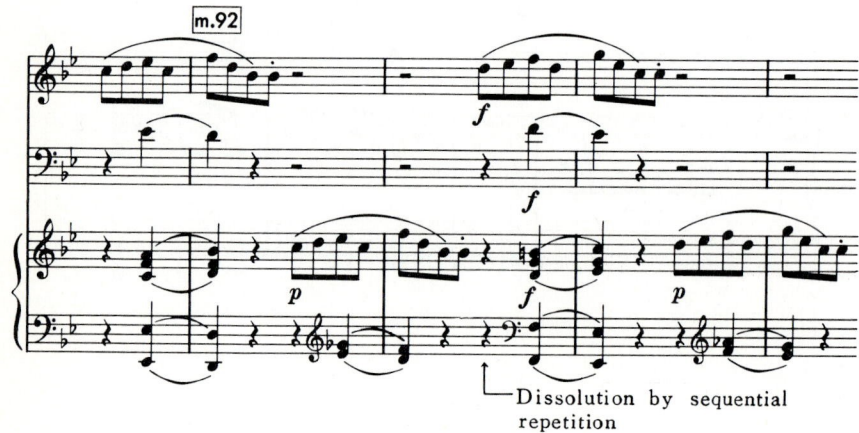

takes off at m. 100 in a modulating sequence of 5th relations—G minor, C minor, F, B-flat—leading to E-flat at m. 108. The theme of the first digression enters in E-flat, its first phrase directed to a cadential modulation into F minor. Here, the phrase begins again (7.1k) over the tonicized F.

Now the music is led into an elaborate development (7.1l) of the chief motive of the first digression,

Ex. 7.1k

Ex. 7.1l

again in sequence, leading to C minor at m. 127 (7.1m). Still another sequence on the same motive (m) leads to a cadence in F at m. 131 (7.1n). Note the use of stretto imitation (Chapter 12) during this phase of the development.

The retransition which follows brings back motives of the rondo theme, in anticipation, again taking F:I as a dominant in B-flat by the addition of the dissonant minor 7th (E♭, m. 139). This dominant is sustained, as in the previous retransition, and it leads directly into the thematic return. (Note the elision at m. 131: the piano's imitating thrust intrudes upon the cadence.)

Ex. 7.1m

Ex. 7.1n

The third statement of the rondo theme, mm. 145–62, has the same form as the original statement.

The transition into the return of the first digression, mm. 163–76, is built of the same material as its earlier counterpart (Exx. 7.1b, c, d), but the tonal direction is altered because the first digression will now appear in the tonic. Where the transition originally pointed to F, it now remains in B-flat, although there are superficial tonal elaborations (7.1o) succeeded by the firm retonicization of B-flat.

While there is some variation in register, the return of the theme of the first digression is essentially unchanged except for the transposition into B-flat. (See mm. 177–193.)

Again, there is a retransition (mm. 194–213); it begins as before except for the difference of key. Example 7.1p should be compared with 7.1f. At m. 208 there

Ex. 7.1o

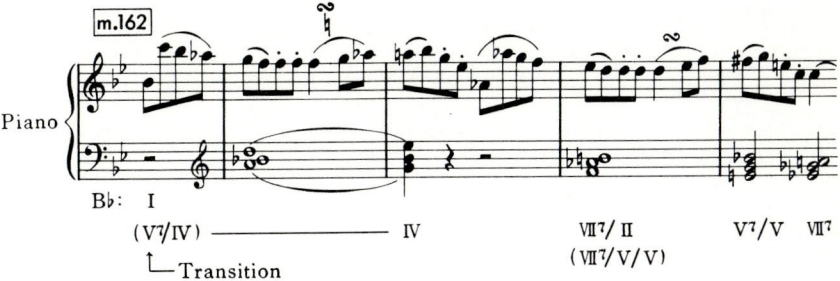

Ex. 7.1p

is an abrupt change from the course of the earlier retransition. The former developmental passage, which would at this point be somewhat redundant, is sacrificed in favor of a longer, more elaborate cadential affirmation of B-flat (see the chromatic approach to the I_4^6 in Ex. 7.1q).

The final statement of the rondo theme begins at m. 214. In keeping with common practice, the theme, having been heard three times previously, is now abbreviated. Its two central motives are treated imitatively without tonal fluctuation (7.1r). Again, the imitation is in stretto, comprising a brief development in lieu of a complete final statement. The imitation continues to a strong cadence at m. 230 (Ex. 7.1s).

The section from m. 230 to the end is the coda. Here, the motive of the first digression is recalled, while a B♭:I pedal is sustained under it. There is stretto like that of the second digression (see Exx. 7.1t and m). At m. 238 the pedal breaks into a final cadential flourish of tonic and dominant harmonies.

Ex. 7.1q

Ex. 7.1r

Ex. 7.1s

m.229
p
p
p
Coda

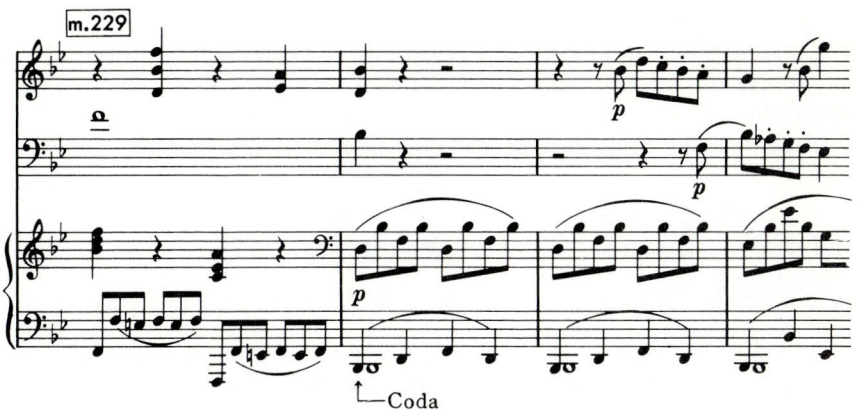

Ex. 7.1t

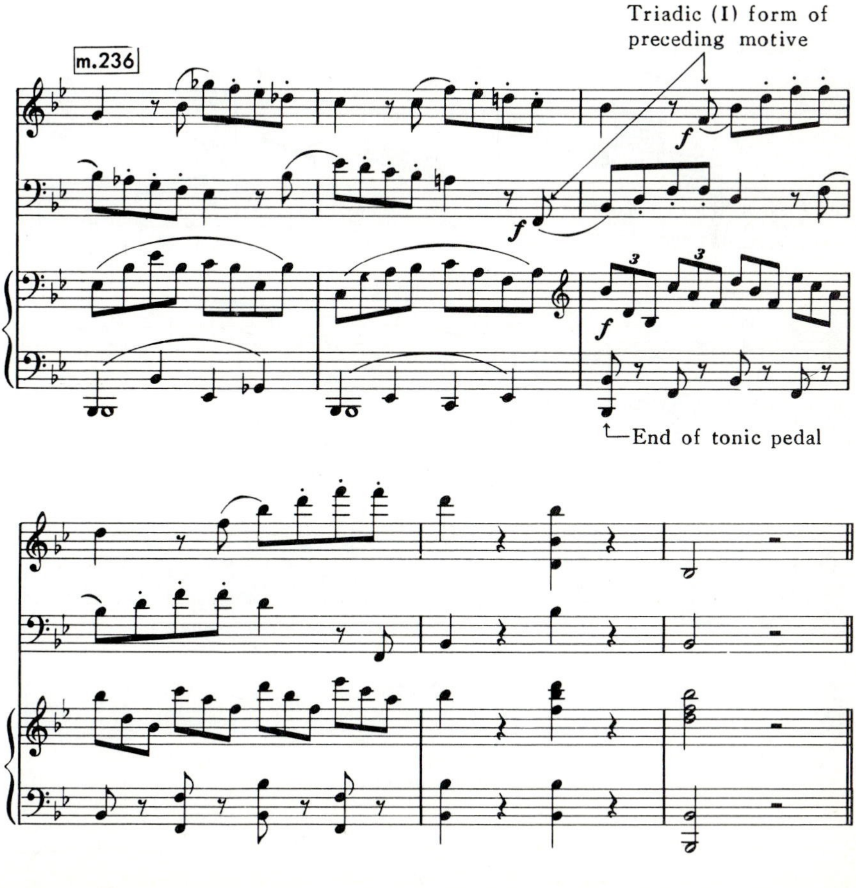
Triadic (I) form of preceding motive
m.236
f
f
3
3
f
End of tonic pedal

PROKOFIEV, SONATA NO. 4 IN C MINOR
FOR PIANO, OP. 29, FINAL MOVEMENT

The closing movement of Prokofiev's Fourth Sonata for piano, written in 1917, is a
clear example of twentieth-century application of the form and principles of the
sonata-rondo.

The movement begins with a rondo theme of the following basic motives:[1]

The Prokofiev theme, like the Mozart, is heard as a double period, as indicated in Ex. 7.2a. The form is symmetrical, the first notated bar an anacrusis to the

Ex. 7.2a   Prokofiev, Piano Sonata No. 4 in C minor, Op. 29, final movement.
Reprinted by permission of the copyright owners, Boosey & Hawkes Music Publishers
Limited.

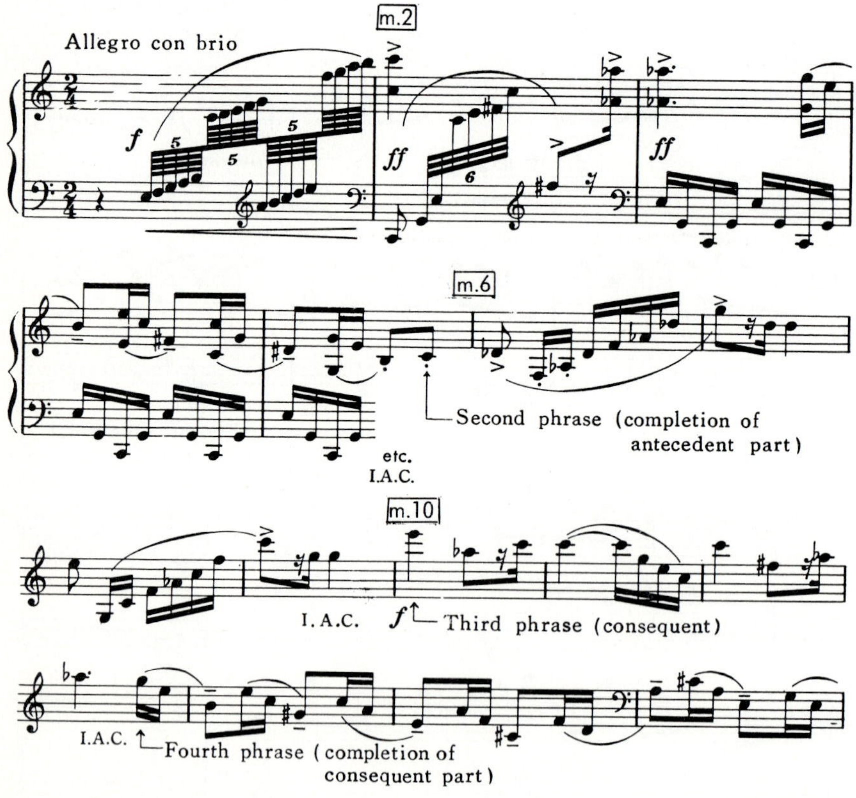

[1]Reprinted by permission of the copyright owners, Boosey & Hawkes Music Publishers Limited.

Ex. 7.2a (continued)

P.A.C. └─ Repetition of consequent
(phrases 3+4)

p   P.A.C.

initial "phrase downbeat." The antecedent part extends to m. 9, and consists of two phrases of equal length; the consequent portion, also of two phrases, extends to m. 17, and is repeated (to m. 25) with minor, surface variants. (The theme might also be read as a single period of two 8-measure phrases, the second repeated, depending upon one's sense of punctuating delineation at m. 5 and at m. 13 or 21.)

The harmonies are essentially traditional elements containing nonharmonic dissonances, often unprepared, adding harmonic color and mobility. (For example, m. 2 is C:I with F♯ and A♭ as auxiliary neighbors, both resolving to G in m. 3.)

The transition is sequential: a pattern of 4 measures (itself sequential, as is apparent in the bass line) is repeated, transposed. In the process, the sense of C as tonic is for the moment dispelled. Example 7.2b shows only part of the sequential repetition.

Ex. 7.2b

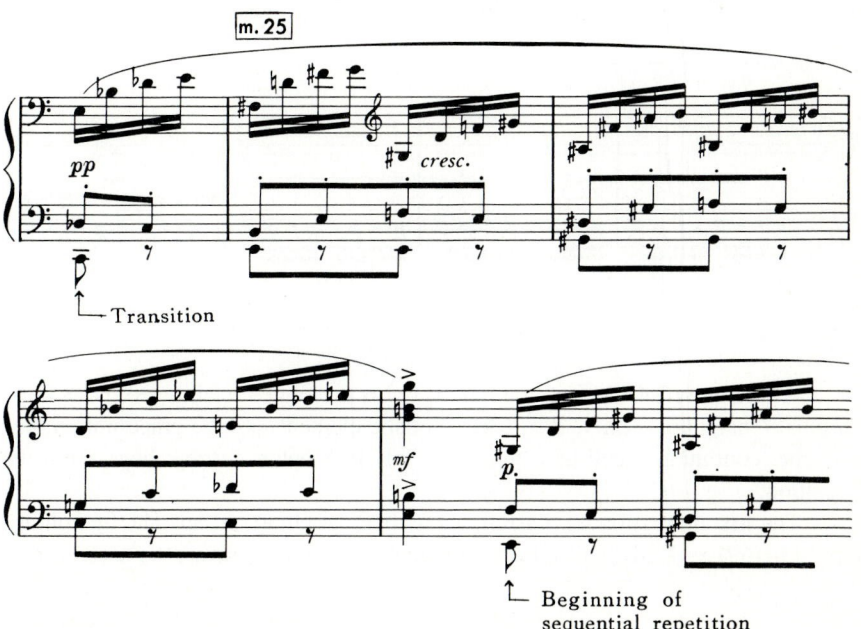

m. 25

pp   *cresc.*

└─ Transition

mf   *p.*

└─ Beginning of
sequential repetition

The transition leads to an appearance of the motive of mm. 6–7, on C♯. The C♯ harmony, as f♯:V, progresses diatonically to IV, the latter over B, thence to G:V$_9$ (f♯:IV=G:III; see mm. 35–37). The D is emphasized as dominant of the approaching tonal region: the digression is to appear, conventionally, in G. The transition consists largely of symmetrically related units, on the precedent of the original 4-measure sequence pattern, but it ends with a 6-measure segment over the D pedal—a subtly decelerating (i.e., shorter to longer) rhythmic factor of preparation (Ex. 7.2c).

Ex. 7.2c

At the outset of the first digression, G:I is prolonged, elaborated by its upper chromatic neighbors (Ex. 7.2d). Characteristic elements are the grace-note motive and the continuing, trill-like figuration of 16th-notes carried over from the transition.

The first digression is, in form, a symmetrical phrase group. The first phrase, mm. 43–46 (Ex. 7.2d), is itself divisible into 2-measure motives; the second, mm.

Ex. 7.2d (*continued*)

└ First digression, first phrase

47–50, is also divisible into halves, ending with a relatively strong cadence; the third, mm. 51–54, corresponds to the first phrase; and the fourth, mm. 55–58, is rhythmically akin to the second phrase, but different in contour (see Ex. 7.2e).

Ex. 7.2e

└ Second phrase

└─Fourth phrase

A retransition follows (m. 59), taking up the motive of the first digression and modulating in rising chromatic successions richly elaborating the fundamental V (of the digression) to I (of the forthcoming theme).

Ex. 7.2f

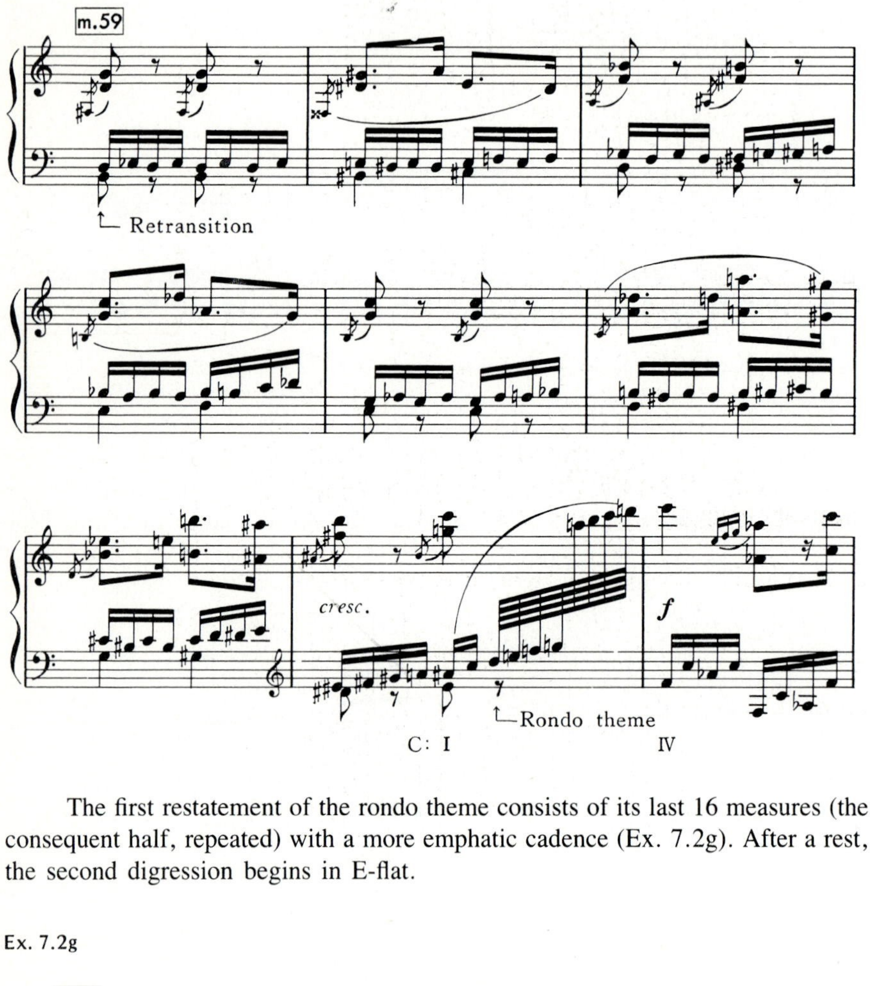

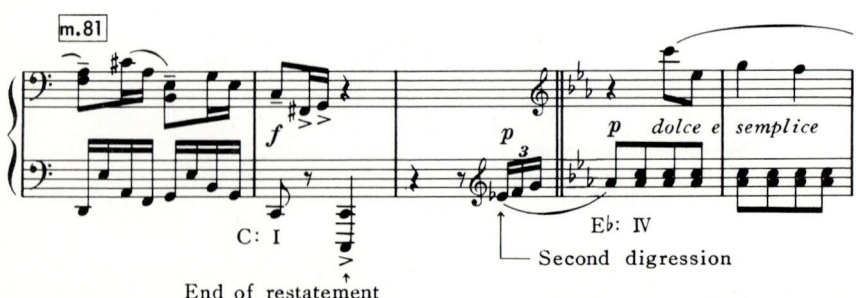

The first restatement of the rondo theme consists of its last 16 measures (the consequent half, repeated) with a more emphatic cadence (Ex. 7.2g). After a rest, the second digression begins in E-flat.

Ex. 7.2g

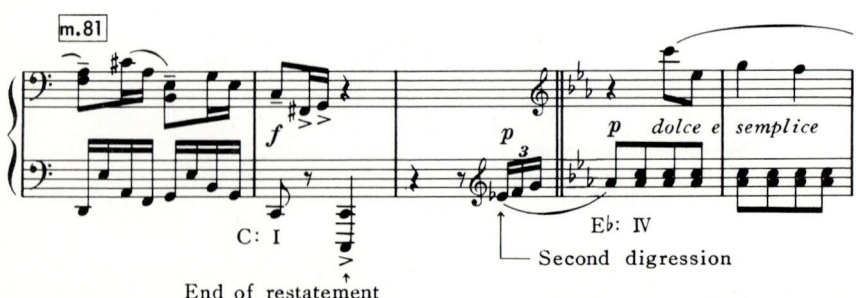

The middle section, unlike that of the Mozart example discussed earlier, employs a new, strongly contrasting theme. It has the form of a simple ternary of three nearly equal parts. It is, as expected, the larger of the digressions, 50 measures long. At its close, it moves directly into the second reprise of the rondo theme. In Ex. 7.2h, the thematic material is shown in short excerpts from each of the three parts of the ternary; in the return of the opening phrase (mm. 118–122), the accompanimental pattern is varied.

Ex. 7.2h

Again, the rondo theme is limited in restatement to its consequent 8 measures, repeated as before, this time with a further repetition of the latter half of the consequent (total length: 20 measures). Here, Prokofiev uses some variation in accompaniment as well as melodic ornamentation.

The following transition, beginning at the anacrusis to m. 154, is extended to 24 measures. It is built of the same material as its earlier counterpart, but at its center there is an unexpected reminiscence of the second digression, abandoned to a sequential repetition of the transition's first 8 measures. The movement is of course toward and around C, whose linearized dominant and tonic triads can be seen as underlying bases for the successions comprising the sequence (Ex. 7.2j).

Ex. 7.2i

Second restatement

Ex. 7.2j

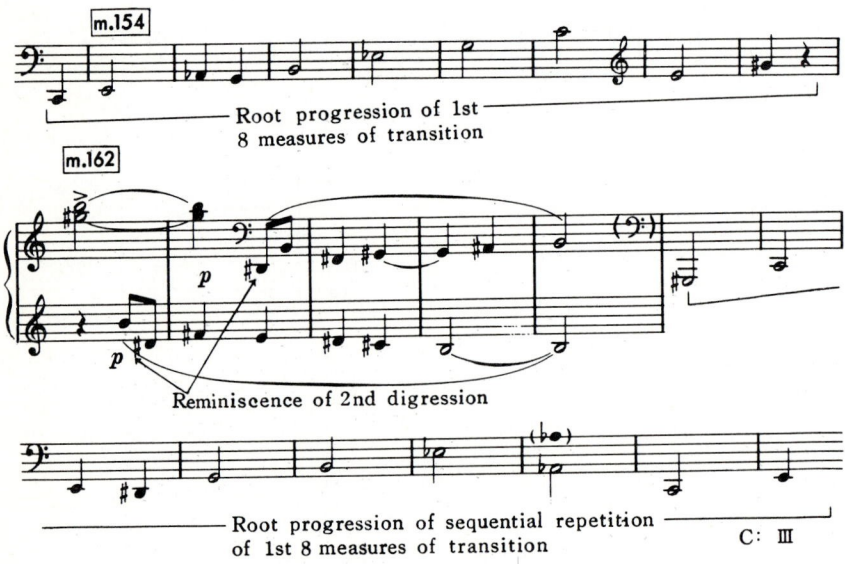

The first digression, *B,* is now restated with its length unchanged. There is considerable variation, however. Its sonorities are now amplified, and it is enunciated *fortissimo.* Moreover, the elements are contrapuntally inverted—the former treble is now the bass. And the material is transposed to the tonic, according to the traditional formula.

The retransition is as before, except that it remains in C. As a preface to the final statement of the rondo theme, Prokofiev now takes the original motive of mm. 2 and 3,

Ex. 7.2k

Restatement of first digression

C: I

unused since the beginning in its definitive form, and develops it in sequence. It is treated brilliantly, evoking an impression of climax. The motive is stated twice, moving up by step, the subsequent 2 measures repeating only the anacrusis fragment, in a process of acceleration complementing the pitch rise and crescendo. In Ex. 7.2l the upward sweep of the anacrusis is represented by a diagonal dash. The sketch shows melodic and root successions through the 6-measure passage just described, immediately preceding the final statement of the rondo theme.

Ex. 7.2l

Rondo theme,
final statement

The antecedent of the original theme now appears, vigorously launched by the preparation outlined above; the 16th-note accompaniment is dropped to a lower octave, in a dramatic, sonorous transformation. The original period goes on into the consequent half (where, it will be recalled, the earlier restatements had begun) with accompanimental variation and melodic ornamentation of the sort already employed. Into the 15th measure of the theme the music corresponds in form and substance to the initial statement; after this point, the theme's cadence is inflated for emphasis—necessary to its present function in conclusion of the movement. The basic V-I progression of the final bars is explicit.

Ex. 7.2m

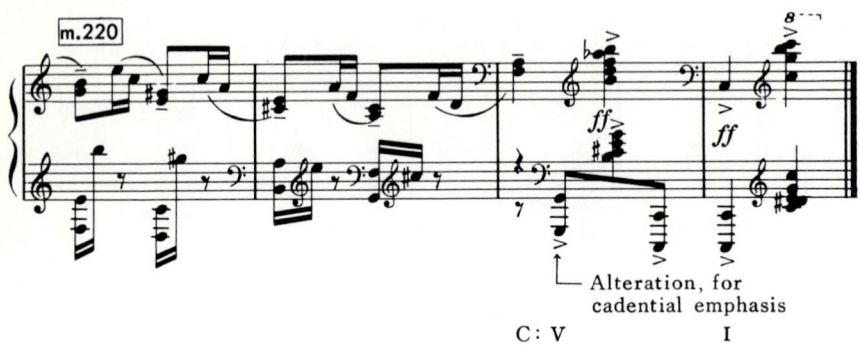

Alteration, for
cadential emphasis

C: V   I

HISTORICAL SIGNIFICANCE OF SONATA-RONDO FORM

Sonata-rondo form is of great importance in the late eighteenth and early nineteenth centuries, and of diminishing importance thereafter. The extended rondo, including the seven-part form having an exterior resemblance to the sonata-rondo, has a continuing vitality, but the specificities of the traditional form, with its conventional tonal implications, are not widely applicable to the music of the twentieth century. Nevertheless, the strictly conformant Prokofiev movement, and other examples to be cited below, show that the use of sonata-rondo form covers a broad historical range not excluding the present time.[2]

The strict sonata-rondo, then, is associated especially with the classical tradition, more particularly with the music of Mozart and Beethoven. For this reason, the examples given for reference and supplementary study are concentrated heavily in the classical period.

EXERCISES

1. Find and analyze one or more examples of sonata-rondo. In your analysis, consider the following problems.
    a) Mark the appearances of the rondo theme. How do they compare in form? What variation techniques are used?
    b) Compare the transitions approaching the first digression and its restatement as to (a) material used, (b) length, (c) tonality, and (d) degree of correspondence between the two.

[2]*Extended rondos* of seven and more parts are referred to in Chapter 5 (see p. 137), and excluded from discussion here except for the particularities of the sonata-rondo. Extended rondos with relatively free tonal relations (see the fourth movement of Hindemith's *Sinfonietta* in E for orchestra) are more common in the twentieth century than is the orthodox sonata-rondo.

c) In what respects are the rondo theme and the first digression contrasted? In what respects similar?

d) Is the middle digression taken up largely with new material? If so, consider it in relation to question c, above. If it is developmental, trace the materials developed and the tonal references which occur.

e) Look for devices of retransition, as enumerated in preceding chapters, in the passage preceding the second restatement.

f) Where does the coda begin? If it is entered by dissolution, locate the point in the final rondo statement at which dissolution begins. If it is set off by a cadence, evaluate harmonic and rhythmic qualities of that cadence.

g) What unusual features do you observe? Does the form differ in any of its details from the norms outlined in this chapter?

2. The finale of Haydn's Piano Sonata in C (Hob. XVI:48) was cited as an example in Chapter 5. What features relate it to the sonata-rondo? What aspect of the thematic material renders unlikely the use of the formal sonata-rondo plan?

3. Study a number of Beethoven examples of sonata-rondo form (finales of piano sonatas and other multimovement works).

a) What observations occur to you regarding Beethoven's treatment of the final statement of the rondo theme? Give several examples to support your finding.

b) Do you observe a standard tonal scheme, or is there considerable variation from work to work?

4. Analyze the finales of Beethoven's first two sonatas for violin and piano, Op. 12. How many of the remaining violin sonatas of Beethoven have final movements in sonata-rondo form?

5. Look among Viennese classical concertos for specimens of the sonata-rondo.

6. Study one or more of the following, taking special note of irregularities— unexpected developments, interpolations, extensions, variations—as interesting and provocative bases for study.

Beethoven, Concerto No. 2 in B-flat for piano and orchestra, Op. 19, final movement

Concerto in D for violin and orchestra, Op. 61, final movement (Consider liberties of form, key, and character in the final statement. How is the cadenza worked into the form?)

Sonatas in F and G minor for cello and piano, Op. 5, Nos. 1 and 2, final movements

Sonata in E-flat for piano, Op. 27, No. 1, final movement (Note interpolation from slow movement.)

Sonata in E minor for piano, Op. 90, second movement

String Quartet in F, Op. 18, No. 1, final movement

Symphony No. 2 in D, Op. 36, final movement (Consider similarities to single-movement sonata form.)

Brahms, Piano Concertos in D minor, Op. 15, and B-flat, Op. 83, final movements (In each, what compensations do you find for absence of the final formal restatement of the rondo theme? Which movement has a thematic complex as first digression?)

Edvard Grieg (1843–1908), Concerto in A minor for piano and orchestra, Op. 16, final movement (Compare the Brahms movements cited directly above.)

Mozart, Concerto in G for flute and orchestra, K. 313, final movement (Note the use of ornamental variation.)

Concerto in G for violin and orchestra, K. 216, final movement (Note interpolation of *andante* material. Why does Mozart insert an "extra" reminder of the rondo theme at m. 315?)

Concerto in D for violin and orchestra, K. 218, final movement (Again, note interpolations, and use of introductory material throughout the form.)

Concerto in E-flat for piano and orchestra, K. 271, final movement

Piston, String Quartet No. 3, third movement (Note Beethoven-like omission of final statement in favor of strong, but brief, reprise of primary motive during coda, at m. 280.)

Schubert, Sonata in A, D. 959, final movement (Give special attention to the brilliant, developmental second digression.)

7. Examine form in the final movement of Beethoven's Symphony No. 8 in F, Op. 93.

    a) Show that the theme is a small ternary.

    b) What is unorthodox in the tonality of the entry of the first digression (especially in relation to its preparation)? Consider the same question as to the recurrence of this material later in the movement.

    c) Discuss motivic preparation of the rondo theme in its restatement at the upbeat to m. 98. How is this restatement dissolved into a developmental middle section?

    d) What, in the recapitulative division of the form following development, is suggestive of single-movement sonata form?

    e) Trace materials and techniques of development in the extensive coda (from the double bar of mm. 379–80).

8. Consider, in one or more of the following works, traditional sonata-rondo form.

    Beethoven, Sonata in A for cello and piano, Op. 69 (Compare the finale with the corresponding movements of the two sonatas listed above—Op. 5, Nos. 1 and 2.)

    Mozart, String Quartet in D, K. 575, final movement

    Haydn, Symphony No. 101 in D, final movement (Why would strict sonata-rondo form be extremely unlikely in this movement?)

    Vincent Persichetti (b. 1915), Symphony No. 4, final movement

8

CONCERTO

The concerto is not a form, but rather a medium of application of various forms and procedures. Comprehensive treatment of such diverse procedures, changing considerably with the concerto's historical development, would reach far beyond the present, limited context.

The variants on traditional forms evident in that colloquy of sonorous elements by which the concerto is defined, thematic and tonal content shared and distributed in many different ways, reveal those forms in special, distinctive aspects. And the means by which composers have handled solo and orchestral components in the unfolding of the tonal-thematic scenario are interesting and instructive. Forms in superior examples of the concerto are, in Tovey's apt statement, "adapted to make the best effect expressible by opposed and unequal masses of instruments," and "modified so as not merely to fit those conditions but to make them a special means of expression."[1]

It is arguable that the sonata for disparate instruments (piano and violin, for example) poses issues of integration and distribution comparable to those of the concerto, but unlike the quartet, for example, which in its finest manifestations aspires to realization as a "single" instrument. Several considerations in the composition of the sonata duo are indeed analogous to those of the concerto (for example, condensations for avoidance of redundancies, modes of dialogue and other exchanges). But these problems arise especially acutely in the latter, with its extreme

---

[1]Donald Francis Tovey, *Essays in Musical Analysis, Volume III: Concertos* (London: Oxford University Press, 1936), p. 6.

sonorous contrasts, and with the conventional expectation of virtuosic display by the soloist.

Some particular approaches to form in the concerto, as specimens of problems and solutions, will be demonstrated in this chapter. This limited objective can best be achieved by examining formal events in several movements of different types and styles, following some brief commentary concerning terms, basic problems, and certain conventional procedures which have characterized the concerto at different points in history.

THE CONCERTO PRINCIPLE AND ITS EARLY MANIFESTATIONS; THE CONCERTO GROSSO

The technique of opposing, commonly in alternation, two sonorous elements (a principle termed *concertato*) is one of great importance throughout the baroque period. Indeed, the origins of the concerto, especially in works (choral as well as instrumental) of Italian composers, are to be found in the second quarter of the seventeenth century, from which point the term "concerto" can be understood to refer increasingly consistently to the *concertato* technique in instrumental works. Earlier applications of the term have diverse meanings.[2]

In the baroque period, the solo element of the concerto is often a small group of instruments, termed *concertino;* or at times each of its members is designated *primo* or *principale* to distinguish it from its counterpart of the *ripieno* (literally "full") or *concerto grosso* (translatable, in this restricted sense, as "large ensemble," as opposed to the diminutive *concertino*). In the type of baroque concerto characterized by a small body of solo participants, the larger instrumental group is called *concerto grosso;* the term came to be applied to the genre itself, which enjoyed great vogue in the later seventeenth and early eighteenth centuries. (See the discussion of ritornello procedures, pp. 107–09.)

The solo concerto, which appeared at about the same time as the concerto grosso, subsequently assumed preeminence in pre-classical and classical literatures; the works of Bach's sons, Carl Philipp Emanuel and Johann Christian, are of primary importance in the direct progression to the solo concerto of the classical period. While "concerto" thus essentially means "solo concerto" after the baroque, the principle of the concerto grosso survives in the occasional classical *symphonie concertante* (in Italian, *sinfonia concertante*), for a group of soloists with orchestra, written by Haydn and Mozart among others.[3]

---

[2]For a brief account of the earliest and related antecedents, see Donald J. Grout, *A History of Western Music*, pp. 317–18 and 397–99. Arthur Hutchings's *The Baroque Concerto* (London: Faber, 1961) is a broad survey of some depth of inquiry and insight respecting style and stylistic development, as well as elements of structure and compositional idiom in individual works and bodies of works.

[3]The concerto grosso has enjoyed some resurgence in the twentieth century. That of Ernest Bloch (1880–1959) is an example, as are some works called "concerto for orchestra" by such composers as Bartók and Elliott Carter (1908–).

The analysis of content in examples from the early history of the concerto through the baroque reveals pronounced differences in the role of the solo, between largely figural parts on the one hand, and thematic exposition and development on the other, the latter arguably a feature of more sophisticated and convincing integration. Indeed, the solo (or concertino) in many specimens is overtly preoccupied with "nonthematic" active figuration (see the Handel movement discussed on pp. 108–09), with primary thematic material left to the ripieno.

Some practices observable in Handel's great Concerti Grossi of Op. 6 can serve as a summary of functions of the two groups.[4] These practices cover the entire gamut of degrees of concertino exposure, from the complete absence of a concertino group, to prominent concertino functions of genuine thematic substance. Handel's Op. 6, No. 7, in B-flat, can be cited as a "ripieno concerto" in which all movements are played throughout by the orchestra (further examples are No. 10, in D minor, throughout; and the first and third movements of No. 4, in A minor, among others). In the latter category are No. 1, in G, third movement, a beautiful specimen featuring two solo violins in imitative interaction and, at another level, in dialogue with the ripieno; the second movement of No. 2, in F, skillfully integrated and featuring phased tutti entries under the solo; No. 3, in E minor, first movement, a good example of regularity of ritornello, solo and ripieno elements thematically distinct; No. 5, in D, third movement; No. 8, in C minor, fifth movement (a *siciliano* of memorable thematic interchanges); No. 10, the fifth movement; and No. 12, in B minor, first movement.

Examples might be cited from the same opus in which the solo, while conspicuously exposed, is largely figural and relatively nonthematic: No. 3, third movement, in which the solo parts employ only 16th-note figurations; No. 6, in G minor, fourth movement; No. 11, in A, fourth movement; and No. 12, second movement. Finally, examples of very meager solo exposure of any kind are the fifth movement of No. 1, where the role of the solo is that of doubling the tutti except in four one-bar interjections; No. 2, third movement; and No. 4, second movement, a fugal context in which the solo component is restricted to very brief interjections.

These remarkably diverse compositions embrace an expansive variety of genres and forms: fugues, binaries, dances, "free" forms, and occasional variation (e.g., Op. 6, No. 12, third movement, a *larghetto* with variation).

Bach's realization of the concerto grosso is evident in the *Brandenburg Concertos,* the genre's consummate achievement. A survey of techniques in these inexhaustibly rich works can scarcely be sought here. The third and sixth are essentially orchestral pieces, for richly divided strings, the latter dispensing with violins as well as winds. A notable example for analysis at the opposite extreme is the fifth, in D. Its third movement is a fugue in which the concertino (flute and violin) hardly doubles the ripieno at all, although the solo instruments at times double one another in assertive thematic statements against the full sonority of the orchestra. What little unison or octave doubling there is between concertino and ripieno is incidental and

---

[4]Footnote 4, Chapter 5, identifies an accessible modern reprinting of the Handel Concerti Grossi.

rarely strict (mm. 177–87 are exceptional). The keyboard of the continuo is active not only in its characteristic role of defining the rhythm and deepening the sonority, but in thematic exposition as well, and it emerges in the first movement in an expansive solo, without orchestra (*senza stromenti*), preceding the final ritornello. The second movement is for the concertino pair and continuo only. All told, the fifth is a true concerto in the highest sense of *concertato* opposition, exposition, and amalgamation.

FURTHER HISTORICAL PERSPECTIVES

The evolution of the baroque concerto might be traced along such lines of compositional treatment and formal integration as those touched upon in the above discussion of Bach and Handel. Tendencies of relatively inane technical flourish in the solo, but also of emergent functions of true thematic definition and full collaborative participation, are evident in the violin concertos of Antonio Vivaldi (c. 1680–1743), a central figure whose works were of great interest to Bach, who transcribed a number of his violin concertos.

Substantial functions of the solo can be seen as in one sense concommitant with emergent homophonic textures of classical style and increased exposure of thematic materials in upper textural voices. Such textures provide a fortuitous perspective for the solo in its contention with the orchestral mass. Similarly, prominent statement of themes by the soloists is understandably a feature of slow movements of the baroque concerto, while in *allegro* movements thematic exposition tends to be assigned more to the orchestra, the solo doubling treble voices of the tutti, released at points of cadence for episodic passages of incipient motivic development or virtuosic fingerwork.[5] Tempo can thus be a factor in conditioning content in the solo part, active figuration more likely in faster movements, and slower rhythms conducive to thematic elaboration.

In works of the high baroque, evidence can be seen of two specific evolutionary tendencies in concerto history: one is an increasing tendency of multimovement types to adopt standard three- or four-movement form (the later solo concerto almost invariably consists of three); the other is a development away from suite-related pieces of dance traditions toward movements conditioned by the more abstract premises of sonata elements.

In the classical period and later styles, the concerto, like other genres (solo, chamber, and orchestral), becomes a vehicle for forms typical of the multimovement sonata: single-movement sonata form, rondos, and ternaries espe-

---

[5]A good example for consideration of these points is No. 257 in A. Schering, ed., *Geschichte der Musik in Beispielen* (Leipzig: Breitkopf and Härtel, 1931, and New York: Broude Bros., 1950), a concerto for violin and string orchestra by Torelli.

cially, with such forms as variations serving exceptionally as bases for the concerto.[6]

The vast literature of the solo concerto is summarized in standard reference sources; much of it is quite well known, an indication of the popularity of the medium.[7] The large majority of solo concertos are for piano or violin with orchestra; only occasional works employ the cello or one of the treble winds or horn (and exceptionally other instruments) as soloist, though the variety of solo media increases in the twentieth century. The remarkable viability of the solo concerto extends up to the present, and the repertoire includes a number of widely performed twentieth-century masterworks. A few of assured significance are Bartók's three for piano, and his concerto (1937–38) for violin; Stravinsky's for violin and for piano with wind ensemble; Schoenberg's concertos for piano and for violin; and Berg's for violin.

FUNDAMENTAL ISSUES
AND CONVENTIONAL APPROACHES

The essential problem of the concerto is that of establishing for any given set of conceptual materials and premises a suitable model and sequence of sharing by the two protagonists (solo and orchestra) in the tonal-thematic narrative—whether in dramatic opposition, in complementary roles of principal agent and supportive subsidiary, or (rarely) in a true fusion of unified purpose.

The principle of obvious sonorous alternation evident in the ritornello procedure of many baroque concertos (see pp. 107–09) has been mentioned as one common solution in the literature of the concerto grosso.

Moreover, the classical and post-classical solo concerto, almost invariably in three movements (fast, slow, fast), often adopts the formula of the so-called *double exposition* (see also pp. 234–37) in the first movement (and at times in other movements). Here, the orchestral tutti sets off with its presentation of exposition materials, at times (as in Mozart) maintaining an underlying unity of tonic key. A "second" exposition is then undertaken by the soloist typically with orchestral accompaniment, exchanges, or interjections; it usually proceeds from the tonic to

---

[6]Examples of variation procedures in the concerto are Franck's *Symphonic Variations* for piano and orchestra and *Rhapsody on a Theme of Paganini* by Sergei Rachmaninov (1873–1943) (see p. 297).

[7]A summary tracing of the literature is given in Apel, *Harvard Dictionary*, 2nd ed., pp. 192–95. Major solo concertos of the nineteenth century are discussed in overview in Paul Henry Lang's preface to *The Concerto (1800–1900)* (New York: W. W. Norton and Co., Inc., 1969). Neither recent nor significantly analytical is Abraham Veinus, *The Concerto* (London: Cassell, 1948), a study of interest for its immersion in many literatures, some off the beaten track, treated historically and anecdotally. One might also mention Hans Engel, *The Solo Concerto*, trans. Robert Kolben (Cologne: Arno Volk, 1964), which gives descriptive comment about many works of the eighteenth and nineteenth centuries, some of them little known.

the dominant (or relative major) tonal region for the second thematic element and cadential materials, the solo often yielding to the orchestra at the exposition's close, prior to formal development. There may be variants on this essential outline: the solo may precede the orchestral tutti either with the primary thematic statement (as in Beethoven's Fourth Piano Concerto, with its starkly mesmerizing piano statement at the outset), or with commanding flourishes (as in Beethoven's Fifth Piano Concerto, where the solo's brilliant "extemporizing" on introductory harmonies ushers in the orchestral exposition). In a sense the double exposition is an expansion of the historical ritornello procedure. But the increasing prevalence of the sonata idea in the solo concerto of the later eighteenth century patently requires more than the mere alternation of substance and sonority.

It might seem that the traditional literal repetition of sections seen in many forms—the binary form, the single-movement sonata form, the *da capo* aria, and others—would lend itself easily to the dual medium of the concerto, perhaps employing the principle of double variation (Chapter 10, pp. 318–19). But so pat a standardization of approach is not evident in the practices of composers. To quote Tovey again: "On a large scale a too facile alternation between solo and tutti produces forms too sectional for the high organization required in first movements . . . ."[8] Clearly, the assignment of entire, large divisions to one of the two participants would be a denial of the point of the concerto's duality of function and interaction, its integrated duologue of subtle lines of exchange. The concerto represents, at best, a counterpoint of sonorous elements of competing substance, solo and orchestra joined in circumstances of broadly purposeful amalgamation and continuity.

By no means is the challenge of the concerto idea consistently met. There are times when inappropriately severed flights of the solo seem awkwardly encumbered by the orchestral presence, or when, on the other hand, the solo seems to assert itself only because it is there, in superficially active ostentation lacking the conviction of true integration and motivation arising from the implicit demands of posited materials. These issues are, to be sure, most critical in large sonata forms; simpler movements use "more sectional forms, in which solo and orchestra alternate more simply than in the first movement."[9] Yet the Brahms movement traced below, the second movement of the Double Concerto, is a supreme example of balanced and subtle interchange far from mere direct alternation marking the boundaries of formal divisions, here in a context of ternary form.

It has been noted that one frequent approach in the earlier concerto, whose challenges are surmounted most successfully in the best works of Vivaldi, Handel, and Bach, has been to relegate the solo or solo group to primarily figural material, often quite exhibitionistic, a circumstance in which the solo can function, however vacuously, in marking important directions of *tonal* structure. A survival of the tendency of virtuosic ostentation appears in the cadenza of classical and later works, typically in the outer movements, in which the movement's structural thrust and

[8]Tovey, *The Forms of Music* (New York: Meridian, 1956), p. 15.
[9]Tovey, *Essays*, Volume III, p. 24.

continuity are temporarily halted. The practice of such interruptive display is somewhat curtailed in later phases of the concerto's evolution.

In the literature's most notable specimens, composers have coped mightily with the provocative issues of the concerto, even while accepting conventional assumptions of the solo's virtuosic aspect. In the genre's supreme manifestations—in Bach, in easily half of the piano concertos of Mozart, in the piano concertos of Beethoven (especially the Fourth and Fifth) and in his Violin Concerto, and in Brahms (particularly the Second Piano Concerto, but notably in all four concertos)—persuasively integrated formal structures arise from particular conditions and materials.

When traditional forms are thought of as to particular processes (see pp. 403–04), in which areas of *statement* are opposed to areas of relative fluctuation in *development and transition,* applications of such processes in the concerto can be viewed as to common approaches constituting a perspective for the study of individual works. Such a broad summary would, for example, regard thematic statement in the concerto as the potential function of solo, orchestra, orchestra accompanied by figural or other elaborations in the solo, or solo with orchestral accompaniment (e.g., a simple harmonic underscoring). Or, thematic statement may be by the two protagonists alternating (e.g., one having antecedent, the other consequent, or one repeating the other's statement, in variation) or of deeply fused coactive roles. Big events, like perorative codas involving developmental review, or ending movements involving intense developmental procedures, are, understandably, often the responsibility of the tutti, or of conjoined, collaborative functions, as in the Bartók movement discussed below.

Processes of development and transition tend, as we have seen, to involve fluctuation and fragmentation; in the concerto, such areas are likely to entail colloquies of an accelerated frequency of motivic exchange. The solo's cadenza, a special manifestation of development which usually interrupts the course of events at a late point in the coda, has been mentioned above as the occasion for especially severe problems of continuity.

Much can be learned by serious analysis of particular works, each on its own terms. While such an observation applies to all discussion of forms in music, it seems that the concerto is especially resistant to principles of generalized applicability. What follows is an examination of formal outlines in three individual concerto movements which reveal disparate, interesting solutions to the special problems of the medium in a variety of formal types. Presumably any examples chosen at random would prove instructive; the choices here are, quite simply, favorite movements.

The analytical commentary focuses on three aspects of the form. First, major divisions in the form are listed, with discussion of the roles of solo and orchestra in each. Second, a classification of kinds of function in solo and orchestra is given. Third, areas of predominance of solo or orchestra, and of combined activity of the two, are cited. Since only a few examples can be quoted, consideration of the three analyses requires that the musical events be followed carefully in the full scores.

MOZART, CONCERTO IN A FOR PIANO
AND ORCHESTRA, K. 488, FIRST MOVEMENT

Mozart's piano concertos, in particular those following the composer's move to Vienna in 1781, are among the authentic treasures of the literature. In the present context, we can but glimpse this significant corpus through the first movement of one of the greatest, K. 488, in A. Analysis of single-movement sonata form in its first movement is given here as an outline of events and processes in major sections, regarded as to functions of solo and orchestra.

The "first exposition," to m. 66.   The classical convention of "double ex-position" has explicit application here. The piano is silent throughout these 66 measures, and it is left to the orchestra to set forth principal materials: the theme associated with the tonic area, mm. 1–18, a double period of which the strings state the 8-measure antecedent, while winds predominate in a 10-measure consequent; the expected transition (mm. 19–30[10]); a second thematic element (mm. 31–46), a period of 8-measure phrases, its antecedent in strings and its consequent having winds added gradually, thus expressing timbral contrast akin to that of the first theme; and a sectional codetta (mm. 47–62). The transition in this initial exposition, as usually in Mozart, sustains the tonic key throughout, despite superficial fluctuations; it introduces a motive of great vitality, related (stylistically rather than literally) to "appoggiatura" formulations occurring in all of the movement's themes, as indicated in Ex. 8.1a.

Ex. 8.1a   (See also Ex. 8.1f.)

**transitional motive
(mm.18-19):**

**motive of theme consequent
(mm.5-6):**

**second theme motive
(mm.30-31):**

**codetta motive
(mm.46-47):**

---

[10]A recurrent technique in the movement is a kind of elision in which pronounced changes of texture and sonority occur *at* the point of cadence, so that the transition, like later divisions, appears to begin with m. 18. But here, and later, the actual impetus of motivic entry is in the bar following, and numbers of measures given for the beginnings of formal divisions are stated accordingly in these cases.

The codetta has the unmistakable content of cadential process: the G♮ (m. 46) leaning toward the cadential IV (m. 49, etc.); relatively peremptory motivic content—here, another appoggiatura shape (into m. 47, over a tonic pedal, the motive varied by ornamentation at m. 52, woodwinds and violins in opposing directions, etc.); momentary avoidance of resolution (by VI, at m. 52; by interposition of V$^6_5$, at m. 59); and a final 4-measure section of explicit cadential articulation (in which the rising-3rd motive with which the codetta began is extended over 2 bars, 63–64). The orchestra functions here largely as tutti, suggestive of the ritornello tradition, yet including exchanges between strings and winds, notably in the aforementioned motivic development at mm. 52ff.

The "second exposition" (mm. 67–137).   It is in the second exposition that the two protagonists enter into their *concertato* interplay. The initial theme is structured as before (see mm. 67–82), in the tonic, although the consequent portion lacks its original extension (compare mm. 79–82 with mm. 13–18). Here, thematic statement is the role of the piano solo, in ornamental variation, while the orchestra functions subordinately in accompaniment, chiefly in the consequent portion (Ex. 8.1b). (But note how the strings approach the consequent, into m. 75, by upbeat imitation of the solo's cadential figure.)

The solo predominates in the transition (mm. 83–98): thus, an initial tutti is cut off by the solo's entry at m. 87, at which point the orchestra is reduced to accompaniment and doubling. This time, of course, the transition is directed toward a sustained E:V (mm. 93ff.). The reader will find it of interest to compare harmonic content in the two transitions: for example, m. 23 with m. 87, m. 26 with

Ex. 8.1b   Mozart, Concerto in A, K.488, for piano and orchestra, first movement (Allegro).

Ex. 8.1b *(continued)*

m. 90, etc. Of particular interest in interaction of solo and orchestra is the former's ornamental doubling of strings, then of woodwinds, at mm. 93–98, during the prolonged E:V (Ex. 8.1c).

Ex. 8.1c

Ex. 8.1c (continued)

The second theme now appears, in accord with the sonata principle, at the dominant (mm. 99–114), a 16-measure period as before. Here, as in the first theme, solo and orchestra function contrastingly in antecedent and consequent parts. The antecedent is straightforwardly assigned to piano, while in the consequent the orchestra takes over the expository role with the solo doubling in ornamental variation (m. 107, etc., Ex. 8.1d).

The materials of the closing section (mm. 115–37) are now at the dominant, with exact harmonic duplication to m. 129 (cf. m. 61), after which the earlier cadence is amplified significantly (cf. mm. 61–62 and 129–137!). The original 4-bar final section is omitted. In this repeated codetta, the piano enjoys *general predominance consistent with its important role in the second exposition.* In mm. 114–20, it presents primary motivic material, the orchestra accompanying; the two engage in motivic dialogue in mm. 120–24 (Ex. 8.1e). Following this point the piano's motivic material largely dissolves into elaborate figuration, especially following the avoidance of cadence at m. 127. The solo continues to predominate to the end of the exposition, the orchestra lending harmonic support in broad cadential articulation.

The development (mm. 138–78). Not unexpectedly, it is in the development section that the interplay between solo and orchestra is of greatest interest. The

Ex. 8.1d

Ex. 8.1e

present development (from m. 137) is almost exclusively taken up with its own, distinct theme (Ex. 8.1f), relatively little attention being paid to exposition materials which have by now been extensively displayed.

Ex. 8.1f   Theme 1, Theme 2, and development theme (all at dominant):

Ex. 8.1f *(continued)*

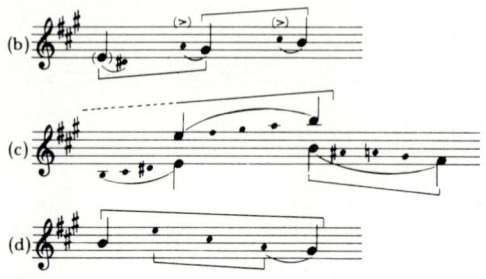

The first bars of the development are drawn from earlier transitional material (cf. mm. 18ff.), with interpolation (mm. 141–42) of elements appropriated from mm. 29–30. At m. 143, the cadence is abruptly denied. There is silence, followed by statement of the new theme's first phrase.

Although some surprising affinities can be seen in the study of this theme in relation to others (see Ex. 8.1f), these are best viewed as of a stylistic basis rather than of literal connections in which the present theme would be seen as derived from earlier ones.

Following the first developmental impetus (tutti), and the new theme's 6-measure phrase (strings), the solo enters with the same phrase in ornamental variation (Ex. 8.1g), slightly extended; during the solo's statement, strings participate

Ex. **8.1g**

only in definition of the cadence into m. 156. There is now a sequence on a motive (woodwinds, mm. 156–58) extracted from the theme:

The sequence follows a line of descending 3rds, its interim arrival points E, C, A, F, D, with the final succession (F to D) accelerated—i.e., occurring in reduced time. A further sequence, on a variant of the same motive treated imitatively (mm. 170ff.), is of descending steps: D, C, B, A. During these characteristic developmental episodes, solo and orchestra function in active dialogue, woodwind statements in the first sequence answered by strings in ornamental doubling, the piano unaccompanied at the point of acceleration (mm. 166ff.). The second sequence again features motivic statements in woodwinds (imitating one another), the solo now devoted to accompanimental figuration supportive of strong harmonic directions toward retransition. What is evident here is an ideal equilibrium of exchanged function and content between the solo and orchestra, as between orchestral segments themselves.

The retransition (mm. 178ff.) typically sustains the primary dominant, here as an explicit pedal all the way to recapitulation at m. 198. The developmental piano figuration accompanying motivic entries in woodwinds has led to an augmented 6th (m. 177) directly preceding retransitional entry of the A:V, at which point strings assume the role of motivic statement, still preoccupied with the same idea, extracted from the development theme. As this motive persists, over the dominant pedal, strings and winds engage in dialogue, the solo elaborating the wind entries (mm. 180–86, partly shown in Ex. 8.1h), then becoming predominant (mm. 186ff.), its figurations over the dominant pedal defining the final cadential articulation. The orchestra is now reduced to sustained chords of dominant harmony and its neighboring chromatic auxiliaries. To the ultimate dominant articulation, taken from strings by winds, with continuing piano figuration, D♮ is added, in intensification of the tendency toward recapitulative tonic resolution.

The recapitulation (mm. 198–244).   A factor of variation between recapitulated themes (mm. 198–213 and 228–44) is a *reversal of antecedent and consequent roles for piano and orchestra.* That is, the first is characterized by antecedent in orchestra (strings with woodwind doublings of certain motives) and consequent in ornamental variation in the solo (mm. 206–13), the orchestra accompanying in "simpler" versions of melodic and harmonic elements (Ex. 8.1i). The second theme, on the other hand, has antecedent in the exposed solo, while in the consequent the piano has active ornamental doubling decorating an orchestral statement (melody in woodwinds, harmony in horns and strings).

The transition (mm. 213–28) now holds to the tonic, but its material is largely that of the parallel section in the second exposition. (As to tonal content, compare the D♯ of m. 90 with the D♮ of m. 221; or the V of V at m. 93 with the V in m. 223.) A tutti flourish is elided with the thematic cadence as before, but the solo intervenes at mm. 217ff. (Compare mm. 22 and 86.) Here the piano has elaborating passage

Ex. 8.1h

Ex. 8.1i

work expressing, with harmonic undergirding in the orchestra, the motion toward, and prolonging, the primary V.

The coda (mm. 244–314), and renewed development.   The coda derives, as often, from earlier codetta material (cf. mm. 114ff.). Content traceable to the amplified cadence of the second exposition (following m. 129) leads to material clearly associated with that of the development: the aborted cadence (mm. 259–60, analogous to mm. 141–42), and the contrasting theme, a signal that the coda is to be significantly developmental. In the coda's first section, the solo leads the way, largely, with erstwhile closing motives and figuration over harmonies preparing the thematic entry. There are fragmentary exchanges between piano and strings (mm. 250–53), and the orchestra provides supportive doubling of harmonic progression, imitating at moments the solo's motivic statements (mm. 245, 246).

A second section brings relatively forthright statement of the development theme; now the roles, as compared with the theme's original appearance, are reversed, with piano stating the first phrase, modestly varied (cf. the imitations of m. 264 with their original, inverted, form at m. 146), and woodwinds its subsequent variation, in which the solo participates subordinately (Ex. 8.1j). The second phrase, thus a repetition in variation as initially, is extended by motivic repetition over V (cf. 271–72 with 153–54, or with 266) and, further, by VI (at m. 275) and

Ex. 8.1j

chromatic reapproach to V. After m. 275 the orchestra yields to cadential figuration in the solo, against intermittent harmonic doubling in the orchestra. The presentation of the theme is in the tonic (originally it appeared at the dominant, as though an element of the second tonal group); thus it is in keeping with the sonata's recapitulative procedure.

The third section (mm. 284–89) is an interpolation of originally transitional material, its brass underscoring sonorously appropriate, seeming to herald the movement's end; but this too is aborted (mm. 288–89) by the unfulfilled cadential drive which has heretofore announced the development theme, as now it prepares that theme's final entry, at the tonic (m. 290). *The solo is absent through all of this,* and the tutti statement of the theme, *piano,* is interrupted by dissolution (m. 293) on V of V, which persists for 2½ irresolute measures, thence leading to the climactic cadential six-four (m. 297) and fermata which signal the solo's cadenza.

The thematic dissolution and cadenza can be considered a fourth section of the coda (mm. 290ff.), a final surge of development, of which the cadenza is an aspect. In obvious preparation for the cadenza, the piano has been silent, as it is in the fifth section (mm. 299–314), which is composed of familiar closing motives. A final cadential avoidance (m. 303) leads quickly to emphatic tonic arrival at m. 306. Now appears, in elaboration of I, the final 4-bar section of the original codetta (see m. 62), then 5 measures of consistent tonic harmony elaborated only superficially, by V, in the penultimate measure.

Summary.   These details of exchanges of function by orchestra and solo reveal the composer's skillful and subtle manipulations of the medium. Thematic statement is balanced between the two in a pattern far from the tedium of systematic alternation. Quite naturally, the full orchestral forces are used at points of climax and conclusion. In developmental passages, there is interaction at close temporal intervals; textural mobility is thus enhanced simultaneously with accelerated tonal and motivic activity. The development's preoccupation with fresh thematic material is appropriate in view of the dual exposition of earlier materials; it makes possible a fairly complete recapitulation in which the two protagonists exchange functions in ways that complement prior relationships of antecedent and consequent segments. Such reversals of role are themselves means of variation by which redundancies are avoided. Materials associated with transition and conclusion are assigned largely to the tutti, in reminiscence of ritornello procedure. The accompanimental role of the solo often includes ornamental doubling of slower-moving orchestral voices, while that of the orchestra consists commonly of harmonic underpinning; in both circumstances significant motives are exchanged as subjects of dialogue and imitation.

BRAHMS, CONCERTO IN A MINOR
FOR VIOLIN, CELLO, AND ORCHESTRA,
OP. 102, SECOND MOVEMENT

The Brahms movement is a compound ternary. The following account indicates types of *individual and collaborative functions* of the two solos and orchestra, with examples cited. Again, reference to the score is essential.

Some brief prefatory comment might be made with regard to certain highly interesting aspects of structure in the Brahms movement. The thematic melody (solos, mm. 3ff.) is broadly based on the 5th scale degree: its upper and lower auxiliaries (the latter chromatic, G♯) are prominent in the first phrase, while the second (mm. 11–14, the first having been repeated) has as its basis a step descent to the 5th degree (C, B, B♭, A; see Ex. 8.2a).

Phrases throughout undergo extensions in their variant recurrences. For example, see mm. 17–18, 24–26 (involving hemiola by motive repetition in half-note values), 46–50, 52–53, to cite a few examples, all of these subject to comparison with earlier occurrences, and all occasions for vitalizing asymmetries. The means of transitional tonal fluctuation is a further item of particular interest, especially that of retransition to the *A* section's return (mm. 63–79), which is by way of F–f modal change yielding D♭ (= C♯), a basis for enharmonic reintroduction of the primary

Ex. 8.2a Brahms, Concerto in A minor, Op. 102, for violin, cello, and orchestra, second movement (Andante).

leading-tone. Finally, a full accounting of motivic development, references to which are here limited to the discussion of concerto procedures, must be left for independent study; it is especially important in transitional areas, and in the coda (mm. 100ff.).

The movement's primary theme, that enunciated in the A section,[11] is given in condensation as Ex. 8.2a, where repetitions of units and extensions are omitted. The illustration gives the upper-voice melody in its fundamental three phrases, here superimposed for ease of comparison.

Note, in the example, that the second phrase, Ab, ''mirrors'' the first, Aa, in a remarkable compositional resource of unity and contrast; the inversion is a ''tonal'' one, adjusted to express II (preceded by its dominant, through the D♯ in m. 11) and V, with Brahms's characteristic modal alteration of the 6th degree, by which the underlying descent to A is intensified.[12]

Following is a listing of solo and orchestral functions in the form, with examples briefly described.

Thematic projections by the solo(s).   The most striking example is the first part of the movement, in which the solos are joined in intense melodic statement of the entire theme of A, in the rich sonority of octave doubling. Notable is the

[11]With the compound ternary's three major divisions represented as A, B, and A', and with minor divisions within each of these represented as a, b, and a', the following derivative scheme of symbols is utilized here: (Introduction); Aa–Ab–Aa'; Ba–Bb–Ba'; A'a–A'b–A'a'; (Coda). (This does not account for immediate repetitions.)

[12]Another subtlety of variation is the elaboration of the motive of m. 4 at m. 16, where the 1st scale degree (as d¹ and d² in the solos) is introduced, pointing to the tonic cadence which will articulate the first large division in the form. The solos of m. 16 alone are related more immediately as variants on this same motive (Ex. 8.2a).

"heterorhythmic" nature of the doubling at relatively climactic points, m. 16 (Ex. 8.2a) and mm. 26–27. The orchestra is generally accompanimental, but with intermittent participation in melodic statement, noted below. At the return (*A'*, mm. 79–99, extended from 4–4–4–5 to 4–5–4–7), the solos perform comparably, again with surface variation in the doubling at key points (e.g., mm. 95–96).

Solo(s) subordinate, yet having motivic interpolations.   Reference here is to mm. 63–78, the retransition to return of the first ternary (*B* to *A'*). The solos are silent up to a point, but they provide motivic statements (of *B* material; cf. m. 39 and m. 63, etc.), in retrospection, and at the midpoint (m. 71) in anticipation of forthcoming material of *A*.

Solo(s) active with the orchestra, in modified (usually ornamental) doublings.   Section *Bb* is a good point of reference (mm. 39ff.); here, the solos elaborate motives having simpler ("reduced") representations in clarinet and flute. The timbres alternate: solo violin is tied to clarinet, solo cello to flute. Section *Ba'* (mm. 51ff.) is a further example: the solos have ornamental variation of concurrent statements in the woodwinds (Ex. 8.2b). Solo violin thus decorates woodwind statements, while the solo cello functions analogously for the string pizzicato which imitates and extends the motive's final notes. In the coda (mm. 100ff.) comparable technique is in evidence, as in *B*, again with alternation.

Solo(s) developing extracted motives.   There is a brief, retransitional expression of F:V in section *Bb* (see mm. 47ff.); here the solos, joined at the upbeat to m. 48, largely in 6ths, spin off and develop an increasingly fragmented final motive from the solo cello's mm. 45–46 (Ex. 8.2c), within the F:V implication.

Another instance, of many, is at the upbeat to m. 109, from the cello's $e\flat^1$, a reminiscence of the *A* motive, beautifully integrated into the coda in its diminution and augmentation forms (the latter at mm. 112–13, Ex. 8.2d). Moreover, the brief retransitional "cadenza" at mm. 73ff. is an arpeggiation of D:V impelled by and further developing the *A* motive; the analogous occurrence in the last bars (114–15, on I and IV) is a further case.

The orchestra in introductory preparation.   Perhaps the most striking instance occurs in the first 2 measures. As can be seen in Ex. 8.2a, the theme's first 4 notes are a sequence of rising 4ths, beautifully anticipated by horns and woodwinds in mm. 1–2, with characteristic temporal suspension expressed by the fermatas, and with the solos silent. Measure 69 is comparable (in the retransition to *A'*). Here, brass and low strings carry out the same function, introducing the solo's climactic presentation of the motive at m. 71. Note too that the violins and violas share in this function, in a merging of *A* and *B* motives.

Ex. 8.2b

The orchestra in direct thematic statement.   The function of the orchestra is, in section *B, comparable to that of the solos in A*. At mm. 31ff., the winds
(Ex. 8.2e) have primary statements of motivic material, strings minimally suggesting its harmonic basis. At mm. 39ff. the orchestra has a ''reduced'' motivic
doubling noted earlier, its statements increasingly elaborate (mm. 43–47) as they
progress. With *Ba'*, mm. 51ff., winds have the burden of statement as before (Ex.
8.2b).[13]

[13]The middle division of the overall ternary is in F, relative of the tonic minor; hence, tonal relations broadly conceived are an expression of the minor tonic triad, comprising the primary tonic factors D
and A together with the F of the *B* section.

Ex. 8.2c

3
3
and
to
etc.

Ex. 8.2d

m.109
Fl.
Cl.
Bn.
Solo Vln.
Solo Vc.
Vln. I
Vln. II
Vla.
Vc.
Db.
f
dim.
f dim.
dolce
p cresc.
pizz.
p

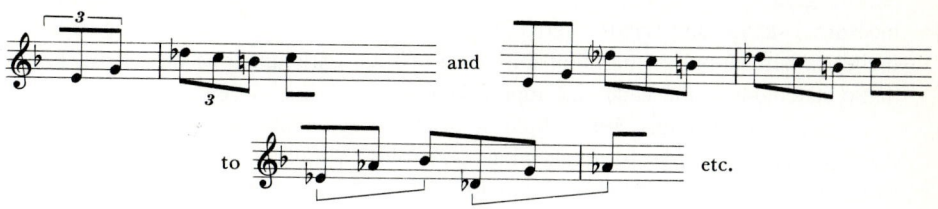

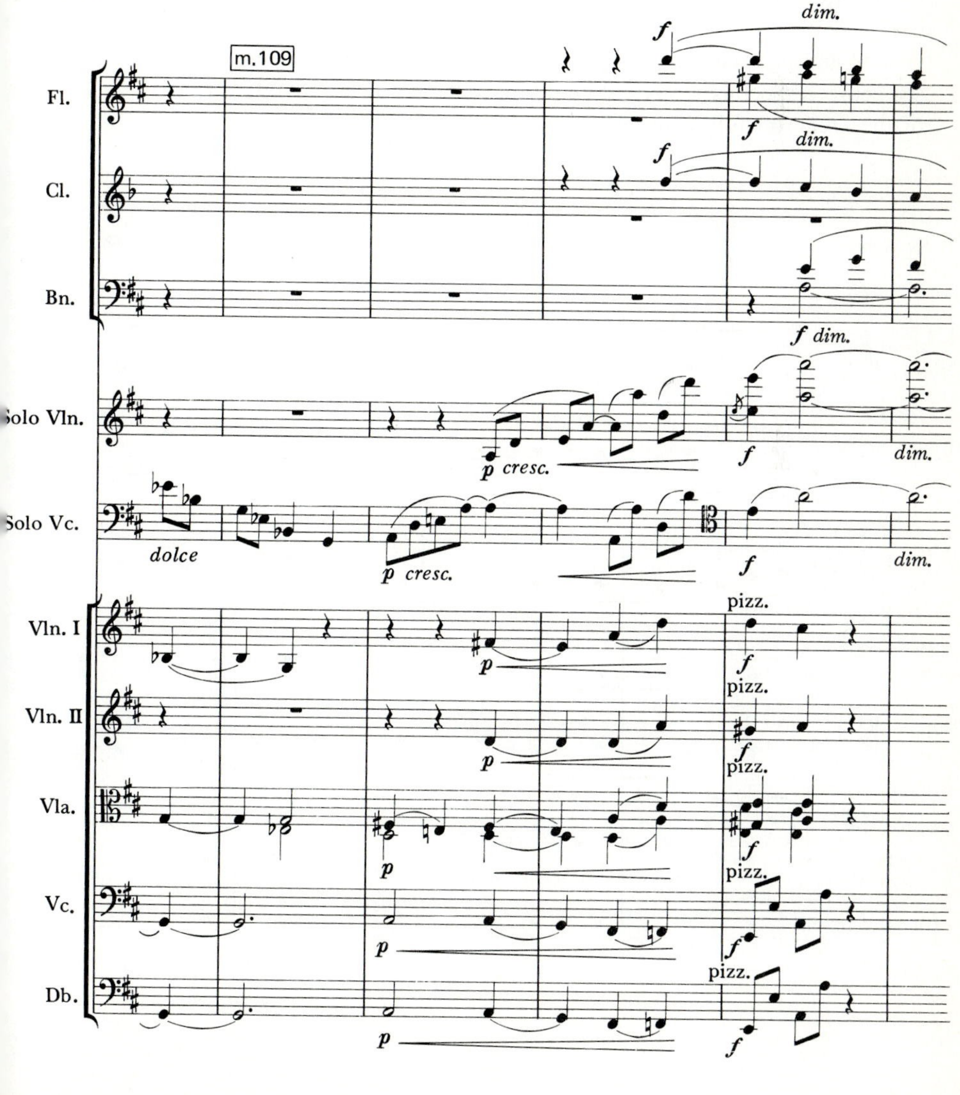

Orchestra in subordinate accompanimental functions.   In *A*, the orchestra greatly enriches the theme melody in intermittent doublings in alternate measures, strings and winds alternating unit by unit. But the essential role of the orchestra here is one of harmonization and textural enrichment of the solos' thematic statement at the cadential approach into m. 30 (Ex. 8.2e).

In section *Bb* (mm. 39ff.), the role of the strings is one of lean harmonic accompaniment of motive forms in winds and solos. Similarly, in *Ba'*, mm. 51ff., string pizzicato chords are subordinate to motivic statements, although the chords, as pointed out, echo the motive's conclusion (Ex. 8.2b). In *A'*, mm. 79ff., orchestration is varied, *motivic forms woven into a basically accompanimental orchestral fabric*. For example, see the elaborating orchestral cello part of m. 89, or the mirroring orchestral violin part of m. 93 (Ex. 8.2f), and like instances. In the coda, as expected, the orchestral function involves much accompaniment and, as at mm. 104–11 and especially at the final cadence, relatively forthright harmonization. (But see below respecting motivic significance in the apparently purely harmonic content of the orchestra following m. 104.)

Ex. 8.2e

Ex. 8.2e (continued)

Orchestral development of motives, and ornamental doublings.   The retransition to *A'*, taken as a whole up to the solo "cadenza" following m. 72, is a development of *B (a,b)* motives molded into chromatic-enharmonic tonal redirection serving also to reintroduce the solos. [There is a compelling progression in sonority here: woodwind solo pairs with strings (pizzicato), to strings (arco) with bassoons, to tutti.]

Ex. 8.2f

Examples have been given (8.2b, d, e, f) of an apparently accompanimental orchestra involving as well motivic elaboration and interjection. Further to this, see first and second violins of, for example, m. 80 as converging in elaboration of the concurrent solo parts, or m. 82 in the same light (Ex. 8.2g). And the woodwinds function in elaboration of the solos' held-back motive in mm. 83–84, by pitch extensions. A further example is the augmentation in low strings at m. 79. All of these are discreetly blended into a fundamentally accompanimental texture.

In the coda, virtually every note in the orchestra, perhaps excepting the final cadential chords, is a factor in motivic reminiscence of some kind, initially of *B* material in the woodwinds, *A* material in the strings. (The strings from m. 104 to m. 110 can be heard as an "elongation" of the *Ba* motive, in imitation of the solos just preceding!)

Orchestra in a subordinate role, yet enhancing and defining form in significant aspects.   Some references pertinent to this aspect of orchestral func-

Ex. 8.2g

tion in the movement have already been given, having to do with motivic variation and development within essentially accompanimental contexts. A further, interesting note might have to do with the "timbral" articulation of form, as for example in A, where form is expressed in distributions of orchestral timbres as well as thematically and tonally (Ex. 8.2h). As is suggested in the diagram, the pattern is at once one of variants in sectional repetitions, and one of "concentric" arrangement around an area of string predominance.

Ex. 8.2h

a:strings   - - a: winds   b:strings   a´:strings   b:winds   a´:strings

Summary.   The movement consists of constant interaction of a number of kinds: statement followed by response or variation, concurrent statements (orchestra having one version, solos another), motivic interpolations (as responses, anticipations, elaborations) interwoven into accompanimental textures, and alternations of function such as those noted in the foregoing examples. Form is expressed here in timbral and sonorous contrasts and recurrences as well as in thematic and tonal events. The distribution of roles is ideally balanced; between solos and orchestra, the issue is of relative predominance and constant, subtle interplay rather than distinct separation.

BARTÓK, CONCERTO NO. 3 FOR PIANO
AND ORCHESTRA, THIRD MOVEMENT

The Bartók example is a five-part rondo, its two digressions both fugal in texture. This study will identify areas of relative primacy of the solo or orchestra, as well as areas of relatively active interchange and of collaboration in tightly codirected functions. An objective is thus *to describe the form in the special terms of the concerto.* Unfortunately, very little of the music can be quoted; reference to the score is therefore imperative in tracing the following analysis.

The idiom is powerfully tonal, the expression of tonality (strongly E-centered) at times overt, even subject to roman numeral analysis of harmony invigorated by dissonances, and at other times in quasi-traditional harmonies interpretable as to tonal function, and at all times manifestly felt in lines, of the surface and underlying the surface.

Some parenthetical reference will be made to tonal structures and implications. For example, the rondo theme characteristically ends with a codetta, yielding to transition except at the movement's end. An instance of this follows m. 54[14] and it is of potent tonal affirmation: a prolongation of I by a diminished-3rd (m. 55), F over D♯, and by opposing lines moving toward the explicit V-I of m. 65, through the upper voice's succession E–F–F♯ (m. 58)–G–B–E, in a tonal course of palpable inevitability. (See Ex. 8.3a.) Comparable motion is then renewed. Over an E pedal, there is a chromatic rise now to B♯ (over E, m. 76), suggestive of V of IV in E and at the same time pointing toward the C♯ basis of the first digression, which enters at m. 91. Comparable tendencies can be studied through the movement; they delineate Bartók's tonal language.

Piano solo in the rondo theme (mm.1–54 and 207–27).   The piano states the theme's 8- and 4-measure units, and its extended concluding unit (following m. 32), in big chords preceded by a 3-measure introductory upbeat flourish. The orchestra's role is one of accompaniment, in elaborations discreetly underscoring

---

[14]Measure numbers here count the first bar of the movement as m. 1; in the published score the second and third movements are numbered consecutively.

the piano's tonal content and animating the theme by rhythmically irregular articulations . It takes over the expository function in small segments (e.g., woodwinds of mm. 20–23, where the piano assumes the role associated with strings in preceding bars), and at times acts in supportive, "slower" doubling of the piano (as in woodwinds at mm. 32–38), at other times in opposing motivic counterpoints (strings at mm. 32ff., or strings and winds of mm. 45ff.). But throughout this early stage, the piano's role of thematic statement is foremost, as it is in the later, abbreviated return of the rondo theme following m. 207, where orchestral texture and sonority are exceedingly transparent against a piano statement in which originally full chords are reduced to octaves and 15ths.

Piano solo in the fugato of the first digression (mm. 91–116, 132–55, 169–84).   The orchestra is silent as the piano launches the fugato[15] with subject and answer (the subject's descending 5th answered by the complementary, traditional 4th). The solo continues with an episode (mm. 107ff.), its two voices tracing tonally explicit step ascents from C♯ to G♯ (mm. 106–16).

A second area of piano predominance in the fugato is that of mm. 132–55: free canon on a subject variant, at the harmonic interval of the 10th and the time interval of 1 bar, to m. 139, a cadential episode leading to the subject entry of mm. 147ff. (here mixolydian on F), and thence to the cadence of m. 155, elided with subject entry in the orchestra.

Measure 169 finds the piano again exposed in free canon on a subject derivative, now inverted, at temporal and harmonic intervals as before, and with subordinate orchestral interjections. This leads to a B pedal (mm. 177–84, corresponding to that of 143ff.), a brief episode of relative coequality of piano and orchestra, with chromatic lines in both directed toward the C♯ and G♯ of the forthcoming subject entry in the orchestra (m. 186).

Orchestral predominances in the first digression fugato (mm. 116–32, 115–69, 185–206, 290–314).   The third and fourth subject entries are assigned to violins and violas, solo and orchestra thus *sharing equally in the fugato exposition*. Here the piano is reduced to chordal accompaniment, but it takes on emergent motivic substance (mirroring the viola's subject) in the final bars of this section, mm. 129–32, in preparation for its approaching canon. At mm. 155–69, the orchestra has its canonic counterpart, on a subject derivative in inversion, winds entering at 2-measure intervals with the piano accompanying.

Later phases of this first digression feature the orchestra again, in its turn. This can be seen at mm. 185–206, in the fugato's final entry and stretto on mirrored subject fragments, at 1- and 2-measure distances in a process of dissolution preparing reentry of the rondo theme. In this phase, the orchestra gathers to a climactic tutti tonally preparing the coming thematic statement (see for example the violin, ascending toward the solo's pitch of entry at m. 207), the piano silent, wait-

---

[15]Fugato and related imitative procedures are discussed in Chapter 12.

ing. In general, in the first digression, solo and orchestra alternate in prominence (of statement) and subordinacy (of accompaniment and interjection).

Orchestral function in the fugato of the second digression (mm. 290–314).   The second digression is a ternary whose second section is another fugato. Here (compare Mozart) is an excellent example of orchestral primacy against the piano's figuration, the latter underscoring in brilliant display essential pitch directions of the orchestra's subject entries. Following exposition of the subject, with answers (m. 298, m. 306) at the 6th, all confined to strings, woodwinds enter in mirror imitation of the third entry, at 1 bar, and through all of this the piano maintains its vigorous accompanimental activity.

An approaching subject entry in the piano, on B, is here prepared in part by a "leaning" C pedal, from m. 306. As a matter of orchestration, it is notable that certain instruments have function analogous to that of the solo—one of lines harmonizing subject entries while doubling their essential notes; orchestral parts having this function (e.g., viola and cello, mm. 306ff.) are, to be sure, lacking in the piano's density of rhythmic activity. The context is in general one clearly comparable to classical technique in which the tutti is concerned with thematic statement while the solo *elaborates and complements that statement* by virtuosically active figuration.

The orchestra's predominance in initial 8-measure units of the rondo theme's final formal statement (mm. 390–405, 452–69).   The theme's final statement (but for a concluding, retrospective reference in the coda) is grandly prepared by the entire ensemble in a passage to be discussed presently; the statement itself (mm. 390ff.), given this preparation, requires big orchestral sonority. Under the upper-voice melody's E, lower voices project C♮and C♯-related elements reminiscent of the tonal orientation of the first fugato, at the same time suggestive of VI and II (see horns, V of II to II) in anticipation of ultimate cadential directions. At this point, and following the orchestra's rendering of the theme's first two 8-measure units, thematic reference continues developmentally (conjoined roles in further statement are discussed later). The orchestra has the theme in a massive tutti, *fortissimo,* at mm. 452ff. (note the V–VI progression by which it is ushered in, mm. 451–52, the VI now on C ♮).

Fusions of directed activity often in cadential and developmental phases.   A final analytical approach has to do with areas of relative *coalescence and unity of function between solo and orchestra.* (The general focus of present discussion is on comparatively mobile areas of transition and development, although reference is also to thematic exposition in the second digression.)

Recurrent codetta-transition material following the rondo theme (mm. 54–90, 227–54).   The two passages referred to here conclude the first two rondo entries (**AB**A**C**A); the third entry yields to extended development and ultimately to an abrupt and extreme change of pace in the coda, earlier codetta material woven into its concluding measures.

The codettas are unequivocally E-centered. Example 8.3a depicts the characteristic essential lines, the solo-orchestra dialogue, and the point of redirection into transitional fluctuation. The recurrences of E constitute an implied pedal which becomes literal in the transitional segment (mm. 66ff.); the piano's terse responses come repeatedly to E; and arrival points in violins and upper woodwinds (mm. 55–58, 60, 61) describe an E-based triad. Measures 227 to 254 are altogether comparable to those given in the example, except that while the latter embody linear progression to A♯ (=B♭) in preparation for a B♭-based digression, the former lead to an upper-voice B♯ (m. 76) in anticipation of the earlier, C♯-based, fugato. In both cases, codetta might be said to be elided with transition: the elisions at m. 66, and at m. 239. Example 8.3a should, again, be studied in relation to the full score; it portrays, in a context of rich *concertato* interaction, an emphatically tonal expression typical of Bartók.

Ex. 8.3a   Bartók, Concerto No. 3 for piano and orchestra, third movement.

Copyright 1947 by BOOSEY & HAWKES, Ltd. Renewed 1974. Used by permission.

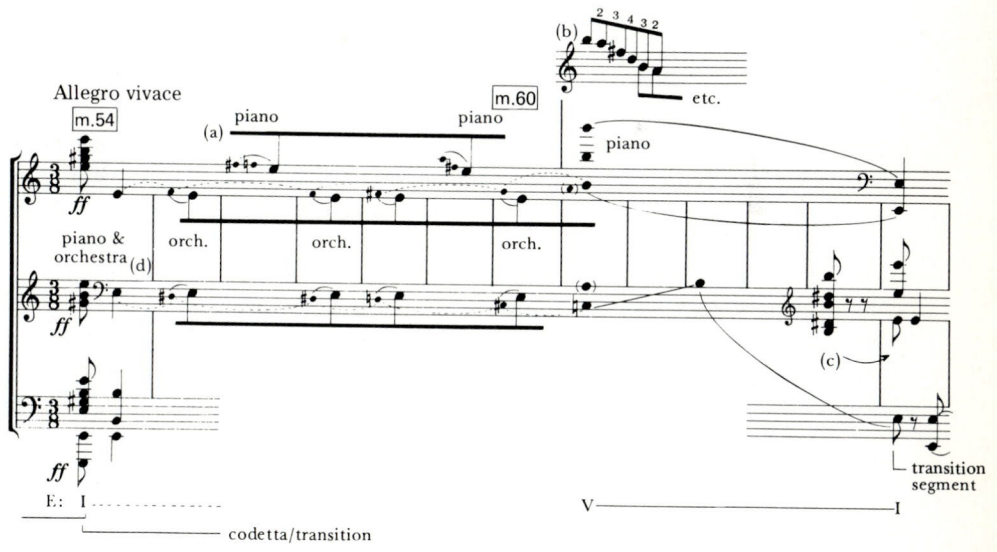

(a)   In the sketched portion, only E is stemmed.

(b)   The descending piano arpeggiation (of E:"V") is a pentatonic formulation, symmetrical in the ordering of intervals, as indicated.

(c)   The arrow denotes dominant-tonic succession.

(d)   Dotted slurs trace the opposed chromatic lines elaborating the motion from E to B.

Motivic content in these rapid exchanges consists of the theme fragment of mm. 4–5, mirrored (e.g., in violin and cello, mm. 54–55). The codetta cadence itself is by solo and orchestra together: swift and emphatic descent in the piano's double-octaves (spanning the distance from b³ to EE), and an explicit V–I succession in the orchestra. In the transition, the piano *becomes in a sense an orchestral instrument,* doubling the timpani, while the orchestra carries out the critical process of tonal change.

Outer segments of the second digression ternary; retransition to the rondo theme (mm. 255–89, 315–90).   The contrasting thematic statement arising at m. 255 is, of all thematic elements in the movement, *most explicitly a duo of solo and orchestra,* with B-flat as tonal center. In the strings occurs a subject to be treated imitatively following m. 265, while the piano has simpler textures becoming imitative. At mm. 284–91, both participants function, complementarily, in chromatic progression to A♭, then G, in transition to the ternary's middle fugato, the piano rising, the woodwinds descending, in basic linear direction.

Piano and orchestra collaborate comparably at the final subject entry of that fugato, mm. 315ff. Here, the piano has an expansive simultaneous statement of two forms in exact mirror relation, underlying chromatic voices ascending (the lower) and descending (the upper) by the characteristic tritonal distance from B to F (dominant of the approaching return in B-flat). The orchestra accompanies, and (in woodwinds) imitates motivic elements of the subject. Interestingly, the prominent interval C–A♯ (=B♭) is tonally suggestive both of the B of the subject entry and the F of its conclusion. The process here is one of statement yielding to retransition; in keeping with the latter function, mm. 322–35 are of relatively fixed harmony in B-flat (I, V), assigned to the orchestra. The return, *a'* of the ternary (mm. 336ff.), has piano and orchestra in deeply conjoined roles as before.

Measure 346 brings the piano to the fore in tight imitation on subject material, as the orchestra describes a tonal course (F♯, G , C) toward the C pedal of mm. 360ff., which, with A♯/B♭, is to point toward the primary tonic (i.e., suggesting E:V). In this further retransitional process, texture undergoes distinct simplification. Even the active piano, at m. 356, is reduced to octave doubling and fragmentary repetitions, with residual imitations in the orchestra (woodwinds of m. 362, violins of m. 366, horns of m. 367).

An intense stir of conjoined activity follows, one that is well characterized as a massive *upbeat to the rondo return* at m. 390. From m.382, strings have a sustained harmony (activated by tremolo and crescendo) which is a chromatic preparation for C♯, G♯, and B, which comprise the forthcoming harmonization of the E-based theme. The whole is a splendid example of calculated orchestration. The piano is *clearly part of the orchestra here,* its upward sweep (of 2-measure, intervallically symmetrical units) best regarded as "doubled" in the woodwinds in modifications of its patterns, all within the encompassing, vigorous impulse of anacrusis. The passage includes explicit tonal preparation for E analogous to the chromatic "leaning" of the strings toward m. 390 (see above); thus, the ascent begins with D♯ in all parts, the last 2 bars, 388–89, featuring F♯ and B in addition to the D♯

leading-tone. *Nowhere in the movement is the ensemble as a whole a more persuasively coalesced unit.*

Developments interrupting and extending the final rondo statement (mm. 406–52, 470–506).   A hundred measures of development intrude upon and enlarge the final statement of the rondo theme, which thus goes beyond perfunctory return. Deviation begins following two 8-measure, regular thematic units, at mm. 406ff.; the insistent C♯ continues while the solo varies the theme in big chords and extreme registral leaps, the chords doubled in string pizzicato. The area following m. 416 is essentially one of texturally activated harmony (and generally slowed harmonic rhythm), the activation by the piano in, again, a ''classical'' convention of surface arpeggiations, with intermittent motivic interjections in solo and orchestra (woodwinds, mm. 416–19; brass and woodwinds, 420–21; piano, 428–29, etc.). Tonally, this development suggests E, but resolution is delayed; the E is a pedal combined with F♯ (in ''B:V''?), D (in a dissonant E:I?), and other destabilizing factors. Against a pedal E and F♯, the piano's lines, at mm. 444ff., articulate a strong approach to B, for the V of m. 451, ushering in further statement in the orchestra.

The orchestra's statement, extended by motivic repetition, is interrupted by the piano for further development at m. 470, in a process comparable to the preceding development, yet more active. Piano and orchestra are fully unified in activity marking inexorable tonal movement toward, yet stopping short of, E, implied in the formulation of m. 504 (D♯ over F), where all activity ceases for a 2-bar hiatus.

Coda and further development and thematic recollection (m. 507–end: presto).   It is of significance that in these final developments, piano and orchestra collaborate in some of the movement's most compelling amalgamations of sonorous forces. The first part of the coda, departing from E:V, is essentially nonthematic, the piano's chords defining a relentless (if now frustrated) tonal course complemented by woodwind punctuations and string figures marking, at intervals, key harmonic factors, in the context of a climactic interruption in cadential drive toward E. (In a sense, m. 504 can be related directly to its ''outcome'' at m. 583, the intervening bars a developmental delaying action in which solo and orchestra join.) Details must again be neglected, but Ex. 8.3b represents a summary of tonal direc-

Ex. 8.3b Tonal expansion in the Bartók coda.

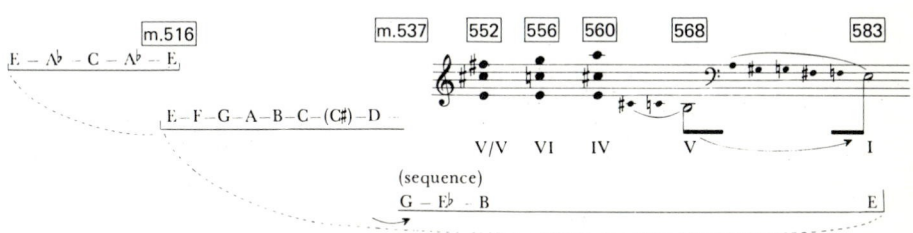

tions in this segment of the coda; their governing logic is patent and obvious. In the diagram, letters represent tonics of passing reference, or at any rate parenthetically tonicized harmonic roots (at 2-, 3-, 4-measure intervals). One of these, C♯, is a marked prominence (mm. 528–31), but not a triadic root. The example portrays in summation a process by which the structure is directed, through foreground elaborations, toward realization at m. 583 of the goal clearly indicated, yet denied, at m. 504, where the coda starts. The whole process is a kind of cadenza in which solo and orchestra participate in an ensemble of emphatic synthesis.

At the final stage, following m. 584, solo and orchestra exchange fragments of the rondo theme, now finally recalled, as in earlier codettas, potently balancing the foregoing, relatively nonthematic episode. Again, but in a more local context, E is approached and withheld: in the orchestra's bass succession (G, F♯−), following m. 596; and in the piano's reiterated double-octave descent to F♯at the same place. The final authentic cadence is, too, a function of both players, articulating the tonally explicit V (mm. 615ff.) and I (m. 623), now elaborated at the surface in foreground V-I articulations, and in the piano's upward chromatic sweep, E to e⁴, over a span of five octaves, woodwinds joining in the final thrust. Bartók's orchestration transparently exposes the piano in this concluding gesture, even while all forces are profoundly integrated in the binding process of ultimate resolution.

Summary.   In the outer segments of the second digression, the solo and orchestra participate coactively in thematic statement. Elsewhere, areas of thematic exposition generally give predominance to one or the other, with the opposite member accompanying, supporting, elaborating, and interjecting. Areas of most active and consistent interchange, and of the deepest fusion of functional participation, are often climactic—associated with intensely directed development, especially in the coda—and cadential.

EXERCISES

The following questions and projects are intended for supplementary study of major works in which issues of the concerto are treated in various ways. Questions raised here can be explored equally or comparably in other examples. The particular methods of discussion and study employed in this chapter are applicable to some of the following, and to many additional works that the reader might identify for study.

1. In the first movement (Allegro assai) of Vivaldi's Concerto in G, Op. 7, Book 2, No. 2 (Fanna 203) for solo violin, strings, and continuo, consider:
   a) variations in the ritornello returns (abbreviation, ordering of motivic material, tonality, etc.);
   b) the E minor ritornello segment yielding to an accompanied solo in extensive development;

    c)   projections of the solo as motivically reflecting the first ritornello statement, and the economy of materials in the movement as a whole;

    d)   areas of predominance of solo or tutti, and roles of the opposite participant;

    e)   areas of relatively nonthematic solo activity, and tonal directions in these;

    f)   the solo of mm. 117ff. as interrupting, yet representing, the ritornello;

    g)   means of achieving cadential emphasis in the final tutti.

2.   Study one or more of Bach's transcriptions for harpsichord (BWV 972–73, and 975–76) of Vivaldi violin concertos, of which one is the G major concerto mentioned above. Identify changes in surface characteristics—textural, registral, or other. What reasons can you adduce for these, and what conclusions regarding their structural and expressive implications?

3.   Bach, Concerto in E for violin, strings, and continuo, BWV 1042; first movement (Allegro).

    a)   Compare this movement with the final one (Allegro assai) as to regularity of alternation and opposition of solo and tutti in the latter, with its explicit ritornello and tonic recurrence.

    b)   Discuss subtleties of solo–tutti interaction in the first movement (e.g., frequency of exchange, solo emergences within tutti segments, ongoing developmental roles and relative predominance as distinct from direct alternation).

    c)   What is the nature of the solo's functions in the middle section in C-sharp minor and G-sharp minor; accompaniment? elaboration? motivic development? imitation? all of these?

    d)   Consider the complex of motivic ideas in mm. 1–11 as to their subsequent development. Argue that virtually every note is traceable to this source, if this seems plausible to you.

    e)   How does the orchestra participate in the major solo segment at mm. 21ff., a development leading to the dominant?

4.   Beethoven, Piano Concerto No. 4 in G, Op. 58, third movement (Vivace; a sonata-rondo).

    a)   Consider how thematic elements are exchanged in variation from the outset, through the "ritornello" tutti of mm. 32ff. and the piano-tutti colloquy of the transition.

    b)   Consider solo and orchestra roles in the digression (B) theme at mm. 80ff.

    c)   What significance in the form would you ascribe to the piano figurations, orchestral chords, and orchestral motivic interjections in mm. 110–59? (Do you find any motivic substance in the piano part here?)

    d)   Compare the original rondo material's realization in the concerto medium with that of its first return.

    e)   In what sense(s) does the development derive from the first transition?

    f)   During much of the development, the solo is preoccupied with brilliant figuration. Where is its content motivic? Measure 248? 287? Elsewhere?

    g)   What is omitted in the piano's statement at mm. 299ff.? Why?

    h)   In the retransition at mm. 347ff., a subordinate, accompanimental orchestral role evolves into one of substance in preparation of thematic statement. Where and how?

    i)   At the varied return of A, mm. 416ff., there occurs a delightful collaboration between solo and orchestra. Describe the role of each participant in the theme's variation.

j) Discuss solo and orchestral roles in developmental phases of the coda following m. 443, including the reason for the piano's relatively subordinate role after m. 471.

5. In the first movement of Beethoven's Fourth Piano Concerto (Allegro moderato), study the roles of piano and orchestra throughout the exposition, considering devices of variation, extension, development, rhythmic contrast and progressive change, tonal structure, pacing of exchange, and other factors which appear to you to be of interest and significance. (Compare the "double exposition" of Mozart's K. 488 first movement.)

6. Again with reference to the first movement of Beethoven's Fourth Piano Concerto, outline a critical-analytical case for the especially convincing integration of solo and orchestra in the overall form.

7. In the third movement (Allegro) of Beethoven's Third Piano Concerto, consider the relationship between solo and orchestra in the developmental elaboration by which the final returns of the sonata-rondo are varied.

8. Refer to the third movement (Allegro) of Beethoven's Violin Concerto. What developmental areas and processes do you find, especially in the coda, and what is the nature of solo and orchestral functions in these? (The middle section of this sonata-rondo consists largely of thematic statement.)

9. The second movement (Allegro appassionato) of Brahms's Piano Concerto No. 2 is a rare occurrence of scherzo and trio in the concerto literature. Discuss solo and orchestral roles in the scherzo's varied return.

10. Compare functions of the solo in the ternary slow movements of Brahms's two piano concertos.

11. What kind of rondo is the fourth movement (Capriccio) of Stravinsky's Concerto in D for violin and orchestra? Compare the theme returns, and the roles of solo and orchestra in these.

12. Paul Henry Lang refers to the *Konzertstück* for piano and orchestra, Op. 79, by Carl Maria von Weber (1786–1826), as a programmatic work in a tradition of one-movement concertos in an "operatic vein." [16] Study the work's form in this light.

13. Discuss cyclic, single-movement form in the Piano Concerto No. 1 in E-flat by Franz Liszt (1811–86), considering functions and interactions of solo and orchestra.

14. How successfully, in your view, could the first movement (Allegro affettuoso) of Schumann's Piano Concerto stand alone as a "complete" piece, as the composer originally intended? Do you feel that further, significant scope is brought to the solo part in its relations to the orchestra in the added movements? If so, how?

15. Compare the realization of single-movement sonata form in the first movement of one of the following Mozart piano concertos with that of K. 488: K. 466, in D minor; K. 491, in C minor; or K. 467, in C major.

16. Study the evolving role of the piano in the second movement (Adagio religioso) of Bartók's Piano Concerto No. 3; the movement is a ternary with variation.

17. Certain Bach solo keyboard pieces are at times described as of "concerto"

---

[16]Lang, *The Concerto (1800–1900)*, p. xvi.

style. How might such a characteristic pertain, for example, to the Prelude of the *English Suite* No. 3 in G minor? What implications would you see for performance?

18. Study Bach's Concerto in C for two harpsichords and string orchestra as to a "profile" of predominance and subordinacy of the orchestra, comparing the three movements in this light.

19. Review a number of Handel's organ concertos, noting the mixtures of sonata and dance movements, and the varying kinds and degrees of solo exposure (as in this chapter's summary of his Concerti Grossi of Op. 6).

20. Consider the cadenza in the first movement (Allegro molto appassionato) of Mendelssohn's Concerto, Op. 64, in E minor, for violin and orchestra, as to its function and place in the form.

21. Describe the imitative interactions between solo and orchestra in Bartók's (1938) Violin Concerto, first movement (Allegro non troppo).

9

OSTINATO FORMS

The Italian word *ostinato* means precisely the same as its English cognate, *obstinate*. And it is in the ostinato forms of music that the principle of repetition is applied in its most direct and uncompromising manner. The technique of ostinato repetition, while a primitive and obvious means of extending music in time, is nevertheless capable of a high degree of intensity and expressiveness when endowed with subtle control and imaginative means of variety. Ostinato technique is the basis for some of the finest compositions in our musical heritage, as examples cited in the present chapter will show.

The origins and interrelationships of specific ostinato forms (chiefly *chaconne* and *passacaglia,* defined on pp. 271-74) are not well understood, and troubling confusion persists despite considerable research and analysis. The device of ostinato repetition can be traced at least to the thirteenth century, as in the *pes*[1] of the famous "Sumer is icumen in," but commentators differ widely as to the evolution of the passacaglia and chaconne and the meanings of terms used in reference to them. Robert Nelson's *The Technique of Variation*[2] is an excellent account of the confusion that prevails concerning the nomenclature and history of forms built on the ostinato principle, and a remarkably thorough and perceptive discussion of many examples of those forms.

Antecedent dance types called "passacaglia" and "chaconne," from sixteenth- and seventeenth-century Spain (and possibly from more distant Mexican sources), do not embody the principle of ostinato repetition itself, rather imparting

---

[1]Literally "foot" in Latin, the word *pes* denotes the repeated bass motive, or ostinato, of the cited example.

[2]Robert U. Nelson, *The Technique of Variation* (Berkeley: University of California Press, 1948).

certain qualities of mode (minor), meter (triple), and tempo (slow) to many, not all, specimens of the later forms. That such qualities do not apply universally to the ostinato forms of tonal music is evident in, for example, the finale of Brahms's *Variations on a Theme of Haydn*, which is a passacaglia in major mode and duple meter. (See p. 272.)

The use of an introduction is not widely observed in ostinato forms, probably because the vast majority of examples begin with a straightforward, often monophonic statement of the ostinato theme—such a statement being itself an introductory gesture. Similarly, the coda is relatively uncommon in ostinato forms. While codettalike elaborations and the emphatic broadening of final cadences may be expected, the rigidity of the ostinato technique does not seem to permit an even modestly discursive closing section. Ostinato forms are by definition essentially expository and repetitive, and thus provide little occasion for concluding peroration. (The coda extending the final variation of Beethoven's *Thirty-two Variations in C minor* is an exception.) A separate concluding form, such as a fugue, is, however, sometimes appended to the ostinato series.

Possibly because of the attenuation of tonality in contemporary music, and the resultant deepened significance of unifying repetitions, at least for many composers, ostinato procedures are extremely important in music of the twentieth century, especially in extended works. This is often (as in Bartók and Stravinsky) to be seen in incidental applications of ostinato technique, as well as in formalized passacaglia and chaconne types adhering to traditional models.

CHARACTERISTICS OF THE OSTINATO

When it is the basis for an extended form, the ostinato is a theme of at least a complete phrase, usually of from 4 to 8 measures. It is often in triple meter.

Ex. 9.1   Hindemith, String Quartet No. 4, Op. 32, final movement.
      © 1924 B. Schott's Soehne/Mainz, Germany. Renewed 1952. Used by permission.

Useful distinction may be made between an "ostinato motive," an "ostinato phrase," and an "ostinato period." The ostinato motive occurs in some sixteenth- and seventeenth-century examples of ostinato form (Ex. 9.9), and in movements in other forms which nevertheless contain ostinato passages. Example 9.2 shows a three-voice ostinato motive of such limited application. Unlike the type quoted as Ex. 9.1, the incidental ostinato is not primarily associated with the bass voice.

Example 9.3 is an ostinato period, while Ex. 9.4 shows an ostinato phrase. In the slow Bach theme, the descending portion seems clearly consequent to the

Ex. 9.2   Bartók, String Quartet No. 3, first part.

Ex. 9.3   Bach, Passacaglia in C minor for organ.

Ex. 9.4   Monteverdi, L'incoronazione di Poppea, aria, "Ma che dico, o Poppea"

initiating 4-measure phrase built around g, despite the pervasive unity of the whole as a melodic expression of the C minor triad.

The ostinato is often simple in structure and comparatively neutral in expressive character—a foil for developments in other voices. On the other hand, certain melodic configurations of ostinati, frequent in the seventeenth and early eighteenth centuries, are associated with particular expressive qualities. Chromatic descent is an example of such affective, idiomatic usage: see Ex. 9.5, and the celebrated lament of Dido from Purcell's *Dido and Aeneas,* Ex. 9.18.[3]

---

[3]For discussion of the common melodic structures of the early ostinato, the reader is again referred to Nelson's *The Technique of Variation,* Chapter 3.

Ex. 9.5 Bach, Crucifixus from the Mass in B minor

The ostinato theme often ends on a nontonic harmony—particularly on the dominant, as in Ex. 9.5. In passacaglia and chaconne forms the theme is repeated in direct contiguity, usually without interruption, at the same tonal level. The melodic ostinato is generally found in the bass voice, but the pitch level may change while the tonality remains constant, and registral movement of the ostinato is a valuable source of change.

If a "passacaglia" treats the theme imitatively and at changing tonal levels, it may be closer to fugue than to true ostinato form, despite its title. (See the first movement of William Schuman's Symphony No. 3, where the "ostinato" is presented one half-tone higher with each appearance, moving freely from voice to voice.)

FURTHER EXAMPLES OF OSTINATO THEMES

Example 9.6 is from one of the organ chaconnes of Dietrich Buxtehude (1637–1707). It appears at the outset of the piece in a contrapuntal setting. The bass melody embraces the span between tonic notes an octave apart. Its second statement has a nearly identical setting, the first true variation coming with the third. It is of interest that the dotted rhythms which mark the third statement are introduced *at* the cadence, before that statement actually begins.

Ex. 9.6 Buxtehude, Chaconne in E minor.

Example 9.7 is built on an 8-measure harmonic theme with a descending chromatic succession in the bass yielding two chromatic harmonies: the V_7 of IV in m. 3, and the German 6th chord in m. 5. The theme is a single phrase, marked by a steady rise of the top voice in forceful contrast to the descending movement of the bass. The contrary motion is underscored by the *sforzando* at its conclusion. After this, the intensity is abruptly dispelled at the authentic cadence.

Ex. 9.7 Beethoven, Thirty-two Variations in C minor, WoO 80.

Example 9.8 shows a complex, chromatic ostinato theme from the late romantic period. It is like the two preceding examples in mode and meter and, like the Beethoven, it is 8 measures in length; unlike either, it concludes on dominant harmony.

Ex. 9.8   Reger, Introduction, Passacaglia, and Fugue for two pianos, Op. 96.

THE GROUND

Like so many words used in the description of music, the term *ground* is widely current and yet lacking in precision of meaning. It may refer to an ostinato motive, phrase, or period, to the resultant ostinato form, or specifically to ostinato form in English music of the sixteenth and seventeenth centuries, music which is based on the reiteration of a *ground bass* (regarded, in this sense, as synonymous with bass ostinato).[4] The ground bass is often an exceedingly simple pattern; Ex. 9.9, from the first volume of *HAM*, is a very early specimen. A ground of this type (here a

Ex. 9.9   Anon., My Lady Carey's Dompe (c. 1525).

Reprinted by permission of the publishers from Archibald T. Davison and Willi Apel, *Historical Anthology of Music: Oriental, Medieval, and Renaissance Music* (Cambridge, Mass.: Harvard University Press, copyright 1946, 1949, by the President and Fellows of Harvard College, © renewed 1974 by Alice D. Humez and Willi Apel).

[4]"Basso ostinato variations from this period [seventeenth, eighteenth centuries] appear under five chief names: ground, folia, bergamask, passacaglia, and chaconne. Although it is customary to speak of each type as having distinct characteristics, there is considerable overlapping among them. Such ambiguity is especially apparent in the passacaglia and chaconne, whose interconnection is historically very close. It can also be seen in the name *ground,* which is sometimes used generically to include all basso ostinato variations, sometimes to refer to a specific English variation type, sometimes to denote the bass subject itself; when *ground* is used to denote the bass subject itself the word is synonymous with *ground bass,* or *basso ostinato.* All five species, except the English ground, may be traced back to prototypes in dance music. The exact relation between dances and variations is in all species obscure; the most definite connection exists in the folia and bergamask, both of which are constructed upon the basses of the original dances, and sometimes upon the melodies as well.

"The ground, using the name in its more restricted sense to mean a definite English variation type, dates from the sixteenth century." From Nelson, *The Technique of Variation,* p. 66.

reiteration of tonic and dominant notes) is rather like a "drone" bass (see, for example, the Musette in Bach's *English Suite* No. 3).

Example 9.10 consists of two excerpts from "A Ground" by Thomas Tomkins (1572–1656), one of the English composers represented in the *Fitzwilliam*

Ex. 9.10   Tomkins, A Ground.

Later:

Virginal Book (c. 1620). The two quotations show wide disparity in harmonization of the ostinato,

The second passage employs canon on the ostinato melody between the two upper voices. In this work, the ostinato appears in the upper voices a good part of the time.

The literature of the English ground provides some of the most memorable examples of ostinato form, especially in the works of Henry Purcell. Purcell's grounds are often well-developed phrases; Ex. 9.11 shows an unusually vigorous and disjunct ground, its structure comprising an initial ("upbeat") thrust toward c^1, thence an underlying step descent to c. Purcell's skill in maintaining continuity over the seams between ostinato repetitions is unsurpassed in any period (see Ex. 9.18).

Ex. 9.11   Purcell, Ground for harpsichord, from Ye Tuneful Muses.

THE PASSACAGLIA

The *passacaglia*, the most important of the ostinato forms, consists of a continuously reiterated bass ostinato, the setting for which is varied with each appearance. The ostinato, typically a phrase, usually appears in the bass voice without accompaniment at the beginning of the passacaglia, or with only a meager setting, after which the repetitions of the ostinato follow in direct succession with changing accompanying parts.

Possibilities for contrast lie, of course, mainly in the other voices; such contrast is vital in view of the relentlessness of the repetition. Example 9.12 shows varied repetitions of a small segment of the ostinato of a passacaglia by Ernest Bloch. The quotations illustrate changes in the ostinato itself as well as in the con-

Ex. 9.12 Bloch, String Quartet No. 2.

trapuntal fabric. The former appears in an upper voice, at m.10, and is embellished in the bass at m. 18.

In view of the large number of statements of an ostinato theme, the ways in which motion is maintained over the repetitions are significant. As in so many facets of musical structure, a paradox is evident here: the static quality of iteration opposed to animating factors of continuity. The following is a listing of a number of means by which marked segmentation is avoided.

1.   The ostinato itself may, in tonal works, end on the dominant, with the implicit motion of unresolved harmony directing the attention to the next ostinato statement (Ex. 9.5).
2.   In an ostinato which ends on the tonic, the final harmony may be avoided or upset by the use of dissonance (Ex. 9.18d).
3.   Rhythmic motion is usually continued at the ostinato cadence. In Ex. 9.13, the use of suspensions and other devices of rhythmic impetus sustains the forward thrust. Such impulsive techniques as stretto and syncopation may also be used.

Ex. 9.13   Brahms, Variations on a Theme of Haydn, Op. 56a, finale.

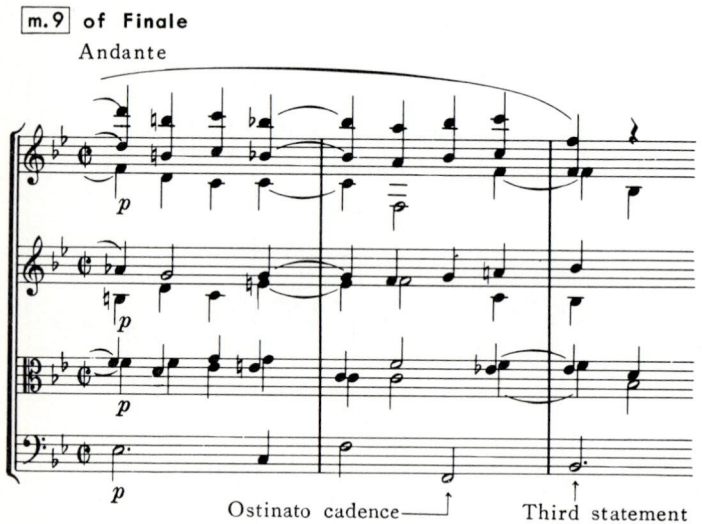

4.   Several contiguous statements may be accompanied by corresponding material. This technique of relating adjacent segments motivically tends to establish division into units larger than those defined by the individual ostinato repetitions themselves. This technique can be seen in almost any passacaglia or chaconne.
5.   A sense of large-scale progress and contour of motion may be established by the use of gradually faster rhythmic values throughout the course of the form or any major part of it, or by the broad shaping of such comprehensive lines of action within any element (such as textural accrual and reduction). For illustration of points 4 and 5, the finale of Brahms's *Haydn Variations* is an excellent example for study.

6.   A variation may begin simultaneously with or earlier than the cadence of that preceding, creating an elision joining two adjacent statements of the ostinato. (See Ex. 9.16.)

The tempo, meter, and mode of the passacaglia often correspond to the dance from which it is thought to be derived; however, as already demonstrated, there is nothing to preclude the occurrence of moderate or animated tempo, duple meter, and major mode in the passacaglia, especially that of later styles. The harmonic rhythm, traditionally, is relatively slow; the texture is often at least partly imitative (Ex. 9.14).

Ex. 9.14   Bach, Passacaglia in C minor for organ.

Fourth statement

Contrapuntal imitation

THE CHACONNE

The chaconne corresponds closely to the passacaglia in form and technique. Indeed, composers have applied the terms indiscriminately, and writers differ concerning the possibility and nature of distinguishing criteria.[5]

    The one distinction which is useful and significant—one worth establishing for terminological clarity despite persistent confusion in the literature of and concerning ostinato forms—defines the chaconne as based upon a multi-voiced *harmonic* ostinato, as distinguished from the *melodic,* single-voiced ostinato of the passacaglia, the latter normally without harmonization in its first entry. Since this is a major distinction with important ramifications for the resultant variations, there is justification for differentiating the two terms. Example 9.15, like Exx. 9.6 and 9.7, shows a chaconne ostinato theme at its first appearance.

    Because it is the harmonic structure which gives essential identity to the chaconne ostinato, harmonic change is less likely to be a substantial resource of varia-

---

[5]Coeuroy even attempts a very dubious distinction on the basis of tonality: "It (chaconne) differs from the passacaglia in that it maintains a single tonality, while the passacaglia involves modulations." From *La Musique et ses formes,* p. 52. The above translated by the author.

Ex. 9.15 Brahms, Symphony No. 4, fourth movement.

tion in this form.[6] However, surface modifications of the preceding theme are evident in Ex. 9.16 (see particularly the ostinato's 4th and 5th measures).

Continuity of motion at cadence points is as important in the chaconne as in the passacaglia, and similar means are used to counteract the partitioning effect of ostinato iteration.

Ex. 9.16 Brahms, Symphony No. 4, fourth movement.

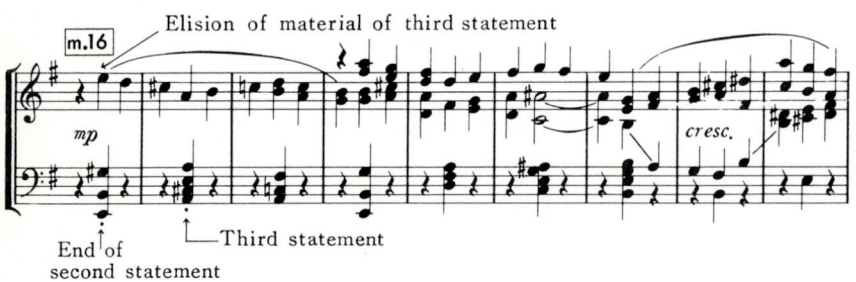

In both forms, the final statements may be made more emphatic and conclusive by dynamic, rhythmic, and other means. In Ex. 9.17, from a twentieth-century passacaglia, intensity is developed by *progressive changes of rhythm and tempo over the course of the movement*. Cadential amplification, whether by durational extension, sonorous expansion, or other devices, is common; some examples include codettas, or other concluding appendages—even complete, distinct forms such as the fugue which ends the following example.

[6]As can be seen in the Brahms, the essential harmonic nature and basis of the chaconne ostinato do not preclude independent, distinctive recurrence of one of its voices as a significant melodic entity. Note that the top voice is maintained intact in the variation, two octaves below its original appearance. (The Brahms theme may be compared with that of the Beethoven Variations cited as Ex. 9.7.)

RIEGGER, SYMPHONY NO. 3, FINAL MOVEMENT

The passacaglia from the Third Symphony of Wallingford Riegger (1885–1961) moves with increasing urgency and carefully spaced changes of tempo, meter, and surface rhythm toward a contrasting final fugue. As it progresses, the passacaglia develops also in textural richness and complexity. The form begins with the 5-measure ostinato given in Ex. 9.17a; the second appearance is marked by the addition of a syncopated upper voice.

Ex. 9.17a   Riegger, Symphony No. 3, final movement.
            © 1957 by Associated Music Publishers, Inc., New York. Used by permission.

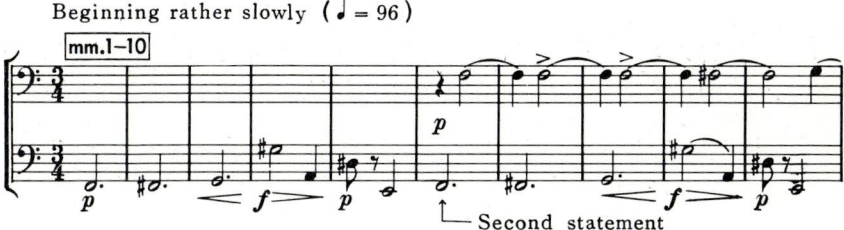

At m. 56, the texture has developed further (Ex. 9.17b), and each motivic articulation is impelled by crescendo, continued syncopations, shortened rhythmic values, and strategic doubling of the ostinato in 8th-notes (bottom staff of the quotation) as aspects of a broad tendency of progressive action.

Ex. 9.17b

At m. 91, the tempo changes to allegro, and the ostinato is broken into very short, impulsive motives articulated at a quickened pace of dynamic contrast. The absence of upper-voice activity compensates for the increase in tempo.

Ex. 9.17c

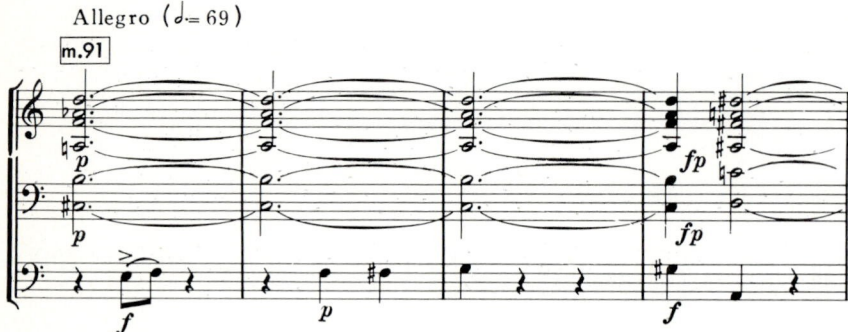

A variation in meter is introduced at m. 109, in a context of rhythmic urgency but reduced dynamic intensity.

Ex. 9.17d

The subject of the fugue which concludes the passacaglia (and thus the Symphony) is derived from the ordered set of notes on which the bass ostinato was built. (See Ex. 9.17e.)

OSTINATO FORMS AS VARIATION SETS

The term *variation* has been used a number of times in the foregoing discussion of the ostinato forms. Its appropriateness is evident, since the ostinato technique is that of taking a given thematic entity and repeating it with alterations in certain of its

Ex. 9.17e

elements—textural setting, rhythm, mode, and others. The principle of a variation series on a given theme is thus explicit in the passacaglia and chaconne, and it is important to recognize the ostinato forms as variation series.

Moreover, we should recognize a characteristic of the ostinato variation forms which sets them apart from the vast majority of variation sets of other kinds. This is their *continuous* structure, in which there are likely to be no breaks between statements of the theme. Chapter 10 deals with types of variation sets in which there is more often deliberate interruption at the end of each variation. These are described as *sectional* variations.

In tonal music of the periods in which ostinato forms occur there is a necessary interdependence between bass line and harmony. Thus, in the passacaglia as in the chaconne, the harmony to which the ostinato is set is *relatively* fixed, restricted in its variational possibilities. On the other hand, in the freer tonal structures of the twentieth century, harmony is increasingly a subject of variation.

PURCELL, LAMENT OF DIDO
FROM DIDO AND AENEAS

A justly famed passacaglia, universally cited and quoted, is the lament of Dido from Purcell's opera *Dido and Aeneas,* one of the most masterly and affecting examples in the literature. Its bass ostinato, or ground, is an intense chromatic phrase of 5 measures, in triple meter and slow tempo, descending from tonic to tonic. The first phrase of the voice part overlaps the end of the ostinato.

At the next ostinato cadence, the voice part is forcefully drawn into the subse-

Ex. 9.18a Purcell, Dido's Lament from Dido and Aeneas.

quent statement by demands of the text, whose verb "create" must be joined to the object which follows ("no trouble") (Ex. 9.18b). Further, a VI$_6$ is substituted for the usual I at the beginning of the bass theme.

Ex. 9.18b

We see here, as in the illustrations that follow, that the piece's form and its subtleties of continuity are powerfully conditioned by the text. After a repetition of the opening music and text, the voice again enters at the point of the ostinato cadence ("Remember me . . . ''), moving through the cadence and establishing a link with the following statement (Ex. 9.18c). The cadence is attenuated by the rhythmic motion of the voice part, and by the voice's entry on the 5th scale degree.

The suspension seen in Ex. 9.18c at the beginning of the emerging ostinato statement is one of a series contributing to an approaching peak of intensity. The next ostinato cadence finds the tonic harmony dispersed immediately (Ex. 9.18d),

Ex. 9.18c

Ex. 9.18d

weakening the cadential effect and supporting the voice part in its rise to the climactic g². Again, there is overlap between the solo part and the ostinato phrase.

The solo part coincides cadentially with the bass only at its final cadence. Following this, the ostinato has two further appearances (one is shown in Ex. 9.18e),

Ex. 9.18e

Ex. 9.18e *(continued)*

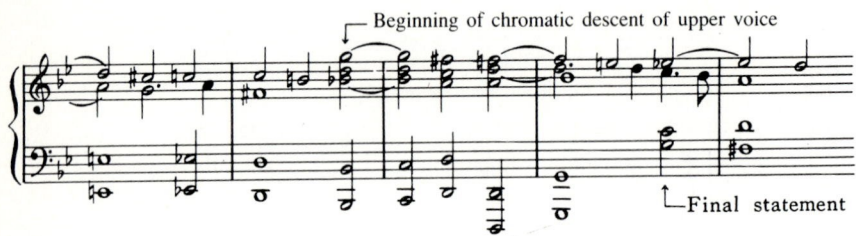

making a total of nine. In the final variations, a great deal of chromaticism and nonharmonic embellishment are used. The final chromatic descent of the top part, a reminiscence of the ostinato melody in a contrasting rhythm, starts *before* the end of the penultimate ostinato phrase. The pull of its descent, often enforced by dissonance in its relationship to the bass, has the effect again of partially concealing the cadence through which it passes.

EXERCISES

1. Prepare an analysis of the second movement of the Stravinsky Septet (1953).
   a) How many recurrences of the ostinato are there?
   b) Is the succession of ostinato statements interrupted at any point?
   c) How is the ostinato itself varied? Compare the rhythmic placement of notes in its first and final statements.
   d) Discuss the overall form as to the broad lines of rhythmic activity.
   e) What correlation do you see between faster motion and simpler texture? Which sections are more contrapuntal? Compare the textures of the first and last statements.
   f) Exceptionally, Stravinsky emphasizes the breaks between ostinato appearances. Where is this not true? Explain. What compensating factors of continuity do you see?
   g) What factors contribute to the sense of finality in the last several measures?
   h) How does the movement seem to center on A?
2. On the basis of research in sources available to you, write a short paper dealing with the historical origins of forms based on the ostinato principle.
3. Compose an ostinato theme—harmonic or melodic—and at least one or two varied restatements.
4. Among works cited in this chapter, or in others, find additional examples of the following:
   a) A device for bridging the cadence ending an ostinato statement.
   b) A 4-measure ostinato.
   c) An ostinato of an odd number of measures.
   d) Use of contrapuntal imitation in an ostinato variation.
   e) Significant variation in harmony.

5. Which of the following, performed in moderate tempo, do you feel might serve best as a passacaglia theme? Why? What advantages or problems would you foresee in each one?

6. Look over some of the works mentioned in this chapter or select some analysis projects from the following list. Is the work an example of incidental use of ostinato or is a full ostinato form developed? If the latter is true, to which type does the example most closely conform? What are the means by which motion is maintained to counteract the static implication of ostinato? Does there appear to be a long-lined, controlled development within some element in the overall plan? By what techniques are the ostinato statements varied?

John Blow (1649–1708), *Venus and Adonis,* finale of Act II

Chopin, *Berceuse* for piano

Franck, Chorale No. 2 in B minor for organ

Handel, *Susanna,* opening chorus

Arthur Honegger (1892–1955), Symphony No. 2, second movement

Jean-Baptiste Lully (1632–87), *Amadis,* final chorus

Ravel, Trio in A minor for piano, violin and cello, third movement

Max Reger (1873–1916), Introduction and Passacaglia in D minor, Op. 145, for organ

Schoenberg, *Pierrot Lunaire,* No. 8, "Nacht"

Stravinsky, *Histoire du Soldat* (To which sections does the present study apply?)

Webern, Passacaglia for orchestra, Op. 1

7. Find in one or more of the following sources examples of ostinato technique and ostinato form.

a) *Historical Anthology of Music,* Vol. II

b) Couperin, *Pièces de Clavecin*

c) Bach, Sonatas and Partitas for solo violin

d) Handel, Suites for harpsichord

8. Find a Handel chaconne for harpsichord in which there are 62 variations on the theme. What is the extent of harmonic invariance in these variations?

9. Look up the passacaglia in Act I of the opera *Wozzeck,* by Alban Berg. List the devices by which the composer modifies the ostinato theme in its several appearances.

10

VARIATIONS

Variation styles in major historical periods are significantly identifiable as to (1) particular techniques of thematic transformation, and (2) the relative degrees of variance and invariance of specific theme elements. For example, adherence to one key throughout the typical variation set before the late nineteenth century would be such a determinant of stylistic classification. Further examples would be the usual changes of tempo and mode in the classical variation; variability of form in many works of, roughly, the past century; the embellishment of theme melody by surface decorations in the melodically-harmonically-fixed variations of the classical and early romantic periods; and other specific devices. Such broad observations are useful in any commentary concerning variation procedures in particular styles, allowing of course that no generalizations of variation technique can apply inflexibly in any given corpus of music, nor even throughout any particular example of theme with variations. Examples will be cited in this chapter which are in certain respects exceptional with regard to stylistic terms of reference.

A variation and the theme from which it derives are certain to share at least one common element. A starting point in the analysis of form in a variation set is therefore the identification of those theme elements which are constant, strictly or in elaboration, in each variation of the series. Such an investigation presupposes a thorough familiarity with the structure of the theme—its form, melody, motivic content, harmony, and all other distinguishing, variable elements.

The techniques of variation are, of course, of enormous significance in virtually all music and all forms. The list of musical genres in which variation plays a part is inexhaustible; the following examples are only a reminder of the universality of variation in music. (See too Ex. 5.27, as one of many pertinent illustrations.)

1. In the mass of the fifteenth and sixteenth centuries, a given plainsong melody is often the basis for all movements, with that melody appearing in varied form in each. This can be studied, for example, in masses and magnificats of Giovanni da Palestrina (1525–94). The technique often involves retention of melodic interval succession with modification of metric structure according to inflections of the text.

2. Variation techniques are basic to the variation suite (Chapter 11).

3. Occasionally movements in the baroque suite are paired, one a variation (Fr., *double*) of the other. An example is found in the first of Bach's *English Suites,* which includes two courantes, the second having two *doubles*—repetitions in variation.

4. Commonly in the chorale prelude (Chapter 12), a given phrase is repeated with modified setting. Thus, as a single example among multitudes, the first chorale phrase in Bach's organ prelude on "Allein Gott in der Höh' sei Ehr'" (*Clavierübung,* Part III, No. 8), appearing initially at m. 13, is repeated at m. 46 in an inverted contrapuntal setting.

5. A multimovement work comprised of a number of quasi-independent, self-contained forms is, when based on a common theme, in a sense a set of variations on that theme; Bach's *Art of the Fugue* is an example.

6. A strophic song in which the strophes, while nearly identical, are slightly varied, is a further case of the use of variation. An example is the change of mode in the second stanza of Schubert's "Der Wegweiser" from *Die Winterreise;* another is seen in the introductions to the andante stanzas of Papageno's song in Act II of Mozart's *Die Zauberflöte.*

7. An orchestral work often involves a modified doubling of an instrumental part, another example of the incidental use of variation. (See Chapter 8, pp. 246-54, where this technique is evident at a number of points in the discussion of the slow movement of Brahms's Double Concerto. Modified doubling—the performance of an ornamental version of a theme against the simple theme—is common in the relation of solo to orchestra in the concerto.)

8. In the *da capo* aria and other *da capo* forms (Chapter 4), the return of the first part is often modified. (Extemporized ornamentation of the *da capo* by the singer was practiced in, for example, baroque opera.)

9. Indeed, any form in which repetition occurs—especially those, like rondo forms, in which numerous restatements of a theme take place—is likely to employ variation techniques. An excellent illustration of this principle, to supplement those cited in other chapters, is the third movement of Beethoven's String Quartet in A minor, Op. 132; this movement is a five-part rondo with variations of the rondo and digression themes: *ABA'B'A''* coda.

The variation series, in which several forms of the same basic idea are presented in succession, is, of course, an ideal solution to the requirements for unity and variety, provided that the elements of contrast are balanced. (Constant and extreme tempo change among variations would produce distractingly poor distribution in tempo structure, for instance. Another would be the clustering of slow and fast statements, or the regular, predictable alternation between slow and fast.)

Historically, the variation principle is prevalent to the point of universality, and especially so in music in which tonal fluctuation as a source of contrast is not widely exploited—for example, that of the sixteenth and seventeenth centuries. And variation on a theme is current in much music of today, including that in which tonality is negated or obscured. The concept and practice of variation form is more than four centuries old—a longer uninterrupted history than that of any other large instrumental form. While even earlier examples are extant, the real development of variation form begins in the early sixteenth century, especially in the lute and keyboard music of Spain and England, respectively. Early Spanish variations are called *diferencias.* Many examples of early English variation sets have come to us in the *Fitzwilliam Virginal Book,* mentioned in the preceding chapter. Some of the examples included in this chapter are drawn from early and recent literatures.

In summary, not only is the systematic form of theme with variations the oldest of all formal procedures in the history of instrumental music, but the principle of variation is the most universal solution to the fundamental requirement for unity and variety. Themes with variations are basic in other arts as well—for example, in dance choreography.

In no area of music theory is confusion of terminology more persistent and widespread. For example, the term "melodic variation" can mean variation in which the melody of the theme is retained in its original form, in which it is retained with embellishment, or in which it is abandoned. A variation which retains the theme's harmony, form, and melody, with the latter ornamented, is called "ornamenting variation," "ornamental variation," "embellishing variation," "decorative variation," "melodico-harmonic variation," "figural variation," and "melodic variation"—a partial list of applicable terms.

The following discussion establishes a terminology designating those *basic* elements of the theme—*form, melody,* and *harmony*—which, in variation, remain fixed. An example of such a term is "melodically-harmonically-fixed variation." Since traditional variations, with few exceptions, involve its uniformity from theme to variations, retention of *form* is specified in terminology only when it is the sole element among the three determinants remaining fixed. The more recent variation in which form is quite commonly modified is called "free variation."

A theme with variations may be one of the movements of a multimovement work (Beethoven, Piano Sonata in A-flat, Op. 26), or the variation set may constitute an entire, independent composition. The frequent reference to music of Beethoven and Brahms in the following pages indicates the importance of these masters in the history of variation forms, and the vitality and brilliance of their contributions to that history.

THE THEME

As might be expected, the theme for a variation series is usually stated at the beginning. However, there are occasional exceptions to this rule. There may, for instance, be a short introduction, or even an extended one if the work is large. Example 10.1 shows an introduction to a variation movement. The suggestion of G minor in the opening bars is a devious twist, since the movement is in E-flat. And what follows the introduction is the bass of the theme, which might be called variation 1, followed by two variations on the bass; the full theme, complete with upper-voice

Ex. 10.1 Beethoven, Symphony No. 3 in E-flat, Op. 55, final movement.

melody, arrives only after three variations in which its harmony and other elements gradually emerge as adumbrations of what is to come.

Other introductions to variation sets are the 8 measures which begin the *Rhapsody on a Theme of Paganini,* Op. 43, by Rachmaninov, and, at another extreme, the introduction to *Don Quixote,* Op. 35, by Richard Strauss (1864–1949), a gigantic development of one of the work's variation themes.

In Ex. 10.2, the theme is first suggested, after the brief introduction, in a nebulous outline consisting of its harmonic roots, somewhat in the manner of the Beethoven example cited as Ex. 10.1. Apel refers to a variation such as this as a "negative variation"—an excellent characterization.[1]

In his Piano Variations, Aaron Copland "reverses the usual procedure by putting the simplest version of the theme second, naming 'theme' what is, properly

Ex. 10.2 Rachmaninov, Rhapsody on a Theme of Paganini, Op. 43, for piano and orchestra.
Copyright renewed 1962 by Charles Foley, Inc. Used by permission.

[1] *Harvard Dictionary of Music,* 2nd ed., p. 895.

Ex. 10.2 (continued)

—Theme m.33

speaking, a first variation. The idea was to present the listener with a more striking version of the theme first, which seemed more in keeping with the generally dramatic character of the composition as a whole."[2]

A very unusual specimen, *Istar,* Op. 42, by Vincent d'Indy (1851–1931), presents the variation series in order of diminishing complexity, with the theme appearing at the end.

The theme is normally relatively simple in form and content, constituting a foundation upon which the variation series is to build. It is frequently a period (Brahms, *Variations on a Hungarian Song,* Op. 21, No. 2), a binary form (Bach, *Goldberg Variations*), or an incipient ternary (Schubert, Impromptu in B-flat, Op. 142, No. 3). But the only general observation that can be made is that it is of small proportions, usually not exceeding 32 measures in length, and often shorter. Example 10.3 is a symmetrical simple ternary, whose third part corresponds to the first in melody, while opposing it in tonal direction (f♯-A, A-f♯).

Ex. 10.3 Brahms, Variations on a Theme by Robert Schumann, Op. 9.

[2]Copland, *What to Listen for in Music,* p. 159.

The theme may be composed specifically for variations (Ex. 10.1), or it may be borrowed from a traditional or popular source (Ex. 10.4) or from the music of another composer (Exx. 10.2, 10.3). The theme quoted in Ex. 10.4 is an adaptation from music of the Roman liturgy.

Ex. 10.4 Norman Dello Joio, Variations, Chaconne and Finale (1947).

A composer sometimes borrows his variation theme from previous works of his own. An example is Schubert's variations on his lied "Die Forelle," used as the basis for the fourth movement of his *Trout Quintet* in A major for piano and strings, Op. 114.

A variation series may be based on two themes, or a "double theme," as in Ex. 10.5. Here the tonic is shared while one part is in major, the other minor. In this work, the two parts of the theme are varied in alternation according to the following

Ex. 10.5 Haydn, Variations in F minor, Hob. XVII: 6.

pattern: first, second, variation 1 on the first, variation 1 on the second, variation 2 on the first, variation 2 on the second, variation 3 on the first, and coda. The resemblance to rondo form scarcely needs mention.

Examples of variation series with two themes are Strauss's *Don Quixote,* in which the themes are intended to represent the knight and Sancho Panza, and the second movement of Beethoven's Piano Trio in E-flat, Op. 70, No. 2, whose two themes are contrasted in mode. The slow movement of Beethoven's Symphony No. 5 in C minor may be described as a variation series on two themes.

Sometimes the theme, more or less in its definitive form, is recalled in the course of the variation series, or restated at the conclusion. An example of the former technique, again showing parallels to rondo form, is the fourth movement of Mozart's Quintet in A for clarinet and strings, K. 581. The reprise of the theme at the end, in a quasi-ternary design, is seen in Haydn's String Quartet in D, Op. 20, No. 4, second movement. The theme, which is 18 measures long, is recalled up to its 17th measure at the conclusion of the series, at which point it dissolves into a coda.

THE SECTIONAL VARIATION SERIES

Although a few of the works mentioned in this chapter have continuous form, in most specimens of theme with variations the theme and each of the variations are followed by clear cadential breaks of indefinite length, forming a sectional series in contrast to the continuous form of ostinato variations. The performer naturally does not exaggerate these breaks, lest continuity and relationships within the series be impaired. A composer can, of course, indicate that there is to be no break in the form, as Aaron Copland does in his Piano Variations.

A further distinction between ostinato forms and the sectional theme with variations is that in the latter the theme melody is often a primary object of attention in the variations, even though it is from time to time relinquished. The usual theme for a sectional variation series is of greater length, moreover, than that of the ostinato forms.

We may consider briefly a few works that present problems of classification in the terms outlined above. In the *Goldberg Variations* (Ex. 10.21) of Bach, the upper-voice theme melody disappears altogether during the variations, which are built on the theme's bass line and harmony, but are sectional rather than continuous. Something comparable may be said of the *Diabelli Variations* (Ex. 10.13) of Beethoven, although in this work the composer develops melodic motives of the theme, which is not of distinctive melodic character, in addition to the retention, in most of the series, of theme form and harmonic outlines. The Piano Variations of Copland, which are continuous rather than sectional, are an eloquent discourse on the principal motive of the theme,

rather than on its bass line or harmony, as would be the case in conventional osti-nato forms.[3]

Rarely, transitions are used in the sectional variation series. Thus, there is continuous motion through cadences in the *Diferencias Cavallero* by Antonio de Cabezón (1510–1566), included in the first volume of *HAM* (pp. 145–46). Despite this, its sectionalization is quite pronounced. Transitional passages in variation series whose fabric is frankly continuous are, of course, more usual. (See mm. 108–116 of the final movement of Beethoven's Third Symphony, a transition linking the first complete theme statement with the first of the fugal variations.)

An even rarer feature is the use of an introduction to one of the variations; such an introduction precedes variation 12 of the *Enigma Variations* of Edward Elgar (1857–1934).

One of the most interesting areas of analysis with respect to the theme with variations is the consideration of the overall plan which gives profile and cumulative shape to the total series. The composer may achieve this by gradual increase (and/or subsidence) of motion, of dynamic intensity, of brilliance of color, of textural complexity, of degrees of prominence of the theme, or in broad lines of diminishing or increasing complexity in any element. Control of such factors may be extremely important in the unity of the composition—as important as interrelationships among variations and theme, or transitional links.

Such a sense of total shape and progress can transcend the cadential interruptions in the musical flow, as in Ex. 10.6, which employs an obvious yet effective device: the gradual increase in surface rhythmic motion from variation to variation.

Ex. 10.6 Handel, The Harmonious Blacksmith (Air and variations from the Suite in E).

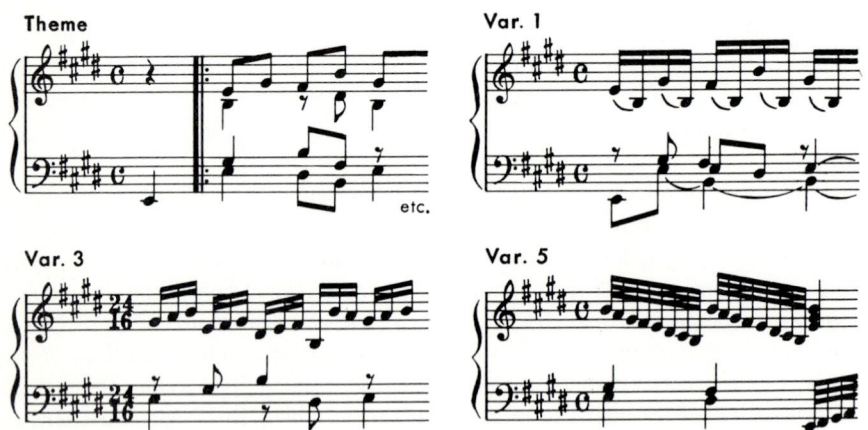

---

[3]A further anomaly in relation to the above stipulations may be seen in the *strophic bass* of certain seventeenth-century cantatas and other works. Here, the bass line—as a kind of ostinato theme, but of greater length than that of the usual passacaglia—is repeated with each textual strophe with varied accompaniments, but the overall structure is sectional rather than continuous. (See among Monteverdi's *scherzi musicali* the aria for soprano, solo instrument, and continuo, ''Et è pur dunque vero,'' whose strophic bass appears seven times with changes in its superstructure.)

EXAMPLES OF FIXED THEME ELEMENTS

Form; the fixed-form variation[4]

While it goes without saying that any element of the theme may, in a variation, remain fixed, it can be observed in the historical practice of variation form that primary significance attaches to the retention in variation of any or all of three basic elements: form, harmony, and (upper-voice) melody. Indeed, omitting many examples from the past century or so, it is possible to characterize virtually any traditional example of theme with variations as having invariable form from theme to variation, often with melodic, harmonic, or melodic-harmonic retention as well. (Rarely, however, is any combination of fixed elements retained consistently throughout an entire variation set.) In romantic, classical, and pre-classical examples, the form of the theme undergoes modification in the variation series in only occasional instances. The following classification of traditional variations suggests itself:

1. Those having *fixed form*, with the original harmony and melody decisively altered or relinquished (rare, and applicable only to occasional *individual* variations; see the Brahms examples cited below).
2. Those having *fixed form and melody* (generally an upper-voice melody as distinct from a bass ostinato, discussed in Chapter 9), with the theme's harmony decisively altered or relinquished.
3. Those having *fixed form and harmony*, with the melody decisively altered or relinquished (very common).
4. Those having *fixed form, harmony, and melody*, with any one of these varied slightly[5] or with variation applied to other theme elements (very common).

Categories 2, 3, and 4 above occur in individual components of variation sets and in groups of such components or even through entire sets.

When we consider the theme as a composite of many elements, of which the above are the most basic in traditional variation treatment, we avoid the mistake of equating "theme" with "melody." Morris commits this error in discussing Bach's *Goldberg Variations:* "This work is a masterpiece of its kind, but I confess it seems to me somewhat of a strain on terminology to speak of it as a 'theme and variations.' The theme itself—a highly rococo little dance in binary form—is completely ignored; all that is kept is the binary structure and the basic harmonic progressions."[6]

---

[4]Other terms that could conceivably apply to the variation set in which the theme's form is constant are "uniform" (in its literal sense) and "isomorphic." But these, like the rejected "structurally-fixed," imply the preservation of form *and* other elements of theme structure.

[5]Obviously no absolute distinction can be made between the "decisive" (essential) and "slight" (superficial) variation of an element. "Retention" in variation implies the presence of features that bring the whole original element readily to mind. The appearance of melodic outline, with new embellishments, has this effect and is very common. In harmony, again "retention" must imply adherence to a basic outline and distinguishing features, such as beginnings of phrases and, especially, cadences, if associability is to be felt. (Example 10.7 is a case in point, and many of the examples cited in this chapter are concerned with these distinctions.)

[6]R. O. Morris, *The Structure of Music*, p. 71.

Thus, Morris recognizes Bach's retention of the theme's form and harmony (together, it is assumed, with its bass line), but considers that with the dismissal of the upper-voice melody the "theme" is "completely ignored."

The reader may question the apparent exclusion of rhythm in the above delineation of three "basic elements," since certainly rhythm is one of the vital distinguishing elements of any theme. But rhythm and meter are regarded here as primarily aspects of melody, harmony, and form.

Since fixed thematic form is a feature of nearly all variations until the late nineteenth century, we define the *fixed-form variation* as that in which form is the *only* basic element remaining invariable. This is, as noted above, a rare circumstance.

Traces of the original harmony or melody, or both, are nearly always present in the fixed-form variation. In Ex. 10.7, form is clearly the principal tie between theme and variation—the chief basic element of the theme which is preserved. Harmony conforms only very limitedly, and is radically altered and reduced. Of the theme melody, it is primarily the 16th-note motive which is discreetly woven into the canon.

Ex. 10.7   Brahms, Variations and Fugue on a Theme by Handel, Op. 24.

Another example that might be described as a fixed-form type is variation 6 of the Brahms *Variations on a Theme of Haydn*, Op. 56. Here, the theme's melody and harmony are retained at phrase beginnings but radically altered at cadences. Furthermore, the middle section (third and fourth phrases) of this variation violates the melody and harmony so severely that for all practical purposes neither element remains fixed.

Form and melody;
the melodically-fixed variation

The term *melodically-fixed variation* refers to that procedure in which melody and form are retained while harmony is decisively altered.[7] Example 10.8, from a lute book of 1538, is among the earliest specimens of theme with variations. (The complete piece can be seen in *HAM*, Vol. I, pp. 130–32.)

Ex. 10.8   Luis de Narvaez, Diferencias sobra O Gloriosa Domina.

> Reprinted by permission of the publishers from Archibald T. Davison and Willi Apel, *Historical Anthology of Music: Oriental, Medieval, and Renaissance Music* (Cambridge, Mass.: Harvard University Press, copyright 1946, 1949, by the President and Fellows of Harvard College, © renewed 1974 by Alice D. Humez and Willi Apel).

For further study of the melodically-fixed variation, see *Versos del sexto tono*, by Antonio de Cabezon, also in *HAM* (Vol. I, pp. 144–45): in its four sections, the *cantus firmus* (literally "fixed melody") moves through the four textural voices, soprano to bass. Two further examples are the next item in the same volume, Cabezon's *Diferencias Cavallero*, and (in Vol. II, pp. 24–26) a set of keyboard varia-

---

[7]The type commonly termed *cantus firmus* variation is clearly related, but as a category marked by more or less straightforward retention of theme melody with or without (and often with) its fundamental harmonization unchanged, and with such factors as texture and registral placement subject to variance. The *works* cited in the present context are in general of the *cantus firmus* type, while *individual components* of these works, cited in Ex. 10.8 and accompanying comment, are melodically-fixed variations as more narrowly defined here. A further case in point is the second movement of Haydn's String Quartet in C, Op. 76, No. 3, where theme melody recurs with only incidental decorations. But in the Haydn, harmony is largely fixed as well; variation 4 has the most significant changes of harmonization, yet even here it is doubtful that essential outlines can be said to be altered.

tions by Samuel Scheidt (1587–1654), particularly variation 4. The melodically-fixed variation, strictly defined, is infrequent, and is found chiefly in early literatures.

Form and harmony;
the harmonically-fixed variation

The *harmonically-fixed variation* is vastly more common than the fixed-form or melodically-fixed types. We have seen that harmonic retention is a feature of many ostinato variations. It is also a feature of many baroque works, including Bach's *Goldberg Variations,* and many individual variations of the classical period, as well as of many variations of the nineteenth century. The majority of nineteenth-century "character variations" are of this type. It must be understood that harmonic retention admits subsidiary variation, but with the "essential harmonic outlines"—the focal points of phrase harmony—preserved. Inevitably, changes in such elements as texture and tempo involve adjustment in harmonic rhythm, occasional simplification or enrichment of the harmony, and comparable alterations.

An example of the harmonically-fixed variation is shown as Ex. 10.9. It will be seen that the theme's melody is dropped. (Again, reference is to the *upper-voice* melody; it is understood that in the harmonically-fixed variation the *bass* "melody" is usually retained along with the original harmony.) The harmonic structure is largely maintained, although in m. 3 of the variation a new augmented-6th chord is used to introduce the cadential dominant. The use of this embellishing chromatic harmony is encouraged by the slower tempo, and by its higher accessibility in the minor mode.

Ex. 10.9   Mozart, Ten Variations, K. 460, on Come un agnello by Sarti.

IV⁷
(Germ. 6th)

Further examples are the *Abegg Variations* in F, Op. 1, of Schumann and the variation movement of Beethoven's String Quartet in C-sharp minor, Op. 131.

Form, melody and harmony; the melodically-harmonically-fixed variation

The rather cumbersome designation *melodically-harmonically-fixed variation* is adopted here (in preference to Nelson's "melodico-harmonic") because implicit in the former term is the specification that all the basic elements remain *fixed*, with variation dependent upon minor alterations in these elements or in variation of other theme elements.

Like the preceding category, the melodically-harmonically-fixed variation is of great importance in view of the sheer volume of works (especially in the eighteenth and early nineteenth centuries) composed according to this principle. Many of the variations of Mozart, Haydn, Beethoven, and Schubert—to mention only the most significant names of the classical and early romantic periods—are of this type.

In the melodically-harmonically-fixed variation, the theme melody is constant at its chief points, and its main outlines preserved. In some cases a profoundly transformed melody is built upon the original outlines. But often the retention of the theme melody in this type of variation involves its embellishment by the addition of auxiliary notes around its essential outlines. It is for this reason that this category is often designated "ornamental variation." Melodic ornamentation is a fundamental characteristic of the melodically-harmonically-fixed variation. (See Ex. 10.10.)

Ex. 10.10   Mozart, String Quartet in A, K. 464, third movement.

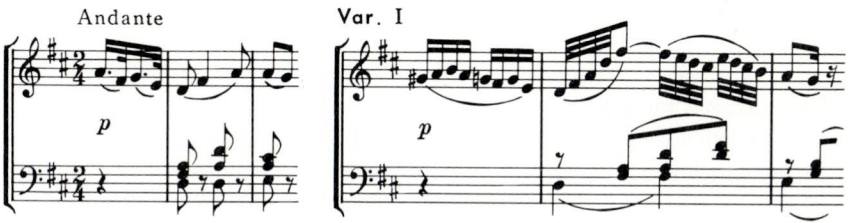

Retention of the melody may involve, in addition to ornamentation, incidental fragmentation, often with contrapuntal or other developmental treatment of its important motives. In Ex. 10.11, minor variation in the form results from such fragmentation, which causes a delay in the otherwise straightforward statement of the embellished chorale melody.

Other examples of the melodically-harmonically-fixed variation are found in the variation movements of Schubert's *Trout Quintet;* Beethoven's Quartets in A, Op. 18, No. 5 (see variations 1 and 3) and C-sharp minor, Op. 131 (see variation 3); and Haydn's Quartet in B-flat, Op. 55, No. 3, in which variation 2 treats the primary motive of the theme melody imitatively.

Ex. 10.11 Bach, Chorale Variations on Sei gegrüsset, Jesu gütig.

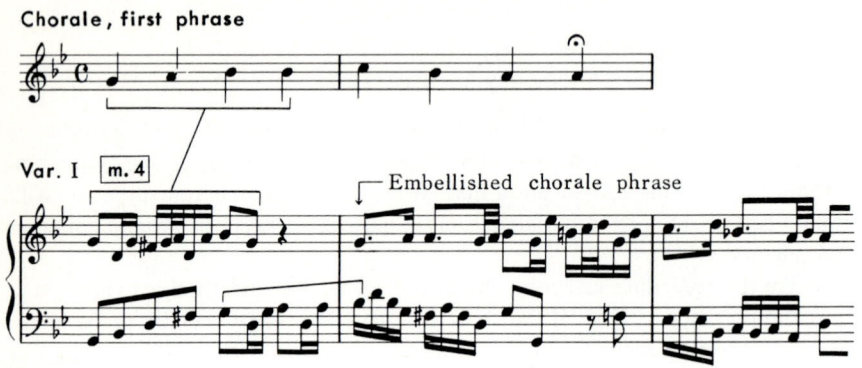

Motive as a fixed element; the free variation

In all four categories of variation just discussed, form is a constant element. It is in the free variation of the late nineteenth and twentieth centuries that all three basic elements—form, melody, harmony—are often largely dismissed, with the only residual link between theme and variations that of a theme motive or motives, retained as a source of free development or as a point of departure in the variations.

Examples of earlier free variation are found in the final movement of Beethoven's Symphony No. 3. A motive derived from the theme's bass,

becomes the basis for a development (see m. 211) which can be properly regarded as a free variation rather than an "episode" or interruption of the series; and the fugal variations (mm. 117 and 278) on the above motive and its inversion are free.

Example 10.12 is included to illustrate the use of a theme motive taken as a point of departure for a twentieth-century variation whose form represents an alteration upon that of the theme (given in part as Ex. 10.2). In the variation, the motive which pervades the entire theme,

becomes the point of departure for a variation of totally contrasting character. As is seen in Ex. 10.12, the motive is inverted.

An excellent work for further study of variations freely deriving from theme motives is the colorful *Variaciones Concertantes* for chamber orchestra, by the Argentine composer Alberto Ginastera (b. 1916).

Ex. 10.12   Rachmaninov, Rhapsody on a Theme of Paganini, Op. 43, for piano and orchestra.
Copyright renewed 1962 by Charles Foley, Inc. Used by permission.

Other fixed elements in theory and practice

The classification of variation techniques, discussed in the foregoing pages, is based on degrees of variance and invariance of melody, harmony, and form (with rhythm understood to be a factor in all three elements); these fundamental thematic determinants are treated with considerable consistency within particular styles and periods in the history of variations.

Other elements of the theme are of course subject to retention or variation. Some normally are fixed, except in the free variation; one such element is tonality, which is usually constant through an entire series in traditional variation form. At the opposite extreme, certain elements may be fixed only rarely—for example, the theme's coloration (timbre, dynamic level, register), which is likely to change in subtle ways in nearly every variation, even when the medium is a solo instrument. Other theme elements—meter, mode, tempo, texture—may occasionally be fixed but in nearly all cases change considerably during the course of a variation series, though without any predictable stylistic patterning or regularity. The following sections of this chapter will refer to examples from many works in illustration of ways in which particular theme elements are subjected to variation while others remain fixed.

EXAMPLES OF THEME ELEMENTS IN VARIATION

Form

The foregoing section dealing with theme motive as a fixed element refers as well to variation in form, for when the formal plan is altered as to its *type* a motive of the theme often becomes the sole or principal binding factor between theme and variation. Variation in formal plan, the exception in most traditional styles, becomes the rule in more recent variations.

Variation in form is of several possibilities. The form of the theme may be altered in its relative proportions—for example, by the introduction of asymmetry or modification in the degree of asymmetry (Ex. 10.12); or the *kind* of form represented by the theme may be changed—binary may become ternary, or a period may become a fugato, as in the *Eroica* examples cited; or what was a set form may become a fantasylike free form. With respect to the first of these points, we are speaking not of total length but of *relationships* of parts. In one kind of variation of form, the nature of the design—the type of form—remains constant while proportionate relations are altered, in a procedure analogous to that of enrichment of a melody by surface elaboration. In another, the formal plan is itself altered.

In Ex. 10.13, variations 12 and 22 are made asymmetrical, the former by the omission of the repeat of the first part of the original binary, the latter by the extension of the second part. An example of actual change in the kind of form—in this case, binary to fugue—may be seen in the penultimate variation of the same series.

Ex. 10.13   Beethoven, Thirty-three Variations on a Waltz by Diabelli, Op. 120.

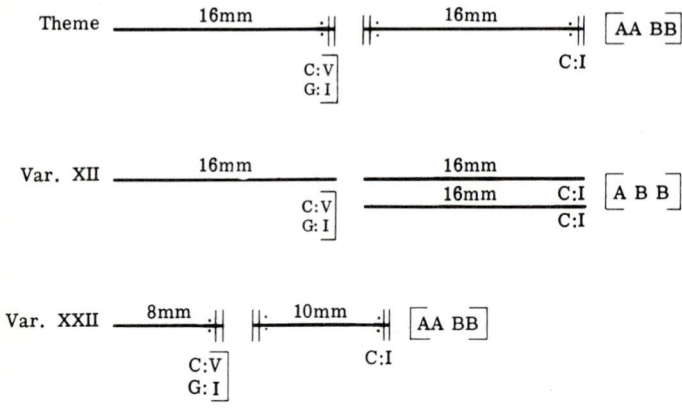

The form of the final variation in a traditional series is often extended or otherwise modified to allow for coda or codetta. In the last of Mozart's *Twelve Variations on* "Je suis Lindor," K. 354, the conclusion of the original form is dissolved into a codetta with cadenza. The means by which such freedoms are taken with theme form are relevant in the development toward the later free variation.

Examples of free variation may be studied in the *Enigma Variations* of Elgar, in which, for example, variations 2, 6, 7, and 9 should be compared with the theme of that series.

Karl Eschman, in his discussion of the modern variation, closes his chapter with a succinct, summary statement: "In short, the form has been added to the possible 'variables' in modern variations."[8]

[8]Karl Eschman, *Changing Forms in Modern Music* (Boston: E. C. Schirmer, 1945), p. 129.

Harmony

Just as the theme melody, as a retained element, may be ornamented without disruption of its outline (Ex. 10.10), the harmony of the theme is very often, in variation, changed slightly. (See Ex. 10.14, which shows how the original harmony may be embellished by passing and neighboring chords.)

Ex. 10.14   Weber, Eight Variations on an air de ballet from Vogler's Castor and Pollux.

Melody

Example 10.10 illustrates melodic embellishment, the most frequent kind of melodic variation, and Ex. 10.11 shows melodic ornamentation as well as fragmentation and momentary textural dispersal and imitative treatment. In such instances, primary identifying features of the melody—its characteristic motives, its basic profile, or both—are preserved.

There are, of course, many other means of varying the theme melody. For instance, the line may be presented in altered rhythm or altered pitch succession, or in augmentation or diminution, or it may be stated in mirror inversion. An example of the latter technique is quoted as Ex. 10.15, which includes canon.

Another which is suggested for study is variation 2 of Schoenberg's *Variations for Orchestra*, Op. 31; this variation begins as a canon between solo violin and oboe on an inversion of the theme melody, rhythmically altered.

When the melody is in its essentials omitted from the variation (see Ex. 10.9), a new melody may be introduced over the original harmonic-structural framework.

Ex. 10.15 Ginastera, *Variaciones Concertantes*.

Copyright 1954 by Hawkes & Son (London) Ltd. Reprinted by permission of Boosey & Hawkes, Inc.

Further examples of this technique are seen in the opening variation of the third movement of Beethoven's Piano Sonata in E, Op. 109, and in variation 7 of Brahms's *Haydn Variations* (Ex. 10.24).

Meter

Variation in such elements as meter, mode, tempo, and dynamics may, especially when treated collectively, change the theme's character radically. Such profound transformation of the theme appears with regularity for the first time in the variations of Beethoven, whose works in many respects predict the broad latitude of later techniques. Example 10.16, a sixteenth-century example of variation in meter, rep-

Ex. 10.16 Nicolaus Ammerbach, *Passamezzo antico*.

Reprinted by permission of the publishers from Archibald T. Davison and Willi Apel, *Historical Anthology of Music: Oriental, Medieval, and Renaissance Music* (Cambridge, Mass.: Harvard University Press, copyright 1946, 1949, by the President and Fellows of Harvard College, copyright renewed 1974 by Alice D. Humez and Willi Apel).

Ex. 10.16 (*continued*)

Saltarello

resents in at least this basic sense a transformation of theme character. (The *salta-rello*, a lively Italian dance of the period in triple meter, often appears as an "after-dance" in alliance with the *passamezzo*, a dance in duple meter.)

Surface rhythm

The interdependence of thematic elements (e.g., texture and timbre, harmony and modality), rendering somewhat deceptive and often difficult their separate consider-ation, is most pronounced with respect to rhythm. Rhythm is an aspect of all ele-ments, each element suggesting and representing a specific feature of rhythmic ef-fect. Thus, rhythm is an aspect of tempo, tempo of rhythm; rhythm is an aspect of meter, meter of rhythm. Rhythm as a feature of unit relations and proportions has been important in consideration of all the forms we have treated.

Short of extensive exploration of rhythmic implications, we can only suggest areas in which surface rhythmic uniformity and modification enter into variation technique. Surface rhythmic motion is an obvious and basic determinant of musical character, since the rate of melodic, accompanimental, contrapuntal, and harmonic activity determines the musical "pace" (an aspect of tempo).[9] Such surface rhyth-mic activity may be lessened (as in the so-called negative variation, Ex. 10.2) or increased (as in Exx. 10.6 and 10.8) as one source of variation.

In Ex. 10.17 by John Munday (d. 1630), the rate of beat-succession is unchanged, as are harmony, form, mode, meter, timbre, and dynamic intensity. The folksong melody is varied negligibly. Principal alterations include the simplification of texture and the introduction of 16th-notes into the accompanying lower voice, felt as a considerable change.

The interrelationship of harmony and rhythm, with modification of harmonic rhythm as a variation device, is seen in Exx. 10.7 and 10.14. Textural change, often a product of rhythmic differentiation among voices, can be described as a kind of rhythmic variation (Ex. 10.21). Melodic ornamentation represents an alteration of

---

[9]*Tempo* is, in one sense, the rate or frequency of beat-succession—the "tempo" which is indica-ted by metronomic figures. In another sense, tempo is related to the degree of internal motion, the *activity* interspersed among the beats. Thus, a piece at ♩ = 96 in which the motion is primarily in quarter-notes has the effect of being "slower" in tempo than a piece at ♩ = 96 in which the primary unit of motion is the 16th-note.

Ex. 10.17   Munday, Variations on Goe from my window.

No. 7

melodic rhythm (Exx. 10.10 and 10.11). Variation in characteristic *patterns* of melodic rhythm in a theme can be seen in Ex. 10.15, where the difference of long-short is lessened, with a "smoothing out" effect in the variation. The alteration of any distinctive rhythmic feature within any element has significance as rhythmic variation of a kind.

Color (timbre and related factors)

When the medium is a relatively homogeneous one—a solo instrument or an ensemble of like instruments—color is determined by register, by dynamic intensity and articulation, and by special effects such as muting. Color and dynamic intensity (*pianissimo, forte,* etc.) are, of course, impossible to set apart, since changes in the manner and intensity of articulation are certain to affect timbral quality, and vice versa.

Color change is obviously of the greatest significance in a medium of broad palette such as a chamber ensemble of unlike instruments, or the orchestra. But striking resources are at the composer's disposal in a homogeneous medium. Attention is called, for example, to the unforgettable *pizzicato* statement of the theme in the cello, against sustained accompanying chords in the upper voices, in variation 6 of Brahms's String Quartet in B-flat, Op. 67, final movement, a case of varied timbre and articulation.

Example 10.18 shows the theme of Don Quixote in Strauss's tone poem as it appears in variation 7. Programmatically suggesting the Don's flight through the air, the theme is thrust in brilliant eruptions through the strings (supported by harp and winds) into the highest violin octave.

Ex. 10.18   Strauss, Don Quixote.
      Reprinted with permission of copyright owner, C. F. Peters Corp., New York.

Tonality

Tonality is not generally a variable element until after the middle of the nineteenth century. (It is one of the neoclassical features of the variations of Brahms that tonality generally remains fixed through his variation series.) Again it is Beethoven who frequently breaks away from the principle adhered to in the traditions which preceded him. In the *Diabelli* series, variation 5 modulates to the mediant minor rather than to the dominant, and the fugal variation is in the key of E-flat rather than the tonic C. The *Eroica* variations, basically in E-flat, traverse such secondary regions as D, C, and G minor. Moreover, the composer's Variations in F, Op. 34, include variations in D, B-flat, G, E-flat, and C minor, with the final variation returning to the original tonic. These references suggest an important distinction between alteration in tonal structure within a variation, and variation in which the theme's primary tonality is changed.

Example 10.12 shows a twentieth-century excerpt in which a key distant from that of the theme is employed in a variation.

Mode

Variations 15, 21, and 25 of Bach's *Goldberg* set employ change of mode, being in G minor rather than G major, while the variations in Handel's Harpsichord Suite in E (Ex. 10.6) eschew change of mode entirely. In the late eighteenth and early nineteenth centuries it became a general rule that a variation series included one variation in mode. An example is shown as Ex. 10.19; another is to be seen in Mozart's

Ex. 10.19   Brahms, Sextet in G, Op. 36, for strings, third movement.

String Quartet in D minor, K. 421, final movement, variation 4. (See also Ex. 10.27e.)

In more recent styles, modal scales other than the conventional major and minor are occasionally significant as a source of variation.

Tempo[10]

Tempo change is a vital facet of variation technique in all styles of music. It is difficult to imagine that the alteration of any single element can have so profound an

---

[10]"Tempo" is here regarded in the "metronomic" aspect only, the frequency of beat-succession. (See footnote 9.)

effect upon the expressive character of the theme. The variation literature shows that tempo variation is decisive in its effect upon the theme even when other elements remain relatively stable. In the fifth variation in the final movement of Mozart's Quartet in D minor, K. 421, all theme elements are fixed except form (after 8 measures there is a brief development, followed by a coda) and tempo.

In variation sets of the melodically-harmonically-fixed category of the classical period, there is almost inevitably an adagio variation toward the middle of the series, and a concluding allegro variation, often quite brilliant. Examples are easily found.

Dynamics

Change in dynamic intensity as a source of variation is so apparent that an example is hardly necessary. Change of dynamic quality, regarded as an aspect of thematic "color," is of course usually accompanied by other changes, although reduction or intensification of dynamics alone would drastically affect the theme's original character. Like that of other variable elements (for example, tonality) the variation in dynamics may be extreme (for instance, when *piano* becomes *forte*) or subtle (when only certain dynamic indications are changed or suppressed). In Ex. 10.20, the main variation techniques are those of meter, timbre and sonority (strings in theme, *tutti* in variation), tempo, and dynamics, the last clearly allied to changes in articulation of performance.

Ex. 10.20   Elgar, Variations in G minor on an Original Theme, Op. 36.
Reproduced by permission of Novello & Co., Ltd.

Texture

The most compelling means of variation in texture is the adoption of such contrapuntal techniques as fugal imitation, canonic imitation, inverted counterpoint, and the like (see Chapter 12). Homophony in the theme thus becomes polyphony in the variation, sometimes simply by the introduction of free accompanying counterpoints. Variation of this kind is therefore often called "contrapuntal variation." Famous examples are found in the *Goldberg Variations* of Bach, in which every third member of the series, beginning with variation 3, is a canon. Alteration in the nature and complexity of texture is a fundamental variation technique.

A single citation is given as Ex. 10.21. In it, the harmonies and bass of the theme are fixed while the texture is modified to include 2 voices in canon at the unison, with an accompanying bass which is not a part of the canon.

Ex. 10.21   Bach, Aria with Thirty Variations (Goldberg Variations)

Further reference may be made to Exx. 10.7, 10.11, and 10.15, as well as to variation 5 of the sixteenth-century *Diferencias* of Luis de Narvaez, cited in Ex. 10.8.

Textural variation may also involve modification of the accompanying fabric within a prevailing homophonic style to introduce varying degrees of internal motion and density or a higher or lower complexity of pattern in inner voices.

The variation shown in Ex. 10.22 preserves the homophonic character of the theme, but reduces its textural density. The theme's pedal point is abandoned, as are such original inner-voice counterpoints as the ascending broken triads of mm. 1-2 and the descending-step motive of mm. 3-4.

Ex. 10.22   Brahms, Variations in D on an Original Theme, Op. 21, No. 1.

Theme

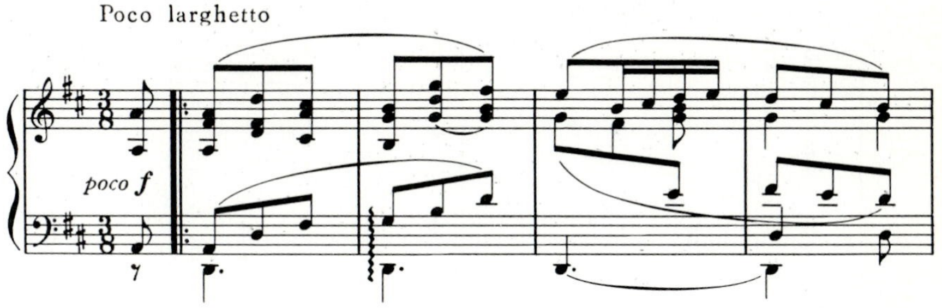

Poco larghetto

Var. II

Più mosso

Character

The theme's character is the product of all its elements with the exception of tonality, although tonal fluctuation (not usually a feature of brief variations) would also have an effect upon expressive character.

It is the most pervasive elements—tempo, dynamics, meter, mode, rhythmic pattern—that have the strongest effect upon thematic character. Extreme change of one or more of these may totally alter the expressive nature of the theme. In Ex. 10.23, there is little or no variation in tempo, mode, harmony, melody (as pitch succession), texture, and form. But the meter is changed and the rhythms are "spread out," with syncopations of the theme eliminated and constant motion introduced. The changes in dynamics and the timbral effect of the warm, high cello register opposed to the dark accompaniment are also factors in the character change, as is the introduction of conjunct motion in the melody.

The term *character variation* often denotes that variation type in which theme characteristics are modified so as to give the variation the character of a specific musical genre, such as a type of dance. This type of variation is especially a feature of the romantic tradition, although the label is sometimes applied to earlier specimens. (See Nelson's *Technique of Variation,* p. 6; see also Ex. 10.16 in this chapter.)

Ex. 10.23   Brahms, Piano Trio in C, Op. 87, second movement.

Example 10.24, from Brahms's *Haydn Variations*, shows the adoption in variation of the qualities of a *siciliano* (a seventeenth-century Sicilian dance in rather slow tempo and compound meter, often featuring dotted rhythms). In the same series, variation 5 is a scherzo—also a character variation.

A more general application of the term "character variation" refers to any variation in which the expressive character of the theme is profoundly transformed.

Ex. 10.24   Brahms, Variations on a Theme of Haydn, Op. 56a, for orchestra.

Ex. 10.24 (*continued*)

Var. VII

Treatment of the variable elements
in the practice of variation

It is clear that most variation sets are concerned with not one but a variety of tech-niques, ranging from invariability of all three basic elements to modification of all of them. Similarly, any single variation of any period acts upon the theme in a num-ber of ways, usually transforming several of its elements. Thus, a combination of variable elements is treated in each variation; and some elements, like texture and color (the latter here understood to include timbre and other determinants of the quality of sound), are altered to some degree in nearly all variations.

In Ex. 10.25, form, meter, tonality, and mode are fixed elements in Etude IV. The harmony corresponds with that of the theme although displaced here and there

Ex. 10.25   Schumann, Symphonic Studies, Op. 13.

by the requirements of the canon. The upper-voice melody is retained in variation; varied elements include surface rhythmic patterns, color, tempo, dynamics, and texture. Articulation seems in this case to require separate mention as a varied element, although it can be viewed as an aspect of melody, rhythm, dynamics, color, and texture—in a sense integral in each of these.

Occasionally, material appearing prominently in a particular variation is drawn, not from the theme, but from an earlier variation. This technique, frequent in Brahms, tends to draw the variations of a series into larger units, further interconnecting the individual segments in the overall variation form. (See Ex. 10.26. Page 290 includes reference to various related factors of interconnection and broad directions in comprehensive form and structure in the sectional variation.)

Ex. 10.26 Brahms, Variations on a Theme of Haydn, Op. 56a.

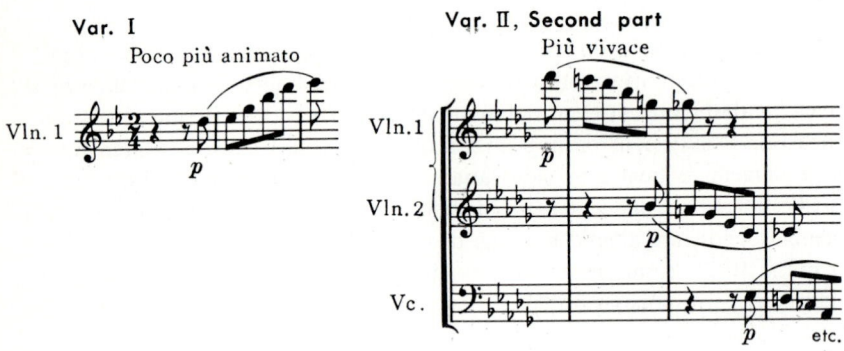

CODA AND OTHER APPENDAGES

"A free fugue is a favorite solution of the problem of the coda in a set of variations. The momentum produced by the revolution of true variations in the orbit of the theme gives the key to the whole problem. A fugue solves it by flying off at a tangent. Very sublime is the way in which Beethoven [in the *Diabelli Variations*], after letting his fugue run its torrential course, returns to the orbit of his theme in an ethereal little minuet with a short coda of its own which, sixteen bars before the end, shows signs of beginning to revolve again."[11] The fugue with which Beethoven ends this work is based on a subject extracted from the opening bars of the theme melody.

Another example of a fugal finale to a set of variations is in Brahms's *Variations on a Theme of Handel*, Op. 24. We have seen in Chapter 9 that Brahms ended his *Haydn Variations* with a passacaglia, whose bass ostinato is derived from the

---

[11]Tovey, *The Forms of Music*, p. 244.

Haydn theme. This series is also a good illustration of the reprise of the original theme at the end—in this instance a major portion of the theme—in its original form but in a much more emphatic, climactic delivery and with the original theme codetta expanded at the end. The reprise of the theme is an extremely useful, rounding device; it is a reminder of the pure source out of which the variation series, in this case a monumental one, emerged.

The fugue is particularly appropriate as a conclusion to variations. The fugue (Chapter 12), in its textural accumulation toward developed intensities of stretto and other accelerations, may be viewed as reflecting an analogous, if structurally disparate, development of drive and complexity in the variation set itself. The fugue thus signifies withdrawal to a minimal beginning in fugal exposition, from which progress resumes, in a different context, toward further culmination within a condensed span of time.

A theme with variations may close with the appendage of a free finale, related or unrelated to the theme, like that which provides so spirited a conclusion to the Schumann *Symphonic Etudes,* Op. 13, or the same composer's *Abegg Variations,* Op. 1, with its finale *alla fantasia.*

Another technique, mentioned earlier in connection with variation in form, involves the enlargement of the final variation by the addition of a codetta, a cadenzalike concluding section, or an expansive coda which develops thematic material. The first of these may be seen at the conclusion of Schubert's Impromptu in B-flat, Op. 142, No.. 3, where the codetta consists mainly of abbreviated theme restatement and cadence repetitions; in the variation movement of Haydn's *Emperor Quartet* in C, Op. 76, No. 3, where a 4½-measure codetta is appended to variation 4; and in the variations of John Munday from which Ex. 10.17 is drawn. The use of a cadenza in the concluding section is associated with Mozart's keyboard variations (see p. 298) and can be observed in his *Twelve Variations on an Allegretto,* K. 500; here, variation 12 is extended by avoidance of cadence, and by the addition of a cadenza and theme reprise. The literature is replete with examples of the big coda. Brahms's *Variations on a Hungarian Song,* Op. 21, No. 2, has its 13th variation dissolve into such a coda, with a precise reprise of the theme in the final bars, extended from 8 to 9 measures for slight cadential broadening. The coda to Beethoven's *Eroica Variations* incorporates material of the introduction as well as the theme, putting both to powerful use.

BRAHMS, QUINTET IN B MINOR
FOR CLARINET AND STRING QUARTET,
OP. 115, FINAL MOVEMENT

Generally speaking, the Brahms movement is a series of harmonically-fixed variations, but as we have by now learned to expect, so general a statement is unlikely to apply to the entire group. Thus, certain of the variations retain major points of the theme melody in transformation or ornamentation and belong in the category of the melodically-harmonically-fixed type; this applies to variation 3 and, especially, to variation 5.

The theme is in two parts. The first is a period of 2 parallel phrases of 8 measures each; melodically they are nearly identical but the first moves to b:V, the second to D:I. Part II has the same form, but its consequent matches the opening phrase of Part I—the earmark of incipient ternary form. The total length is 32 measures, the second part repeated. In Ex. 10.27a, which shows key instrumental parts only, harmonic analysis of the antecedent of Part II is given at both secondary (D) and tertiary (G) levels of tonality.

Ex. 10.27a Brahms, Quintet in B minor, Op. 115, for clarinet and strings, final movement.

Ex. 10.27a (continued)

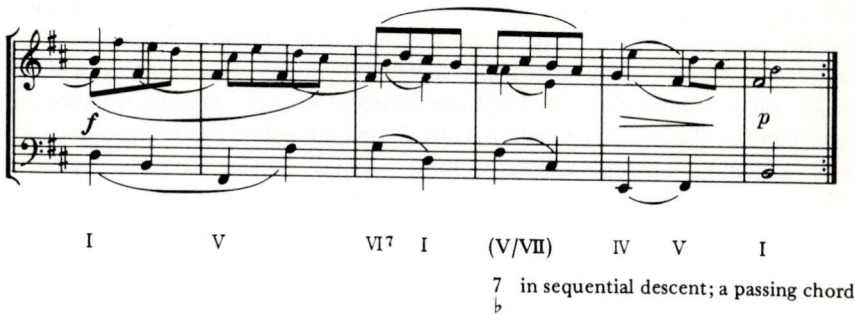

I   V   VI⁷ I   (V/VII)   IV   V   I

7 in sequential descent; a passing chord
♭

    The first variation is fixed in harmony and form (there are minor harmonic changes at certain points, such as mm. 36, 44, and 48). Often the cello alone, as at the beginning of the variation, outlines traces of the theme bass and melody and represents the theme harmony. The "linking motives" of the theme, originally in the clarinet and setting the motion ahead at points of punctuation, are present in an expanded form. The harmony of the middle section is rigidly fixed; that of the reprise is retained but again with minor alterations.

    The first variation increases texturally as it develops. Brahms plays upon two motives, as he often does in variations: one of them is in the violin and clarinet parts in the quotation (the clarinet, imitating the cello, has the motive in a more disjunct form); the other is in the viola—a two-note anacrusis motive which has a vital animating function.

Ex. 10.27b

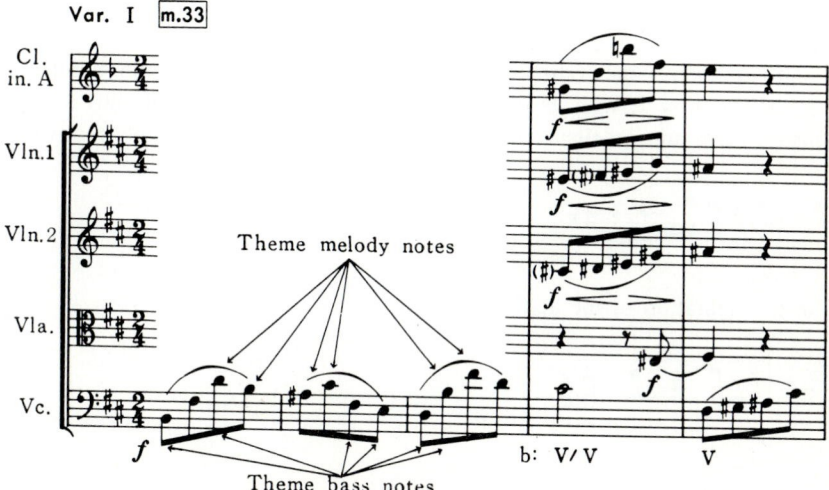

There is important rhythmic change in variation 2, with syncopation in the accompanying inner parts, part of it created by dynamic accents in mm. 2, 4, etc. The music is more dramatic than the preceding as a result of these rhythmic qualities and the potently directed falling or surging motive in clarinet and cello. Melodically, the variation presents essentially new lines built on the theme's form and harmony. Momentum is developed and intensified (even with stability of tempo) by syncopations, the rising and falling motives, and the unbroken 16th-note articulation. Variation 2 is harmonically fixed, despite minor changes—largely in intensified dissonance, and it is characterized by a marked stability of bass line at cadential points.

Ex. 10.27c

In variation 3, the 16th-note motion continues in the same tempo, but the urgency of variation 2, with its irregular stresses, is subdued. Despite this reduced intensity, there are impellent anacrusis rhythms both in the 16th-note motives,

and in the figuration of the accompaniment,

The fidelity of the bass line should again be noted. The device of melodic ornamentation is apparent in Ex. 10.27d, in which notes of the original theme melody are indicated in the first violin part. It is not unusual that the middle variation should thus recall the theme melody, as does the final one. Moreover, the harmony of variation 3 is especially close to that of the theme.

Ex. 10.27d

Variation 4 is a change in mode. The opening motive of the theme melody is transformed to become

and it is used imitatively, together with another form of the same motive, creating the first significant change in texture, complemented by the contrapuntal association of second violin and viola. In a metronomic sense, the tempo is still constant. The 16th-note motion continues but there are steadying factors: the dismissal of anacrusis rhythms and syncopations, and the increased prominence of 8th-note and dotted-quarter-note motives. Thus, the relaxation after variation 2 continues, suggesting that the intensity of the series is at its peak with variation 2.

It can be seen in the quotation of the opening of Part II (Ex. 10.27e) that the syncopation of variation 2 is recalled, but without comparable force—a kind of ripple in the subsiding motion. While the harmony and bass are again in general correspondence with the theme, two significant changes might be noted: (1) the dominant pedal introduced at mm. 133–36 (affecting theme harmony only at m. 135); and (2) the middle cadence on d♯:V, a consequence of use of the major mode and the increased distance of D, the original relative major. Still, the harmony clings to the original theme patterns remarkably closely. Where theme harmony revolved around a subsidiary center of G, we now have G-sharp minor (mm. 17–20 compared with

Ex. 10.27e

145–48); just before the reprise the music leads back to the dominant of B. Details should be studied carefully, as should the movement of the bass line in relation to that of the theme.

Now the higher textural density and complexity of variation 4 are relinquished, and the minor mode is restored. The tempo continues to be stable, but variation 5 introduces the first change in meter, and the most significant variation in color, with a new form of the melody in the richest register of the viola and a pizzicato elaboration of the theme bass in the cello. It is in this variation that the nearest approach to character variation is achieved, largely through the alteration in meter.

In Ex. 10.27f, notes of the original theme melody and bass are pointed out.

Ex. 10.27f

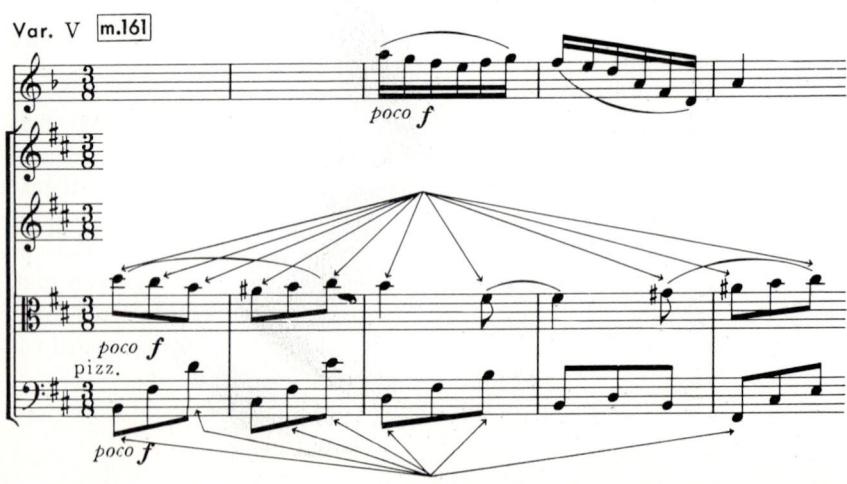

The clarinet motive is developed as a diminution of the opening notes of the viola melody; both, of course, refer to the theme.

As stated before, this variation is the one that is most definitely in the melodically-harmonically-fixed category. The transformation of the theme melody continues into Part II, but with reduced fidelity. It is worth noting again that the theme melody is most conspicuously recalled in the middle and final variations.

Again, the harmony is generally fixed. Changes that should be noted occur at the cadence to Part I, and at the point of variation of mm. 23–24 of the theme, where harmonic direction is preserved but with alteration in the harmonic rhythm and in the root progression itself.

Double variation (see discussion following) is exemplified in these variations, especially clearly in variation 5; the second half of Part II is, as usual, a reprise of the opening, but it is much enriched in color and texture.

The repetition of Part II of variation 5 concludes in a half-cadence for direct motion into the coda. The tempo is slightly relaxed, and the meter changes to 6/8—in a sense combinative of the original 2/4 and the 3/8 of variation 5; it is also a return of the meter of the first movement.

The coda dwells mainly on theme motives of the first movement of the Quintet, but it includes reference to the opening of the variation theme melody:

This motive, clearly allied to the variation theme (compare the viola part in variation 5), bears a striking resemblance to one of the motives of the first movement,

now recalled.

VARIATION PRINCIPLES FREELY APPLIED

We have referred to the combination of variation principles with other procedures of form in music, as for example the use of variation in theme restatements in the rondo, or in strophic forms, to which instrumental variations are very closely allied (see pp. 123-27, as well as p. 284 in this chapter).

Similarly, variation is commonly used in free forms. A famous example is the final movement of Beethoven's Ninth Symphony, in which the familiar "Ode to Joy" theme and its variations are intermingled with introductory and transitional passages, recitativelike statements in the low strings, recollections of themes of other movements, contrasting themes, and many dramatic episodes, including fugal sections on subjects derived from the theme, in effect free variations (as at m. 101).

Many other examples can be found. Haydn's symphonic slow movements are often rather freely constructed—often monothematic, sometimes in composite or hybrid forms, with variation techniques appearing conspicuously in theme restatements in rondolike or quasi-ternary forms. In the slow movement of his Symphony No. 95 in C minor, the theme (Ex. 10.28) is followed immediately by variation, with the melody transferred to the cellos. This is followed by a digression in the parallel minor, based on the theme and characterized by silences and a sense of hesitancy. Now the theme returns in part, unadorned, after which there is a complete variation in shorter rhythmic values. A coda, also based on the theme, closes the movement.

Ex. 10.28   Haydn, Symphony No. 95 in C minor, second movement.

DOUBLE VARIATION: VARIATION ON VARIATION

Variation themes are often in binary and small ternary forms, with their customary repeats. These repeated sections may be written out in further variation (Ex. 10.27 and Ex. 10.29). Nelson describes the *double variation* as the ''use, within a single

Ex. 10.29   Brahms, Variations on a Theme of Paganini, Op. 35, Vol. 1.

Theme (first 4 measures repeated literally)

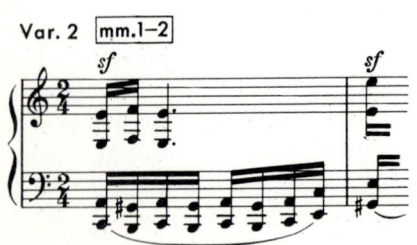

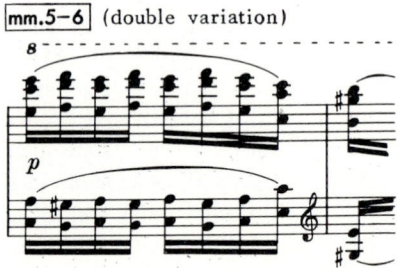

variation, of varied restatements to take the place of literal repetition in the theme''[12]—variation on variation. The principle of double variation can apply to any theme unit which appears in the theme more than once, whether literally and contiguously or not, and of whatever size. Thus, further alteration in the reprise in a variation on a ternary theme is a form of double variation. Example 10.29 shows a theme repeat written out in double variation.

EXERCISES

1. Prepare an analysis of a theme with variations, giving particular attention to the theme elements which might be varied. How would you characterize the form of the theme? If you feel it is a good theme for variation, explain why. What theme elements are fixed in each of the variations? With reference to the variable elements of the theme, list the techniques actually used by the composer. What overall shape (in rhythmic motion, dynamic intensity, textural growth, etc.) can be observed? Are the variations of increasing complexity? Does the theme return in its original form at any point? How is the series concluded? You may analyze one of the many works cited in this chapter or one of the compositions listed below.

    Bach, *English Suite* No. 6 in D minor, Sarabande with *double*
    Chorale variations and partitas on *Christ, der Du bist der helle Tag; O Gott, du frommer Gott;* and *Ach, was soll ich Sünder machen*
    Five canons on Vom Himmel hoch

    Bartók, Concerto for violin and orchestra, second movement

    Beethoven, Piano Sonata in F minor, Op. 57, second movement
    Sonata in G for violin and piano, Op. 96, final movement
    String Quartet in E-flat, Op. 74, fourth movement
    String Quartet in E-flat, Op. 127, second movement

    Boris Blacher (1903–75), *Variations on a Theme by Paganini,* Op. 26

    Luigi Boccherini (1743–1805), Quintet No. 6 in C, Op. 30, for strings, final movement

    Britten, *Variations on a Theme by Frank Bridge,* Op. 10
    Young People's Guide to the Orchestra

    William Byrd (1543–1623), "The Carman's Whistle" and other virginal variations

    Chopin, Variations, Op. 2, on *Là ci darem la mano* from Mozart's *Don Giovanni,* for piano and orchestra
    Variations on a Theme from Halévy's Ludovic, Op. 12

    Frederick Delius (1862–1934), *Appalachia*

    Dvořák, *Symphonic Variations,* Op. 78

    Fauré, Theme and Variations in C-sharp minor for piano, Op. 73

    Ross Lee Finney (b. 1906), *Variations for Orchestra*

    Franck, *Symphonic Variations* in F-sharp minor for piano and orchestra

    Harris, String Quartet No. 2

[12]Nelson, *The Technique of Variation,* p. 8.

d'Indy, Piano Sonata in E, Op. 63, first movement

Kodály, *Variations on a Hungarian Folksong* for orchestra

Mendelssohn, *Andante con Variazioni* in E-flat, Op. 82, for piano
    Variations in B-flat for piano, Op. 83
    Variations in D for piano and cello, Op. 17
    Variations Sérieuses in D minor for piano, Op. 54

Mozart, Serenade in B-flat, K. 361, sixth movement

Luigi Nono (b. 1924), *Variazioni Canoniche* on the row of Schoenberg's *Ode to Napoleon,* for orchestra

Rachmaninov, *Variations on a Theme by Chopin* for piano, Op. 22
    Variations on a Theme by Corelli for piano, Op. 42

Ravel, *Bolero*

Reger, *Variations and Fugue on a Theme by Telemann* for piano 4 hands , Op. 134

Schubert, String Quartet in D minor, second movement

Stravinsky, Octet for wind instruments, second movement

Tchaikovsky, *Six Pieces on a Single Theme* for piano, Op. 21
    Variations on a Rococo Theme for cello and orchestra, Op. 33 (variations separated by a recurring ritornello)

Vaughan Williams, *Fantasy on a Theme by Thomas Tallis* for double string orchestra

2. Make an outline of the first chapter of Nelson's *The Technique of Variation.*

3. Find as many examples of sectional variation form as you can in each of the following sources:
   a) The piano sonatas of Beethoven
   b) The string quartets of Haydn (for example, the first movements of Op. 2, No. 6; and Op. 3, No.2)
   c) The piano sonatas of Haydn (for example, Hob. XVI:27, 28, and 31)
   d) Works of Franck
   e) Harpsichord pieces with *doubles* by Rameau
   f) Keyboard music in the twentieth century
   g) Chorale variations of the seventeenth and eighteenth centuries, including works of Johann Pachelbel (1653–1706) and Buxtehude
   h) The *Tabulatura Nova* of Samuel Scheidt
   i) The *Fitzwilliam Virginal Book*

4. Write your own variation on a Mozart theme of your choosing.

5. Find an example of variations by Schubert on a binary theme. Take one of the variations in which repeat signs are used and write out the repetition as it might occur in a double variation.

6. Find examples of the following:
   a) A form-fixed variation (as defined in this chapter)
   b) A melodically-harmonically-fixed variation
   c) Variation in meter
   d) Variation in tonality
   e) Variation in texture involving use of contrapuntal imitation

    f)   Free variation

    g)   Character variation

7.   Compare rondo form and theme with variations as seen in the Allegretto con variazioni of Mozart's Clarinet Quintet, K. 581.

8.   Select one of the leading motives (leitmotivs) from Wagner's *Der Ring des Nibelungen* and trace some of its varied appearances. What variation techniques do you find to be especially important?

II

SUITE

This is the only chapter devoted primarily to a multimovement form, although Chapter 6 deals in part with the multimovement sonata. The forms and techniques observed in individual movements of the suite are treated at length in other parts of this book.

The suite and the sonata are the two chief multimovement types in the history of instrumental music. As might be expected, they are not firmly separable; for example, the minuet which occurs in many sonatas comes from the suite, and the suite sometimes includes movements of abstract character which would not be out of place in the symphony or other sonata medium.

The suite is the major multimovement form of older instrumental music, having its highest manifestation in keyboard music of the century before 1750. No discussion of traditional approaches in the forms of music is complete without reference to the suite; yet an essay of this kind is problematic since the suite is standardized only to a very limited degree. Even in the baroque period there is much variation in content and ordering of the suite from composer to composer and among national styles. Moreover, the suite of most recent styles is of such diversity that it resists all but the most general commentary.

A consequence of the rise of dance forms in the secular music of the medieval and renaissance periods, the suite may be described as an aggregation of dances and dancelike movements, often highly idealized, interspersed with occasional contrasting movements which are not dances or dance-derived but which usually reflect the general grace, lightness, and comparative brevity of expression which characterize the suite. That dance forms should enter so significantly into the history of art music is not surprising in view of the inevitability and universality of the alliance of dance and music.

The arrangement of the suite is, broadly viewed, extremely free. Within the baroque period the most significant standardization of movement sequence is found in the suites of J. S. Bach, and even among these there are considerable disparities in intermovement relations.

The form of the suite's individual movements is usually binary, as pointed out in Chapter 2. (The discussion of binary form should be reviewed.) In those instances in which the form of the dance movement is not binary, it is most often periodic or ternary. The use of compound ternary form in dances paired in *alternativo* style has been treated in Chapter 4.

As in the multimovement sonata, the problem of unity in the suite (apart from that which is a consequence of consistency of harmonic style, prevalent use of binary forms, and the like) is one of considerable difficulty. Many suites might not suffer from the exchange of, say, the *allemande* of one with that of another of the same style and tonality. In the evolution of the suite, however, certain significant practices of intermovement unity can be discerned: (1) the use of the same key for all of the movements; (2) the occasional use, as in the variation suite, of a common motive; (3) a unity of extramusical subject, as in programmatic suites; and (4) a comprehensive intermovement profile articulated in balances and contrasts imparting to the full sequence of movements an overall tempo-structure, dynamic contour, or broad configuration traced through other elements, in subtle compositional control of the sort observed in many variation sets (Chapters 9 and 10). Contrast of substance and character among suite movements, within stylistic uniformity, is vital in view of the absence, usually, of marked diversity within binary forms, and in the context of intermovement constancy of tonality.

ORIGINS OF THE SUITE

It is impossible to deal conclusively with the history of the suite in this chapter, and the reader is again urged to consult standard reference dictionaries, especially the *Harvard* and *New Grove* dictionaries.[1]

Dances are included in many sixteenth- and seventeenth-century collections of lute and keyboard music. In Chapter 10 reference was made to the sixteenth-century custom of joining dances in pairs, with contrast of meter (the first duple, the second triple, as a rule), contrast of tempo (the second dance usually faster), and affinity of theme. The second dance is sometimes called by the German word *Nachtanz* (literally, "after-dance") or designated *proportio,* from *proportio*

---

[1]Stanley Sadie, ed., *The New Grove Dictionary of Music and Musicians* (London: Macmillan, 1980).

tripla–a reference to its usual triple meter. (See Ex. 10.16, from a *passamezzo-saltarello* pair.)

Other dances frequently paired in the sixteenth century are the *pavane* and *gaillarde*—the former a slow, stately dance in duple meter, probably of Italian origin, and the latter a lively triple-meter dance. Later the *allemande* and *courante* form a dance pair which is ultimately incorporated into the mature suite. The dance pair of the late fifteenth and sixteenth centuries is extremely important in the evolution of the suite. The pairing of dances of common theme but opposing character ''was common to all countries of western Europe in the early sixteenth century, and was the germ out of which the seventeenth-century dance suite grew.''[2]

Some early sixteenth-century European publications of lute and keyboard music contain, in addition to dance pairs, ''suites'' of three or more dances grouped together, although it is not always clear whether the intention was that the group should in performance constitute an aggregate. One of the earliest of these, a publication of 1508 by the Venetian printer Ottaviano dei Petrucci, contains dances for lute in sets of three. Another lute collection, published in France in 1529 by Pierre Attaingnant, contains dances in groups of three or more. A German clavichord collection of 1571 by Elias Ammerbach contains, in addition to dance pairs, a ''suite'' of three movements.

English virginal books of the sixteenth century include dances, sometimes of polyphonic texture and occasionally with variations; an example of the latter is Byrd's ''Five Variations on a Galliard'' in the *Fitzwilliam Virginal Book*. Ensemble suites for viols, called ''lessons,'' are found in late-sixteenth-century and early-seventeenth-century English sources; examples are *Consort Lessons for Six Instruments* (1599) by Thomas Morley and *Lessons for Consorts* (1609) by Phillip Rosseter, both significant works in a movement that culminates in the suites of Purcell in the late seventeenth century.

Thus, instrumental collections in the sixteenth century often included dances, dance pairs, and occasional larger groups of dances, and lead toward the late seventeenth-century maturation of the dance suite.

The performance of instrumental excerpts from stage works, strung together in a kind of suite with the prelude or overture at the head, enjoyed a great vogue in seventeenth-century France, notably in the works of Lully. Many of the dances occurring in the operas and ballets of Lully, dances of both peasant and court origins, assumed important places among the *Galanterien* (optional dance group of lightest character) of the baroque suite.

As the suite evolved and became an established, highly popular form in late seventeenth-century music, dance movements tended to become more and more stylized; the basic group—*allemande, courante, sarabande,* and *gigue*—achieved in the high baroque a level of refinement and sophistication which sometimes ob-

---

[2]Homer Ulrich, *Chamber Music: The Growth and Practice of an Intimate Art* (New York: Columbia University Press, 1948), p. 69. Chapter 4 of Ulrich's book is a useful, although not recent, treatment of the history of the suite.

scured their dance origins, while those of the optional group—*bourrée, passepied,* etc.—retained more of the original dance character and simplicity of texture.

During the late seventeenth century the suite spread rapidly over Europe, becoming the vehicle for a large share of the instrumental art music of the time. In this period there is standardization neither of movement sequence nor of the number of movements in the suite. Qualities that appear relatively universal are the unity of key among the movements and, to a lesser but significant extent, a prevailing homophonic style with a clearly edged surface of melody which is at times richly ornamented. In the later baroque, the texture becomes more polyphonic, especially in certain movements, notably the allemande and gigue.

In an interesting general observation, Willi Apel comments on the various national contributions to the suite's evolution: "The development culminating in Bach's suites represents an interesting example of international cooperation. Briefly stated, Italy contributed the early development (16th century), England the gigue, Spain the saraband, France the great wealth of 17th-century dance types, and Germany the allemande as well as the concept of the suite as a unified . . . musical form."[3] The French dance groups, sometimes called *ordres,* often seem somewhat arbitrarily arranged as to tonality and dance type (Jacques Chambonnières, c. 1597–1672; Louis Couperin, 1626–61; and later composers), while German suites of the seventeenth century more often appear deliberately ordered for group unities, contrasts, balance, and performance length (for example, suites of Johann Hermann Schein, 1586–1630). The principal figure in the seventeenth-century suite is the German composer Johann Jacob Froberger (1616–67), whose keyboard suites are marked by an elegance, textural richness, and expressiveness which bring into carefully ordered and balanced form the outstanding qualities of the several national styles with which they are contemporary.

THE BAROQUE SUITE

The antecedents of the suite as well as its later developments are best viewed from the period in which it became established in its most definitive form and most universal acceptance, the late seventeenth and early eighteenth centuries. The following is a summary of characteristics of the baroque suite.

1. The individual movements continue to be commonly in binary form, although some are periods or incipient binaries, some are ternaries, and some (particulary non-dance movements) are free in form.
2. The inclusion of non-dance movements introduces an important source of contrast in form and style. Among the types to be found are *airs, intermezzi,* pieces with evocative titles (as in many of the French *ordres,* including those of François Couperin), rondos, fugues, ostinato forms, and preludes of varying types.
3. Unity of key throughout a suite continues to prevail. There are exceptions to the rule,

---

[3]*Harvard Dictionary of Music,* 2nd ed., p. 815.

such as the use of relative keys in dance pairs and, for further example, early *sonate da camera* of Arcangelo Corelli (1653–1713), in which the slow movement is occasionally in a different key.

4. Contrasts of tempo and meter are vital in the ordering of the suite. A typical arrangement is allemande–courante–sarabande–gigue, having a metric sequence of duple–triple–triple–compound duple, and a tempo sequence of, frequently, moderate–fast–slow–fast.

5. The majority of baroque suites are for keyboard, but important examples were written for chamber ensemble (for example, English works by such composers as Matthew Locke [c.1630–1677] and later Purcell) and for orchestra, culminating in the brilliant orchestral suites of Bach.

6. *Explicit* thematic unity, or cyclic procedure, is not a prevalent feature of the baroque suite except in *doubles* (Chapter 10) and in the variation suite.

7. The number of movements varies widely, from as few as three to over twenty in some of the French *ordres*. Most suites of the baroque consist of four to six movements.

8. The allemande, courante, sarabande, and gigue, in whatever order, gradually become established as the basic nucleus of the baroque suite. They form an ideally balanced distribution of expressive elements, with the sarabande fulfilling the function of slow movement. In addition to the basic group, optional dances are inserted *ad libitum,* many of them from French opera and ballet sources. The dances of the optional group constitute another important element of contrast, tending to be less stylized, more symmetrical, more sectional in form, simpler in texture, more straightforward in expression, and lighter in content.

The order of the basic group varies considerably. In Froberger the sequence is often allemande–courante–sarabande (ACS), with the gigue (G) appearing as an optional movement before or after the courante, and the sarabande concluding the suite. Ultimately, in the later baroque, the gigue and the sarabande exchanged positions, as in the suites of Georg Böhm (1661–1733) and Bach. Still, the location of the optional group (O) varies: in Pachelbel, for example, the order is commonly ACOSG; in Bach, it is ACSOG, with an introductory movement often added at the beginning of the suite. Further variation in the order of the basic group is seen in Corelli: for example, prelude–A or C (sometimes both)–S–G or *gavotte.*

A later section of this chapter considers specifically the suites of Bach and Handel, in whose works the form has its highest flowering.

THE INTRODUCTORY MOVEMENT

An introductory movement, whatever it is called, is especially in the keyboard suite often freer in rhythm, texture, and form than the later movements; it may be assembled of a number of contrasting and corresponding sections, and may employ an improvisatory, rhapsodic style which differs strikingly from that of the dance movements of the suite proper.

Example 11.1 is the sort of prelude that conveys the impression of playing

Ex. 11.1   Handel, Suite No. 1 in A for harpsichord.

extempore, in a free and tentative manner, with idiomatic passagework and with tonality strongly affirmed.

The prelude may command attention with brilliant virtuosic display. A case in point is Ex. 11.2, the beginning of the Prelude of Bach's first *English Suite,* whose opening 2 measures are made up of rapid tonic- and dominant-oriented figures comprising an amplified upbeat to the a^2 of m.2, from which, in m. 3, the principal imitative subject descends. (An arresting, forceful beginning far removed from the baroque period is that of Debussy's *Suite Bergamasque* for piano.)

Specific types of introductory movement occurring in suites and partitas of Bach are discussed in a later section.

Ex. 11.2   Bach, English Suite No. 1 in A, Prelude.

SOME IMPORTANT COMPONENTS
OF THE BAROQUE SUITE

The movement types listed below are some of the most basic of the baroque suite; they include the four (ACSG) which constitute a relatively fixed nucleus as well as a few of the less universal dances used among the *Galanterien*. All of the listed dances are found in the suites of Bach, although not all the dances used by Bach are listed here. The reader will easily find descriptions and examples of dance forms other than those included below, and is urged in this connection to consult the *Harvard Dictionary* concerning undefined dance names occurring in this chapter (and including especially types found in Bach suites: *anglaise, loure, passepied, polonaise, siciliano,* and others).

The descriptions given here are in general based upon the characters of the dances as they appear in the baroque suite. It must be understood that many dances, whether peasant or aristocratic, underwent extreme evolutionary changes before arriving at the sophistication seen in the art music of major composers. For instance, the sarabande, which is a dignified movement in slow tempo in the baroque suite, is thought to have been a tumultuous dance in its early history. It must be acknowledged, finally, that there is little that can be said in general description of any given dance form that cannot be contradicted by an unorthodox example.

Air[4]

The *air* (It., *aria*) is, as might be assumed, a movement of lyric style: a melody of often songlike character against a relatively simple background, the texture usually homophonic. Although often designed to accompany dances in seventeenth- and eighteenth-century French opera and ballet, the *air* as it appears in the suite is not a dance form.

Frequently in the baroque period the melody of the air is ornamented. A movement of this kind, often intense, is of great importance as a source of variety in the suite. Example 11.3, from a modern suite for violin, shows the slow, *cantabile* character of the air.

Ex. 11.3   Stevens, Suite for solo violin, third movement.
© 1958 by Halsey Stevens. International copyright secured. Used by permission.

[4]The French terms are used here, except in the case of the minuet (Fr., *menuet*), in preference to such English terms as *jig* and *saraband*.

Ex. 11.3 (continued)

Ornamented reprise (measure 56):

A very famous baroque example is the air from Bach's Orchestra Suite No. 3 in D, whose movement sequence is that of French overture, air, gavotte I, gavotte II and *da capo* of the first, bourrée, and gigue. The second movement is best known as "Air for the G-string" in a much played transcription for the violin. Another air was quoted in excerpt as Ex. 2.3.

Allemande

One of the primary dances of the baroque suite, usually the opening movement when there is no prelude, the allemande is moderate in tempo, and it is in simple duple meter, sometimes of a sumptuous, flowing quality. It usually has an anacrusis, of variable length—from a single 16th-note to as many as 3 notes. (It is not difficult to find allemandes without anacrusis: the sixteenth-century example by Claude Gervaise in *HAM,* Vol. I, is a case in point.)

In addition to Ex. 11.4, reference may be made to Exx. 2.5 and 2.12.

In English sources like the *Fitzwilliam Virginal Book,* the name appears in such forms as *alman* and *almagne*. While the dance is known to be of German origin, it is not certain that the allemande of the baroque suite has a basis in actual dance. In the baroque suite, the allemande is more usually polyphonic in texture than any of the other movements except the gigue.

Ex. 11.4   Handel, Suite No. 10 in D minor for harpsichord.

Bourrée

A French dance, apparently from the Auvergne, the bourrée is a good example of an optional dance which entered the baroque suite from stage works of Lully. It is comparable in some respects to the gavotte, but has an anacrusis of only a quarter-bar and is somewhat more animated. It is in simple duple meter; rhythms like ♩ ♫♩ ♩ are characteristic.

Found in the *French* and *English Suites* of Bach, the bourrée is sometimes followed by a second bourrée and a *da capo* repeat of the first.

Ex. 11.5 Bach, Suite (Ouverture) in F.

Courante

This dance movement is of two types in the baroque suite—one of them French (*courante*), the other Italian (*corrente*). Both types emerged in the seventeenth century and were taken into the basic dance group of the suite.

The *courante* has an anacrusis of 1 to 3 notes, is in simple triple meter (often 3/2), more moderate in tempo than its Italian counterpart, somewhat more contrapuntal in texture, and often characterized by dotted rhythms. Example 11.6 shows a typical feature: the use of *hemiola* (the temporal juxtaposition of simple triple and compound duple meters, 3/2 and 6/4 in this case), a rhythmic device which occurs often at cadential points in the courante and occasionally within the phrase as well. (See also Ex. 2.9.)

The *corrente,* as its Italian name suggests, is a dance of "running" movement; its meter is usually 3/4 or 3/8 and its tempo quite lively. As might be expected in view of its faster motion, the texture is often simpler and more homophonic than that of the courante, although many examples contain contrapuntal imitation (see Bach's fifth *French Suite*). The anacrusis, when present, is comparable to that of the courante. Example 11.7 is testimony to the fact that many sonatas of the period include dance movements; this one contains a gigue as well.

The name given by the composer (or editor) is not always in accord with the actual character of the music. In the fourth *French Suite*, Bach uses the title "Courante" for a movement whose texture, motion, and meter suggest the corrente, although the dotted rhythms and restrained tempo might be considered features of the courante. There is no reason why a movement cannot combine features of both

Ex. 11.6   Creston, Pre-Classic Suite, Op. 71, for orchestra, first movement (reduction).

Ex. 11.7   Vivaldi, Sonata in A, Op. 2, No. 2, for violin and figured bass, third movement (figured bass realized by F. David).

forms; and indeed the two names are, while in general practice denoting significant differences of style and texture, of the same root and literal meaning.

Excellent examples of the courante can be found in the suites of Frescobaldi. Bach's *English Suites* include examples of the French type, as do the second and fourth harpsichord *Partitas;* the Italian form is seen in the *French Suites,* Nos. 2, 4, 5, and 6, and in the *Partitas,* Nos. 1, 3, 5, and 6.

Gavotte

The *gavotte* is a graceful French dance, moderate in tempo, and of simple duple meter. Its most distinctive feature is the presence, except in very early examples, of a half-bar anacrusis which is often repeated with every phrase. The phrases are typically short, often of 2 measures. Example 11.8 illustrates these features and also shows the French practice of titling dance movements. (See also Ex. 11.13.)

Ex. 11.8   F. Couperin, La Bourbonnoise, gavotte from Premier Ordre.

Here again is a dance of the optional group which came into fashion with the stage works of such French composers as Lully and Rameau. Actually, the gavotte continued to flourish in French opera of the later eighteenth century and beyond.

This dance is often paired with a second, the *musette. Musette,* like *loure,* is originally the name of a French instrument of the bagpipe type, and the musette as a dance form (that is, *à la musette*) occurring in association with the gavotte is characterized by a drone. Usually the gavotte is repeated following the musette, the total form being a compound ternary. Bach's third *English Suite* contains an example; in the sixth *English Suite* the second gavotte is also of musette character, although simply titled "Gavotte II." In the first of these the drone is a sustained note; in the second, it is repeated in remarkable animation on the second half of every beat.

Example 11.9 shows a twentieth-century composer's use of the baroque gavotte-musette pair with *da capo.* In Ex. 11.9, the drone (on G) and the gavotte-like features of the musette are clearly apparent.

Gigue

Another of the basic group, the *gigue* (It., *giga*) is of sixteenth-century English or Irish origin. Its distinctive features are quick tempo, compound meter (usually du-

Ex. 11.9   Schoenberg, Suite for piano, Op. 25, second movement.

ple, occasionally triple), frequent wide leaps, and, in the baroque suite, imitative texture.[5] Example 11.10 shows the beginnings of Parts I and II of a Bach gigue. In addition, the reader may consult Exs. 2.6 and 2.11.

Part II of the gigue binary, as seen below, often starts with a new exposition of the motive using a mirror inversion of the original.

Exceptions to the principle of compound meter are found in Bach's first *French Suite* and sixth harpsichord *Partita*. In the former, the meter is 4/4; in the latter, 4/2. In both there is a prevalence of dotted rhythms in more moderate tempo than usual, although both of these anomalous examples conform in the use of imitation and inversion in the second half. In general, metric irregularities in the harpsi-

Ex. 11.10   Bach, English Suite No. 4 in F, final movement.

m.25

<hr>

[5]Apel's *Harvard Dictionary* entry on gigue (pp. 346–47) distinguishes between the more common French type (compound meter and imitative texture, as illustrated in Ex. 11.10) and a rarer Italian type, of faster tempo and nonimitative texture (for example, the *giga* of Bach's first *Partita*). Apel also notes exceptions to the characteristic compound meter, citing examples by Froberger in 4/4 meter.

chord suites of Bach are more apparent than real: where the meter is 3/8 (fifth *English Suite,* second and third *French Suites*) each pair of measures is, to the ear, obviously analogous to a single compound duple measure. In the first *Partita,* the notated meter signature is 4/4 but triplets are used throughout.

The Italian *giga* of such composers as Giovanni Battista Vitali (c. 1644–92), Corelli, and their contemporaries is sometimes set apart as a distinct genre, having faster motion and simpler, less imitative texture. Most of Bach's gigues, like those of Froberger and Handel, are of the French type, with fugal texture, but this is not invariably true; in this respect too the gigue of Bach's first *Partita* is exceptional.

The gigue is usually the final movement of the baroque suite, despite such exceptions as Bach's second *Partita* and many of the suites of Froberger.

Minuet

The minuet is the most familiar of all the dances of the baroque suite, because of its survival in later chamber music, symphonies, and solo sonatas, and because of its association (despite its rustic origins) with courtly dance and ceremony in the seventeenth and eighteenth centuries. Again, the works of Lully were an important vehicle for the popularization of this dance type.

It is a stately dance in moderate tempo and in triple meter. In the baroque period the minuet characteristically lacks an upbeat, although the upbeat does appear in some minuets by Lully and often in those of classical multimovement sonatas.

The minuet is often paired with a second minuet, followed by the first *da capo.* The second of the pair is frequently called the *trio,* as in Bach's third *French Suite* (see pp. 87–89). The performance of minuets in *alternativo* form is seen even in the early baroque. Example 11.11 is from a twentieth-century example; it, too, is followed by a ''trio'' and *da capo* return.

Numerous minuet examples have been cited already, including Exx. 3.19 (a

Ex. 11.11   Piston, Suite for oboe and piano, third movement.

later, rather free interpretation of the minuet), 4.6, and 4.20. It is the only dance of those discussed here to have survived significantly in later periods.

Sarabande

Apparently of Mexican origin, the *sarabande* came into Europe through Spain in the early sixteenth century, and thence into vogue in France and England a century later.[6] It is of slow tempo (the only slow dance in the basic group of the baroque suite), and triple meter, usually 3/2 or 3/4. It begins without anacrusis. ♩ ♩. ♩ | ♩ 𝅝 is a typical rhythm; the slight cessation of motion and consequent agogic accent on the second beat are characteristic of the sarabande. (An exception may be seen in Bach's third *French Suite*.)

The sarabande of Bach's sixth *Partita* shows an especially high degree of idealization and refinement. The memorable sarabande illustrated in Ex. 11.12 was written in the first year of the twentieth century.

Ex. 11.12   Debussy, Suite Pour le Piano, second movement.

Permission for reprint granted by Editions Jean Jobert, Paris, France, copyright owners, and Elkan-Vogel Co., Inc., Philadelphia, Pa., agents.

THE SUITES OF BACH AND HANDEL

It is in the suites of Bach and Handel, the two giants of the baroque period, and especially in those of Bach, that the form is seen at its zenith, enjoying a degree of importance which it attains in no other age.

In most of the suites of these two composers the basic group, ACSG, occurs in that order, although this is less true in Handel than in Bach. A prelude or other introductory movement is used in some of the suites of both, and the most usual place for one or more of the optional dances is between sarabande and gigue.

The four orchestra suites of Bach begin with *French overtures* of the type associated with Lully: opening *grave,* rather fast fugal section, and sometimes a brief concluding passage, again *grave,* with dotted rhythms normally dominant in

[6]A case for the Mexican origin of the *sarabande* is made by Robert Stevenson in "The Sarabande, a Dance of American Descent," *Inter-American Music Bulletin,* July 1962, pp. 1–13.

the slow sections. In these suites there is no fixed order of a basic group, as there is in the harpsichord suites. The movement sequence of the third Suite appears on p. 329. Another example, the Suite in C, has the following movements: French overture, courante, gavotte, *forlana* (a Venetian dance of spirited character in compound duple meter, often compared to the gigue), minuet, bourrée, and concluding passepied. Some of the movements have a second dance, often in three voices and occasionally in related keys, and *da capo* repeats (the gavotte, minuet, bourrée and passepied of the C major Suite). A *double* follows the polonaise of the second Suite. Some of the movements in these suites are uncommon; there is, for example, a *badinerie*—a dancelike movement of humorous quality—as finale of the Suite in B minor. The Suite No. 4 in D concludes with a *réjouissance,* a piece of vigorous motion in triple meter.

Inevitably, attention ultimately focuses on the six *French* and six *English Suites* and the six *Partitas*. In the summary of movement sequence, given below, upper-case letters (ACSG) are used to represent the basic group. Optional dances and other movement types (needed definitions will be found in the *Harvard Dictionary*) are abbreviated as follows: a, air; ang, anglaise; b, bourrée; bur, burlesca; c, capriccio; g, gavotte; l, loure; m, minuet; p, passepied; pol, polonaise; pr, introductory movement (prelude or other); r, rondeau; and s, scherzo.

French Suites	*Key*	*Movement Sequence*
No. I	d	A, C, S, m-1, m-2, G
No. II	c	A, C, S, a, m, G
No. III	b	A, C, S, ang, m, trio, G
No. IV	E-flat	A, C, S, g, m, a, G
No. V	G	A, C, S, g, b, l, G
No. VI	E	A, C, S, g, pol, b, m, G

English Suites

No. I	A	pr, A, C-1, C-2 with 2 *doubles,* S, b-1, b-2, G
No. II	a	pr, A, C, S with *double,* b-1, b-2, G
No. III	g	pr, A, C, S with *double,* g-1, g-2 à la musette, G
No. IV	F	pr, A, C, S, m-1, m-2, G
No. V	e	pr, A, C, S, p-1 *en rondeau,* p-2, G
No. VI	d	pr, A, C, S with *double,* g-1, g-2, G

Partitas

No. I	B-flat	pr, A, C, S, m-1, m-2, G
No. II	c	pr *(sinfonia)*, A, C, S, r, c
No. III	a	pr *(fantasia)*, A, C, S, bur, s, G
No. IV	D	pr (overture), A, C, a, S, m, G
No. V	G	pr, A, C, S, m, p, G
No. VI	e	pr (toccata), A, C, a, S, g, G

We may draw certain conclusions regarding the types of movements used in these suites and the sequence in which they appear. The basic group appears consistently in the order ACSG and is complete except in the second *Partita,* which has no gigue. The optional group is placed between sarabande and gigue except in the fourth and sixth *Partitas,* where a non-dance movement titled *air* or *aria* is inserted between courante (or corrente) and sarabande. The number of movements in the optional group varies from two to four, the larger number found in the sixth *French Suite.*

The *Partitas* and *English Suites* have introductory movements. The study of form in these preludes is extremely rewarding, since the prelude is in some cases the longest and most challenging movement of the suite. We shall make some summary comments respecting the introductory movements of the *Partitas,* leaving their rich details, and those of the corresponding movements of the *English Suites,* for the reader's independent study.

The first three *Partitas* have inventionlike opening movements (the "invention" is discussed in Chapter 12). The first might, in fact, be compared with Bach's two-voice invention in the same key. Like a typical invention, this first prelude is sectionalized by cadential arrival points on related tonics, here dominant and relative minor. The prelude of the second *Partita,* called "Sinfonia," is in three sections. The first is marked by strong dotted rhythms and homophonic texture, and ends on the dominant; the second, andante, resembles an invention despite the failure of the initiating motive to recur strictly; the third, rigorously imitative, is in a contrasting triple meter, and ends in an 8-measure codetta.

The opening movement of the third *Partita,* labeled "Fantasia," is a 2-voice invention; its 2-measure subject is imitated canonically at the octave and subsequently treated in sequential development, at times in fragments. The whole is, typically, sectionalized by cadences on related tonics.

The French overture which opens the fourth *Partita* is characteristically slow in its first section, with dotted rhythms and homophonic texture typical of the form. The subsequent fugal section, on a 2-measure subject, includes two contrasting episodes in which the texture becomes abruptly thinner and more homophonic, and in which the subject in its full form is relinquished, to reemerge assertively where the fugal texture is resumed (mm. 48 and 104).

The movement which begins the fifth *Partita,* in G, is titled "Praeambulum." Like some of the preludes of the *Well-Tempered Clavier,* it is mainly homophonic. Its character is unpretentious and uncomplicated; often it is improvisational in style, as in the section beginning at m. 5. Occasional areas of 2-voice counterpoint (see m. 21, for example) contrast with the pure homophony of the theme, which recurs strictly at mm. 17 (in D), 41 (in E minor), and 65 (in C). Unity derives from motive repetition and development, as well as from a characteristic tonal plan in which modulations orbit in closely related tonal regions around the G tonic.

The toccata which begins the last *Partita* is a brilliantly wrought ternary design: its flanking sections (mm. 1–26 and 89–108) are relatively homophonic, and improvisational, yet rich in double counterpoint.[7] The middle section, starting at m. 27, is a 3-voice fugue, beginning with a full exposition (I-V-I) of its 3-measure subject. Episodic developments are preoccupied with the subject's opening motive of three 8th-notes, and are relentless in the baroque standard of constant rhythmic articulation of the surface. An anomaly in the fugue is that, adjusting to the material surrounding it, it begins in E minor and ends in B minor.

In these eighteen suites, the optional movement appearing most frequently, excluding preludes, is the minuet, which occurs in nine of the suites. The gavotte is second in frequency, appearing in six of the suites. Four of the suites have airs and four have bourrées, while the passepied is used twice. Other optional movements—anglaise, loure, polonaise—have one appearance each, as do non-dance movements titled scherzo, rondeau, capriccio, and burlesca. All of the latter four types are found in the *Partitas,* which are in many ways the most anomalous of the harpsichord suites.

The Handel keyboard suites are not as well known as those of Bach, with the exception of the fifth, in E, which contains the "Harmonious Blacksmith" variations (see Ex. 10.6), and the ninth, in B-flat, which contains the aria theme used for a brilliant set of piano variations by Brahms (see Ex. 10.7). The composer called the suites "lessons," in the English tradition. The first eight were published in 1720 and the second eight in 1733. The basic group order ACSG is observed for the greater part in Nos. 9–16, which, like the *French Suites* of Bach, are written without introductory movements.

Of the first eight suites, only No. 4 has the four basic movements in the characteristic sequence. In some, no more than half of the basic group is present, and in No. 2 no dance movements occur at all (its movement sequence is Adagio–Allegro–Adagio–Fugue). The seventh, in G minor, includes a passacaglia in addition to an andante, an allegro, and a sarabande. There are several fugues among the movements of the sixteen suites of these two volumes. Suites Nos. 1–8 have preludes. Because of the frequency and even occasional predominance of non-dance movements, the suites of Handel are sometimes regarded as hybrids, and some even as sonatas rather than suites. In any event, all of the works are valuable for the study of multimovement form.

Except for the occasional compound ternary (formed by paired movements with *da capo*), simple ternary, or rondo, the components of the suite of Bach and Handel are in binary form. This excludes the preludes, which we have seen even in a limited sampling to be of a wide variety of styles, types, and forms, and some of the many non-dance movements of the Handel suites. Unity of key throughout the suite is the rule though exceptions occur (see the two minuets of Bach's fourth *English Suite*).

---

[7]There are interesting passages of double counterpoint (see p. 359 for definition), as in mm. 9–11. Especially striking is the relationship between m. 22 and its contrapuntal inversion at m. 23: in the latter the notes occur in their original sequence but in different octaves; consequently the melodic intervals are radically transformed, in a variation procedure suggestive of twentieth-century serial technique.

Even the optional dances lose something of their original innocence in the later development of the baroque suite. For comparison, a gavotte by Lully is shown in a brief excerpt together with the opening of the gavotte from Bach's fourth *French Suite* (Exx. 11.13a and b), over whose usual rhythms Bach weaves a fabric of tight motivic unity, with imitation at the octave. The Lully example is clearly of dance character and in fact intended as music for dance, utterly homophonic, and without such sophistications as motivic repetition and development—in all of these features opposite to the Bach example.

Ex. 11.13a   Lully, Cadmus et Hermione, gavotte from Act V.

Ex. 11.13b   Bach, French Suite No. 4 in E-flat, fourth movement.

Further comparison could be made between the sarabande of Lully's *Le Ballet de l'Amour Malade* (*première entrée*)—texturally uncomplicated, unadorned, of danceable quality—with, say, that of Bach's third *English Suite*.

THE LATER SUITE

After the baroque period the suite is eclipsed by the emerging multimovement sonata form of classical keyboard, chamber, and symphonic music. The suite does not, however, disappear; although it ceases after the mid-eighteenth century to have the reasonably definitive form it had known, vestigial traces of the form are important in later genres, including the sonata itself. Moreover, the suite again becomes an important vehicle of expression in the twentieth century.

Any definition of the later suite must be very general. "The later uses of the word 'suite' comprise almost all sets of pieces mainly in forms smaller than those of the sonata, especially such pieces as have been selected from ballets or from incidental music to plays."[8] "On the whole, the suite in the nineteenth century no longer had as fixed and definite a form as in the eighteenth. Any series of loosely connected pieces of entirely different types (with the exception of the sonata form) could now be linked together in a suite."[9]

Dance forms, ancient and modern, continue to have an important part in the suite; where non-dance movements are involved, distinction can be made only on the basis of relative movement length and relative lightness or weightiness of content. Certainly the presence or absence of pronounced thematic contrast and development within movements is a factor in both of these criteria. Thus, while the suite after the baroque loses much of its vitality and definition, it continues in related forms (see below) and in recent periods comes back into practice much less universally but with importance as a multimovement work of light, sometimes dancelike character, consisting of movements which lack the expansive and vigorous thematic manipulations and tonal fluctuations of the sonata.

Certain nineteenth-century composers sought consciously to bring about a recrudescence of the baroque type of suite, but their works are virtually unknown today. We may mention Franz Lachner (1803–90), who wrote orchestra suites, and Julius Otto Grimm (1827–1903), whose *Suite in Canon Form* for strings seems worthy of more than a passing glance.

The practice of assembling pieces from stage works into suites usually preceded by the original prelude or overture is still a vital practice. Examples include George Bizet's (1838–75) *L'Arlésienne,* incidental music to a play, later molded into an orchestra suite; Tchaikovsky's Suite from the *Nutcracker* ballet; Stravinsky's Suite from the ballet *Firebird*; Elliott Carter's Suite from the ballet *The Minotaur.* Such suites often are compounded of rather extensive movements sometimes with substantial thematic development. But the term "suite" is deemed appropriate here in view of their descriptive or programmatic intent, and a consequent relative negation of purely abstract, musical significance. Often strict dance forms are included, especially in suites extracted from ballets. A suite of this kind naturally involves recasting of the original music with appropriate cuts, bridges, rearrangements of sequence, changed endings, and the like.

While in modern suites the baroque concept of invariance of key is commonly abandoned, the unity of related tonics orbiting a central tonic remains an important factor. Effective contrast is still vital in the ordering of movements, and explicit intermovement connection is often fortified by reference to a central, extramusical subject (Nicolai Rimsky-Korsakov [1844–1908], *Sheherazade*) or the cyclic use of common thematic elements among the movements (Alexander Borodin [1833–87], "Polovtzian Dances" from *Prince Igor*). The latter also affords an example of the

---

[8]Tovey, *The Forms of Music,* p. 235.
[9]Hugo Leichtentritt, *Musical Form* (Cambridge, Mass.: Harvard University Press, 1956), p. 94.

use of indigenous ethnic dances and folk materials in suites of strongly national character which begin to appear in the late nineteenth century. An American example is seen in the *Indian Suite,* Op. 48, of Edward MacDowell (1861–1908).

Many recent suites incorporate the rhythms and character of baroque and pre-baroque dances in new tonal-harmonic styles: Ravel's *Le Tombeau de Couperin;* d'Indy's *Suite dans le style ancien* (two of whose movements are ''Sarabande'' and ''Menuet''); Debussy's *Petite suite,* which includes a *menuet* and a *cortège*—a solemn march—as well as a titled piece, *En bateau,* in the manner of early French *ordres;* Schoenberg's Suite for piano, Op. 25; and Bartók's *Dance Suite* for orchestra.

We have mentioned that in the recent dance suite the repertory of dances is greatly broadened. Examples are the polka in Dvořák's Suite for orchestra, Op. 39, and the fox-trot of Alfredo Casella's (1883–1947) Five Pieces for string quartet (1920). Walter Piston's Suite from *The Incredible Flutist* includes both old (minuet, siciliano) and new (tango—free, in 5/8 meter) dances, and Gunther Schuller's (b. 1925) Suite for woodwind quintet has a ''blues'' movement between the opening prelude and concluding toccata.

In summary, the later suite consists of relatively short, light, often descriptive movements, sometimes fancifully titled, freely assembled for balance and contrast as well as, in some cases, for unity of narrative or extramusical subject. The movements are often dance forms or dancelike pieces. The suite is usually written for orchestra or for keyboard or some other solo instrument, but relatively rarely for chamber ensemble. This is not surprising considering the depth of intellectual engagement commonly associated with chamber music since the late eighteenth century.

THE VARIATION SUITE

The variation suite is a series of dances and other suite movements built on a common theme, a procedure related to the dance with *double* and the sixteenth-century dance pair. In some variation suites there are movements which do not employ the otherwise common theme.

The variation suite has significance as an effective solution to the problem of intermovement unity. Tonal as well as thematic unity generally prevails; the result is a multimovement form in which the individual components are tightly interconnected, with contrasting elements lending interest and profile as in any multimovement work.

Bach approaches this principle closely in the *Partita* in B minor for solo violin, in which paired dances are related by the use of harmonically-fixed variation. The sequence of A-C-S-bourrée is extended in that each movement is followed by its *double.* Example 11.14 quotes from the final movement and its subsequent variation.

A series of variations on a dance movement (as seen also in Byrd's *Five Vari-*

Ex. 11.14 Bach, Partita No. 1 in B minor for solo violin, fourth movement and double.

Tempo di Bourrée.

Double.

ations on a Galliard, mentioned earlier) may be judged a kind of variation suite, although what is usually meant by the term is a series of disparate dance types united by the use of related thematic material.

The variation suite is as old as the suite itself. The German composer Paul Peuerl published suites in 1611 in which the movements are related by common motives. Some of the suites of Schein's *Banchetto musicale* (1617) show a degree of intermovement motivic correspondence. Composers who wrote variation suites for orchestra include Andreas Hammerschmidt (1612–75) and Johann Kuhnau (1660–1722). An unusual specimen in this tradition is Buxtehude's Suite (sarabande, courante, gigue) on the chorale "Auf meinen lieben Gott."

A nineteenth-century example is the piano work *Six Pieces on a Single Theme,* Op. 21, by Tchaikovsky; this set was listed in Chapter 10 for the study of variation.

THE SUITE BY OTHER NAMES;
RELATED MULTIMOVEMENT FORMS

In all periods in which the suite has existed it has been known by other names in various national styles, and some of its features have often been incorporated into coexisting related forms.

In the seventeenth and eighteenth centuries the Italian word *partita* (Ger. *Parthie, Partie*) sometimes means suite, although its more proper meaning is variation. Bach uses it in both senses: the chorale variations for organ are sometimes called partitas, while six suites for harpsichord and three for solo violin bear the same title. We have seen the use of the word *lesson* for the early English suite and *ordre* for French dance collections.

In the baroque, both the chamber form *sonata da camera* and the *concerto grosso* often contain dance movements. The distinction between the *sonata da camera* (as "suite") and *da chiesa* (as "sonata") is not to be oversimplified; for example, the latter may have a giguelike movement as its conclusion and the former sometimes has *chiesa* movements in addition to those in the domain of the strict suite.

Dance movements are found also in, for example, the *concerti grossi* of Torelli and Muffat. Bach's *Brandenburg Concerto* No. 1 in F includes a polacca as well as a minuet. (See also, in this connection, Chapter 8, p.229.) *Concerti grossi* in which dance movements are prominent are sometimes called *concerti da camera.*

In the late seventeenth and early eighteenth centuries, suites preceded by a French overture were frequently called *ouverture* (Muffat, Georg Philipp Telemann, 1681–1767). We have noted this practice in Bach's designation of the *Partita* in B minor from the *Clavierübung.*

In the classical period there came into fashion multimovement works for chamber ensembles of string and wind instruments consisting of as many as eight and ten movements, some of them dancelike, and most in small forms, exhibiting a light, diverting character. These works were variously called *divertimento* (Fr., *divertissement), notturno* (not to be confused with the nineteenth-century piano salon piece), serenade (It., *serenata), and* cassation. The relationship of these genres to the earlier suite is based less on the prevalence of dance movements than on the brevity and relaxed, entertaining character of the movements.

The divertimenti of Haydn and Mozart, which often contain two minuets, indicate a popularity never again achieved by this type of work. Mozart wrote three cassations—K. 62, 63, and 99 (each of the latter two having a march and two minuets). Haydn's *Feldpartiten* and notturni (2 *lire,* 2 clarinets, 2 horns, 2 violas, and double-bass) are specimens of the same type of piece. Mozart's Serenade in D (*Haffner),* K. 250, has three minuets; his *Eine kleine Nachtmusik,* K. 525, is an extremely well-known example of the same species. Beethoven wrote serenades (Opp. 8 and 25); Schubert's Octet in F, Op. 166, is a similar work; Brahms wrote serenades for orchestra, the one in D, Op. 11, containing two minuets. Later comparable works are Dvořák's Serenades in E, Op. 22, for strings, and in D minor, Op. 44, for mixed ensemble, as well as Elgar's Serenade in E minor, Op. 20, for strings.

EXERCISES

1. In addition to the works cited in this chapter, make a study of several of the following. Try to see and hear a variety of types, without necessarily reviewing all of the music in detail.
    Bach, Suites for solo cello
    Bartók, Orchestra Suites, Op. 3 and Op. 4.
        Suite for piano, Op. 14
    Bizet, *Petite suite* for orchestra (from *Jeux d'enfants* for piano duet)
    Bloch, *Suite symphonique*
    Ferruccio Busoni (1866–1924), Suite from *Turandot* (opera by Busoni), Op. 41
    Casella, Concerto for string quartet
    Luigi Dallapiccola (1904–75), Partita for orchestra
    Irving Fine (1914–62), Partita for wind quintet
    Charles Griffes, *Roman Sketches* for piano, Op. 7
    Handel, Suites No. 4 and No. 12 in E minor for harpsichord
    Gustav Holst (1874–1934), *The Planets*
    André Jolivet (1905–74), *Suite delphique*

Ulysses Kay (b. 1917), Suite for orchestra
Křenek, Two Suites for piano, Op. 26
Darius Milhaud (1892–1974), *Suite provençale*
Modest Mussorgsky (1839–81), *Pictures at an Exhibition*
Persichetti, Serenade No. 5 for orchestra, Op. 43
Piston, Partita for violin, viola, and organ
Ravel, *Ma mère l'oye* (orchestral or 4-hand piano version)
Riegger, *Suite for Younger Orchestras,* Op. 56
Albert Roussel (1869–1937), Piano Suite, Op. 14
    Suite in F for orchestra, Op. 33
    Petite suite for orchestra, Op. 39
    Concert suite from the ballet *Le Festin de l'araignée*
Schuller, *Contours* for small orchestra
Schumann, *Papillons* for piano, Op. 2
Halsey Stevens (b. 1908), Suite for clarinet (or viola) and piano
Stravinsky, *March, Waltz, Polka* and *Galop* for small orchestra (1919)
    Suites from the ballets, e.g., *Petrushka, L'Histoire du soldat, Pulcinella*
Tchaikovsky, Suites Nos. 1, 2, and 3, Opp. 43, 53, and 55, for orchestra

2. List the dance forms mentioned but not described in this chapter, along with their defining characteristics. Refer to the *Harvard Dictionary* or other sources.

3. Analyze intermovement contrast and unity and such factors as overall tempo-, texture- (or other element-) shape in a suite of your choosing.

4. Study one of the following groups of suites to determine (1) which movements are in binary form, (2) whether unity of key prevails, and (3) to what extent dance movements are used.

   a) Bach's suites for solo cello

   b) Handel's first eight suites for harpsichord

   c) The solo violin and cello suites of Bloch

   d) Any two of the *ordres* of F. Couperin

5. Find an example of variation suite and make a study of the variation techniques used.

6. Compare form, rhythm, texture, and general character in four or five sarabandes of different composers and periods (for example: Frescobaldi, Bach, Roussel, and Dallapiccola).

7. Make the above comparison with a group of gigues, including an example by Goffredo Petrassi (b. 1904).

8. Why is the aria "Lascia ch'io pianga" from Handel's opera *Rinaldo* characterized as a sarabande?

9. Do you feel that Bloch's Suite for viola and piano (or viola and orchestra) is appropriately titled? Give reasons for your answer. Similarly consider the composer's *Suite modale* for flute and piano.

12

FUGUE AND
RELATED GENRES

Is the fugue a form? Certainly it exhibits, over some three hundred years, important common features of form: the initiating exposition of a thematic subject, recurrence of the theme, episodic development and tonal flux in areas central to the structure, and tonic (usually with thematic) return in the final stages. These are form-defining characteristics, if we consider that form has as one of its essential bases the *plan* of tonal and thematic events marking the directions of (expository and developmental) action. Like other forms, the fugue unfolds in a ''narrative'' or ''scenario'' embodying an ordering of circumstances, conditions, materials, and stages of occurrence of identifiable kinds capable of broad generalization. That is what this chapter is about.

Obviously all forms vary in realization. The schematic definition of the prototype is always fictional, yet always true. The features by which fugue is defined are as valid as anything that can be said of any form; the subject exposition, development, and restabilizing recurrence, within a unified tonal configuration, in themselves define fugal form.

There are usually distinct sections—two, three, or more, interconnected (in the single, as opposed to double fugue) by a common subject. If we recall that tripartition normally implies a third, rounding section recalling the first part's content and tonality (*ABA*), it will become apparent that a ternary concept of fugal form is not supportable in the same sense. Tonally, however, the fugue's form is rounded. And it is reasonable to regard the form as consisting of three *stages* of events, or processes: (1) the exposition of the subject material; (2) tonal variation with subject recurrence in single entries or groups, usually interspersed with episodes developing subject fragments; and (3) the return to the tonic, with the subject recurring in the tonic at least once. Such stages may involve more than three sections, and are often defined by cadential articulations *as well as* by distinct identifying factors of content and procedure.

The baroque is a period of unsurpassed achievement in fugue, and the form is, like the suite, best viewed from that vantage point, the period of its greatest universality. Somewhat less common in the nineteenth century, the fugue assumes a renewed vitality in the twentieth; yet, the dominant association of eighteenth-century practice of fugue is seen in modern tendencies to regard fugue-writing as "neobaroque."

This chapter outlines in detail the organization and anatomy of fugue as seen in major phases of its existence. Before proceeding, we may quote a few words from Karl Eschman, who expresses well a view that sees in three primary forms of music three basic processes of musical development, "three fundamental procedures which may be used, if a form of some type is to result: (1) we may repeat the idea with a difference (variation); (2) we may develop some part or all of the idea in a process of germination, induced by its inherent potentiality acting within its environment (the environment in the Sonata-form is in part, at least, furnished by conflict and contrast with other musical ideas), and (3) we may imitate it and extend its ramifications in a horizontal structure of more than one stratum; that is, we may present the idea in contrapuntal 'flight' or fugue."[1]

ORIGINS OF THE FUGUE

Although much remains to be learned about the historical evolution of forms based on imitative counterpoint, it is likely that evolution would be traced from polyphony of the thirteenth century, and would include such fourteenth-century canonic forms as the *rota* and *rondellus* (types of medieval round) and *caccia* (It. for "chase"; see No. 52 in *HAM*, Vol. I). An important place in that history would be occupied by the great fifteenth-century Flemish polyphonic school of such composers as Johannes Ockeghem (c. 1420–1495) and Jacob Obrecht (c. 1450–1505), examples of whose works will be found in the *Historical Anthology*. The reader should consult these examples, as well as the commentary that accompanies them.

Josquin des Prez, whose sacred and secular vocal works represent the culmination of the fifteenth-century Flemish school, must be reckoned a figure of monumental significance in the early history of polyphonic music. Josquin's motets are frequently sectional, with each section exposing its own subject, in a technique later seen in direct predecessors of the fugue.

The immediate background of the baroque fugue lies, of course, in the sixteenth and early seventeenth centuries. Motets, chansons, madrigals, and masses of this radiant period of modal polyphony exemplify many of the techniques of contra-

---

[1] *Changing Forms in Modern Music*, p. 150. Copyright 1945 by E. C. Schirmer Music Company, Boston, Massachusetts, and reprinted with their permission.

puntal imitation and development which found their way into the fugue of the eighteenth century. The structural techniques of the motet and chanson found new expression in instrumental forms like the *fantasia, canzona,* and *ricercar* for organ by such composers as J. P. Sweelinck (c. 1562–1621), Frescobaldi, and Froberger, as well as in the English ensemble fantasy which found ultimate expression in Purcell.

These instrumental forms were, like some vocal forms which preceded them, typically multisectional, their several parts varied in subject and texture. The ricercar by Andrea Gabrieli (c. 1520–86) in *HAM* (Vol. I, No. 136) illustrates the imitative, multisectional form. Ultimately, the monothematic ricercar became a direct precursor of the baroque fugue, and the term was often used interchangeably with "fugue" (see Bach's *Musical Offering*). An example by Johann Krieger (1649–1725) appears in *HAM,* Vol. II, as No. 249.

The immediate development toward the baroque fugue is seen in German fugal literatures of the late seventeenth and early eighteenth centuries, those preceding and contemporary with the young Bach (see, for example, Nos. 215, 234, and 236 in *HAM,* Vol. II). Many of these, including some of the "fugues" of Buxtehude, are sectional forms resembling the earlier canzona and ricercar, with contrasting themes and textures.

A majority of the examples in this chapter are culled from the fugues of Bach. It is in Bach, of course, that imitative counterpoint reaches an apogee of inventive and expressive capacity; his canons, fugues, and chorale settings exploit the means of imitative polyphony within a framework of tonal architecture and balance as never before or since. The typical Bach fugue grows out of the germinal subject, finding variety in an endless resource of variation and development, consummately controlled in a perfect equilibrium of horizontality and verticality, of interdependence and independence of voices, of the ebbing and rising movements of lines of pitch and of other element-structures, and of infallible direction of tonal-harmonic progression.

THE SIGNIFICANCE OF IMITATIVE COUNTERPOINT AS A MOTIVATING, UNIFYING TECHNIQUE

While it is germane to the nature of polyphony that the separate strata or voices are often concurrently opposed in rhythm, direction of line, timbre, and coincident surface material, they are at the same time frequently related thematically (in imitation) at varying distances. Thus, in the midst of contrasting elements, there is paradoxical yet balancing unity among the voices in the use of similar or identical motives interacting "diagonally," separated in time.

The employment of imitative counterpoint is vital in many forms and genres, some of which, like mass and oratorio, are represented here only to the extent that their component movements exemplify the principles of fugue or other forms arising out of systematic imitative procedure. We have already observed the importance of imitative devices as resources of development in largely homophonic forms like those of the sonata and the suite.

FUGUE

Except for wider tonal latitudes (such as dismissal of the principle of subject response at the 5th, the fluctuation of tonality beyond the traditional range of closely related regions, and occasional atonality) most of the characteristics uniting fugues of various periods are applicable to contemporary music as well as to that of the eighteenth and nineteenth centuries. Standard, definitive features of fugue are examined in detail in the following pages.

Although textural freedoms are more common in some fugues (the organ fugues of Bach, or orchestral fugues, such as the final movement of the *Brandenburg Concerto* No. 2 in F) than in others, texture tends, by and large, to be fixed throughout the typical fugue. For textural contrast, individual voices drop out from time to time, and are accounted for by rests. (Bach's 4-voice fugue, *WTC*, Book II, Fugue 5 in D, has all voices in play through about 39 of 50 measures, and is thus a "dense" fugue; during these 39 measures there are, of course, shorter rests from time to time in one voice or another.)

And although there may be subsidiary phases of homophonic texture (Ex. 12.1), again as contrast, or of momentary emphasis on harmonic verticalities, fugal texture is in general polyphonic. In fugues by such nineteenth-century composers as Mendelssohn and Schumann, chordal texture is more frequent than in eighteenth-century styles. In Ex. 12.1, the middle voices are devoted to straightforward harmonic articulation as homophonic accompaniment to the top voice, which is doubled in 3rds and 6ths; the entire movement occurs over the fixed pedal A.

Ex. 12.1 Bach, Prelude and Fugue in D minor for organ, BWV 539.

The fugue is a concentrated and intensely active form, usually relatively brief. Its intensity is without doubt one reason for its brevity; another is its compactness—the fact that generally all of its motivic material emanates from a single, limited, sometimes minuscule source.

The fugue begins with an exposition of the subject. Throughout the form the subject is recalled at intervals, often in varied form. Occasionally, contrasting motivic material intervenes among subject statements, as at times in Bach's organ fugues, or in fugues of orchestral and choral works.

There is tonal flux in the modulatory episodes and in the practice of subject statement at changing tonal levels. In most cases, there is relative tonic stability at beginning and end, with modulation concentrated in interior parts. The statement of the subject in the tonic at the end of the fugue is a nearly universal feature of the form, and a coda or codetta is sometimes appended.

The romantic spirit of the nineteenth century saw the fugue more freely, resisting submission to its most rigorous disciplines, creating the possibility of its adaptation to a new environment in the *free fugue*, more consistent with the subjective, dramatic impulses of the romantic tradition. The following features characterize the free fugue: less consistency of textural character and density; use of chordal strata in place of single lines (a technique seen in the final movement of the Stravinsky *Concerto for Two Solo Pianos*); chordal harmonizations of subject material (as in the Franck *Prelude, Chorale and Fugue,* just before the B major section near the end), and, in general, more frequent homophonic writing; introduction of contrasting thematic materials, in sonata or rondo fashion; increased length; and pronounced interruptions, including tempo changes, with or without resumption of the fugue. An example is the Fugue in E minor, No. 1 of Mendelssohn's Op. 35, which among many of the above features incorporates a chorale in chordal style just before the final section of the fugue. Freedoms of other kinds are to be seen in modern fugues; for example, the first movement of William Schuman's String Quartet No. 3 includes the augmented form of the subject in the initial exposition. (See related comment on pp. 362–63.)

Many of the devices typical of the fugue—invertible counterpoint, stretto, subject permutations, sequence, and others—are noted in the following pages.

The subject

The subject determines the character of the fugue; in the subject reside in essence the expressive qualities that are to unfold in the fugal development. Be it somber, majestic, jocose, or whatever, the subject determines the character of the entire work.

The subject is generally short—often 1 or 2 measures—but its length can vary from a few notes to several bars (Ex. 12.2).

Ex. 12.2a Bach, WTC I, 4 in C-sharp minor.

Ex. 12.2b   Bach, Chromatic Fantasy and Fugue.

To bear repetition, and to hold attention through the densities of the fugal texture, the characteristic subject is striking and distinctive in melodic and rhythmic content. Often, as an aspect of mobility (see below), it is asymmetrical in the distribution of component units (*WTC* I, 14; II, 14).

The subject is commonly self-propulsive, lacking a strong cadential ending (unlike many themes of homophonic forms), thus a vehicle of continuity. Internal unity is typically a product of such factors as unbroken motion (Ex. 12.3a), explicit

Ex. 12.3a   Bach, Toccata and Fugue in D minor for organ, BWV 538.

relations among individual motives (Ex. 12.3b), and persuasive encompassing contour, as for example of up-down (Ex. 12.3a), or the Stravinsky example's essential uniformity of linear placement (its extreme leaps notwithstanding) followed by descent. Such unities of shape and gesture as are seen in these two examples are of the essence.

Ex. 12.3b   Stravinsky, Symphony of Psalms, second movement.
Copyright 1941 by Russischer Musikverlag; renewed 1958. Copyright & renewal assigned to Boosey & Hawkes, Inc. Revised version copyright 1948 by Boosey & Hawkes, Inc. Reprinted by permission.

In Ex. 12.3a, the subject is propelled by suspensions and syncopations. There is no internal punctuation, and its cadence is characteristically suppressed by the overlapping entry of the answer.

In the Stravinsky subject, the notes C-E♭-B-D occur four times, after which there is a transposition and reordering of the same note-series. Or, considering the natural punctuation points in the subject (see brackets), the first bar constitutes a basic motive which is varied by diminution and extension. The final bar is a repetition, transposed, of the preceding motive from its first B♮, as indicated.

Still another structural principle is at work in the final bar of the Stravinsky subject. If we count the number of half-steps in each of the six intervals, the result reveals an ordering of graduated interval sizes: 9–10–11, 8–9–10, and the end of the subject forms an "augmented 6th" whose natural (traditional) resolution is to G, the first note of the answer.

In traditional examples, the tonic and dominant scale degrees and the notes of the tonic and dominant triads are pivotal. Traditional subjects often begin and end on tonic-dominant factors. In Ex. 12.4, tonal uncertainty is countered by the occurrence of notes of the tonic triad at metrically strong points.

Ex. 12.4   Franck, Prelude, Chorale and Fugue for piano.

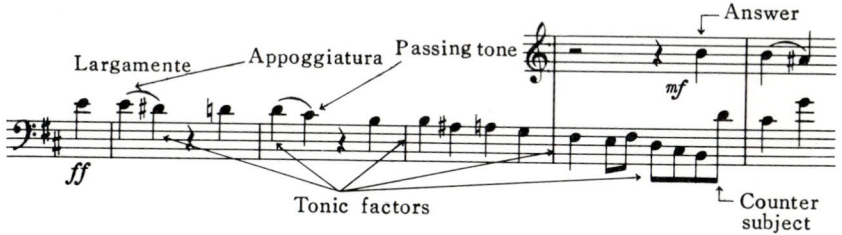

Traditional subjects vary in modulatory character, degree of conjunct motion, extent of chromaticism, and in overall shape around a climactic or turning point; such a point may be marked by articulative stress, duration, pitch level, approach by leap, implied harmonic dissonance, approach by melodic dissonance, by its function as the point toward which linear motion is strongly directed (Ex. 12.5), or of any combination of these factors. In Ex. 12.5, the climactic note is the culmination

Ex. 12.5   Bach, Prelude and Fugue in E minor for organ, BWV 548.

point of the preceding harmonic-melodic "wedge"; it is also the highest pitch, and is approached by the widest leap.

In a particular fugue, the subject's length may be identified, as far as possible, by determining where the answer enters, by looking for a point of tentative "settling" (a point of metric prominence, a note of the tonic, or a point of hesitation), and, most importantly, by comparison of all the entries in the fugue to find the point to which most are in conformity. The determination of exact subject length can be problematic (see *WTC* I, 9).

The many subject quotations in this chapter will serve to illustrate further the above points, some of which clearly apply more particularly to the baroque fugue than to that of modern styles. It must be said, finally, that the superiority of Bach in the literature of the fugue is in the captivating richness of invention and persuasive power of his fugue subjects as much as in the inerrant craft of contrapuntal manipulation and development in his works.

The answer

The first statement of the subject may be in any one of the voices, with its imitation, the answer, appearing in another. The answer may follow immediately after the conclusion of the subject (Ex. 12.7), may enter with the final note of the subject (Exx. 12.3a, 12.6), or may follow after a "link" of one or more notes has intervened (Ex. 12.2b).

Ex. 12.6   Hindemith, Ludus Tonalis, Fugue No. 9 in B-flat.
© 1943 by Associated Music Publishers, Inc., New York. Used by permission.

The traditional interval of imitation is the 5th above (or 4th below)—the dominant level—and the answer is frequently an exact transposition of the subject at that level. When this is the case, it is called a *real answer* (*WTC* I, 1).

If the imitation at the 5th is not exact, the answer is called *tonal*. Textbooks often strive over the why and how of tonal answers, sometimes provocatively.[2] In some cases, either a tonal or real answer is clearly possible, and the composer made an arbitrary choice. In Ex. 12.7, Bach sets out on what appears to be a real answer, then suddenly shifts to avoid modulation (the subject progression ♭ answered by ♭). He could, in a real answer, have submitted to modulation, as is often done, quickly cutting it off in a *transitional episode* to prepare the third entry, as seen above.

[2]See, for instance, George Oldroyd, *The Technique and Spirit of Fugue* (London: Oxford University Press, 1948), Ch. 5.

Ex. 12.7 Bach, Fugue in A minor for harpsichord, BWV 947.

as is often done, quickly cutting it off in a *transitional episode* to prepare the third entry, as seen above.

It is important to observe that the effect of the traditional tonal answer is almost invariably the *strengthened affirmation of the tonic key and the tonic harmony* as the focal point of the exposition. The exposition may (and, indeed, usually does) include secondary tonal regions, but it always asserts and revolves around the tonic; transitory fluctuation leads back to the tonic, reaffirming the principal center. What is sought is the prolongation of the tonic center and the tonic harmony into the answer, even though secondary modulation often occurs before the answer is concluded.

When the subject ends on a note of the tonic harmony, suggesting harmonic conformity in the answer, with appropriate intervallic adjustment, the dominant note is often answered by the tonic (a 4th above) rather than by the supertonic, the ''real'' imitation. Though this is by no means an absolute formula, it is an exceedingly common procedure for a certain kind of tonal answer; see the following examples.

Ex. 12.8 Bach, chorus, Sei grüsset, from the St. John Passion.

Ex. 12.9   Bach, Cantata no. 33, Allein zu dir, Herr Jesu Christ.

Ex. 12.10   Bach, WTC I, 22.

Ex. 12.11   Bach, The Art of the Fugue.

Thus, the ''gravitational pull'' of the tonic center is not in this circumstance compromised by imitation at the dominant level.[3]

Another way of regarding this type of tonal answer is to consider that the tonic and dominant split the diatonic scale unevenly. To proceed with imitation at the 5th without disturbing the stability of the tonic scale, with its unequal ''halves,'' requires the pattern 1–5, 5–8 and consequent unequal intervals in the adjustment which theory characterizes by the term *tonal answer*. In summary, tonal unity in the exposition, and the avoidance of early tonal-harmonic fluidity at the point of subject-answer juncture, are vital traditional principles.

Two further examples follow. In 12.12a, the subject (derived from the first phrase of the chorale) is built on the notes

Ex. 12.12a   Bach, Fughetta on Allein Gott in der Höh' sei Ehr', BWV 677.

[3]The practice of tonal answer of this type is often traced to the modal past in which a subject centering on the final and dominant of a mode (for example, d-a in the dorian), answered at the 5th, would in the consequent plagal range center on the low point of the plagal ambitus (here, a) and the *final* of the plagal form (here, d).

which affirm tonic harmony, progressing from 1 to 5; the answer is made to progress from 5 to 1 (cf. Ex. 12.7), with the interval of a 4th responding to that of a 5th
in the manner described above. Example 12.12b represents another type of tonal
answer. Here, the subject is made to move harmonically from I to V, without modulation; the answer is made to move harmonically from V to I, automatically
preparing the next entry, by the single intervallic adjustment to which attention is
directed in the quotation. (Minor disparity between major and minor 2nds is occasioned by the firm retention of the original leading-tone D♯.)

Similarly, a tonal answer may be necessary to restore the tonic after a
superficially modulating subject. A subject moving from tonic to a tonicized dominant may be followed by an answer going equidistantly from the subdominant to the
tonic; 4–1 as a response to 1–5. (See Ex. 12.13, as well as Bach's Organ Fugue in
C, BWV 547.) In Ex. 12.13, only the first note of the answer is at the 5th. Rarely is
Bach's answer at the 4th throughout (but see Ex. 12.18).

Tonal and real answers may be mixed, even within the initial exposition (Ex.
12.14).

Within internal expositions during later stages in the fugue, tonic stability is
less important and thus tonal response is less likely. The type of answer within such
groups is governed by the harmonic environment of the moment.

In modern fugues, and to some extent in those of the nineteenth century, the
tonal answer is used infrequently, reflecting the diminished significance of tonal orientation in general. The answer may occur at any interval and is more often real
than it was in the baroque.

The term *answer* applies only to the immediate response to the subject within
a full or partial exposition. Thus, single subject entries corresponding in interval
structure to an original tonal answer are *tonal entries* rather than answers (Ex.
12.23).

In the final analysis, every tonal answer requires study on its own terms since
each case suggests its own reasons and methods; only a few of the more usual circumstances have been outlined above. (Some examples make for extremely interesting and instructive speculation. In the A minor fugue, *WTC* II, 20, Bach might
have used a real answer except for the desirability of using the tonic note, which
appears only briefly in the subject itself, and avoiding the unorthodox V_4^6 which
would have been caused by strict imitation at the 5th.)

Efforts to characterize composers or periods with respect to prevalences of
tonal or real imitation usually come to naught. In Bach's *WTC*, 27 of 48 expositions
have tonal answers.

The countersubject; the free contrapuntal associate; invertible counterpoint

The originating voice continues after the subject is stated, forming a counterpoint to
the answer. If this counterpoint appears more than once in association with the subject entries in the course of the fugue, it is a *countersubject*. Otherwise, it is simply
a *free contrapuntal associate of free counterpoint*—the latter a term applied to any

Ex. 12.12b Brahms, Sonata in E minor, Op. 38, for cello and piano, final movement.

Ex. 12.13   Bach, Fugue in G-sharp minor, WTC I, 18.

Ex. 12.14   Bach, Prelude and Fugue in G for organ, BWV 541.

Ex. 12.15   Hindemith, Sonata No. 2 for organ, third movement.

fragment of line not derived from subject or countersubject. The countersubject often contrasts with the subject in rhythm and direction, although the two may be motivically and otherwise related (Exx. 12.4, 12.16).

Ex. 12.16   Bach, Fugue in G minor, WTC I, 16.

Theoretically, a 4-voice fugue may have two or three countersubjects, the first appearing with the answer to the first subject statement, the second with the following subject entry, and the third with the second answer; but this is unusual. *WTC* I, 2 has two countersubjects, as does the fugue cited in Ex. 12.17.

Since the voices cannot always appear in the original relationship, a countersubject must function suitably either above or below the subject—must be *contrapuntally invertible* (or *interchangeable*) with the subject.[4]

Ex. 12.17   Bach, Fugue in A-flat, WTC II, 17.

[4]For detailed discussion of invertible counterpoint, see Walter Piston, *Counterpoint* (New York: W. W. Norton and Co., Inc., 1947), pp. 167–87; Kent Kennan, *Counterpoint*, 2nd ed. (Englewood Cliffs, N.J.: Prentice-Hall, Inc., 1972), pp. 111–21; or other basic sources.

Ex. 12.17 (continued)

Answer ⟶   C.S. 1   End of exposition ⟶
                C. S. 2

While space does not permit a full exploration of this subject, we may explain briefly that the *interval of contrapuntal inversion* is determined by adding the distances between the voices in the two versions: if the voices are originally a 6th apart and, in inversion, a 3rd apart *at the corresponding point,* the inversion is said to be "at the octave"—the sum of the 6th and 3rd: [music] . In eighteenth-century counterpoint inversion is most often at the octave or 15th (double octave), 12th, or, more rarely, at the 10th. Inversion at intervals other than the octave or octave-multiple (15th or 22nd) produces significant change of harmonic implications (for example, in inversion at the 12th, a 6th becomes a dissonant 7th); thus, contrapuntal inversion, when practicable, is a useful source of harmonic variety. Inversion at the 15th is shown in Ex. 12.17. In *WTC* II, 16, the reader may compare m. 60 with m. 5 to see inverted counterpoint (2 voices, thus *double counterpoint*) at the octave, 10th, and 12th. Inversion at other intervals, extremely rare in traditional counterpoint, is a mark of freer styles and thus is common in contemporary polyphony.

The fugal exposition

The *exposition* is the first part of the fugue; it consists of subject statements, once in each voice with, occasionally, an added entry in the originating voice. A cadence is usual at the conclusion of the exposition, or following a subsequent episode. Whether or not there is such cadential punctuation, the exposition is regarded as a distinct structural entity in view of its singular function. The usual traditional pattern is tonic level to dominant level (T–D) or subject-answer (S–A), in a 2-voice fugue; T–D–T (S–A–S) in a 3-voice fugue; and T–D–T–D (S–A–S–A) where there are 4 voices. But occasionally such regularity is violated, as in Ex. 12.18, whose pattern is SAASS.

Between answer and subject, for tonal-harmonic adjustment and preparation of the tonic re-entry, there may be a brief *transitional episode* (called "codetta" in some texts) of the kind pointed out in Ex. 12.18.

While a fugue almost always begins with the single-voice statement and systematic exposition of the subject, in freer examples the exposition may be preceded by an introduction of some kind. Beethoven's *Grosse Fuge* in B-flat for string quartet, Op. 133, is a free fugue with an introduction in several parts. Other introduc-

Ex. 12.18   Bach, Prelude and Fugue in D minor for organ, BWV 539.

tions occur preceding the fugues of William Schuman's String Quartets Nos. 2 and 3, and in the fifth of the author's *Five Pieces for Small Orchestra*. The fourth fugue of Roy Harris's String Quartet No. 3 begins with a statement and brief development of the subject by all instruments, after which a normal exposition occurs. The unusual beginning of the fugue of Stravinsky's *Concerto for Two Solo Pianos* is a further case in point.

The counterexposition

The *counterexposition* is a subsequent pair or group of entries of subject and answer, often separated from the initial exposition by an episode, and remaining within the original tonic-dominant sphere. The counterexposition is sometimes only partial, involving fewer than all of the voices, and its subject-answer ordering may be irregular. The final movement of Bach's *Brandenburg Concerto* No. 5 in D completes its exposition (SASA, with a 4-measure episode between subject and second answer) at m. 13, after which a cadential episode leads to the dominant key and an entry in A at m. 17. Now a longer episode precedes a full counterexposition at m. 29 (SASS, with, again, a 4-measure episode separating the third and fourth entries). There may be a series of counterexpositions, as in Bach's Organ Fugue in C, BWV 547.

As may be seen in either of the above examples, the counterexposition does not begin again with a single voice, but maintains the developing density and textural activity.

Episodes; techniques of development

Where no subject entry is in progress, there is an *episode*. When not merely cadence-forming *(cadential episode),* or brief and simply transitional (within the exposition, the *transitional episode*), an episode is an area of tonal movement, of often substantial explorative manipulation of subject or countersubject motives. Example 12.19 illustrates subject fragmentation and sequence, the most fundamental traditional techniques of episodic development.

Ex. 12.19   Bach, Fantasy and Fugue in G minor, BWV 542.

Two fugal episodes may correspond in material, possibly inverted contrapuntally, as in Ex. 12.20.

A subject-centered fugue may be virtually devoid of episodes. Thus, in *WTC* I, 1, the subject is relinquished only for the formation of cadence at m. 14, m. 23,

Ex. 12.20   Bach, Fugue in C-sharp major, WTC I, 3.

and mm. 26–27; there are no real episodes. On the other hand, episodes may be extensive and occasionally may even introduce distinctive material not explicitly related to that of the exposition. An example is Bach's Organ Fugue in E minor, BWV 548, whose subject was quoted as Ex. 12.5; at m. 59 there begins a long episode of new figuration, an episode which recalls the subject only briefly at widely-spaced intervals. Another illustration appears as Ex. 12.21.

Ex. 12.21   Bach, Fugue in E minor, WTC I, 10.

When not explicitly derived from subject or countersubject material, episodes may be built upon other motives of the exposition, as in *WTC* I, 15. In this fugue, the transitional episode within the exposition, mm. 9–10, furnishes material for later episodes.

Episodes should not be confused with actual interruptions in which the fugal content and progress are suspended and later resumed. Such interruptions, common in the post-baroque free fugue, have been mentioned in connection with Mendelssohn's Op. 35. They are characterized by such departures as radical textural change, change of tempo, character, and material. A further example of such nonepisodic interruption may be seen in Franck's *Prelude, Chorale, and Fugue* for piano. In m. 154 of the fugue, a homophonic, cadenzalike section brings in a development of the second movement theme, which continues to m. 178, at which point the fugue re-enters in combination with the second movement theme. Measures 154–78 can hardly be said to constitute an episode in the fugue.

Successive entries and entry groups

As the fugue unfolds beyond the exposition and any counterexposition, it begins to move tonally, and to alternate between episodes and subject statements or groups of statements and answers; or, further counterexpositions might occur, as in Bach's *Leipzig* Organ Fugue, BWV 547, to some extent restricting the form to the tonic-dominant tonal sphere.

The subject–answer internal entry group shown in Ex. 12.22 has imitation at the 4th, the interval established in the initial exposition. It is surrounded by episodes, the preceding one, largely sequential, being 14 measures long. Another example of subject-answer internal entry group may be seen at mm. 12–16 of *WTC* I, 16, where tonal answer is used.

Ex. 12.22   Hindemith, Ludus Tonalis, Fugue No. 2 in G.
© 1943 by Associated Music Publishers, Inc., New York. Used by permission.

We may distinguish among (1) counterexpositions, defined as subject-answer groupings within the tonic-dominant orbit; (2) internal expositions, removed from this restricted tonal range, yet having subject answer(s) at the interval initially established (Ex. 12.22); (3) internal entry groups lacking such answers; and (4) single entries—either *tonal* (where conforming in interval structure to an established tonal answer) or *real entries*. Example 12.23 illustrates a single internal tonal entry, preceded and followed by episodes.

At times one encounters unanticipated events. In Bach's Organ Fugue in C minor, BWV 546, unusual developments occur at m. 59, where a new "subject," of 1 measure, appears in imitation at the octave, later to be extended and combined with the original subject (see mm. 86ff., or 92ff.) in the manner of a double fugue.

Ex. 12.23   Bach, Fugue in C minor, WTC I, 2.

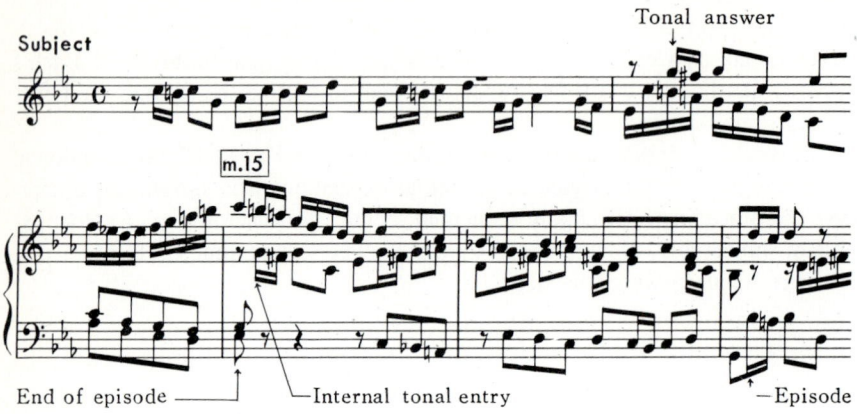

It is, in fact, a kind of double fugue, whose second subject has an irregular exposition and evolution, its full shape emerging only when it is joined to the original subject. Another irregularity would be the statement of the full subject in sequence, repeated contiguously in a single voice, rather than in more usual imitation (*WTC* I,3).

Subject variation

Given the monothematic character of the single fugue, and the procedure of subject repetition as its basis, means of varying the subject are of great importance. The transposition of the subject is such a resource, and requires no explanation.

Mirror inversion is practiced a great deal, sometimes strictly (with precise fidelity to original interval sizes) and sometimes freely. Example 12.24 illustrates mirror inversion, as well as homophonic composition of the accompanying figuration—characteristic of the free fugue.

Example 12.25 shows two subject forms in stretto (p. 369): the first is a rhythmic alteration and mirror, the second a rhythmic alteration of the original form. An exceedingly powerful use of the technique of foreground rhythmic alteration is seen in the second movement of Stravinsky's *Symphony of Psalms*, rehearsal no. 14.

The fugue section of the Prelude to Bach's *Partita* No. 6 uses melodic (intervallic and rhythmic) alteration in ornamentation of the subject at mm. 69–71. The reverse of ornamentation may be seen in Bach's Prelude and Fugue in G for organ, BWV 541, where the end of the subject,

Ex. 12.24 Brahms, Variations and Fugue on a Theme by Handel, Op. 24.

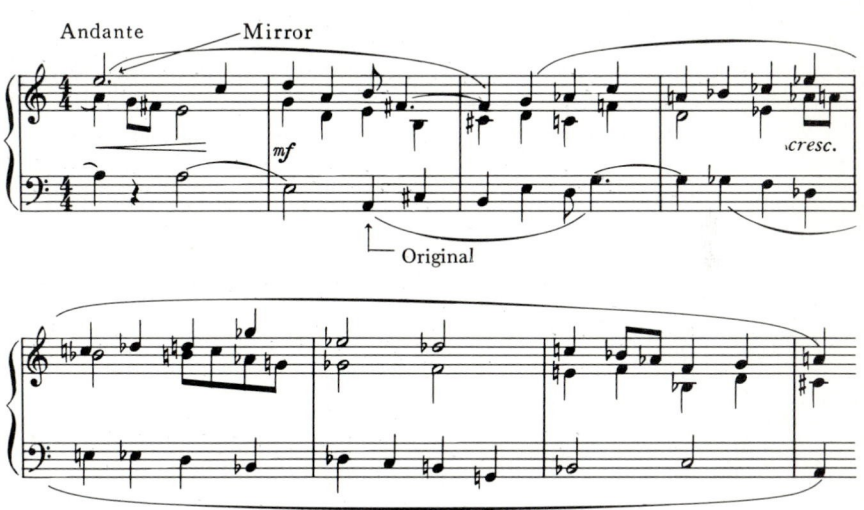

Ex. 12.25 Hindemith, Ludus Tonalis, Fugue No. 3 in F.

© 1943 by Associated Music Publishers, Inc., New York. Used by permission.

is often reduced to

Intervallic variation of a fugue subject, without rhythmic change, is illustrated by Ex. 12.26.

Ex. 12.26   Schumann, Six Fugues on the Name of Bach, No. 2 in B-flat.

Regular *augmentation* is a proportionate lengthening of the original notes in durational value; regular *diminution* is the reverse. Irregular augmentation or diminution, resulting in a kind of rhythmic variation (Ex. 12.25), is corresponding increase or decrease not in a consistent ratio. The fugue from which Ex. 12.27 is taken includes mirror (violin, m. 128) and augmented (violin, m. 146) subject versions. The reader may also refer to *WTC* II, 2, m. 19, and *WTC* II, 9, m. 26. In Ex. 12.27, there is progressive episodic diminution of the subject's head motive; the process of developing intensity is abruptly steadied on a D♯ pedal (m. 193), at which point the coda begins.

Retrograde—the appearance of the notes in reverse order—and retrograde

Ex. 12.27   Dallapiccola, Due Studi for violin and piano, second movement.
Ⓒ 1950 Edizioni Suvini Zerboni, Milan, Italy. Used by permission.

Ex. 12.27 (continued)

mirror forms are relatively rare. Examples are found in the fugue of Beethoven's *Hammerklavier* Sonata, Op. 106, and Bach's *Musical Offering* (retrograde canon). Examples are also found in Hindemith's *Ludus Tonalis:* the second half of Fugue No. 3 in F is a retrograde of the first (see m. 30, the turning point), and much use of retrograde and retrograde mirror is made in Fugue No. 9 in B-flat. Since retrograde treatment tends to obscure the relationship to the original form of the theme, its most likely use is in the transformation of small motives and figures (Ex. 12.28).

Ex. 12.28   Bach, Two-Voice Invention in B minor.

Unorthodox approaches to internal subject entries may occasion melodic vari-ants,[5] and changed harmonic implication at the subject entry can be a resource of variation. Thus, the fugue of Bach's Prelude and Fugue in B minor for organ, BWV 544, has a subject which usually, at its opening, bears tonic harmony; at m. 40, the bass entry is varied to suggest f♯: V.

A given fugue may, of course, employ a striking assortment of variational techniques. Bach's *Leipzig* Organ Fugue, BWV 547, uses mirror and augmented subject forms with great ingenuity. A fascinating fugue from the standpoint of sub-ject variation is the finale of Stravinsky's *Concerto for Two Solo Pianos*, whose second part sets forth the subject in mirror form, and rhythmically altered. Example

---

[5]See Oldroyd, *The Technique and Spirit of Fugue*, pp. 128–29.

12.29 shows an excerpt from a Bach fugue in which the subject appears in three forms concurrently.

Ex. 12.29   Bach, Fugue in D-sharp minor, WTC I, 8.

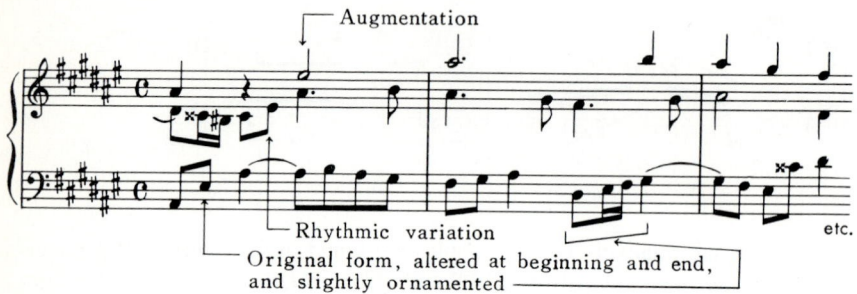

Tonal range; cadential divisions in the form

The basic tonal range of traditional fugue may be expressed as shown below, using the symbols T for tonic, D for dominant, SD for subdominant, and R for relative major and minor keys. Arrows indicate overlapping identities (for example, T is the same as D of SD).

Only rarely would a single eighteenth-century fugue exploit an entire such tonal system. Typical Bach examples are T–D–SD–R–SD of R (third movement, *Brandenburg Concerto* No. 2 in F), T–D–R–SD–SD of R–SD of SD (*WTC* II, 8 in D-sharp minor) and T–D–R–SD–D of R–SD of R (fugue of Toccata and Fugue in F for organ, BWV 540).

Tonal range is one of the most relevant features of style, and it is to be expected that a greater scope of fluctuation will be found in nineteenth- and twentieth-

Fig. 12.1

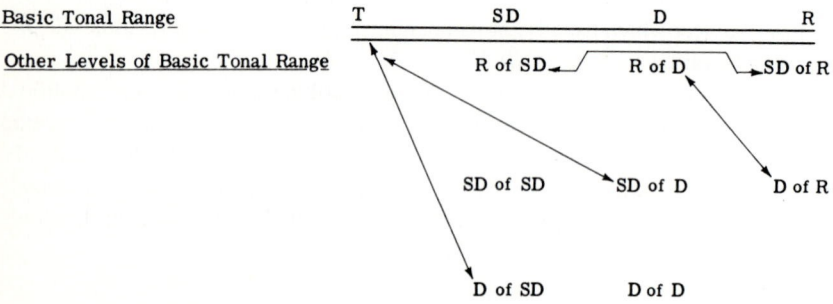

century fugues. (The fugue of Hindemith's Organ Sonata No. 2, basically in A, freely explores such tonal regions as B-flat and A-flat.)

The apparently natural principle that the middle parts would avoid the original tonic and even its dominant, to establish a basis for fresh reaffirmation of the primary tonic at the end, is not always in evidence (see for example m. 39 of *WTC* II, 1). Still, the concept of tripartition has significance in fugue in departure from and ultimate restoration of the primary tonic.

The fugue is a sectional form in which clear but often inconspicuous cadences on related tonics articulate a bisectional (*WTC* II, 2: two sections and coda) or multisectional plan (*WTC* II, 5: authentic cadences on T, D, SD, and R of D). In addition to being consummated harmonically, cadences are frequently marked by a drop-off in textural density and a renewal of the accumulative process, usually with surface rhythmic motion continued. In Ex. 12.30, an ornamented subject entry has just ended, and an episode begins. The suspension and the B♭ dissonance intensify forward thrust.

Ex. 12.30   Bach, Partita No. 6 in E minor, first movement.

Episode
(reduced texture)

Stretto

Stretto is the overlapping of subject entries. Often, stretto involves an abbreviated form of the subject, presenting enough of the original, including its vital head motives, to make it clearly identifiable as a subject entry. Example 12.31 is a stretto on the abbreviated second subject of a double fugue.

Stretto, a climactic device usually of intense effect, appears primarily in the later sections of the fugue. However, in some fugues stretto is a more-or-less constant feature. Examples are the Fugue No. 2 in G from Hindemith's *Ludus Tonalis,* with stretto beginning at m. 24 (hardly a third of the way through), and *WTC* I, 1, in which stretto first appears immediately after the initial exposition. Rarely, a subject may even be in stretto with its first answer; see the fugato "Hosanna" in the "Sanctus" of Mozart's *Requiem,* where the answer enters on the fifth note before

Ex. 12.31   Mozart, Requiem in D minor, K. 626, Part II, Kyrie eleison.

Contraction of subject (middle portion omitted)

the end of the subject. (Stretto is sometimes defined to include only that overlapping *in excess of* any occurring in the exposition.)

Distinction is made between a *total stretto,* involving all the voices, and a *partial stretto.* The closer the distance of imitation, the tighter and more intense the stretto. In Ex. 12.32, the tight stretto on an extension of the subject head motive is intensified by the orchestration.

An example of tight stretto involving the entire fugal texture is seen in *WTC* I, 22. The subject appears in imitations at the time interval of a half-measure in the passage following m. 67.

Ex. 12.32   William Schuman, Symphony No. 3, second movement.
                 Copyright 1941, 1942 by G. Schirmer, Inc. Reprinted by permission.

Ex. 12.32 (continued)

Pedal point

Theoretically, a pedal point may occur anywhere after the exposition, but, like stretto, it is associated with the later stages, or with the coda itself, as in *WTC* I, 2. It is thus, by definition, primarily cadential in function. The pedal point is usually on the primary tonic or dominant, forming a dramatic conflict in its rigidly fixed quality, with harmonic and rhythmic motion over it. Uncommon examples of pedals in related keys may be seen in the first and sixth of Schumann's *Six Fugues on the Name of Bach,* Op. 60. The first of these, at m. 32, has a c:V pedal, and a g:V pedal at m. 25; its fundamental key is B-flat.

A dominant pedal progressing to a tonic pedal, viewed telescopically, may be regarded as forming an inflated authentic cadence. This is seen in Ex. 12.33, an excerpt from a tonal 12-tone work. The V pedal is broken by reiteration of the

Ex. 12.33 Piston, Chromatic Study on the Name of Bach.
     © Copyright 1941 by The H. W. Gray Co., Inc. Used by permission.

Ex. 12.33 (*continued*)

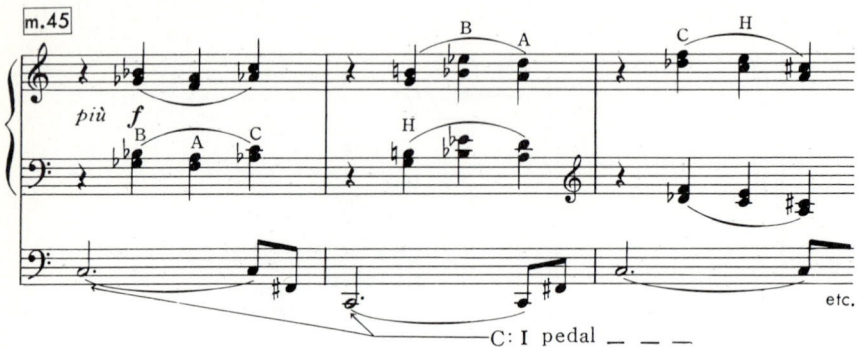

motive B-A-C-H;[6] sequential movement of shrinking pattern repetitions occurs over it (see brackets), descending in whole-tones. The motive, harmonized, continues over the tonic pedal which follows.

Many pedal points will be found in the *WTC*—for example, the 8-measure ornamented V pedal of II, 10. An example of striking length is the V pedal of the fugue of Brahms's *Handel Variations,* beginning at m. 76; here the pedal point is broken and reiterated.

The final stage: elements of return and cadential preparation

The fugue's final stage is marked by reassertion of the primary tonic and, often, by restoration of the definitive subject form, after which there is only very superficial deviance, if any. Frequently it is set off by a half- or authentic cadence *in the tonic,* with a final subject entry or group within the tonic region. At this point, the tonal fluctuation of any episodes is restricted (see discussion of Ex. 12.36).

In the fugue from which Ex. 12.34 is drawn there is a perfect authentic cadence in A minor at m. 63, followed by a harmonically vacillating episode ending in a strong half-cadence in the tonic key, with fermata, at m. 71. This cadence sets off the final stage of the fugue. Several tonic entries follow, some in stretto. Later, there is a compound tonic pedal[7] in conjunction with typical harmonic use of the V_7 of IV in the final bars (see also Ex. 12.35), and a single entry at this subdominant level, appropriate in the harmonic environment of the cadence.

[6]Among German pitch names, *B* is B♭ and *H* is B♮. Thus, the B-A-C-H motive is B♭-A-C-B♮.

[7]*A compound pedal point* occurs in more than one voice. In the Bach organ fugue under discussion here the bass pedal is doubled in the uppermost voice—a combination of the normal pedal with the *inverted pedal.*

Ex. 12.34   Bach, Prelude and Fugue in G for organ, BWV 541.

Ex. 12.35   Bach, Brandenburg Concerto No. 2 in F, final movement.

The coda

The end of the fugue is typically emphatic, sometimes fortified by increased textural thickness (Ex. 12.34). When there is a coda or codetta, it is, as in other forms, a concluding appendage in the tonic, set off by a clear cadence (not infrequently a deceptive cadence). Distinction is appropriate between the coda, an appendage, and the integral final stage itself, with tonic return and other preliminary cadential activity described above.

The coda at times includes a final subject entry, as in *WTC* I, 2. A definitive specimen is that of *WTC* II, 8 (final 3½ bars), whose coda, set off by a perfect authentic cadence, contains two simultaneous subject entries, one the mirror of the other.

Some fugues have closing sections with cadenza figuration—a feature of several of Bach's organ fugues; that of the A minor Prelude and Fugue, BWV 543, includes a brilliant cadenza within the framework of an inflated authentic cadence in the last 6 bars. This is a codetta, lacking thematic substance.

Important in the baroque fugue is the device of embellishing and extending the final tonic with V_7 of IV, the subdominant, and, unless the ultimate succession is plagal as in Ex. 12.35, the concluding foreground V-I.[8] We have seen that this is sometimes carried to the point of including a subject entry at the subdominant level (Ex. 12.34, or *WTC* II, 2, m. 25).

As Ex. 12.35 indicates, the coda is often primarily or entirely homophonic. Bach's *Leipzig* Fugue includes, preceding the coda, augmentations of the inverted subject at the tonic and subdominant levels; its coda, distinctly marked by a perfect authentic cadence, contains stretto on the subject's original and mirror versions over a 6-measure tonic pedal.

HANDEL, CHORUS, HE TRUSTED IN GOD, FROM MESSIAH

The following example from *Messiah,* although in some ways less interesting than, for example, a keyboard fugue of Bach, will illustrate fugal function in a universally familiar work in a distinctive medium. The reader will find other examples of choral fugue in masses, oratorios, and requiems of such composers as Bach, Handel (see also the final chorus of *Messiah*), Haydn, Mozart, Beethoven, Mendelssohn, and Brahms. The following discussion is of necessity cursory and, while brief excerpts are quoted, the complete fugue should be available for reference.

The opening tonic chord affirms the key, "introduces" the fugue, and by its sharp, emphatic articulation sets the subject in motion. The subject itself is on the lengthy side, but nevertheless remains a tight unit, vigorously rising and falling over its octave range. The melodic curve, which peaks soon after the midpoint, is of a common type. Interesting is its basic harmonic implication: secondary high points of *prominence* (duration, leaped approach, pitch) outline the IV triad; yet the underlying tonal basis is c:I, its 3rd and 5th elaborated by factors of the tonally subsidiary

---

[8]The V_7 of IV, an almost omnipresent cadential factor in conventional tonality, *is* the tonic goal, but rendered active, by dissonance, reintroducing a surface IV, then V, in typical cadential elaboration.

IV, in an upper-neighbor relation. The first 2 notes, descending between scale degrees 5 and 1,

suggest that the answer will probably be tonal, responding with a descent from tonic to dominant,

Motivic unity is achieved in part by repetition of the motive

in various forms, as bracketed in the quotation.

The tonal answer, from the second note, is consistently at the 5th, submitting to transitory reference to the dominant, a surface modulation cancelled by the lowering of the F♯ secondary leading-tone just before the third entry; a usual transitional episode is thus circumvented. The counterpoint in the originating voice, accompanying the answer, is designated a countersubject in view of its subsequent recurrences.

Ex. 12.36a   Handel, He trusted in God, from Messiah.

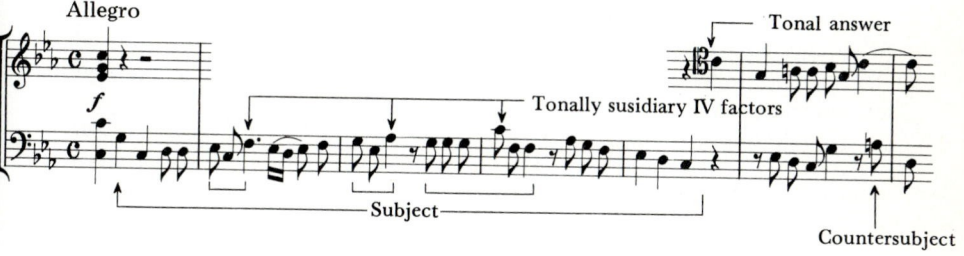

It is interesting that the first notes of the bass, under the tonal answer, are a retrograde of the motive with which the subject began (see Ex. 12.36b). The countersubject affords motivating rhythmic contrast to the subject; at the same time

Ex. 12.36b

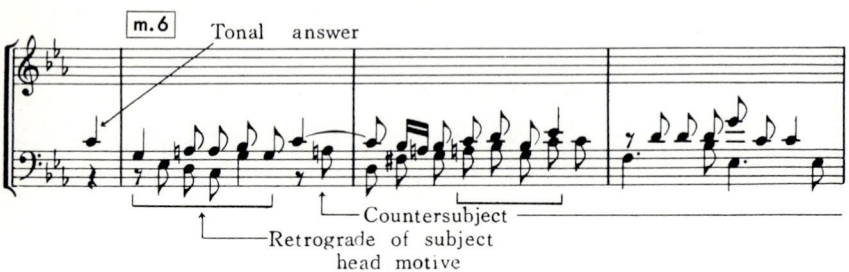

the motive which had been repeated in the subject is worked into the countersubject, along with the characteristic skips of a 5th, as seen in Ex. 12.36b.

The exposition proceeds with perfect regularity, with the voices entering from the bottom up. After the originating voice has completed the countersubject it continues with free counterpoint. The third entry, with countersubject in the tenor, and the fourth, with the countersubject stated freely in the bass, are quoted in Ex. 12.36c to give a view of the conclusion of the exposition. An interesting feature is a false entry of the subject at m. 14, just before the appearance of the second tonal answer in the soprano. In the conclusion of the exposition, m. 19, the tonal structure again leans toward the dominant. But at the cadence a B♮ points back to the tonic, C minor. (Orchestra parts duplicate the singing voices most of the time.)

Ex. 12.36c

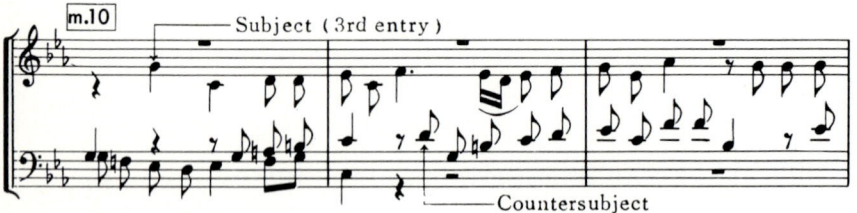

Ex. 12.36c *(continued)*

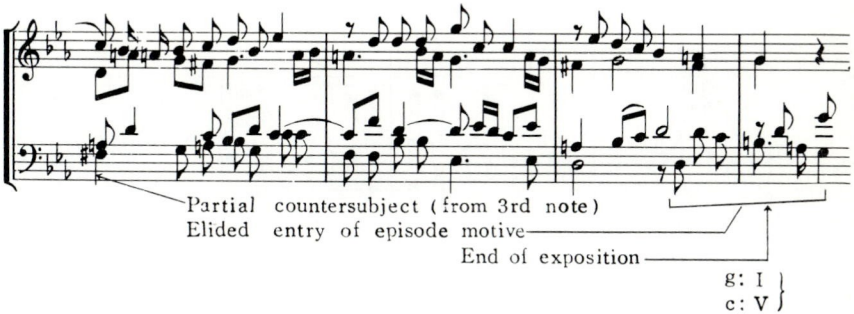

There is no counterexposition. Measure 19 sets the pattern for the fugal episodes, which are based on the motive

a rhythmic variation, inverted, of the subject's head motive. The episode has all the standard qualities: its derivation (although somewhat removed) from the subject, the colloquy among voices, the tonal flux, and sequential repetitions (see Ex. 12.36d). At its conclusion, in B-flat, there is another false entry of the subject, which materializes fully in the alto, together with part of the countersubject, a measure later.

In later entries, the subject is varied a good deal by changes of line and rhythm, and by contraction, without impairing its associable features or cutting it so short, as in the false entries cited above, as to compromise the sense of true "entry." The variants are summarized in Ex. 12.36e (see Exx. 12.36a and b for original and tonal forms of the subject).

The fugal development includes no stretto, no pedal, and very little inverted counterpoint, since the countersubject recurs with determined consistency below the subject. However, a fragment occurs above the subject at m. 43, forming double

Ex. 12.36d

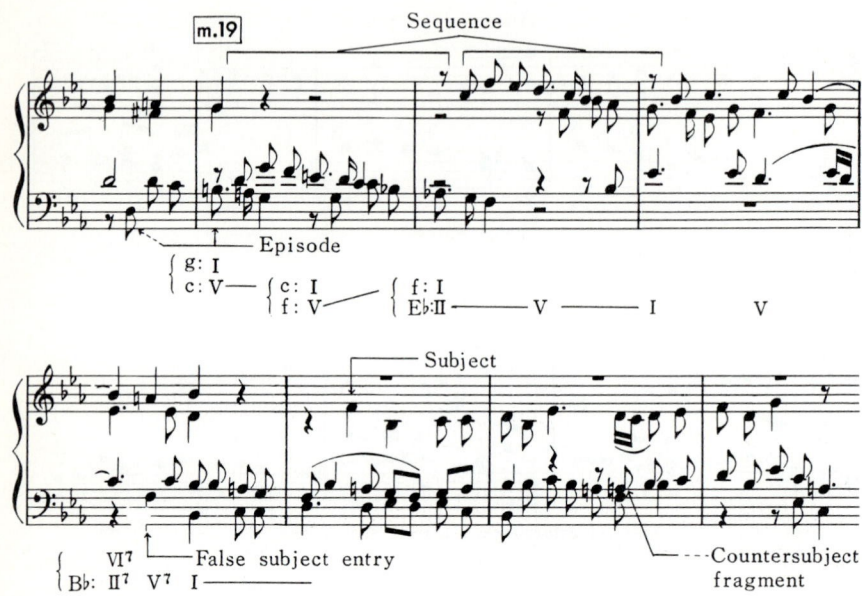

Ex. 12.36e

Ex. 12.36e (*continued*)

Dissolution

counterpoint at the 15th (in Ex. 12.36f, the actual countersubject is shown along with its variation—the former in small notes). Modest double counterpoint is also seen in the episodes (e.g., m. 19, Ex. 12.36f).

Ex. 12.36f

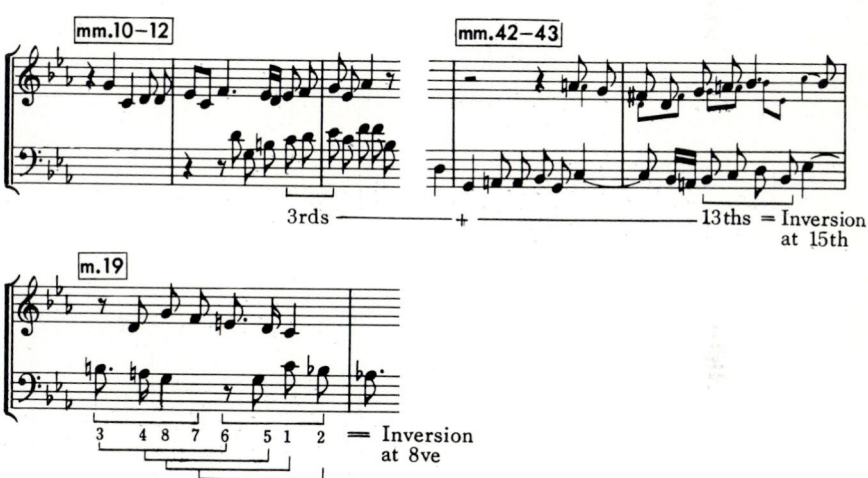

After the first episode, there are subject entries, all of them single, at m. 23 (B-flat, alto), m. 29 (E-flat, soprano), m. 36 (F minor, tenor), m. 42 (G minor, bass), m. 50 (C minor, soprano), and m. 57 (bass). It is interesting to observe the manner in which Handel introduces countersubject fragments in bass and alto under the subject entry in m. 50, and in the alto counterpoint to the entry in m. 29. But the countersubject as a whole is dismissed early in the fugue. The device of false entry, as mentioned in two instances above, is exploited again in m. 28, where the tenor anticipates the soprano entry of the following bar.

Episodes are constructed consistently of the motive seen in Ex. 12.36d, sometimes used sequentially, as in the episode beginning at m. 46 (see also Ex. 12.36d). The technique of episodic dialogue is pronounced in the episodes at mm. 33 and 46.

The tonal range is characteristic. Unusually, the subject itself moves to an emphatic cadence, with alternating formulae in tonic and dominant regions throughout the exposition. Cadences of significant value are at m. 22 (Ex. 12.36d), in B-flat; m. 27, where cadential effect is attenuated by entry of the episode motive; m. 33, an imperfect cadence in E-flat, yielding to F minor; m. 38, F minor, checked by early entry of the episode motive as before, by the alteration of f:I (as B♭:V), and by uninterrupted rhythmic drive; m. 41, half-cadence in G minor; m. 46, the cadence compromised by the above-mentioned devices; m. 50, weak half-cadence in C minor, ending the preceding episode and setting off the final stage; and m. 54, where the tonic is strongly confirmed, having been established in preparation for the tonic entry 5 measures earlier. The tonal range may be summarized as T–D–R of D–R of T–SD; there are subject entries at all of these levels.

The final stage of the fugue brings back the subject at the tonic (m. 50). This is followed by a last episode, end of m. 54, and still another tonic entry at m. 57, dissolved as seen in Ex. 12.36e. Here, events lead to a half-cadence on c:V$_2^4$. The 3-measure homophonic codetta is of a style characteristic of many choral fugues (see the *Kyrie* movement in Mozart's *Requiem*).

Ex. 12.36g

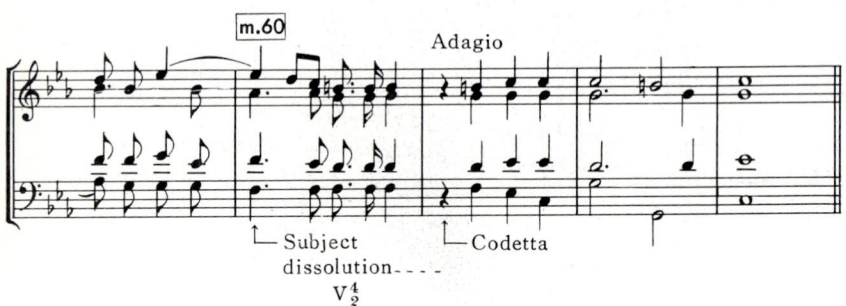

Although many of the sophisticated techniques of fugue are not to be seen in the example, important lessons of form are to be observed in the unity deriving from common elements in subject, countersubject, and episodes; unity and contrast in the control of tonal movement from, around, and to the central tonic; variation in subject appearances; textural contrast achieved by frequent dropping-off at cadential points, and by the use of episodes in which movement of the voices, rather than constant, is taken up with responsorial dialogue on short motive repetitions; the interest of deceptive implication in false entries, which anticipate full entries; systematic recalling of the subject after episodes of moderate length; frequent suppression of cadential punctuation in the interest of directed continuity; and other factors.

MULTIPLE FUGUE

A fugue with two subjects is a *double fugue.* A second subject is distinguished from a countersubject, with which it has much in common, in that it does not appear initially as an accompaniment to the first *answer,* and usually has some degree of independent existence, occurring alone as well as in association with the first subject. An example to which we may again refer is the *Kyrie* from the Mozart *Requiem;* its second subject, on the words *Christe eleison,* appears concurrently with the first subject at the outset, entering a bar later, and arises independently, in stretto, later in the fugue (Ex. 12.31).

When a fugue has two themes *appearing together at the beginning,* each of them recurring exclusively in association with the other, it can scarcely be insisted that the example is either a double fugue or a single fugue with countersubject. The 8th-note associate to the passacaglia ostinato theme in the fugue of Bach's Passacaglia and Fugue in C minor for organ seems of secondary importance—a countersubject to the theme which prevails throughout—and it does not appear independently; yet, this fugue is often characterized as a double fugue.

A second subject must of course be capable of combination with the first, yet it must also present a marked contrast. Thus, in the Mozart, one subject is disjunct, the other conjunct; one features relatively long rhythmic values and dotted rhythms, the other is fast-moving. Some double fugues begin with two separate expositions, one for each subject, later combining them. This is vividly clear in Fugue No. 4 in A of Hindemith's *Ludus Tonalis,* the exposition of whose second subject is at a changed tempo.

Another example, Bach's Toccata and Fugue in F for organ, BWV 540, contains an exposition (SAAS) of a second subject at m. 71; the two subjects are combined at, for example, m. 134. Another with separate expositions is the Mendelssohn Fugue No. 4 in A–flat, Op. 35. A final example of the opposite type, in which two subjects are exposed concurrently, is seen in the 32nd variation of the Beethoven *Diabelli* set.

A triple fugue is, of course, a fugue with three subjects, and a quadruple fugue one with four. The latter is extremely rare, as, indeed, are full forms (separate expositions, later combinations) of either of these. Example 12.37 is taken from a triple fugue in which subjects two and three have a concurrent exposition separate from that of subject one. Subject three differs from a countersubject in its independ-

Ex. 12.37   Hindemith, String Quartet No. 4, Op. 32, first movement.
© 1924 B. Schott's Soehne/Mainz, Germany. Renewed 1952. Used by permission.

Ex. 12.37 (*continued*)

ent appearance (as at m. 133) as well as in its initial presentation with subject two rather than as accompaniment to an answer. The example quotes excerpts from each of the two expositions, and from the combination of all three subjects at m. 203. Note the intervals of imitation in the expositions.

The reader should consult the multiple fugues of Bach's *Art of the Fugue,* VIII and XI of which are triple fugues, the latter using mirror forms of the three subjects of the former. IX and X are double fugues, and the final fugue, unfinished, was intended to be a quadruple fugue. The finale of Haydn's String Quartet in A, Op. 20, No. 6 is a further example of triple fugue.

FUGATO

Fugato, as a noun or adjective, refers to a passage involving fugal texture and imitation in a work or movement which is otherwise primarily nonfugal. Frequently the fugato consists of a fugal exposition only, as may be seen in such examples as the second movement of Beethoven's Symphony No. 7, beginning at m. 183; the opening of Puccini's *Madame Butterfly,* whose 8-measure subject is set out in a 32-measure exposition (TDTD); and the finale of Beethoven's Quartet, Op. 59, No. 3, and the opening of his Op. 131. The fugatos in Mozart's *Requiem,* following the "Sanctus" and "Benedictus," have been mentioned. Examples are extremely numerous.

FUGHETTA

It is incorrect to consider *fughetta* and *fugato* as synonymous. The former term is the diminutive of *fugue* (actually of the Italian *fuga*) and thus denotes a small fugue. The brevity of the fughetta may be the consequence of a very short subject, or of the absence or severe reduction of the usual fugal development. Obviously, the fughetta is far more limited than the fugue in its range of modulation and in its application of developmental and variational techniques.

Examples are variations 10 of Bach's *Goldberg* series and 24 of Beethoven's *Diabelli,* both of these fughettas within binary theme framework. The Bach Fantasies with Fughettas (in B-flat and D) and Preludes with Fughettas (in F, G, D minor, and E minor) are further examples. A modern fughetta occurs as variation 3 in the second movement of Stravinsky's Sonata for Two Pianos.

BACH'S "INVENTION"

The term *invention* was used only rarely and inconsistently before Bach (for example, as synonymous with *suite*), and the word is now usually associated with his 30 well-known harpsichord pieces, even though half of them (those in 3 voices) he called by the name *sinfonia.* It is further testimony to Bach's genius that even in this limited frame of reference the invention must be regarded as an important contrapuntal genre. An invention may be characterized very generally as a study in contrapuntal techniques.

The Bach inventions are sectional, falling into two or more parts, and are based on a unifying recurring motive which is stated and imitated at the outset, and very often restated with imitation at the beginning of the second section. The inventions are short and typically consistent in surface rhythmic articulation and tempo. Often the subject-motive is accompanied at the outset. Prevalent techniques are double and triple counterpoint, sequence, pedal, and motive variation. True binary and ternary forms are exceptional (see the 2-voice Invention in E, cited in the chapter on simple ternary form). Sometimes a ''countermotive'' assumes significance by its frequent recurrence, like the countersubject in a fugue, or the subject-motive may appear initially with a counterpoint of comparable importance (again, the E major 2-voice Invention). A coda or codetta is sometimes added.

While the 3-voice invention is sometimes distinguished from the fugue on the basis of its brevity, the lesser importance of devices like stretto, the accompaniment of the initial subject-motive statement, and its more restricted development and tonal movement, it is unlikely that any absolute distinction can be made. Any attempt to distinguish firmly between fugues and inventions must face such questions as: How short is a fugue? How short is a fugue subject? What integral and important devices are consistently associated with fugue and not with invention, or the reverse?

All subject-motives of the 3-voice inventions are accompanied, and only six of the 2-voice inventions begin with unaccompanied motives. Tonal range varies from simply T–D (2-voice Invention in G) to T–D–R–D of R–SD of R (3-voice in F minor). Some have as few as two sections (2-voice in B-flat), some as many as five (3-voice in E-flat); a few virtually avoid cadential partitioning (2-voice in A); some have closing sections (2-voice in D and D minor). Ten of the 2-voice inventions begin with imitation at the octave, but a few (for example, the one in B minor) answer at the 5th. All of the 3-voice inventions answer at the 5th (sometimes tonally) except those in C minor and B minor. Subject-motive length varies from a half-bar (2-voice in C) to 4 bars (3-voice in A minor); eight have 1-measure subject-motives. In some, certain techniques predominate: *canon* in the 2-voice Inventions in C minor and F, and to a lesser extent in the one in B-flat; *pedal* in the 2-voice Invention in E minor and the 3-voice Invention in G minor, among others; *sequence* (practiced in all) in the 2-voice Invention in A minor and the 3-voice Invention in D, whose subject is itself sequential; *mirror inversion* in the 3-voice Inventions in C and E. The 3-voice Invention in F minor is especially interesting for its use of motive ornamentation and triple counterpoint (4 of 6 possible contrapuntal inversions are used).

Coequal counterpoints to the opening motives are seen, for example, in the 2-voice Inventions in E-flat and G minor, and the 3-voice Invention in F minor. While diatonicism is usual in the Inventions, a few are notably chromatic in line or harmony, including the 2-voice Invention in A minor, and the 3-voice Inventions in D minor and G. The inventions constitute an exceedingly rewarding body of material for study, and the above are only very broad, summary suggestions as to their nature and content. The beginning of an invention is shown in Ex. 12.38, with some of the typical features marked.

Ex. 12.38   Bach, Two-Voice Invention in D minor.

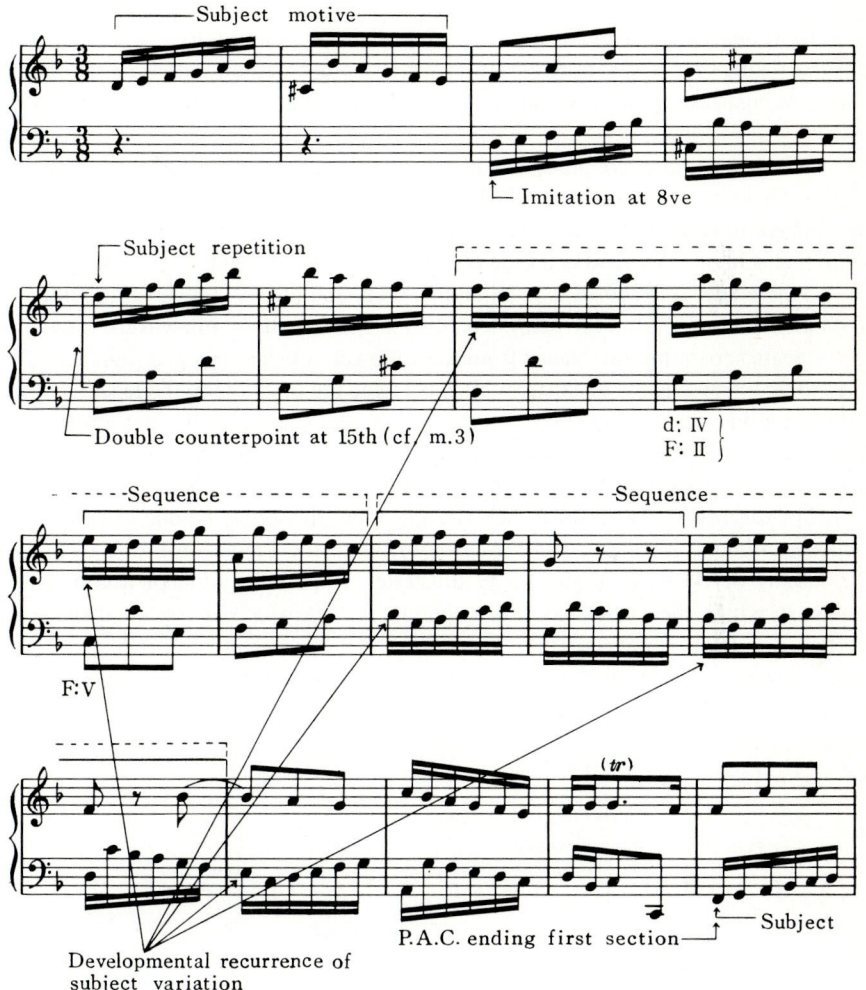

Inventions sometimes appear under other names. Thus, certain of the preludes to Bach's *Partitas* were described in Chapter 11 as inventions or inventionlike. Additional examples may be found among the *WTC* preludes (see Nos. 13 and 18 in the first book). Inventions have occasionally been written in the twentieth century (Bartók, *Mikrokosmos,* contrapuntal studies in Books V and VI).

CANON

The word *canon* (from *kanōn,* Gr. for *rule*) originally referred to a formula or rule for the realization of an imitative line which was not written out. Canonic procedures and genres appear in Western music as early as the fourteenth century (see p. 346).

Canon, an imitative procedure of rigorous discipline, is not capable of general characterization in any sense in which forms are defined: it consists of usually strict, prolonged imitation between two or more voices, but follows no predictable tonal or sectional scheme. A round is a kind of canon. The voice which begins the canon is called the leader (*dux, proposta,* initiating voice) and the second voice the follower (*comes, risposta,* imitating voice). The distance in measures, in measure-fractions, or in beats separating the leader from the follower is called the *time interval.* The *harmonic interval* is the distance in pitch between the first note of the leader and the corresponding note of the follower, a distance which usually, but not always, remains constant throughout the canon. One might thus, for example, speak of a canon at the octave, at the time interval of a measure and a half.

In addition to those voices actually in canon, there may be one or more free, accompanying voices (*accompanied canon*), as in the canons from the *Goldberg Variations* of Bach. Example 12.39 illustrates a particular kind of accompanied canon in which the leader has a homophonic setting which also accompanies the follower.

A *double canon* has at least four voices, and consists of two canons pro-

Ex. 12.39   Franck, Sonata in A for violin and piano, final movement.

gressing simultaneously (Ex. 12.40). The principle can be extended to *triple canon,* an example of which is quoted by Leichtentritt from a chanson of Josquin des Prez.[9]

Ex. 12.40   Mozart, Double Canon, K. 228, for four voices.

In *canon in augmentation* the follower is an augmentation of the leader; in *canon in diminution* the opposite procedure obtains. Increasing discrepancies in the time interval have to be made up by holding back the faster-moving voice by rests or passages of free counterpoint to bring the time interval into conformity as appropriate. Example 12.41 shows canonic imitation of a fugue subject by its augmentation; the subject enters also in a third voice in a free mirror inversion.

Ex. 12.41   Bach, Fugue in C minor, WTC II, 2.

Like other, more esoteric forms of canon, the *retrograde canon* (crab canon, canon cancrizans), in which the follower is the retrograde of the leader, is extremely rare, as attested by the fact that reference is made again and again to the same examples, especially that of Bach's *Musical Offering.* Theoretically, such unlikely types as retrograde mirror canon are possible. The following is from a contemporary retrograde canon.

---

[9] Leichtentritt, *Musical Form,* p. 81.

Ex. 12.42   Dallapiccola, Quaderno Musicale di Annalibera for piano, No. 7.

© 1953 by Edizioni Suvini Zerboni, Milan, Italy. Used by permission.

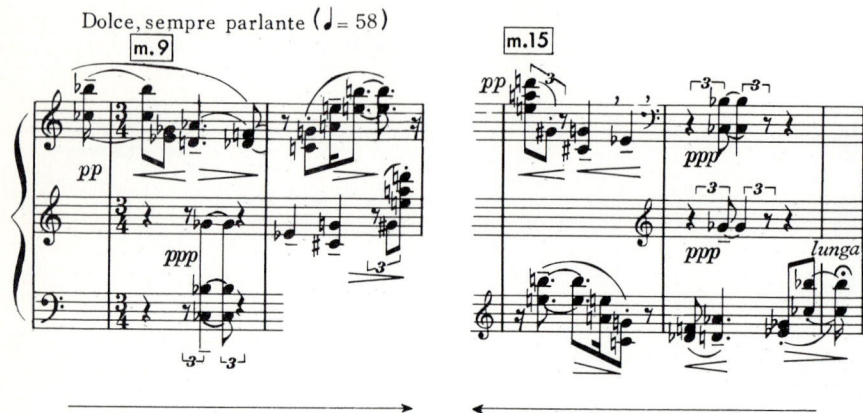

A *mirror canon* (Ex. 12.43) is one in which the follower is the precise inversion of the leader, a canon in contrary motion. (See the Bach *Goldberg Variations,* Nos. 12 and 15.) The inverted imitation in Ex. 12.43 is transposed.

Ex. 12.43   Schoenberg, Suite, Op. 25, for piano, trio of minuet.

Copyright renewal 1952 by Mrs. Arnold Schoenberg. Used by permission of Mrs. Schoenberg for the U.S.A. and Canada and Universal Edition (Alfred A. Kalmus Ltd.) for other countries.

In an *enigma canon* (riddle canon, puzzle canon), the imitation is not given, with clues to the realization provided in the form of clef signs, entry signs, and even literary inscriptions. Several enigma canons are included in Bach's *Musical Offering.*[10] Excerpts from two of them are quoted in Ex. 12.44. In the first, the upper voice (the subject of the entire work) is not part of the canon. The follower of the

---

[10] Solutions to the Bach canons are discussed in *The Bach Reader,* ed. Hans T. David and Arthur Mendel (New York: W. W. Norton & Company, Inc., 1945; rev.ed.,1966).

Ex. 12.44   Bach, A Musical Offering.

lower voice begins on a♭, as indicated by the second clef sign on the lower staff (an F clef, placing f on the top line), and the location of its entry is indicated by the symbol ⸮ . The second canon is more difficult, since the time interval is not given and has to be discovered. The inversion of the clef sign for the follower means that it is to be a mirror of the leader. (It begins ♩♪♪♪♪♩♩ in m. 4.)

In a multivoiced canon, the harmonic and time intervals may vary. In Ex. 12.45, which has a free bass, the second violin imitates at the 5th, the first violin at a tritone, or minor 9th as to the original entry, while the time interval is consistent.

Ex. 12.45   Bartók, String Quartet No. 4, first movement.
Copyright 1929 by Universal Edition; renewed 1956. Copyright & renewal assigned to Boosey & Hawkes, Inc. for the U.S.A. Copyright for all other countries of the world by Universal Edition (London) Ltd. Reprinted by permission.

There are several types of *free canon*. In one, only a note (pitch-class) series is imitated—a method associated with the 12-tone technique. Another procedure would duplicate only durations of notes.

Example 12.46 illustrates two free canons. The first has a follower which imitates melodic intervals but not rhythms (*rhythmically free canon*); the second imitates rhythms but not melodic intervals (*intervallically free canon,* or *rhythmic canon*). The implication is clear that other musical elements—for example, dynamic articulations or textures—might be subjected, independently or in tandem with other elements, to canonic imitation. In Ex. 12.46, accompanying voices are omitted.[11]

Ex. 12.46   Schoenberg, Variations for Orchestra, Op. 31, variations 2 and 8.

A free canon may exercise liberties of varying kinds, avoiding rigid imitation of melodic intervals, ordering of notes, rhythms, and other elements, but maintaining sufficient imitation to convey the impression of canon. In addition to Ex. 12.47, the opening of Bartók's String Quartet No. 1, as well as mm. 6–11 of his Quartet No. 3, might be cited.

In an *infinite canon,* or *round,* the imitation goes on without interruption, re-

---

[11] The second quotation shows the beginning (two principal voices only) of Schoenberg's Variation 8. In the rhythmic canon, the roles of oboes and bassoons as leader-group and follower-group, respectively, are clear. Interval relationships, in which for an instant the "leader" imitates the "follower" in mirror inversion (cf. bassoons, m. 2, from d, with oboes, m. 3, from e^{b2}), are produced by application of the same 12-tone set in both voices and are distinctly secondary to the effect of rhythmic imitation, which, unlike the mirror intervallic correspondence, continues well beyond the quoted passage.

Ex. 12.47   Berry, Duo for violin and piano.

peating in apparently endless succession (rarely, changing tonal level each time, as in the ascending *spiral canon* of Bach's *Musical Offering*), possibly with an alternate ending provided to bring a close. In most canons, the imitation must be interrupted in order to end the canon. Frequently, the imitation is abandoned to free counterpoint at a convenient point, after which the voices join in a cadential progression, possibly followed by a codetta or coda.

Examples of canon are easy to find. A few of special interest are Bach's *Five Canonic Variations on "Vom Himmel hoch"* for organ; the quartet "Mir ist so wunderbar" from Beethoven's opera *Fidelio* (free voices enter after m. 40, and the canon dissolves into the coda); the quartet "E nel tuo, nel mio bicchiero" from Mozart's opera *Così fan Tutte* (a canon in 3 voices with an accompanying bass); and all the canons of the *Goldberg Variations* of Bach. Many sixteenth-century choral works contain canons. Examples of tight canons—canons at short time intervals—are seen in the last movement of Bartók's Quartet No. 4 (m. 285, for instance), the first movement of Mozart's Sonata in D, K. 576 (mm. 27–33), Piston's *Chromatic Study on the Name of Bach* for organ (m. 35), and the opening of Bach's *Brandenburg Concerto* No. 6 in B-flat, where, as is sometimes the case, the time interval occasions a contrasting metric structure in the follower.

The adjective *canonic* is applied to passages in canon during the course of a fugue, sonata development, or other form, as well as to pieces (like the Bach 2-voice Invention in C minor) in which canonic imitation is freely interrupted and resumed. In fact, several of the foregoing quoted examples are canonic passages within large forms which are not primarily canonic.

All kinds of combination of canon types are theoretically possible; more than one type may occur within a single passage, from section to section of a work, or among the several strata of a polyphonic texture.

THE ORGAN CHORALE

The principles of the chorale prelude, chorale fugue, and other types of organ chorale, while associated with the organ, are applicable to other media as well (see, for example, the chorus of Bach's cantata *Jesus nun sei gepreiset*).

The literature of the organ chorale, written on chorale melodies of the Protestant tradition, is one of the most sublime in all polyphony, and the works of Bach in this medium should be known to all who profess serious interest in music. The history of the organ chorale goes back at least to the early sixteenth century, and antecedents, at times on Latin hymns, can be traced to the late fifteenth. (See the *Harvard Dictionary,* under "organ chorale.") That history includes notable works of such composers as Scheidt, Buxtehude, Pachelbel, Bach, and Brahms. The second volume of *HAM* contains organ chorales of Scheidt, Buxtehude, Pachelbel and Bach on the same chorale melody (No. 190).

As with all classifications of musical form, each specimen creates its own problems and solutions. Still, it is possible to list certain fundamental principles in the treatment of the chorale melody, all of them visible in the works of Bach.

One type of organ chorale is only a step removed from the straightforward chorale harmonization known to every student of music. In this simple species the harmonic setting of the chorale is activated by rhythmic embellishment throughout the texture, the chorale tune usually remaining in the soprano. Examples are found in Bach's *Orgelbüchlein,* many of whose chorale melodies are ornamented in this relatively simple style. See Ex. 12.48, in which is evident a typical motivic consistency in the accompanying counterpoints.

Ex. 12.48   Bach, Chorale Prelude on Vom Himmel hoch.

First notes of chorale

What might be described as a standard *chorale prelude* has imitative introductory, transitional, and concluding passages derived from the chorale melody. The chorale phrases are separated by interludes of this sort; the melody appears in longer notes, often remaining in one voice, accompanied contrapuntally. Sometimes the same basic material is used for an introductory section, interludes, and a concluding section, as in No. 4 of Brahms's Chorale Preludes, Op. 122. Example 12.49 is an example of this type, including, as often in Bach, a tonic pedal at the end; however, its opening counterpoint, while derived from the chorale, is not imitative, as it commonly is in Bach.

Ex. 12.49   Hindemith, Sonata No. 3 for organ, second movement (on Wach auf, mein Hort).
© 1940 B. Schott's Soehne/Mainz, Germany. Used by permission.

It will be convenient to draw further illustrations of the organ chorale from a single, broadly representative source, Vol. VI of the Peters edition of Bach's works for organ. Numbers denote ordering in that volume.

Within the classification of chorale prelude represented by Ex. 12.49, No. 1 of the Peters volume (BWV 693) is a short, very clear example, and No. 2 (BWV 649) an unusual specimen within the same category. This work, on "Ach bleib bei uns, Herr Jesu Christ," includes a theme,

derived from the first notes of the chorale melody,

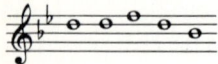

carried in the accompanying voices throughout without the usual imitative treatment. A *da capo,* in which the introductory material functions also as concluding section, makes an overall ternary. No. 6 (BWV 676), on "Allein Gott in der Höh' sei Ehr'," has an introductory section formed of a free bass and 2 voices in canonic relationship, with the chorale melody in a middle voice (beginning at m. 12). Sometimes the upper voice takes the chorale, and sometimes a chorale phrase is articulated in canon with itself (see the third phrase, at m. 78).

No. 9 (BWV 662), still of the same general category, has the same chorale melody,

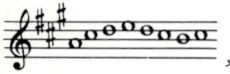

in elaborate ornamentation,

and illustrates as well the common protraction of the final tonic note into a pedal point (here, inverted). No. 30 (BWV 688), on "Jesus Christus, unser Heiland," is striking in its use of canon, invertible counterpoint, and a pervasive motive occurring in four variants:

with the chorale in the pedal voice. No. 16 (BWV 695), even though it is titled *Fantasia sopra Christ lag in Todesbanden,* is a perfectly regular chorale prelude in the approaches outlined above: introductory section, chorale phrases in sequence with contrapuntal accompaniments and separated by imitative interludes, and concluding section, also of imitative counterpoint. No. 19 (BWV 678), on "Dies sind die heil'gen Zehn Gebot', " represents an unusual type of chorale prelude in that the chorale melody is presented consistently in canon with itself.

Opening and concluding passages in the chorale prelude are in nearly all cases integral to the total form. The concluding section—that which follows the final chorale phrase—is generally an unbroken continuation over (or under, or around) the final chorale note, which is sustained as a pedal point. Only rarely is there a codetta or coda, occurring *after* the final phrase and confirmation of the tonic key, and set off from it by cadential punctuation. No. 2 of the Peters Volume (BWV 649), "Ach bleib bei uns, Herr Jesu Christ," comes closer than any example we have considered to having a discrete introduction (ending on a cadence, with fermata, at m. 15) and coda (identical here to the "introduction," beginning with the cadence at m. 46, just before the repeat *dal segno*).

Another type of organ chorale, represented by No. 18 (BWV 685), "Christ, unser Herr, zum Jordan kam," takes a segment of the chorale melody,

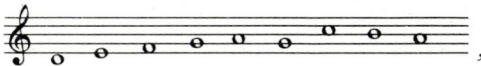

and weaves out of it a free contrapuntal study, not readily accessible to classification (Ex. 12.50).

Ex. 12.50   Bach, Organ Chorale on Christ, unser Herr, zum Jordan kam, BWV 685.

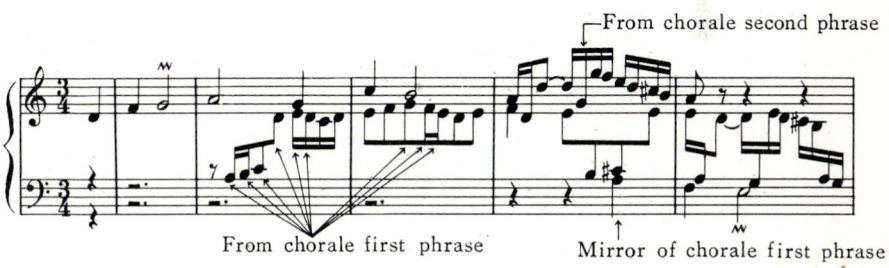

We have referred to that kind of organ chorale which is a fugue (or fughetta), taking its subject from the chorale melody (Ex. 12.12a). No. 11 (BWV 716), a *chorale fugue* (Ex. 12.51) on "Allein Gott in der Höh' sei Ehr'," characteristically adopts the first chorale phrase as subject, and later brings in the second phrase as well, using both in augmentation in the pedal voice in the final 19 measures.

A good example of the *chorale fantasy* is No. 15 (BWV 718), on "Christ lag in Todesbanden." One of its definitively free features is an extensive, rhapsodic development on the opening notes of the fifth phrase of the chorale melody (Ex. 12.52).

Ex. 12.51   Bach, Fugue on Allein Gott in der Höh' sei Ehr', BWV 716.

Real answer

Canonic transitional episode

m.27

Notes of chorale second phrase
as episodic materal

Repetition of **mm.29–32**
in inverted counterpoint
at 8ve

Ex. 12.52   Bach, Organ Chorale on Christ lag in Todesbanden, BWV 718.

Chorale fifth phrase

m.43

etc.

Another is No. 29 (BWV 713), on "Jesu, meine Freude," which begins in the usual fashion of the chorale prelude, breaking away at m. 54 into a section of contrasting meter in which motives of several of the chorale phrases are freely developed. No. 22 (BWV 720), "Ein' feste Burg," is anomalous—often described as a fantasy because of the free movement of the chorale melody from voice to voice, sometimes embellished, and the multiplicity of motives in the accompanying voices, having the effect of breaking the form into diverse sections, often nonimitative.

The *chorale trio*, Nos. 7 and 27 (BWV 664, 655), is a 3-voice organ chorale which freely derives the voices of its contrapuntal fabric from parts of the chorale, whose melody is not usually stated directly, although it may be brought in during the final section. This is the case in both of the cited examples, the first of which concludes with a statement in the pedal of the first two chorale phrases. No. 27 (BWV 655), a trio on "Herr Jesu Christ, dich zu uns wend'," states the chorale in the pedal in the concluding 22 bars. This final section has a brief, imitative introduction, interludes, and a concluding section precisely as in the most standard type of chorale prelude; hence, it represents a merger of the two approaches. Up to these final 22 measures, which are an appended, complete chorale prelude in themselves, the trio consists of relatively free sections punctuated by cadences in closely related keys. It is an abundant display of contrapuntal technique: canon (for example, the upper voices of mm. 22–25); invertible counterpoint (compare, for example, mm. 8 and 9); sequential development of basic motives (for example, mm. 13–14); melodic inverson of the subject (compare mm. 12 and 22); and interpolations of melodic segments derived from the chorale (the initiating subject combines motives from phrases 1 and 3).

The *chorale partita*, a further type of organ chorale, is a sectional series of variations on the chorale melody. (See, for example, Bach's variations—*partite diverse*—on "O Gott, du frommer Gott," BWV 767.)

No. 21 (BWV 705), the "fugue" on "Durch Adams Fall ist ganz verderbt," is not a strict fugue. It consists of a series of sections in which chorale phrases and a *number of chorale-derived subjects* form the basis for canonic and fugal imitation. This is the form which is properly described by the term *chorale motet*, still another classification of organ chorale. No. 14 (BWV 687), on "Aus tiefer Noth schrei' ich zu dir," also represents the chorale motet type. In this work, each phrase of the chorale is preceded by introductory or interlude material derived *from that phrase*. "Aus tiefer Noth" takes the first phrase,

treats it in diminution,

imitates it in mirror inversion,

and then in its original form, as the basis for its introductory section. A similar procedure is followed for material preceding each of the subsequent chorale phrases.

There is an infinite variety of technique and approach in the organ chorales of
Bach and other composers. The above statements should be interpreted as illustrations of some basic methods rather than as exhaustive classifications of types and
resources of form in this richly diverse literature.

EXERCISES

1. Find examples of each of the following.
   a) Fugato
   b) Second countersubject
   c) Real answer in a choral fugue
   d) Episode restated in inverted counterpoint
   e) Subject variations of several kinds
   f) Total stretto
   g) Coda containing a tonic pedal point
   h) Mirror canon
   i) Canon at the 3rd
   j) Chorale fughetta
2. Check as many as possible of the musical examples of Chapter 12 and find
   other examples to illustrate the same points.
3. Prepare an analysis of one work from any of the following sources.
   a) Chorale preludes of Brahms
   b) Bach, Two-Voice Inventions
   c) Bach, *The Art of the Fugue*
   d) Mozart canons—e.g., K. 89a, 229, 230–34, 347–48, 553–62
   e) Hindemith, fugues from *Ludus Tonalis*
4. Find examples of fugal techniques in the eighteenth-century concerto grosso,
   especially in works of Handel.
5. Find examples of any of the following in motets, madrigals, or masses of the
   sixteenth century.
   a) Double counterpoint at the 12th
   b) Imitation at the 4th
   c) Mirror inversion
6. Answer the following questions with respect to a fugue of your choosing or
   concerning one suggested to you. Depending on the style of the work chosen,
   certain questions may not be relevant.

a) How long is the subject?

b) What is the subject's range of pitch?

c) To what extent does the subject move conjunctly?

d) Is the subject divisible into parts? If it is divisible into individual motives, how are they related or contrasting or both?

e) What scale degrees lie at the basis of the subject melody? (That is, how would you reduce the subject to its essential pitches, and what fundamental structure do these articulate?)

f) What are the most obvious harmonic implications of the subject?

g) What distinctive melodic or rhythmic features does the subject have?

h) How would you describe the expressive character of the subject?

i) The fugal texture comprises how many voices?

j) Are all voices brought into play consistently, or infrequently ?

k) Is the first answer real or tonal? If tonal, where are the adj ustments made?

l) If the answer is real, how and where is the tonic restored in preparation for the third entry?

m) Is the answer accompanied by free counterpoint or by a countersubject? Is the countersubject motivically related to the subject?

n) Is there an additional countersubject?

o) How does the countersubject contrast with or complement the subject and its answer?

p) In counterpoints to subject entries, trace the origins of their motives to the subject or countersubject wherever possible.

q) Where does the exposition end? Is there an additional entry in the starting voice?

r) What is the order of voice entries in the exposition?

s) Is there a transitional episode during the exposition?

t) Is there a full or partial counterexposition?

u) Mark all subsequent entries "real" or "tonal" as applicable.

v) Are there subject groups or internal expositions in related keys?

w) Mark all episodes and determine any directions of modulation.

x) In the episodes, find an example of sequence, identifying its basic pattern and the direction and number of transpositions of the pattern.

y) Are there instances of melodic sequence independent of parallel harmonic movement?

z) Determine the sources of motives developed in the episodes.

aa) What is the fugue's tonal range?

bb) Is there any use of pedal points? Tonic or dominant? Where?

cc) Is there stretto? What is the order of voice entries in the stretto, and at what time interval? Is stretto particularly prevalent? Does the stretto engage all voices of the fugal texture?

dd) In subject recurrences, look for examples of augmentation, diminution, mirror inversion, rhythmic alterations, and other variants.

ee) Find examples of double and other multiple counterpoint. At what interval is the inversion?

ff) Do you find canonic procedure other than in subject imitation? At what harmonic and time intervals?

gg) Is the fugue distinctly sectional? Locate cadences and evaluate their properties of punctuation and continuity of motion.

hh) To what extent is the fugue taken up with the subject material? With full subject entries? Is much of the fugue, on the other hand, episodic?

ii) Locate the final entry or entries of the subject in the tonic.

jj) Is there a coda?

kk) If there is a coda, what does it contain? Subject? Pedal? Reduction or thickening of texture? Use of the dominant of the subdominant?

ll) Is the fugue anomalous in any way? What if any particularly striking or unusual characteristics do you observe in the fugue as a whole?

7. Find an example of the use of canon in an art song.

8. Study the use of canonic techniques in "Ricercar II" from the Stravinsky *Cantata* (1952), including the use of retrograde in what the composer labels *cantus cancrizans* and in, for example, the canon between cello and voice at rehearsal no. 10.

9. Listed below are some suggestions for further study and analysis.

Bach, *Brandenburg Concerto* No. 5, third movement
> *Goldberg Variations,* variations in canon
> Mass in B minor, "Kyrie eleison," "Credo," and other movements
> Organ Chorales
> Eight Short Preludes and Fugues for organ, BWV 553–560

Samuel Barber (1910–81), Piano Sonata, Op. 26, fourth movement

Bartók, *Music for Strings, Percussion and Celesta,* first movement

Beethoven, Mass in C, "Cum Sancto Spiritu"
> Mass in D, "Et vitam venturi"
> Piano Sonatas in B-flat, Op. 106, and A-flat, Op. 110, fugal movements

Berg, *Wozzeck,* Act II, Scene 2 and Act III, Scene I

Bloch, Concerto Grosso No. 2 for strings, first movement
> String Quartet No. 3, fourth movement fugue

Brahms, *Requiem,* "Der gerechten Seelen sind in Gottes Hand" (end of Part III)
> Thirteen Canons for women's voices, Op. 113
> Chorale Preludes, Op. 122

Ingolf Dahl (1912–70), *Music for Brass Instruments,* first and third movements

Fauré, Eight Short Pieces for piano, Op. 84, Nos. 3 and 6

Franck, *Prelude, Fugue and Variation,* Op. 18, for organ
> Quartet in D, first movement, mm. 173ff.

Handel, Concerto Grosso in F, Op. 6, No. 9, fourth movement
> *Israel in Egypt,* chorus, "Egypt was glad"
> Six Fugues for harpsichord *(Handel Gesellschaft* edition, Vol. 2, pp. 161–74)
> Six Short Fugues *(H. G.* edition, Vol. 48, pp. 183–90)
> Suite No. 2 in F for harpsichord, fugue

Haydn, *The Creation,* chorus, "Glory to His name forever"

    String Quartets in F minor, Op. 20, No. 5, and C, Op. 20, No. 2, final movements

Hindemith, Piano Sonata No. 3, final movement

    String Trio, Op. 34, fourth movement

    Symphony *Mathis der Maler,* first movement ("Engelkonzert") following rehearsal no. 12

Mendelssohn, *Elijah,* chorus, "Lord our creator"

Mozart, Adagio in Canon for 2 basset horns and bassoon, K. 410

    Adagio and Fugue in C, for string quartet, K. 546

    Fantasy and Fugue in C, for piano, K. 394

    Fugue in C minor for 2 pianos, K. 426

    Fugue in G minor for piano, 4 hands, K. 401

Ravel, *Le Tombeau de Couperin,* second movement

Riegger, Canon and Fugue for organ, Op. 33b

Schumann, Four Fugues for piano, Op. 72

Shostakovich, 24 Preludes and Fugues for piano

Stevens, Quintet for flute, strings, and piano, fourth movement

    Symphonic Dances, third movement

Stravinsky, Septet (1953), gigue

Vaughan Williams, Prelude and Fugue in C minor for organ and orchestra

Verdi, *Falstaff,* finale, "Tutto nel mondo è burla"

13

FORM AND STRUCTURE IN MUSIC

FORM AS TO ANTECEDENT-CONSEQUENT RELATIONS

One sense in which form in music has been conceived in this book has to do with interactive units related as antecedent and consequent. This fundamentally significant relation has been seen to be of potential relevance to the organization of conjoined motives, phrases, and larger units, even to single-movement sonata form (the exposition as ''antecedent,'' in an expansive derivative of the binary principle). The formal property of antecedence-consequence is, indeed, pertinent wherever partitioning involves a second balancing unit which is in its active elements more decisive in content and in finality of arrival.

While other elements (for example, texture, orchestration, dynamic intensity, surface rhythm) often contribute to the expression of antecedence-consequence, the decisive factor in most music is that of tonal orientation, in that extraordinary system of relations by which motion is directed toward the first scale degree, toward the tonic triad, and toward the primary tonic following conditions of relative fluctuation into secondary, subordinate regions.

FORM AS THE "SCENARIO" OF THEMATIC EVENTS

The foregoing discussion and analysis point to form in music also as a matter of thematic ''scenario,'' the statements, developments, and restatements, often in variation, of the motives and themes by which listeners most readily apprehend a composition's integrality and identity. It is thus significantly within the consideration of the thematic scenario that forms are classified as to types and conventions of schematic design and as to degrees of complexity. Moreover, studies of forms in music as to thematic content must often take account of historical evolution. For example, the introduction of opposing themes, like the broadened scope of development, is an aspect of evolving form; the relation of the normative single-movement sonata form to the usually more restricted, monothematic binary reflects such a tendency of evolution. Moreover, we have seen that such usually monothematic forms as the fugue or variation series may expand through broadly ranging, elaborate transformations. The richness of the thematic scenario is thus assuredly not simply a function of the number of disparate motives and themes, whose proliferation can, in fact, severely compromise formal-structural coherence when it is a substitute for integration through resourceful development.

Whatever the circumstances of individual works, the analysis of themes, their component units, and their ultimate dispositions and expansions in development, is an important mode of study by which form is, *in one sense,* to be understood.

PROCESSES BY WHICH FORM, AS AN ASPECT OF STRUCTURE, IS ARTICULATED

A further sense in which form can be regarded has to do with certain basic processes, evident by implication in all the foregoing studies, which remain relevant whether or not a particular design is classifiable according to stereotypical conventions. These processes may be summarized quite simply as to five fundamental formal contexts.

The *process of introduction* lays a basis of tonal (and other elements of) content, and often of expressive "attitude"; it is the process of anticipatory preparation of (usually expository) events to follow. We have seen that introductions can vary from a single "gesture" to an expansive, major division. The introductory process, characteristic of but not limited to the beginnings of forms, is typically tentative and expectant, often establishing dissonant harmony as its basis, restricted or lacking in motivic-thematic content in many particular instances.

The *expository process* is that of statement (and restatement) of thematic-motivic ideas, in their relatively direct and definitive guises, and in an atmosphere of relative stability. Restatement, as we have observed, is likely to involve some elaboration, and at times restricted developmental forays not admitted in original expository statement.

The *process of transition* commonly involves some development, confined as subordinate to the central objective of moving from here to there (or, retransitionally, there to here) often in a relatively brief time. The transitional phase is one of bridging palpably conditions somehow opposed.

The *developmental process* is typically one of intensified activity: the submission of basic materials to searching, digressive exploration from various angles of view, in a course of action directed in accord with broadly projected tonal and other structures. We have noted that the developmental process, at times brief and even perfunctory, can be very expansive indeed. It takes place in a general environment of review of prestated motivic ideas and their further implications, within a binding framework of underlying continuities elaborated in surface fluctuations. The process is thus one of mobile, manipulative treatment in relatively fragmentary and episodic conditions, as compared with those of expository presentation.

And finally, there is the *process of resolution,* of conclusion, of closure. Conclusion may well involve a final review of materials in fundamentally *confined* development, or in peremptory recollection, often over the cadential pedal points. Even where apparently expansive development occurs in a context of conclusive process, it is typically found, and heard, to overlie a broadly cadential tonal basis. In many examples, such a basis is a lower voice elaborating scale degree 5, then 1.

Apart from relations of antecedence-consequence, and those of stereotypical scenarios of thematic design which are the primary subjects of this book, it is primarily by these five processes that form may be defined, and by the probing analysis of processive content, of purposive tendencies involving all applicable structural elements, that form is understood. It must be emphasized that processes of these kinds are relevant however the traced scenario may depart from normative conventions.

Such processes, except for those of expository statement and resolution, may be manifest only limitedly or not at all in any given composition. Moreover, these processes overlap and coincide: any particular example, segment or whole, is likely to embody diverse processive "phases" and orientations, concurrently and over differing spans of activity, within an *essential tendency conforming to a governing, fundamental condition of processive direction.*

While these ideas about form cannot be presented comprehensively in a summary discussion, they are essential to any comprehension beyond the mere classification of conventional formal prototypes, and certainly to the study of unusual examples.

Finally, particular devices by which antecedent-consequent relations are articulated, the thematic scenario unfolded, and formal processes carried out, are a critical concern in the study of distinctions among styles, and of the evolution of styles, in music history.

FREE APPROACHES TO MUSICAL FORM

In their relative independence of established conventional thematic scenarios and tonal designs, certain forms may be regarded as "free," although, to be sure, no form is really free, since any plan which gives order and coherence to a musical structure must incorporate many of those principles which are at the roots of the traditional forms of music.

It could be argued that the analysis of "free" forms is the most valuable study of all. For while the application of a standard design by no means *solves* the problems of form, it does suggest and often determine the nature of many of these solutions. The fascination of studying forms which depart from the norm in fundamental *plan* and *ordering* of events is the discovery and analysis of factors which are independent of standard methods, even though many of the most vital secrets of any instance of form lie in its particular variable details.

At certain points in this book, relatively free forms have been the subject of brief, parenthetical reference (see, for example, the section on irregularities of multiple segmentation in Chapter 3; the discussion of certain of the preludes to Bach's Partitas in Chapter 11; or the reference to the chorale fantasy on p. 395). And the comparatively unpredictable content of given sections in standard forms has frequently been a subject of comment. Among such sections are the concluding parts of certain baroque organ fugues, cadenzas in concertos and other genres, fugal episodes, and developmental areas in single-movement sonata form.

Particular modes of creative license in the treatment of standard forms are important to recall here. The enlargement or contraction of these forms, the use of hybrid approaches (rondolike digressions in fugue; sonata-rondo; or the use of a new theme in rondolike manner in place of the expected development in single-movement sonata form, as in the third movement of Beethoven's Sonata, Op. 2, No. 1), the practice of establishing thematic likeness between usually contrasted groups in the rondo or the sonata movement—these and many other free approaches to standard forms have been discussed, and have often constituted the most provocative aspects of cited examples.

Certain musical genres are *commonly* free in form. Where a text or program is important, the formal plan may rely in some degree on literary content as the determinant of major factors of structural continuity. Or concern with natural speech inflection, notably in song, recitative, and recitativelike passages, may significantly shape musical directions and sequences of activity.

On the other hand, programmatic and textual imagery and structure may be compatible with conventional formal procedures; indeed, this is often the case. Beethoven's Symphony No. 6 comes to mind, as does Strauss's variation set *Don Quixote*. Moreover, where narrative, extramusical circumstances do influence and determine unconventional formal design, the procedures by which form is articulated—thematic development, variation, reprise, universally applicable formal processes, and of course broad tonal continuities—are relevant and basic.

Some issues of comparatively free approaches to form are treated in connection with Ex. 13.1.

THE STRUCTURAL FUNCTIONS
OF MUSICAL ELEMENTS

Any ultimately valid, general concept of the structure of music must have in view *all potentially functional, expressive elements*. The formal "scenario" is one aspect of structure; yet structure is finally to be seen holistically as a total dynamic order comprising all lines of successions of events, directed to and from normative conditions understood as referential for a particular piece, or for an entire stylistic corpus.

The consideration of form as to certain basic processes suggests a complementary view of structural content, a view of the elements of music as commonly expressing certain fundamental tendencies. These tendencies are of (1) *progression,* in a direction of relative mobility, of dissonance (broadly conceived), of acceleration, of relative complexity, and of "distance" from an established, appreciable, normative state (e.g., a homorhythmic texture; or the tonic); and of (2) *recession,* in a direction of resolution, of reduced intensity, of reactive consonance, of deceleration, of comparative simplicity and inactivity, toward the normative, relatively resolutive condition for any given element.[1] In light of these concepts, the principle of antecedence-consequence can, for example, be seen as progression from and recession to the tonic.[2]

Each of the identified formal processes—introductory, expository, transitional, developmental, and resolutive—is decidedly associable with one or the other of the structural tendencies of progression and recession. The factors of such association may be detailed as follows.

The introductory process appears, as a rule, to be limitedly progressive, toward a dissonant, expectant state, yet, being preliminary, relatively firmly within the tonic sphere. Within elements other than the tonal, it is often recessive—for example, in the realm of dynamic intensities. Except when it is merely perfunctory, the introductory process leads toward tentative cadential punctuation, necessarily indecisive in tonality.

The expository process entails progression and recession of chiefly local import, comparatively restrained, in an environment of prevalent stability. While recapitulation is often initially more mobile in some of its elements, resolutive functions are, predictably, prevalent in final thematic statements. Still, certain elements of closing materials, notably those of dynamics and sonorous volume (as distinct from textural or tonal complexities), often increase in intensity. And where final recapitulative statements do range distantly in digressive, progressive actions, a proportionately expansive conclusive process is likely to follow.

The developmental process is typically one of relative instability, acceleration in rate of change, and progression into a form's most distant and animate conditions (e.g., actively imitative textures, farther tonal regions). Transition is related to development, but within more circumscribed aims and restricted temporal spans.

The resolutive process is, of course, essentially recessive, especially within the elements of texture, rhythm, and tonality. Even the most expansive concluding

---

[1]While utterly *static* content is conceivable if unlikely, such a state is presumably unimaginable at the music's immediate surface. Thus, for example, an ostinato motive would manifest stasis only at a near-surface level underlying the motive, which would reflect activity of some degree in its internal organization.

[2]These ideas are extensively explored in the author's *Structural Functions in Music* (Englewood Cliffs: Prentice-Hall, Inc., 1975; reprint, New York: Dover, in press).

sections reflect the underlying imperatives and constraints of cadence, however amplified.

The "function" of an event, as the term is employed here, is its role within a particular process, in an identified, directed tendency, as to its condition more or less, farther or nearer, more or less mobile, in relation to preceding and subsequent events within its particular domain of action. Of profound significance in this regard are the implications of the element of tonality, with its capacities for articulating progressive and recessive motions, however problematic may be the reckoning of distance and position in individual tonal events.

FORM AND STRUCTURE IN THE PRELUDE IN C
FOR ORGAN, BWV 567

The Prelude reproduced as Ex. 13.1a embodies a relatively free form; moreover, it is succinct, and comprises only a few encompassing gestures, richly elaborated. Its relative simplicity permits and requires analytical attention to *form as process,* and to shaping structural attributes beyond form.

The query "What is its form?" is found here, on examination, to be not a particularly useful one; the analyst is instead drawn into examination of details of

Ex. 13.1a   Bach?, Prelude in C for organ, BWV 567 (possibly by a pupil of Bach).

Ex. 13.1a (continued)

Ex. 13.1a *(continued)*

the piece's individual terms of structure, general features of which it shares with other examples from the baroque period. The analysis of structural elements and processes is always a necessity going beyond mere "form"; but in relatively freely formed examples of this kind (prelude, toccata, fantasy, and like genres), the analysis of *processes,* of singular content and formulation, is inescapable.[3] As in many such pieces, the motivic content is here economical and unassuming; this prelude is in a sense more figural than motivic. The brief, perfunctory subject (Ex. 13.1b) is a

Ex. 13.1b

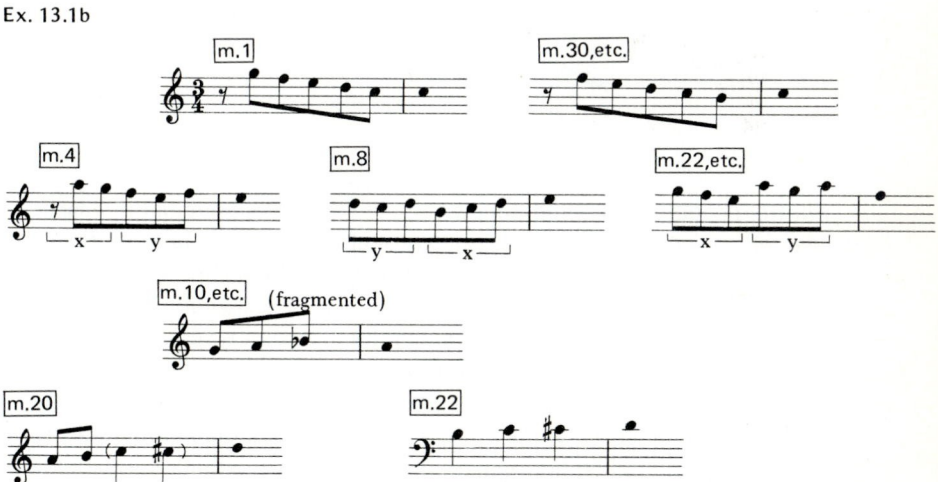

[3]Many published studies of comparable pieces can serve as useful supplementary references; some of these will be found in sources given in footnote 6. The author's *Structural Functions in Music* includes, with many other examples, a discussion (pp. 63–67) of Bach's Prelude No. 1 in C from the first book of the *Well-Tempered Clavier,* the subject of many published analyses which it may be interesting and instructive to compare. The *WTC* example, even more figural than the present organ piece, is an expansive I–V–I succession richly elaborated. Its broad, recessive registral descent is a vital structural principle cofunctioning with tonal and other factors.

Also pertinent here is the author's discussion of structure in Bach's Little Prelude in D minor, BWV 926, in *College Music Symposium* XXI, 2 (Fall 1981), pp. 92–100.

simple step descent spanning a 5th, interpretable as a triad filled in with passing tones.[4]

The Prelude presents a modest unfolding of imitative motivic statement and variation. Its subject is presented and immediately varied at the outset (mm. 1–9), developed, recalled at mm. 16–18, and explicitly restated again in the codetta. The motive in its various forms and derivatives appears in Ex. 13.1b.

The Prelude's phraseology is, typically for its style and genre, relatively lacking in sharp delineation and regularity, as well as in explicit periodic relation in the classical sense. Nevertheless, as in virtually any tonal piece, a principle of antecedence-consequence can be discerned in relations of segments (Ex. 13.1c). The phrasing is asymmetrical, marked by punctuating cadences on I (m. 5, elided, and m. 9—both relatively active); on the unusually prominent VI (mm. 16 and 20, both quite emphatic cadences); and again on I (m. 24, qualified by the upper voice's scale degree 3, thence reascending and descending to a culmination at m. 30, the decisive arrival, elaborated in a brief codetta).

Ex. 13.1c

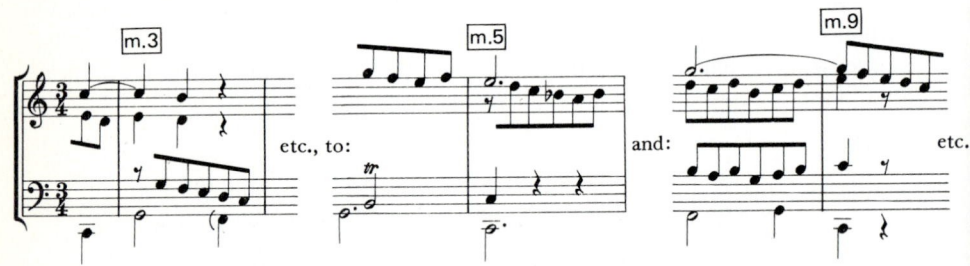

Formal processes. *Expository process* is evident in the initial and subsequent presentations of the motive, in contexts of characteristic textural vitality, of imitation. These are, while active in this sense, contexts in which the textural voices emerge gradually, as the motive enters in a progression of accrual at the time interval of one bar. In the reexposition (mm. 16–18), the composer reverses the order of entries as to registral placement and events now occur in the contrasting tonal region of the submediant. But both expository contexts are marked by relative stability.

The motive's varied form (as in m. 4) and fragments (m. 9, etc.; see Ex. 13.1b), and their derivatives, are subjects of developmental treatment in the prelude's interior segments separating the two expositions and following the second of these. Some facets of the *developmental process* are the superficial yet distinct tonal fluctuation (accelerated at mm. 9–12 and 20–24, the motivic truncation being itself an aspect of acceleration), and the stimulant metric noncongruity expressed in

---

[4]The motive can be regarded as a diminution of the piece's upper voice as a whole, discussed in connection with Ex. 13.1f.

durational accents represented in Ex. 13.1d. Developmental technique also involves chromatic elaboration of portions of the motive's step succession, which occurs following m.20 (see Ex. 13.1b). In the developmental areas, elaborating tonicizations touch the subdominant/supertonic region (mm. 9–11), and the supertonic again at mm. 20–21 and 22–23, in addition to fleeting references to the dominant (mm. 21–22).[5]

Ex. 13.1d

Resolutive process involves a typically inflated authentic (V–I) cadence, fortified and amplified by the chromatic approach to V at mm. 24–27. Outer-voice pedals on the dominant, then tonic, are conspicuous signs of cadential inflation. The process involves motivic elaboration, rigidly circumscribed within V, then I, in a stylistically typical, "retrospective" imitative presentation and textural reaccrual. All of this is contained within the tonic, which predictably (for the style) "leans" toward IV (by means of B♭) then V (modally altered by A♭) in a surface reaffirmation of the authentic cadence within the rigid confinement of tonal resolution. The pedals, moreover, are themselves an aspect of textural recession, as is a good deal of similar motion between inner voices. Thus do aspects of resolutive tendency appear within the element of texture itself.

The tonal framework and its elaboration.   The ordering of formal processes suggests a "narrative" of events unfolding within an underlying, binding tonal scheme. That scheme can also be viewed as to stylistically common 5th-successions preparing and enhancing the ultimate arrival—that is, receding toward I by an inexorable and logical course embracing the greater part of the piece. In the sketch given as Ex. 13.1e, 5th-relations are marked by pointed slurs (these include of course the preliminary V–I). "N" denotes the neighbor relation of F to G, while the dotted "tie" indicates a tonal factor sustained or prolonged, and "overreaching." The notes of the encompassing line of 5th-successions are given as *pitch-classes* independent of specific registral locations, in order to convey an image

---

[5]II, the subject of relatively strong tonal reference in the second of the developmental areas, is at the same time, more locally, IV of the VI from which it directly arises, at m. 20. Thus can be seen an implication of "levelling" in tonal structure: differing tonal functions of individual harmonies, each applicable to a definable contextual span and thus identifiable as to a "level" of significance in an ordered hierarchy.

Ex. 13.1e

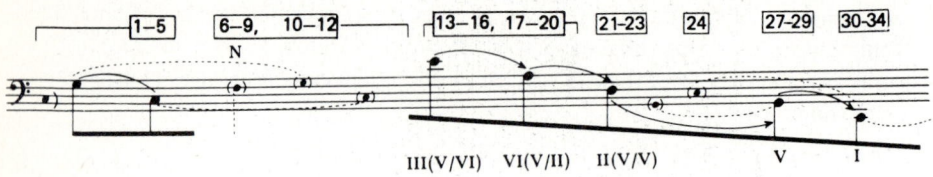

III(V/VI)   VI(V/II)   II(V/V)   V   I

of "descent," of decisive recession toward I. That recession is not, to be sure, in a "straight" line; that is, it is worked out in superficial deviant actions, yet must be heard as an underlying summation of essential tendency from m. 13.[6]

The upper voice is a distinct structural element. Most basically, it can be traced as a descent from g^2 to c^2—a vital factor of underlying tonal expression (Ex. 13.1f). The registral apex, a^2, functions in relation to this frame as a highly active,

Ex. 13.1f

a) Note mm. 23–24 as a diminution of the g^2-e^2 descent.
b) In m. 9, flat; in m. 15, natural.
c) Note mm. 9–10 as a diminution of the f^2-a^1 descent.
d) Preliminary occurrences of g^2 and a^2 in mm. 1 and 4, respectively.

dissonant neighbor to g^2. The strongest representation of a^2 is at m. 7, where it has durational emphasis as well as that of potently dissonant, chromatic harmonization. Transitory appearances of this important pitch can be viewed as "preparatory" and "reverberative"; yet each "overreaches" as part of a basic prolongation of the structural g^2. Further, as shown in Ex. 13.1f, the a^1 of m. 16 is heard as a lower-octave manifestation of this broadly articulated auxiliary.

[6]Although the present examples portray various underlying continuities of tonal structure, it will be apparent to any knowing reader that they do not express or represent the precepts of Heinrich Schenker. But the fundamental idea on which they depend, that of linear affiliations and continuities underlying a composition's actual surface (or foreground of all composed events), must of course be ascribed in the most general sense to Schenkerian theory. Important, useful sources dealing with tonal voice-leading in the Schenkerian tradition are: Felix Salzer, *Structural Hearing: Tonal Coherence in Music* (New York: Dover, 1962); Salzer and Carl Schachter, *Counterpoint in Composition* (New York: McGraw-Hill, 1969); and, more recently, Allen Forte and Steven E. Gilbert, *Introduction to Schenkerian Analysis* (New York: W. W. Norton and Co., Inc., 1982). Heinrich Schenker's most influential treatise, *Der freie Satz*, is available in translation by Ernst Oster, as *Free Composition* (New York: Longman, 1979).

It is apparent that elaborations such as the passing tones represented in Ex. 13.1f are by definition of the surface and near-surface, while the underlying 5th-descent is a factor of relative stability and containment characteristic, by definition, of deeper levels. Such a leveled implication is evident among narrowly drawn segments of the broad line: in recessive descent to a^1 (mm. 7–16) and progressive reascent (mm. 16–22, 27) to a^2 and its resolution, g^2, within framing, orienting occurrences of scale degree 5. All of this constitutes, in undulations of the surface, a structural unity reaching from one end of the prelude nearly to the other. In Ex. 13.1f, solid slurs depict direct connections, dotted slurs underlying associations conceived in simplifications of the actual foreground. Dotted ties similarly refer to under-surface affiliations linking occurrences of a particular pitch.

Example 13.1g is a further representation of tonal structure. Here, that structure is viewed as *a digest of essential harmonic elements* and their connections, in a broadly drawn context of which the upper voice is one factor. Some of the symbols will be clear from stipulations already given, and some are self-evident. Stemmed

Ex. 13.1g

Area of concentrated, accelerated harmonic
fluctuation: "descending" 5ths in
recession toward I.

a) Note m. 19's diminution of this inner-voice descent in 3rds.
b) Notated as eb^1, m. 26.
c) Superficial II–V fluctuation; note mm. 4–5 as diminution of upper voice's descending 3rd from g^2 to e^2.
d) Cadential chromatic approach to V.
e) Elaboration of cadential I (as V of IV).

notes in the sketch mark components of the overall harmonic succession: I, VI–II–V–I. Subsidiary motions (chiefly passing tones), linking and elaborating those primary events by which broad harmonic motion is directed and articulated, are shown as smaller unstemmed noteheads. Parentheses denote implied notes (for example, the c^2 of m. 24). A left- or right-facing square bracket ([or]) indicates a voice interpreted as, respectively, entering or dropping out (for example, the problematic g^1 of m. 24). A measure number in parentheses is an approximation, where some notes have been brought into imposed vertical alignment as an aspect of summarizing in the reduction. Solid slurs and lines connect points of basic harmonic content, enclosing passing tones, where these occur. Revoicings of harmonies, by registral exchanges and shifts, are summarized in the system below the sketch. (These are not, of course, direct connections of voice-leading, but displacements of triadic components as a result of voice-leading.) The arrow indicates dominant–tonic action, primary or secondary, and brackets denote two stages in the 5th-"descent" referred to in connection with Ex. 13.1e; they also indicate groupings in some sense parallel in configuration. The developmental area is summarized on the bottom staff, where however actual pitches are given rather than the pitch-classes of Ex. 13.1e. (The sequence of measure numbers given above the sketch itself reveals this section of the piece as one of distinct acceleration in harmonic and tonal "eventfulness.")

Example 13.1g thus affords a synoptic view which omits details in the interest of a grasp of *essential* structure and broad continuities spanning major segments of the piece and, ultimately, the whole. Further synopsis would, for example, represent mm. 21–23 as a "single" event, the underlying II, redistributed in the motions of voices. Indeed, the prelude can ultimately be heard as an expansive expression of the tonic harmony itself (see the interrupted dotted "ties" attached to the bass C and g^2, suggesting an overreaching of outer occurrences of I), extended in the abundant elaborations of the composed surface.

Progressive and recessive tendencies as structural factors. Examples of local *progressive* action include the two initiating, preliminary assertions of I–V–I (mm. 1–5 and 5–9), critical points of departure for the piece's development. Each of these segments expresses progressive action, though tentative and confined, from I, followed by immediate recession to I from V. It is a typical, initiating verification of the tonic in a context of restricted fluctuation. Yet the second of these mm. 5–9), embracing such mobile factors as chromatic leaning toward IV and V, oes modestly beyond its preceding counterpart, subtly hinting at fluctuant events to me. This second fluctuation (mm. 5–9) is thus an expression of intensified mobil- (as compared to mm. 1–5), all in a context of relative stability (of I) in the over- perspective. This particular relation of the two opening segments is a vital aspect preparation for immediate progressive movement into the important VI-region of . 13ff.

Progressive functions in the developmental phases, going beyond those of the ly expository opening segments, can be suggested in a few examples: accelerated rhythms of harmonic change (e.g., mm. 11–12, at a "countermetric" frequency of half-bars!); a quickened pace of tonicization (pointing toward F, D minor, C, and A—all diatonic to the primary system); and accelerations of chromatic occurrence in interior segments. Further progressive tendencies are seen in the motivic fragmentation mentioned earlier; in textural mobility (resumed at mm. 16–20 in renewed imitation balanced against temporary tonal stability of the prolonged VI); in resumed tonal fluctuation and allied chromaticism in mm. 20–24; in upper-voice reascent (mm. 22–27); and in the chromatic approach to V, mm. 24–27, yet in a governing context of counteractive tonal and textural tendencies of resolution.

Examples of prevailing, or counteractive, recessive tendencies are: relative textural simplicity during phases of tonal-harmonic acceleration (mm. 9ff.), marked by abandonment of imitation and reduction in the number of independent voices (where, often, 2 of 3 voices are doublings); the upper-voice descent from a^2 to a^1 (Ex. 13.1f), contributing to decisive, if interim, cadential arrival on VI, at m. 16; tentative tonal stability (on VI) and a broadly retained upper-voice a^1, at mm. 16–20, a reexpository "pause" in developmental activity; a balancing reduction in texture toward a homophonic condition (mm. 24–27) in the context of opposing, intensifying actions noted above; and the resurgence of the primary tonic in the final resolution.

In any broad, summary analysis much remains unsaid. We have not examined such foreground details as suspensions, which are almost motivic here, and which culminate in the triple suspension of m. 34. And our neglect of such obvious factors as the steady foreground 8th-note motion throughout (except at cadential points) is by no means a denial of the expressive import of such relatively obvious factors. Indeed, one of the most powerful messages to be learned from any analysis, however penetrating, is that the complexities of interesting music, and of the experience of such music, never stand fully revealed. Nor is any single methodological approach sufficient to probe the complex network of lines, tendencies, associations, levels, dimensions, and actions of many interrelated, cofunctioning elements by which interesting music must be defined.

MUSICAL STRUCTURE AND PERFORMANCE

Musical interpretation must be informed by penetrating analysis. Such an assertion, which would require another book for its ample justification and exploration, can be underscored by the identification of specific questions of performance which arise in connection with the above analysis.

Thus, how can such a broad continuity as the 5th-succession toward scale degree 1, or the upper-voice step descent, be realized and clarified in performance of this prelude, if indeed any sort of intervention is indicated? Or, how might the awareness of such factors lead the interpreter to avoid articulations (and what might these be?) which impair such continuities? What special importance do the prominent E–A occurrences (mm. 12–20 and perhaps elsewhere) have in the broad scheme of 5th-succession, and in other functional relationships? Further, what subtle interpretive distinctions (for example, in tempo, organ registration, and articulation), following from understood differences of processive content and function, might be appropriate in dealing with imitative motivic presentations in mm. 1–3 as compared with mm. 30–32? Or between these and the statement of the motivic variant, still within the tonic sphere, following m. 4? Or between any of these and relative acceleration of motivic treatment, and of other elements, in mm. 9–16? Which cadences, in the piece's realization, are to be treated as comparatively active, and which more strongly punctuative, in the light of structural analysis, and how are such distinctions to be expressed? These are, to be sure, only specimens of interpretive problems requiring thoughtful analysis.

The point of this too perfunctory reference to performance is simply to underscore the importance of analysis as a basis for interpretive decision, and to suggest by examples the kinds of issues, and at times true dilemmas of tempo and articulation, which require the elucidation of comprehensive analysis. Every analytical finding has an implication for performance, even when in the end a quite neutral execution appears to be indicated, for such reasons as to allow the discerned implications of process and function to be felt without exaggerated, gratuitous effects which confuse rather than illuminate.

The act of performance, of bringing to a living realization the lifeless symbols on the page, is after all the outlet toward which all important musical activity aspires, the moment of fulfillment to which all serious effort of study and creativity is dedicated. Genuinely illuminating interpretation must arise from the full and deep comprehension of form and structure. Valid performance is a *knowing* projection of the cogent, composed structure as a dynamic organism of directed, interactive lines disposed toward *identified* goals and foci of orientation, and of processes and functions in a holistic perspective which conditions interpretive approach and attitude. These are the necessary considerations that govern the performer's decisions as a work is, sometimes in arduous endeavor, realized in sound.

No doubt the comprehension of structure and interactive relations in a composition is often a matter of deeply assimilated experience and conditioning working as an intuitive basis determining inarticulate choices. But the effort of working out an analysis of structure leads to performance decisions which are relatively free of caprice, which do not rely purely on intuition. Furthermore, analysis is necessary for persuasive instruction, if interpretive needs are to be communicated rationally. And it is an inescapable necessity in resolving dilemmas encountered by every performer. The way to sound decisions of interpretation through analysis is marked by such queries as: "What is happening at this point in the piece, in form and structure?"; "What place does this passage have in a total scheme?"; and "What vital functional tendencies, within which applicable elements, must I be aware of, and by awareness communicate?" There is no assurance that the spontaneous impulse will be valid, yielding a convincing result; and the world of musical performance is replete with evidentiary experience to the contrary.

Interpretive judgments can be classified as of, broadly, two kinds: those of general approach (of prevalent tempo and essential dynamic intensity, of "attitude"), and those of detail (of local modulations of tempo, of dynamics, of precise durations of attacks and pauses, of punctuation and "phrasing," of *points* of continuity and discontinuity in form and structure). Or, classification can be expressed as to matters of tempo, matters of articulation, and a disposing, conditioning attitudinal perspective judged, through analysis, to be appropriate in a particular context.

All details of the performance of a given work are susceptible to rational inquiry into, and evaluation of, place and function in the formal-structural plan, even if at times study suggests more than one apparently reasonable interpretation serving an identifiable purpose. Of course, a further dimension is that of style and the history of styles, as a factor in decisions of many kinds. The chief concern of music theory is the piece itself—its particular attributes of expressive structure, its individual complex of functioning elements. The aim of analysis is to see the art work as a working organism in which every event, in its broad as well as immediate lines of context, has its place in a directed order, its expressive function to be elucidated in informed performance.

THE ATTENUATION OF TONALITY
AS A STRUCTURAL ELEMENT IN LATER STYLES

To deal with techniques unique to twentieth-century music, with all of their ramifications regarding the elements of musical form and structure, and to do so in any meaningful way beyond the mere recital of methods and superficial appearances, would be to extend our discussion far beyond the concerns of this book. It is a fact that most of the *principles* which underlie formal and structural coherence in traditional music remain decisive; yet the means of their application, and the vocabularies of creative expression, have in recent music evolved in directions of profound change at a greatly accelerated pace.

In view of the emphasis upon tonality in the foregoing studies, it might be well at this final point to consider briefly the diminishing significance of that element in certain styles of the past century. We have seen that tonal functions of melody and harmony constitute a virtual sine qua non of traditional musical form. (We may recall the early explanation of the period as having its basis in cadential relationships, rooted in tonal-harmonic function, and its extension in the binary and larger forms, although we have also seen that such basic formal relations as antecedence-consequence are determined by *many* cofunctioning elements.) A multitude of twentieth-century examples cited in this book clearly reveals the extent to which traditional methods have been applied quite explicitly in much recent music; yet major streams of musical evolution in the late nineteenth and twentieth centuries have deeply altered the appearance and significance of the tonal element which is so fundamentally necessary in the articulation of traditional forms.

In much of the music of Richard Wagner (1813–83), like that of other late-nineteenth-century composers, tonality is often in a state of rapid flux, moving freely into the remotest tonal regions within brief intervals of time. Wagner's operas *Tristan und Isolde* and *Parsifal* are often cited in illustration of widely fluctuant tonality (Ex. 13.2); on the other hand, certain of the composer's works (the preludes

Ex. 13.2 Wagner, Prelude to Parsifal.

to *Das Rheingold* and *Lohengrin,* for example) are strongly anchored tonally. In Wagnerian contexts of unstable tonality, compensatory factors are often in evidence: persistent motivic repetition, progressing and receding currents in which other elements (orchestration, rhythm, etc.) are engaged, the alliance of music to textual-dramatic forms, and long-range tonal relations—expressed linearly and in elaborate systems of interrelated subsidiary tonal regions—which underlie and contrast with the fluctuant surface.

The music of Debussy, as of other composers who represent that idiosyncratic turn-of-the-century idiom often reflecting "impressions" of the objective world, is largely an art of detachment, restraint, and understatement. In this sense, it stands opposed to the sonorous extremes, recondite and pretentious symbolisms, and distended forms and structures associated with Wagner. But the challenge to tonality, and with it a radical loosening of tonal bonds, are manifest in *impressionism* too, in very different ways. Where Wagner's inflated structures are marked at times by a

Ex. 13.3   Debussy, Pelléas et Mélisande, Act I, Scene I.

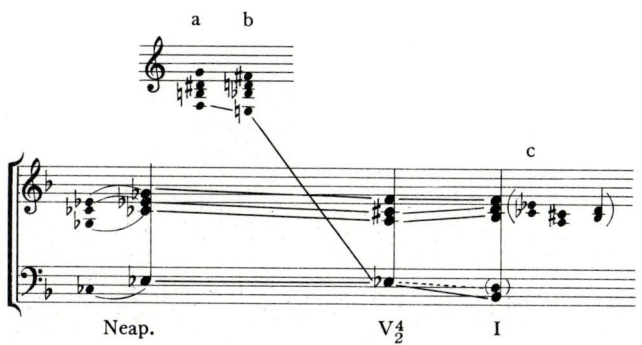

a,b)   Neighbor followed by passing chord of ambiguous whole-tone content briefly obscuring underlying tonal succession.

c)   Inner-voice "encirclement" of tonic factors.

Ex. 13.4   Debussy, Suite pour le Piano, first movement.

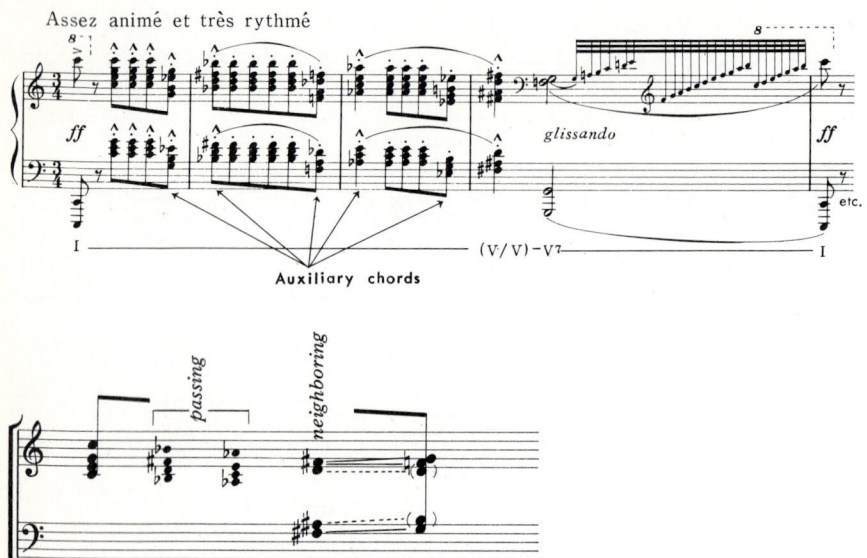

surface turbulent with shifting tonal references produced by tonicizing leading-tones, in Debussy such explicit factors of tonicization are frequently felt only well beneath a surface opulent with unorthodox harmonic color and subtly evasive subsidiary elaboration (Exx. 13.3 and 13.4).

In the music of Debussy, as in that of Wagner, compensatory factors are at work. The music is often vocal-dramatic or descriptive, or derived from dance, its form thus conditioned in part by extramusical associations. Motive repetition, even ostinato, is an important element in this style. Those works and passages of Debussy which are most independent of conventional tonal function are often extremely brief. Still, a subsequent hearing of an apparently problematic passage often reveals an explicit, even rudimentary, tonal succession (Ex. 13.4) overlaid with harmonic embellishment comprising chords whose derivations are essentially linear rather than tonal.[7] Example 13.4 shows a comparable elaboration of a fundamental

----

[7]Such primarily linear factors can be tonally suggestive, too. For example, "neighbor" chord (a) Ex. 13.3 is dominantlike, perhaps anticipating the forthcoming V_2^4, its B♮ "representing" C; and "ing" chord (b) suggests dominant of the dominant.

tonal succession: a progression from I to V is ornamented by auxiliary augmented triads filling linear "space" as passing chords. (See also, in the first movement of Ravel's String Quartet, the firmly sustained V of D minor embellished by auxiliary harmonies in the approach to the second tonal group.)

While in the works of many twentieth-century composers tonality remains a highly important and viable element, many others have felt that its usefulness, in serious question in the late nineteenth-century styles to which we have referred, is spent. Thus, a persistent practice of atonality is current among composers who regard tonal function as an exhausted method. Obviously, atonality poses new questions with respect to musical structure and form. While tonality can scarcely be argued to be indispensable to form—it is one element of many in traditional music—there can be no question that its denial brings forth problems of singular difficulty, occasioned by a long conditioning of response to tonal relationships. A prevalent technique in atonal music is that of serialization of the independent (rather than tonally interdependent) 12 notes (and, at times, rhythms, dynamics, colors, and other musical elements); yet, it is possible that form in 12-tone music, to the extent that it is achieved, derives not from the often imperceptible disposition of ordered 12-note sequences, but from the application of certain of the ancient principles which have brought vitality and unity to music of the past.[8] New idioms thus frequently alter the means of application rather than the principles themselves. And when repetitions of the ordered 12-note sequence become a basis for perceptible unity, the function of such recurrence is exactly analogous to that of melodic-rhythmic theme or motive in traditional music.

There are those who insist that the experience of a tonal center—the product of rhythmic and other relationships as well as of harmony and melody—is inevitable and cannot be suppressed. However that may be, literatures that resist tonality rely upon many of the compensations for its loss or attenuation which we have observed in styles of the late nineteenth century: insistent motive development and reprise, concision and brevity of expression, and association with literary text. Indeed, many of the most compelling atonal works have been written for the stage.

FORM, STRUCTURE, AND VALUE IN MUSIC

We have examined the nature of a number of conventional forms of music, considering some respects in which they provide frameworks for unity and variety. We have considered the technical means by which, in many specific contexts, a skillful and imaginative composer establishes, sustains, purposefully suspends, alters in various directions of fluctuation, and concludes a coherently shaped and motivated work. It may be that we have also seen something of the basis for music's expres-

---

[8]There is today a clearly discernible tendency among composers toward a renewed interest in tonality and tonal methods, and even in such conventions as triadic content and quasi-classical functional relations.

sive appeal and for the seemingly ineffable power of the musical languages of great composers.

If we have been concerned at length with the question "How musical form?", what of the question "Why musical form?" To this inquiry, more than rhetorical in our time,[9] no ultimate, incontestable answer is possible. Form in art (like the structural shaping of other elements) is a choice one makes; that it is the choice professed by all important creative figures until recent, relatively isolated, tendencies of negation is a powerful fact. The value of artistic *order* appears potent and undeniable when we view what music *is* with respect to what it *has been* in the rich literatures which are today's heritage. Even improvisatory styles traditionally concede to the performer certain freedoms of execution and approach only within an understood framework of structure-conditioning terms, bounds, and directive orientation.

Moreover, the perception of organic unities in musical form is a fundamental aspect of the aesthetic experience of listening (or performing), and we have seen that many of the qualities underlying the *what* and *how* of musical communication are illuminated by the study of form in all of its properties. The power of a musical statement lies partly in the strength of the ideas it sets forth, and partly in the weaving of those ideas into a fabric that convinces as their most appropriate development; in these two factors reside whatever "meaning" music has, and they are indissolubly linked. The conception of an ordered yet pliable matrix for his or her ideas is a challenge the serious, resourceful composer does not neglect, much less overtly reject, and the comprehension of form is a challenge that engages the perceptual and cognitive powers of performer and listener in their interpretive roles in the musical experience.

A strong idea demands an enriching, illuminating context—one in which it becomes appreciable as important and rationally disposed in the structure which it generates and by which it is fulfilled. The coherence of syntactic order is of special consequence in an expressive medium whose constituent units do not, as in literature and often in the graphic arts, achieve inner relationship by reference to objective experience. This is the issue to which, in a paramount sense, studies of form in music, like the fertile, richly evolved and evolving forms themselves, are addressed.

EXERCISES

1. Make a comparative study of *three* examples from *one* of the following sources.
   a) Haydn, later symphonic slow movements
   b) Bach, Preludes from the *Well-Tempered Clavier*
   c) Debussy, Preludes for piano
2. Find a piece, possibly contemporary, in which form and continuity seem to you to be unconvincing, or in some sense problematic. Develop a case to support your view.

      question of *aleatoric* composition and performance, one of urgency at the time of this book's
      has paled, yet is still pertinent and provocative.

3. Select, from the following list of works, subjects for study and analysis of form, motivic content and variation, and other elements of continuity and coherence.
    Bach, Fantasies and Toccatas for organ
        Preludes from the *WTC* (for example, 1, 2, 3, and 5 in Book I, 1 and 3 in Book II)
    Bartók, Suite for piano, Op. 14, first movement
    Beethoven, Sonata in C-sharp minor (*Moonlight*), Op. 27, No. 2, first movement
    Berg, Four Pieces for clarinet and piano, Op. 5
    Brahms, "Von ewiger Liebe" and other songs
    Carter, "Recitative and Improvisation" from Six Pieces for kettledrums
        Eight Etudes and a Fantasy for woodwind quartet
    Copland, Piano Fantasy
    Debussy, Preludes for piano (for example, 1 and 2 of Book I)
    Dallapiccola, *Quaderno musicale di Annalibera* for piano (for example, 1, 2, 4, 8, 9, and 11)
    Franck, Fantasy in A for organ
    Hindemith, Sonata for viola and piano (1939), third movement
    Liszt, *Les Préludes*
    Mozart, Fantasies for piano
    Francis Poulenc (1899–1963), *Mouvements perpetuels* for piano
    Prokofiev, Sonata No. 2 for piano, slow movement
    Ravel, *Shéhérazade*
    Schoenberg, Piano Pieces, Op. 19
    Verdi, *Macbeth,* Act IV, Scene 3
    Webern, Four Pieces for violin and piano, Op. 7

Index of Subjects, Names, and Terms

Only the most important appearances of certain frequently-used terms are indexed; these include names of several formal units (for example, *motive, phrase, period*) and terms for fundamental elements and concepts (including *harmony, tonality, chromaticism, dissonance*).

Index of Musical Citations
And Examples

Page numbers in **boldface** refer to musical examples.